NOVALIS

Georg Friedrich Philipp, baron of Hardenberg (1772–1801).
Oil painting by Franz Gareis, Städtisches Museum
Weissenfels.

Novalis

A Romantic's Theory of
Language and Poetry

KRISTIN PFEFFERKORN

Yale University Press
New Haven and London

"Der Tod der Geliebten" is from *Rilke Neue Gedichte* und *Der Gedichte anderer Teil*, Insel Pocketbook 49 and is published by permission.

Published with assistance from the Louis Stern Memorial Fund.

Designed by James J. Johnson and set in Palatino Roman types by The Composing Room of Michigan, Grand Rapids, Michigan.
Printed in the United States of America by Book Crafters, Inc., Chelsea, Michigan.

Library of Congress Cataloging-in-Publication Data

Pfefferkorn, Kristin.
  Novalis: a romantic's theory of language and poetry.

  Originally presented as the author's thesis
(Yale University, 1984).
  Bibliography: p.
  Includes index.
  1. Novalis, 1772–1801—Philosophy. 2. Novalis, 1772–1801—Aesthetics. 3. Novalis, 1772–1801—Knowledge—Language and languages. 4. Romanticism—Germany. I. Title.
PT2291.Z5P4 1987   831'.6   87–10564
ISBN 0–300–03597–7 (alk. paper)

The paper in this book meets the guidelines for permanence and durability of the Committee on Production Guidelines for Book Longevity of the Council on Library Resources.

10 9 8 7 6 5 4 3 2 1

*For my father
and to the memory of my mother*

Er wusste nur vom Tod was alle wissen:
dass er uns nimmt und in das Stumme stösst.
Als aber sie, nicht von ihm fortgerissen,
nein, leis aus seinen Augen ausgelösst,

hinüberglitt zu unbekannten Schatten,
und als er fühlte, dass sie drüben nun
wie einen Mond ihr Mädchenlächeln hatten
und ihre Weise wohlzutun:

da wurden ihm die Toten so bekannt,
als wäre er durch sie mit einem jeden
ganz nah verwandt; er liess die andern reden

und glaubte nicht und nannte jenes Land
das gutgelegene, das immersüsse—
Und tastet es ab für ihre Füsse.

Rainer Maria Rilke, "Der Tod der Geliebten", 1908

Contents

Preface

Most of the texts I have used in preparing this essay were not written in English. For the purpose of achieving a unified presentation I nevertheless decided to give all quotations in English. But since translations frequently either did not exist or were based on interpretations that differed essentially from my understanding of the texts involved, I did my own translations, and, unless otherwise indicated, they are used here. But while I found it fully adequate to rely solely on the translated version of texts in the case of writers other than Novalis, I felt that both scholarly accuracy and aesthetic appreciation of Novalis's fragments, essays, and poems demanded their being given in the original German, as well. I have done so in appendix C. All but one Novalis quotation (which is from the 1929 Leipzig edition), are from *Novalis Schriften, Die Werke Friedrich von Hardenbergs,* 3rd ed., 4 vols., Paul Kluckhohn and Richard Samuel, eds., (Stuttgart: W. Kohlhammer, 1977). I am using the standard system of reference for the works of Novalis in which the Roman numeral indicates the volume, the first Arabic numeral the page, and the second Arabic numeral the line, unless it is preceded by a "#," in which case it is the number of an aphorism or fragment. A quotation that is preceded by an "★" was selected by Novalis for inclusion into a new fragment collection he planned to publish. A quotation that is bracketed by heavy bars "❙ . . . . ❙" Novalis thought in its present form unusable and in need of further work. Slashes "/" were used by Novalis within longer fragments to indicate that a new thought, idea, or subject matter begins.

I wish to express my gratitude to the Graduate School of Yale University for the help and support it has given me during the years of study that led to the writing of the dissertation on which this book is based.

But most particularly I want to thank Professor Karsten Harries who not only first proposed that I work on Novalis but whose teaching and advice were instrumental in returning me to the cultural traditions I had left behind—a return for which I am profoundly grateful. Always generous with his time and knowledge, he contributed far more than can be named or measured. Certainly without his encouragement and the many formal and informal discussions we have had over the years this book would not have been written.

I am also thankful to Professor Rita Terras at Connecticut College whose close reading of the manuscript, many comments, good suggestions, and sound advice, specifically in the area of German literature, have been invaluable. Similarly, I want to express my gratitude to Professor Henry S. Harris of Glendon College at York University, Toronto. His detailed and careful comments were most helpful in revising and editing the manuscript for publication. I am much obliged also to Professor Emeritus Alice Johnson who under severe time constraints proofread the manuscript with painstaking care.

In addition, I am indebted to Connecticut College for awarding me the "Capstone Grant." It made finishing this manuscript immeasurably easier.

And finally, I want to tell my friends and colleagues at Connecticut College—Lester Reiss, Anita and Eugene TeHennepe, and Melvin Woody—how much their lively conversations, good-humored debates, and wonderful meals have meant to me. For their unfailing friendship, interest, support, and forbearance, particularly during the last months and weeks of finishing the manuscript I am deeply grateful.

Abbreviations

E/O   Søren Kierkegaard, *Either/Or*, trans. D. F. and L. M. Swenson (Princeton, N.J.: Princeton University Press, 1971).

FML   Hugo Friedrich, *Die Struktur der modernen Lyrik*, Rowohlts Deutsche Enzyklopädie, ed. Ernesto Grassi, 6th ed. (Hamburg: Rowohlt Taschenbuch Verlag, 1956).

FSW   Johann Gottlieb Fichte, *Von der Sprachfähigkeit und vom Ursprunge der Sprache*, in *Sämtliche Werke*, 11 vols., ed. J. H. Fichte (Berlin: Verlag von Veit, 1846).

HCG   Charles Frederic Harrold, *Carlyle and German Thought* (Hamden and London, Archon Books, 1963), vol. 82, Yale Studies in English.

HSW   Johann Gottfried Herder, *Sämtliche Werke*, 33 vols., ed. Bernhard Suphan (Berlin: Weidmannsche Buchhandlung, 1877–99).

HHL   Johan Huizinga, *Homo Ludens* (Boston: Beacon Press, 1950).

MEE   Maurice Maeterlinck, *On Emerson and other Essays* (New York: Dodd, Mead, and Co., 1912).

PGA   Henry A. Pochmann, *German Culture in America* (Madison, Wis.: The University of Wisconsin Press, 1957).

PLT   Martin Heidegger, "The Origin of Work of Art," in *Poetry, Language, Thought* (New York: Harper and Row, 1975).

TCE   Thomas Carlyle, "Novalis," in *Critical and Miscellaneous Essays* (London: Chapman and Hall, 1869) vol. II, p. 183 ff.

PRT   Paul Radin, *The Trickster* (New York: Schocken Books, 1978).

VNS   Werner Vordtriede, *Novalis und die französischen Symbolisten* (Stuttgart: W. Kohlhammer, 1963).

VGI   Stanley M. Vogel, *German Literary Influences on the American Transcendentalists* (New Haven, Conn.: Yale University Press, 1955), vol. 127, *Yale Studies in English.*

VSS   Silvio Vietta, *Sprache und Sprachreflexion in der modernen Lyrik,* vol. III, *Literatur und Reflexion,* ed. Beda Alleman (Bad Homburg: Verlag Dr. Max Gehlen, 1970).

Introduction

On May 2, 1772, a second child and first son was born to Heinrich Ulrich Erasmus Freiherr von Hardenberg and his second wife, Auguste Bernhardine née von Bölzig. They christened him Georg Friedrich Phillip and called him Fritz. Later he took the pen name Novalis. To his friends, Novalis appeared to be the very incarnation of the Romantic ideal of the artist. A young man of sensitive good looks, he was tall and slender, had wide, hazel-colored eyes, and wore his dark blond hair in long locks. Being of a mostly cheerful and gentle disposition, he was also given to intense and lively conversations that he punctuated with strong gestures made by hands that seemed too large for his build. When at twenty-two he fell deeply in love at first sight ("a quarter of an hour determined me!")[1] with Sophie von Kühn—the child-woman who was twelve and a half years old, and who died only two and a half years after they met, and a year before they planned to be married, on the very day he playfully set for their wedding,[2]—his deep despair and earnest desire to follow her, to die after her,[3] appeared to his contemporaries like life's own offering of the great Romantic theme of love and death.[4] In addition, it was Novalis's declared project to "romanticize" life by making nature, politics, science, and the arts in general more truly poetic. But it was the irony of Novalis's character and of his position in the Romantic movement that, while he strove in theory to romanticize life in all its features, in his approach to his own life and art—and that meant in the essential aspect of his creative personality—he did not have what is generally and popularly understood as a Romantic attitude.[5]

In his view, the creative process is as dependent on a painstaking

1

mastering of artistic craft as it is on inspiration. But craft, for Novalis, is by no means only an imitative skill. On the contrary, excellence of craft allows the artist to succeed in shaping exemplary works. And so Novalis considers it to be among an artist's foremost duties to improve and perfect his skills, no matter how tedious or mundane the discharge of this obligation may be. Yet in Novalis this commitment to the improvement of his skills lives harmoniously, side by side, with a theory of genius and a belief in the artist's superior spirit. Thus his practical emphasis on skill in no way undermines Novalis's belief in genius, nor does it raise doubts in him about the necessity of inspiration for the creation of great works of art in which man is able to express, as well as find, more than is held by the scope of daily life. For only when both these moments come together is the work of art, as a collaboration of the human and the divine, a revelation of the transcendent and infinite in finite terms. For Novalis attention to the craft, then, is the artist's responsibility, since without such craft the inspiration by the muse or the gifts of chance will not find adequate expression. But all the finest tuning and perfecting of the craft, that is, of everything the artist has taught himself or given to himself, will avail him nothing if the muse witholds her gift. Only with the sudden insight offered by chance will the work sing, and not remain dead sound and empty shape. It is, therefore, characteristic of the genius to be possessed of a spirit that can wait until time itself offers up the gifts upon which he will exercise his skills.

The question is whether Novalis's belief in inspiration—particularly as it manifests itself in his belief in the superior poetic nature of wonder tales, dreams, the miraculous, and the magical—is genuine, and possibly based on some experience, or whether it is a poetic conceit that takes the form of a deliberate attempt to return to an earlier Golden Age, when the gods still dwelt among men. If the latter is the case, is such belief not more accurately understood as a measure of the distance from that age than as a sign of belonging to it? In other words, the question is whether Novalis's view of language and poetry is a genuine, though possibly naive, conviction, and simply a fact in his life as an artist, or whether it is an attitude that is affected precisely because the lack of an immediate poetic inspiration is felt, and felt so painfully that a theoretical assertion of it serves, in the shape of hope, as an idealization of what is felt to be absent.[6]

We may find some of the answers we seek by considering how Novalis's development of the impulses contained in Herder's and Fichte's theories of language prompts him to prefer fairy tales, dreams, magical attitudes, and the miraculous in general as proper expressions of the poetical. Yet these nonrational forms of poetic discourse rely for their validity not only on Novalis's particular theory of language, but also on his artistic and religious nature and on the effect Sophie von Kühn's death had on him. Therefore, in order to understand whether, for Novalis, the inspirational view of language and poetry is a simply held belief or a lack, idealized and poeticized into a theoretical claim, we need to know, on the one hand, what Novalis's theory of language means for his understanding of the craft of writing and, on the other hand, what its metaphysical and religious function is. Yet this we can come to know only by understanding what Sophie von Kühn and her death meant in Novalis's life and to his development as an artist.

Only when we have gained some insight into the interrelatedness of these issues can we hope to judge whether Novalis's inspirational view of language and poetry is simply the natural outgrowth of his philosophical, poetical, and religious temperament, or whether it results from an experience of the poetical paradise lost but fervently longed for and, therefore, longingly idealized and represented in a less than genuine attitude as present, or if not as present, as certainly attainable in the future. Yet even if Novalis's views are due to his religious attitude and are therefore part of a straightforward and genuinely held metaphysical position, the question still remains whether an attempt to synthesize the religious and the aesthetic in such a manner that the religious is ultimately subservient to the aesthetic is not always and of necessity the mark of a late age.[7] The question, therefore, is whether a belief in a Golden Age of Poetry, in which man was simply open to the voice of chance, or the muses, or the gods, is not a fiction that comes about because the poet's alienation from the world is about to become apparent to him—and is denied by him and covered over with the nostalgic desire for a time that probably never existed in the manner it is longed for by his fond poetic hope.

These issues may appear to be of a literary rather than a philosophical nature and, therefore, may seem to support the prevalent view (which has only a few notable exceptions such as Dilthey, Barth, or Haering, for example) that Novalis is primarily a writer and poet rather than a philosopher. Yet much in Novalis's various collections of fragments deals with traditionally philosophical concerns: aesthetics, ethics, the philosophy of religion, the philosophy of science, metaphysics, epistemology, and the theory of language all receive his attention. In addition, Novalis's encyclopedic project, the *Allgemeine Brouillon*, as well as several of his short essays, have an entirely philosophical perspective even when traditionally nonphilosophical questions are addressed. Similarly, several of his fictional works are far more interesting philosophically than they are successful as literary creations. If Novalis nevertheless has been largely neglected as a figure in the history of philosophy, this is due no doubt to both the fragmentary nature of his work—very little of it was ever completed—and to his aphoristic or nonsystematic style of presentation. And whereas such a manner of expression has been philosophically acceptable on occasion, as for instance when it sparkles sufficiently with the ambiguous wit of irony or is sharpened by a skeptical and analytic rationality, it has usually been rejected when it is the voice of an entirely syncretic, mystical, and analogical mind concerned with questions of the infinite. For then the aphoristic utterance is judged to belong to the realms of poetry and religion and to be inappropriate for the enterprise of philosophical inquiry. But to dismiss Novalis as a philosopher for these reasons is to subscribe to that narrow preconception of philosophy which Novalis not only challenges by his personal style and approach, but which he programmatically rejects. As a result, Novalis presents philosophers with questions about the philosophic enterprise. I hope my discussion of his work will on the one hand elucidate these questions and on the other hand show their validity. In the process of doing so I hope to help find the proper (and not negligible) place this relatively neglected figure holds in the history of philosophy.

Given the range of Novalis's interests, it should not be surprising that his thought cuts across many fields and defies a clear-cut and narrow compartmentalization. In addition, it is Novalis's avowed aim to synthesize what the increasingly academically defined project of knowledge tends to separate. In my attempt to explicate Novalis, I have chosen to concentrate primarily on his theory of language, since for Novalis language, if its definition is made wide enough, encompasses the universe. This is not a metaphorical statement but a literal description. Everything, each natural and each artificial object and also each subject, is understood by Novalis as a communication and therefore as a form of language. Novalis's theory of language, thus, is neither confined to nor even primarily focused on what a modern philosophy of language would take to be its proper field of study, namely either uttered or written verbal expressions. Since language, then, is not merely a vehicle for carrying meaning or a tool for expressing ideas of beauty, truth, love, and faith, but is itself, in the very being of its various components, the beauty, truth, love, and faith that is expressed, a proper understanding of Novalis's conception of language will have to include questions and problems of aesthetics, epistomology, metaphysics, and religion. It will, therefore, throw light on Novalis's view of man's relation to nature and to art, to other people and to himself, as well as on man's knowledge of this world and his faith in the world beyond. Because of the all-inclusive nature of Novalis's definition of language, my investigation will in part deal with issues which, though they were of central concern to Novalis, would be considered extraneous to the purview of language theory by a narrower and more modern view. But I hope that as a result this essay will contribute, both as historical investigation and as systematic exploration, to the fields of aesthetics, epistemology, and the philosophy of religion.

Since Novalis's thought on language can be viewed from three separate perspectives, it almost naturally groups itself into three distinct spheres of interest. I have structured my investigations accordingly. First, there is language in its relation to time, particularly time's qualitatively-determined and determining aspect. It is dealt with in "Part One" of the essay. Second, there is language and its relation to space, as the prerequisite condition for all nondiscursive understanding and representation. This is dealt with in "Part Two" of this essay. Last, there is the synthesis of these two spheres in the language of faith and poetry which, it will be noticed, is left incomplete, since neither space nor time allow here a fully-developed treatment of the subject. But it will be pointed to again and again in the course of presenting the first two moments and will find in the final chapter of "Part Two," dealing with the metaphysics of fairy tales, its most thorough treatment here.

The esteem in which Novalis is held varies historically, geographically, and individually. The Novalis interpretation holds widely divergent and even opposing views of his work. In part these differences seem to arise as a consequence of focusing either on Novalis's religious and metaphysical stance or on his poetical and aesthetic thought. In order to set the historical framework for my discussion, I will in the first chapter of this essay attempt to give a brief sketch of Novalis's reception by and influence on both the English-speaking world and the French world of letters. The British, as well as the Americans, were primarily interested in Novalis's pre-occupation with night, with death, and with the spiritual power of love. In contrast the French, although they did not ignore Novalis's "metaphysics of night," were far more attracted by his poetic theory and further developed the poetic stance and mood they found expressed there. The effect Novalis, thus, had on modern French poetry and poetics, in turn, excited and attracted modern German thought on poetic theory and came eventually to influence a whole tradition of

Novalis interpretation in Germany. In giving this short historical over-view, the first chapter necessarily differs in aim, method, and subject matter from the chapters that follow. But since it is my contention that the one-sidedness of both the Anglophone and the French-German views of Novalis's work tends to lead to a misreading of it, a brief presentation of the historical context within which and in opposition to which my own views developed seemed necessary, and possibly helpful to the reader. The main body of this essay and of my interpretation of Novalis thus actually begins with chapter two. Here I will argue that Novalis's meta-physics and aesthetics are not only closely interdependent, but form a coherent philosophical stance only if they are seen, on the one hand, as richly interwoven, and, on the other hand, as moving towards a full development in Novalis's religiously grounded philosophy of language.

The main body of literary works Novalis left behind consists of a number of rather extensive collections of fragments, including his philo-sophical studies; two unfinished ambitious fictional pieces, each of which contains at least one wonder tale: *Die Lehrlinge zu Sais* (*The Novices of Sais*) with the story of "Rosenblüthe und Hyacinth"; and *Heinrich von Ofter-dingen* with the stories of "Klingsohr," "Arion," and "Atlantis" (if indeed both these "novels" are not themselves to be classified as wonder tales); a few essays; and a fair-sized sampling of poetry, which includes his two major poetical accomplishments, namely the cycle *Hymnen an die Nacht* (*Hymns to the Night*) and the *Geistliche Lieder* (*Spiritual Songs*). In arguing my view I will rely equally on Novalis's theoretical writings and on his fiction. Only his poems will not receive the attention they deserve. For as pointed out above, it is in his poetry that the synthetic approach is most fully realized, and it is just this approach that must be reserved for treat-ment in the future.

PART I

The Poet and the Heavens

Sophie von Kühn.
Medallion, Städtisches Museum Weissenfels.

Julie von Charpentier.
Chalk drawing, probably by Dora Stock, Hardenberg family in
Oberwiederstedt.

CHAPTER ONE

Some Historical Observations on the Reception of Novalis's Works

BRITISH AND AMERICAN REACTIONS TO NOVALIS'S WORKS

Novalis the poet. Novalis the metaphysician. Despite all his efforts to show that this distinction is essentially spurious, and despite his declared project to synthesize poetry and philosophy, the tradition of Novalis interpretation has tended to deal with the poet and the metaphysician separately—even when recognizing that Novalis's interest lay in not doing so. Thus the individual interpreter or commentator as well as entire schools of poetry influenced by Novalis emphasize either the one or the other. In France, for instance, where the Symbolist writers were much indebted to Novalis, it was usually Novalis the poet and theorist of poetry who was turned to, even when philosophical issues were at stake. In the British and American reception of Novalis, however, the contrary was true. Thomas Carlyle, who first translated Novalis into English and who wrote the first evaluative commentary in English about him, esteemed Novalis for the depth of his thought but considered his poetic gift less significant. Similarly in America, where the Transcendentalists owe much to Novalis, it was Novalis the metaphysician far more than Novalis the poet who was of interest—even if that interest was aroused by Novalis's literary works and even if the people interested were themselves members of the world of literature rather than philosophy.

In his essay "Novalis,"[1] written for the *Foreign Review* in 1829, Carlyle offers the English reader an introduction to both the man and the writer. Basing his discussion on the fourth edition of the two-volume *Novalis Schriften*, edited by Ludwig Tieck and Friedrich von Schlegel, Carlyle

9

begins his article with a comparison of the reading habits of the English and the Germans and comes to the conclusion that,

> It rather seems to us as if, in this respect of faithfulness in reading, the Germans were somewhat ahead of us English; at least we have no such proof to show of it as that fourth Edition of *Novalis*. Our Coleridge's *Friend*, for example, and *Biographia Literaria* are but a slight business compared with these *Schriften*; little more than the Alphabet, and that in gilt letters, of such Philosophy and Art as is here taught in the form of Grammar and Rhetorical Compend. [*TCE*, 184]

High praise, indeed! But even though Carlyle takes the British to task for too superficial an interest, he himself repeatedly comments on the depth and difficulty of Novalis's writings:

> Novalis, a man of the most indisputable talent, poetical and philosophical; whose opinions, extraordinary, nay altogether wild and baseless as they often appear, are not without a strict coherence in his own mind, and will lead any other mind, that examines them faithfully, into endless considerations; opening the strangest inquiries, new truths, or new possibilities of truth, a whole unexpected world of thought where, whether for belief or denial, the deepest questions await us. [*TCE*, 186]

This mixture of admiration for Novalis and of exasperation at his "wild" and "baseless" thought is evident throughout the essay. Carlyle's ambivalence leads him to doubt the possibility of his own enterprise:

> To explain so strange an individuality, to exhibit a mind of this depth and singularity before the minds of readers so foreign to him in every sense, would be a vain pretension in us. [*TCE*, 189]

It seems therefore that Carlyle's interest in Novalis was due not only to Novalis's literary achievements, but was, at least in part, also based on a fascination with Novalis's exceptional fate. For example, Carlyle quotes liberally from Ludwig Tieck's biographical notes and intersperses remarks about the quality and nature of Novalis's life and character among the evaluations of his philosophic and religious stance:

> Naturally a deep, religious, contemplative spirit; purified also, as we have seen, by harsh Affliction, and familiar in the "Sanctuary of Sorrow," he comes before us as the most ideal of Idealists. [*TCE*, 206]

Having set the stage and prepared the reader to expect some difficult, even odd philosophical texts, Carlyle offers his audience translated selections from *Die Lehrlinge zu Sais* (*The Novices of Sais*). Yet his ambivalence, even toward the texts he chooses to translate, leads him to comment about Novalis's view of nature in an ambiguous fashion:

> One character to be noted in many of these, often too obscure speculations, is his peculiar manner of viewing Nature: his habit, as it were, of considering Nature rather in the concrete, not analytically and as a divisible Aggregate, but as a self-subsistent universally connected Whole. [*TCE*,206]

As it turned out, this evaluation was of some consequence and interest to Carlyle's American readers, who found such an idea of nature particularly intriguing, as we shall see when we discuss Ralph Waldo Emerson's relation to Novalis. The other selections Carlyle presents are a lengthy fragment on the history of philosophy, a page of religious fragments, and two pages of short aphorisms on a variety of different subjects offered not because they are what he considers best in Novalis, but because they are, of all things, easily comprehended:

> The reader understands that we offer these specimens not as the best to be found in Novalis's *Fragments*, but simply as the most intelligible. [*TCE*,218]

Carlyle's ambiguity here leaves us uncertain whether he considers Novalis hopelessly obscurantist, or the reader spoiled and ready to digest only light fare, or both. Having given a sampling of Novalis's philosophical speculations along with many warnings of their difficulty, Carlyle turns to Novalis's literary works. He offers the third of the *Hymnen an die Nacht* (*Hymns to the Night*), chosen for a similar reason as the fragments, namely because it is "the shortest and simplest" [*TCE*,220], a rather strange evaluation given that its subject matter is the mystical vision Novalis encountered at Sophie's graveside. Then follow two selections from *Heinrich von Ofterdingen* (*Henry of Ofterdingen*), both of which are descriptions of dreams, with the second being a dream of death and rebirth. It would appear, therefore, that it was neither their shortness nor their simplicity that prompted Carlyle to choose just these passages, but rather their topic. This assumption is further strengthened by the fact that Carlyle was equally fascinated by Novalis's notion of *Selbstthötung*, or self-annihilation.[2] Thus it would seem that it is Novalis's anti-Enlightenment attitude that Carlyle actually values and that leads him to say of both Novalis and his writing:

> There is in it a trace of that simple sublimity, that soft still pathos, which are characteristics of Novalis, and doubtless the highest of his specially poetic gifts. [*TCE*,225]

While ultimately Carlyle finds Novalis's religious and mystical talent and metaphysical position most appealing—even if not necessarily convincing—it is Novalis's intellect he values most:

> We might say, that the chief excellence we have remarked in Novalis is his to us truly wonderful subtlety of intellect; his power of intense abstraction, of pursuing the deepest and most evanescent ideas through their thousand complexities, as it were, with lynx vision, and to the very limits of human Thought. [*TCE*,226]

This "wonderful subtlety of intellect" notwithstanding, Carlyle finds Novalis lacking in ordinary thought patterns, and finds this both attractive and irksome. He would have preferred a mind with a little more everyday clarity and a little less freedom in its habit of associating the most diverse subjects. He therefore takes Novalis to task for a lack of critical evaluation, or the "laxity" of his thinking:

> He *sits*, we might say, among the rich, fine, thousandfold combinations, which his mind almost of itself presents him; but, perhaps, he shows too little activity in the process, is too lax in separating the true from the doubtful, is not even at the trouble to express his truth with any laborious accuracy. With his stillness, with his deep love of Nature, his mild, lofty, spiritual tone of contemplation, he comes before us in a sort of Asiatic character. [*TCE*,227]

But Carlyle finds fault not only with Novalis's habit and mode of thought. He is also critical of his literary or poetic gift and style, the weakness of which he interprets to be a direct result of what he calls Novalis's "softness."

> His chief fault, again, figures itself to us as a certain undue softness, a want of rapid energy; something which we might term *passiveness* extending both over his mind and his character . . . Thus in his poetical delineations, as we complained above, he is too diluted and diffuse; not verbose properly; not so much abounding in superfluous words as in superfluous circumstances which indeed is but a degree better. [*TCE*,227]

These'criticisms of Novalis should not, however, mislead us into thinking that Carlyle's essay has anything like a prevailingly negative tone. On the contrary, its mood is very positive, which no doubt is due to the fact that, as Charles Frederic Harrold says, "what he [Carlyle] missed in current English and French thought—the dynamic element—he found in Fichte and especially in Novalis."[3] For indeed, Carlyle was not only familiar with Novalis's writings and often returned to them, but "after Goethe and Richter [Jean Paul], no German writer is more often quoted by Carlyle than Novalis."[4]

Carlyle finally concludes unambiguously and positively that rather than being regarded as the German Dante—a comparison often made at the time, since the parallels between Dante's relation to Beatrice and Novalis's to Sophie von Kühn could not escape his contemporaries— Novalis ought to be thought of as the German Pascal:

> Both are of the purest, most affectionate moral nature; both of a high, fine, discursive intellect; both are mathematicians and naturalists, yet occupy themselves chiefly with Religion; nay, the best writings of both are left in the shape of 'Thoughts,' materials of a grand scheme, which each of them, with the views peculiar to his age, had planned, we may say for the furtherance of Religion and which neither of them lived to execute. [*TCE*, 228]

I have quoted so extensively from Carlyle's "Novalis" here because it was this essay that first introduced Novalis not only to the British reader but also to the American public. For the American Transcendentalists often found their way indirectly to the German Romantic philosophy of Fichte, Schelling, and Schleiermacher, and even to the idealism of Kant, by way of the writings of Carlyle—especially his essay on Novalis.[5]

Although Carlyle himself was most impressed with Novalis's idea of self-annihilation, it was his representation of Novalis's concept of nature—which, as we have seen, Carlyle thought to be of "a peculiar manner"—that caught the imagination of Carlyle's American readers. For among the important American literary figures on whom Novalis made a lasting impression were Emerson and Thoreau, who both found in nature the same religious meaning, or indeed voice, that Novalis heard.

Emerson, who learned about Novalis first from Carlyle's essay (and possibly also from Coleridge), soon taught himself enough German to read him in the original.[6] In fact, Emerson twice checked out the *Novalis Schriften* from the Boston Atheneum Library, first in 1836 and again in 1851.[7] The fifteen years that elapsed between these two obvious engagements with Novalis's thought are not an indication of any lessened interest on Emerson's part, for in 1830 he had already copied long passages of Novalis's works into his notebook,[8] and he owned and read several of Novalis's works in translation.[9]

Whereas Novalis was not the author most widely read by Emerson, he was directly responsible for one of Emerson's more important essays, *Nature*, which in many ways is a restatement of ideas set forth in *Die Lehrlinge zu Sais* and in the *Fragmente*.[10] But Emerson not only restated Novalis's ideas about nature in another language—English—he also gave to them his own style of thought, organization, and prose.[11] Whereas Novalis's influence on *Nature* thus constitutes a telling example of how his thought shaped—in close and recognizable, yet unacknowledged form—major works of other authors, Emerson at least points to Novalis in *Nature* when he says that "the night shall be my Germany of mystic philosophy and dreams."[12] But this pretty nod in the direction of Novalis neither gives Novalis's name—and thus allows only the initiated reader to recognize Emerson's gesture—nor does it lead one to suspect the extent of Novalis's influence. One of the more ironic consequences of this unacknowledged and unrecognized literary begetting is that Nietzsche, who altogether disliked Novalis and rather fancied Emerson, indirectly paid Novalis a compliment when he copied passages from Emerson's works that were inspired by Novalis.[13]

Whereas Goethe was by far the most admired German author—a judgment the Transcendentalists shared with Carlyle—Novalis engaged their darker, more mystical tendencies:

> The whole Transcendental group found Novalis' writings of profound interest. He was recommended in the *Dial* (July, 1842)[14] and his works were to be found in the personal libraries of Emerson, Alcott, Clarke, Parker, Ripley, Hedge and Margaret Fuller. [*VGI*,86][15]

The passion for German literature among the Transcendentalists was in fact such that they frequently visited each other for the express purpose of reading and discussing German writers. During the year 1833 Margaret Fuller and James Clarke, for instance, met every day to read German together. [*VGI*,67] But others as well took up German, and at Harvard between 1817 and 1842 almost everyone learned enough to read German literature in the original. The most favored authors were Goethe, Schiller, Jean Paul (Richter), and Novalis. But the Transcendentalists not only read these authors, they also wrote about them. The mid-nineteenth-century literary, religious, and philosophical journals printed a wide variety of translations, quotations, comments, and reviews of and about German authors. Although Novalis ranked among those most eagerly read, he was not often cited or reviewed. Still he had his fair share even of the published attention.[16]

Aside from reviews and translations appearing in journals, however,

Novalis also came before the American public in a way that did not make his presence immediately obvious or his voice clearly heard as his own. Several of his aphoristic fragments and sayings were used as mottoes to precede the works of other authors. The editor of the *Journal of Speculative Philosophy*, William Torrey Harris, for instance, used Novalis's *Blüthenstaub (Pollen)* fragment "Philosophy can bake no bread, but she can procure for us God, Freedom, and Immortality" [III,315,#401] as the journal's motto, and that despite the fact that, as Henry A. Pochmann says, "the associated philosophers were no cloistered academicians." [PGA,258] Similarly, writers of fiction and poetry both appended Novalis's sayings to their own texts and followed literary strategies that Novalis suggested and used himself. Most prominent among these was Edgar Allan Poe, who chose the following fragment by Novalis to head *The Mystery of Marie Rogêt*. I quote it here in Poe's translation:

> There are ideal series of events which run parallel with the real ones. They rarely coincide. Men and circumstances generally modify the ideal train of events so that it seems imperfect, and its consequences are equally imperfect. Thus with the Reformation; instead of Protestantism came Lutheranism. [III,341,#411][17]

In addition to using this Novalis fragment as the motto for his tale, Poe also used its insight as the theme that determined the structural and topical strategies of his mystery.[18]

But the most striking resemblance between Poe and Novalis lies in their attitude toward chance events. For Poe, like Novalis, sees in chance occurrences more than merely accidental happenings with no inner coherence or order. It is not clear whether he came to this view because he first found it in Novalis, or whether he found in Novalis an affirmation of his own view and experience. But it is certain that, for both men, similar circumstances in their relations with loved, then lost and idealized women strengthened the tendency to accept chance events as fated occurrences—at least in their literary productions.[19] In any case, Poe's "Calculus of Probabilities" seems sufficiently to overlap with Novalis's idea of chance to make it appear likely that Novalis served as impetus for its conception.[20]

Although the list of those in American literature whom Novalis influenced could be extended—for Melville's flower symbolism, Lanier's musical aestheticism, Fuller's idea of *Poesie* (poetics) as the road to the infinite, and Longfellow's *Voices of the Night* all owe something to Novalis—I hope it is evident by now that for some time during the nineteenth cen-

tury Novalis enjoyed the kind of esteem and recognition in the United
States that are still his not only in Germany but also in France.

What was it then that happened? Why did Novalis's reputation in the
United States diminish so greatly? Why was his star eclipsed so totally?
First, a negative attitude toward Novalis arose within the Romantic tradition itself: Heinrich Heine, in his *Romantische Schule*, criticized Novalis
with the witty and sharp tones of his ironical voice.[21] Second, George
Eliot's "German Wit" made Heinrich Heine something of a German hero
in the English-speaking world, which made his criticism more effective
than it otherwise might have been.[22] Third, the mood of the times
changed. A new appreciation for the sciences and for technology made
the very "softness" that had become associated with Novalis, and that
already Carlyle had found objectionable, entirely unacceptable and even
laughable. Fourth, the association of Novalis with the Transcendentalists
further removed him from any relevancy for the new age in the eyes of the
literary cognoscenti.[23]

But while in some respects Carlyle's and Heine's criticisms correctly
address a weakness or limitation of Novalis's poetic gifts, by far not all of
his literary works are justly so criticized. Both the *Geistliche Lieder* and the
Hymnen an die Nacht without doubt belong to the best that German poetry
has to offer, and the language of the opening chapter of *Heinrich von
Ofterdingen* is unique in its exemplary simplicity. Furthermore, the un-
questionable one-sidedness of Carlyle's as well as Heine's evaluation
presents a false image of Novalis philosophically. Other aspects of his
thought must be taken into consideration if the full measure of his work
and influence is to be correctly understood. Since it is in Novalis's relation
to the French poetic tradition that these other characteristics of his philosophic and poetic nature became most apparent and bore abundant fruit,
let me now turn to consider these and the influence they, in turn, had on
some of Germany's thinking about Novalis.

FRENCH REFLECTIONS OF NOVALIS'S THEORY OF
LANGUAGE AND POETICS

Novalis's avowed project to poetize reality finds expression in his attempts, on the one hand, to give new value to the poet's position within
the framework of national and political concerns and, on the other hand,
to lift the poet in a true apotheosis toward the heavens. This project was
largely rooted in the French tradition, in which poets never lost the an-

cient and classical attitude of understanding themselves as fulfilling a divine mission to mankind, and in which they also perceived themselves (and were perceived by their audiences) as being part of the glory that is France.[24] From Ronsard's description of prose as the language of man and poetry as the language of gods,[25] or Lamartine's pronouncement that "our tears and our blood are the oil of the lamp God commands us to carry before mankind,"[26] to Victor Hugo's claim that "the earth spoke to me: poet! the heavens repeated to me prophet! Go forth! Speak! Teach! Bless!,"[27] French poets understood themselves and their work as being both of universal importance—as essential to all mankind—and as having to play a grand and magnificent national role.

Whereas Novalis certainly agreed that the poet must serve both these ends, his road of glory, in contrast to the classical French tradition's, led inward. Adjusting himself to this newly discovered inner terrain, he spoke with a poetic voice at once more intimate and darker. For in the deep caverns of the soul, light shines only dimly, and the grander voice fitting for public occasions would resound disturbingly, echoing off the walls and covering over what a quieter, stiller voice may discover and reveal. It is into this newly explored region of the self and of poetry and to this new voice that later French poets are thought to have followed Novalis, sometimes influenced by him directly, sometimes following along more indirect paths, paralleling, overlapping, and combining their roads with his.

Victor Hugo, for example, speaking from a dark and hopeless mood, found himself "crushed by the weight of immortality," thus becoming one of the first to sound a tone that later prevailed in the poetry of Vigny, Baudelaire, and Mallarmé.[28]

> The most self assured poet [Victor Hugo] becomes the ancestor of the "poète maudit," as in Germany Novalis becomes the direct predecessor of E. T. A. Hoffmann, with whom the exceptional position of the poet turns into that dangerous isolation in which the way inward leads past the specters of his own soul. [*VNS*, 12]

Yet the genealogy of influence is still more complex than this comment leads us to believe. For Novalis is not only a sort of literary kinsman of E. T. A. Hoffmann (as Hugo is of Vigny, Mallarmé, and Baudelaire), but insofar as Novalis influenced Edgar Allan Poe, and Poe as well as Hoffmann were much admired by the Symbolists (particularly by Baudelaire) and thereby had an effect on the nature of Symbolist poetry, Novalis indirectly becomes the ancestor of Baudelaire and the Symbolist tradition as well.[29] The round dance of poetic kinship and influence finally comes full circle when the French—much like their American cousins—discover in Carlyle a most valuable (and possibly their most important) source of knowledge about German philosophy and poetry.

Although Carlyle's "Novalis" was written in 1829, the full force of its influence was felt in France only considerably later, when that essay came to reaffirm the positive view of German literature that Madame de Staël's book *De l'Allemagne* had originally presented in 1813.[30] Carlyle's essay thus acted as a sort of refutation of Heine's *Romantische Schule*, which had appeared in 1833 in French and had done much to ridicule Novalis and his all-too-German muse.[31] It is likely that Baudelaire knew Carlyle's essay, since he also became acquainted with the works of Poe through British sources.[32] But even if Baudelaire did not read this essay, a sufficient number of his symbolic images bear such a striking resemblance to Novalis's that there is little doubt that he in one way or another knew the latter's work.

Although Novalis's *Schriften* had been available in France since 1837, the first French essay about Novalis did not appear until 1895 in the *Mercure de France*. It was written by Henri Albert, who two years earlier had published his translation of Novalis's *Märchen* "Rosenblüthe und Hyacinth" from *Die Lehrlinge zu Sais* under the title "Conte de Jacinthe et de Feuille-de-Rose."[33] The beginning of *Die Lehrlinge zu Sais* was translated in 1894 by Maeterlinck,[34] who presented the entire work with an appended selection of fragments in 1895.[35] The introductory essay to Maeterlinck's Novalis translation was, in turn, translated into English and presented to English readers in book form together with Maeterlinck's essays on Emerson and Ruysbroeck.[36] But the influence of Maeterlinck's essay remained more narrowly defined than the influence of Carlyle's study, which had sown its seeds far and wide. For Maeterlinck, himself a member of the Symbolist movement, mainly addressed those interested in this movement. But in contrast to other French writers and poets of the period, Maeterlinck found himself drawn above all to Novalis's metaphysical point of view rather than to his poetics. He, therefore, opened his interpretative chapter on Novalis as follows:

> Among the envoys of the human soul, Novalis probably represents one of the most imponderable, one of the most subtle, and one of the most transparent aspects of the superior being silent within the depth of us. [*MEE*,72]

Maeterlinck's essay thus resembles Carlyle's—which he had read—in its preoccupation with Novalis's mysticism, but is rather different in its tone: Maeterlinck enthusiastically and openly endorses Novalis's mysticism. Indeed, the essay begins with Maeterlinck's own musings on the subject of mystical and transcendental thought and gets around to considering Novalis only nineteen pages later, then turning quickly enough to a description of Novalis's life and person. Here Maeterlinck makes a point of questioning the importance of Sophie von Kühn for Novalis's creativity, on the one hand, and on the other hand takes issue with all those who would turn with embarrassment from Novalis's second engagement to Julie von Charpentier. While the former is an odd move, the latter is obviously sensible.

In a final section, Maeterlinck gives thumbnail critiques of Novalis's works and offers the reader the following evaluation of *Die Lehrlinge zu Sais* before presenting his translation of the work:

> There are few works more mysterious, more serene, and more beautiful. It has been said that he [Novalis] climbed I know not what interior mountain known only to himself; and that from the height of this silent summit he saw at his feet, nature, systems, hypotheses, and the thoughts of men. He does not summarise, he dominates without saying anything. In those very profound and solemn dialogues, intermingled with symbolical allusions, which stretch occasionally much beyond possible thought, he has fixed the remembrance of one of the soul's most lucid instants. It suffices that the reader be cautioned that he is here concerned with one of those rare books, where each, in accordance with his merits, finds his rewards. [*MEE*, 113–14]

Novalis himself also used the image of scaling a mountain, but he did so only in order to descend from its height into the metaphoric depths of caves. For the silence that Maeterlinck points to twice as the place and attunement from which Novalis wrote can be found only in the soul-caverns of the inner self. As we shall see, Maeterlinck thus comes close to my own view of the significance of silence in Novalis's voice, but removes himself somewhat from the other French Symbolist poets and theorists of poetry, to whom "silence" connoted a recalcitrance of words to express the ideal, or a withholding of language in general. Mallarmé's symbol of Apollo's white swan, whose wings are pinioned by the waters of the frozen lake, for example, depicts just such a negative silence of language, which he also expresses more directly when he says of his poetry "my art is a dilemma" (*mon art est une impasse*).

The French Symbolists, then, in contrast to the Belgian Maeterlinck, were attracted to Novalis primarily because of a tone and voice the "poète maudit" recognized as his own. Yet Novalis's importance to that tradition is twofold. For although at first he was one of the major influences that gave impetus to its development, he came to serve as an opposing force when he was understood as pointing the way that makes a true symbolist of the "poète maudit."

> For by "Symbolism" we not only mean a specific way to form and use symbols, not only a poetic technique. If that were all, already Baude-laire would have been a pure Symbolist and there would have been no need for any new manifestos and perceptions. Symbolism under-stood as an historically effective movement that shaped its time rather was a distinct attitude towards life, a poetic stance. [*VNS*,26]

And it is this attitude, this new mood vis-à-vis life, this new perception of the poet's position and task that the Symbolists are thought to have found theoretically expressed, poetically implemented, and practically lived by Novalis. For, as Werner Vordtriede observes, "the Symbolists do not continue French but German Romanticism." [*VNS*,32] This, no doubt, is so. Yet it is also true that an essential misunderstanding, especially of Novalis's essay *Monolog*, lay at the foundation of the Symbolists' view of this early German Romanticist. Similarly, later literary historians and critics (for instance Hugo Friedrich or Silvio Vietta, to name but two) also misinterpreted this text and, as a consequence, the Symbolists' relation to it.

In this view—which I do not share—Novalis is thought to have given a first description of the new attitude and voice appropriate for poetry's modern enterprise in his essay on language, the *Monolog*. A short sketch, hardly more than a page, it is credited nonetheless with being the birth-place of the emancipation of language, or at any rate, with being the first theoretical statement about that emancipation. As such it precedes, by half a century or so, the poetry of Baudelaire, Rimbaud, and Mallarmé, who, following Novalis's suggestion, sang with the voice of "autono-mous speech." Understood as a declaration of language's independence from its servitude to objects and subjects, to things and individuals alike, this emancipation is generally thought to have been a freeing of speech to its own nature. Novalis is seen as having originated and first expressed this modern self-sufficiency of poetry by saying it is silly of people to believe that we speak "for the sake of things," since it is actually only when we speak "merely in order to speak," that we utter the most glorious truths, for language is "concerned only with itself." [II,672,4–7] Because Novalis then went on to say that language resembles mathematical formulas that constitute a world in themselves—"playing only with themselves, expressing nothing but their own wonderful nature" [II,672,16]—it is claimed that language purely spoken is, for Novalis, not only a "mere word game," [II,672,3] but a word game with an abstract and cool temper.

Since the manuscript is no longer extant, an accurate dating of the *Monolog* is impossible. But as Richard Samuel says in his introduction to the essay:

> This mentioning of mathematical formulas which "constitute a world for themselves," points, after all, to already advanced studies in Freiberg, as they also manifest themselves in the *Arythmetica Universalis* and in other mathematical fragments. [II,659][37]

Since the *Monolog* is thought to have been written soon after that, it falls in the middle of Novalis's short six-year period of concentrated creative activity (1795–1801). Richard Samuel suggests that,

> The importance, in particular, of this short essay on the self-willed nature and separate world of language lies in the fact that it summarizes *in nuce* Hardenberg's theory of language, and at the same time informs us about Novalis's own form of language, whether it manifests itself poetically or philosophically. [II,659]

Whether one agrees with this statement depends entirely on what one understands the language theory of the *Monolog* to be.

Although there have always been a few interpreters of Novalis who approached his work without any preconceived ideological commitment—for instance, Thomas Carlyle or Wilhelm Dilthey—the majority of Novalis commentators formerly used to be of two sorts: the "true believers" who treated Novalis, both the man and his work, as nearly saintly;[38] and those who had no patience for what they conceived to be the sentimental drivel of a "beautiful soul," a term pronounced with heavy tones of irony and sarcasm that then spill over into the evaluation of Novalis's works in general.[39] It was therefore not only a relief but an overdue obligation when the tradition of Novalis interpretation took on a less emotional tone and began to evaluate Novalis's writings critically.

The credit for this turn of events must go in no small measure to those who, like Hugo Friedrich, first began to analyze Novalis's works in the light of the character and structure of modern poetry—particularly as it was shaped by the French Symbolists, who most obviously and by their own acknowledgment were influenced directly by Novalis's poetical writings and by his thoughts on poetry and language.

GERMAN ECHOES OF THE FRENCH INTERPRETATION OF NOVALIS'S THOUGHT

Since literary and poetic traditions never seem to stay within the boundaries of the language they arise in, literary cross-fertilization has always played a significant part in forming new poetic conventions and directions. But in the case of Novalis, a tradition of interpretation that originated outside of Germany affected critical evaluation as well. For a new appreciation by literary theoreticians and critics of the novel voice and poetics of the Symbolists is responsible for the changed perception of Novalis's role and place in literature both inside and outside of Germany.

One of the first to take such a fresh look at Novalis was, as I have pointed out, Hugo Friedrich. Although not dealing mainly with Novalis, Friedrich's *Die Struktur der modernen Lyrik*[40] set the approach that many were to follow. Pointing to Novalis as the poet who first explored theoretically some of the new interests and directions lyrical poetry was to take up and develop further in the nineteenth and twentieth centuries, Friedrich values Novalis's contributions to aesthetic theory considerably more than to poetry and therefore deals with Novalis's reflections on poetry rather than with his poems.

Identifying the poetic in general with the lyrical, Friedrich claims Novalis set a new tone by interpreting the lyrical subject as a "neutral attunement" (*neutrale Gestimmtheit*) whose creative act is ruled by "cool circumspection" (*kühle Besonnenheit*). [FML,28] Yet, according to Friedrich, in addition to establishing this emotionally controlled and intellectually distanced attitude of the poetic temperament, Novalis also identified the poet with the irrational. For Friedrich attributes to Novalis the view that:

> Fantasy enjoys the freedom "to jumble all images." It is a singing opposition against a world of habits, in which poetical people cannot live, because they are "divinatory, magical people." [FML, 28]

Thus Novalis is said to understand the poet as magician, primarily because, if given free rein, the poet's fantasy is a magical organ. This claim is based on such Novalis fragments as the following:

The imagination is that wonderful sense which can *replace* for us all other senses—and which already answers so much to our willfulness. When the outer senses seem to be subject entirely to mechanical laws—the imagination apparently is not bound to the presence and contact of outer stimuli. [II,650,#481][41]

By means of such a "free" fantasy that has no ulterior goal, serves no purpose outside itself, and follows only its own chance associations in creating poetry, Novalis, according to Friedrich and those who followed his lead, identified poetry with magic and the poet with the magician— who conjures, for those he has enchanted, a world of poetical imagery that in no way relies on, or fears interference from, outer sense impressions or excitations. The importance of such an independent and autonomous imagination is seen to lie in its ability to free art from its bondage to nature, that is, from the age-old model of art as an imitation of nature.[42] But since this fragment is preceded by the observation that the perceivable is attached to the nonperceivable, we must understand Novalis to think of the work of art as the perceivable appearance of a nonperceivable idea, and of the imagination as that organ which is capable of perceiving what our other senses cannot. Written toward the end of August, 1798, after a visit to the Dresden Gallery of Paintings, the fragment obviously refers to the artistic functions of the imagination. It agrees well with Novalis's idea that the artist also uses his senses actively, that is, not as receptive instruments or organs, but as expressive ones:

He [the artist] indeed looks outward and not inward—he feels outward and not inward. The main difference is this: the artist has activated the seed of the self-forming life in his organs—has heightened their sensitivity *for the spirit* and as a consequence is able to bring forth ideas at will—without solicitation—to use them as tools for the modification, *at will*, of the world. [II,574,20–26]

Such Novalis interpreters as Silvio Vietta, for example, see Novalis here following Fichte's suggestion that works of the imagination cannot be grasped except by the imagination itself, and that art—be it musical, pictorial, or poetical—is but an invitation to "self-activity" (*Selbst-thätigkeit*) on the part of the audience. Novalis is thus believed to claim that art requires the active participation of the beholder. But for Novalis not only works of art must be understood in terms of their production. The dynamics of the creative act—our capacity for making, in general— conditions our understanding.

★We know something only—insofar as we can *express*—i.e., *make* it. The more readily and manifold we are able to *produce* it, to *execute* it, the better do we *know* it—We know it completely when we are able everywhere and in all manner to *impart* it, to cause it—to effect an individual *expression* of it in every organ. [II,589,#267][43]

But an artwork that exists essentially only in the process of its creation by the artist or its re-creation by the reader, onlooker, or listener, and that, therefore, has no essentially independent being in itself, must be understood as much more closely allied to the imagination than any traditional understanding of the work of art would require. In fact, one could say that in this view, the work of art becomes the mere occasion for the work of the imagination. The poet-magician's power, then, is seen to lie in his ability to impose *his* will on the reader's or listener's re-creative imagination by causing a perception of things as *he* wishes it by the dictatorial force of *his* imagination alone, that is, entirely independent of any sense-perceptions originating in the exterior world of both the poet and his reader. The poet-magician thus seems to rely on the independence of language from all *external* determination. Indeed, for Novalis's poet, language is said to become what Friedrich calls "self-speech" (*Selbstsprache*), a form of language freed from all determination other than its own imaginative chance directions.

By combining the magical aspects of composing poetry with mathematically precise and constructive operations of rational thought, interpreters such as Friedrich see Novalis as adding a new intellectual severity to the age-old identification of poetry with magic. As a result, it is the magic of chance-ruled fantasy, on the one hand, and of algebraic abstraction, on the other hand, that Friedrich suggests emancipate poetry: "Thematically the writing of poetry relies on chance, methodically on the abstractions of *algebra*." [FML,29][44] But in a world of such autonomous language it is tonal quality that engenders poetic construction, and Friedrich finds that Novalis's reflections anticipate the modern view that,

> Poetry grows out of the impulse of language which, in turn obeying the prelinguistic "tone," points the way in which content accrues; content no longer becomes the actual substance of a poem, but is the bearer of the tonal might and its meaning-surpassing vibrations. [FML,51]

Poetry here is magical, according to Friedrich, because it understands itself as surrendering its substantial being and its origins to the magical powers inherent in language itself, while at the same time acting with mathematical precision in the lesser poetic enterprise of constructing and assigning subsequent meaning to prior sound-compositions.

Insofar then as the *Monolog* serves as *the* text that can and should shape our understanding of Novalis's language theory, the Novalis interpretation that takes its main cue from Friedrich's view of modern poetry as derived from the practice of the Symbolists understands Novalis to have freed fantasy so that its imagery could flow unhampered by objective references and subjective interests. Thus Novalis is seen as relying on chance association alone for poetry's content and on mathematical precision for the order of its poetic sequences, while at the same time subjecting mood to such intellectual distancing that it becomes neutralized into "cool circumspection." By this inversion of the traditional stance, which approached the poetical enterprise with a passionate attunement and with fantasy securely in the service of subjective meaning and objective purposefulness, Friedrich finds Novalis not only "setting modern poetry and poetical theory on a new path" but standing at the beginning of that attitude that regards poetical inspiration with acute suspicion. For inspiration requires the poet to be deeply affected by the spirit with whose voice he sings. Inspiration as enthusiastic and passionate possession denies the poet both the emotional distance of a cool or aloof mood and the independence or freedom of the imagination, which Friedrich thinks Novalis considered necessary above all else for the poet singing with the voice of autonomous speech.

But Friedrich is aware that the magic of an autonomous language and of an entirely free and playful imagination cannot be the only form of magic affecting Novalis's theory of language and poetry. He thinks it likely that Novalis was also familiar with and influenced by the French Illuminati, who proposed a speculative theory of language that held the origin of words to lie in a domain beyond man.[45] In deliberate opposition to the language theories of the Enlightenment (which considered words to have been invented by man for the sole purpose of serving as tools of communication and expression), the Illuminati thought language in its pristine state to be symbolic and to include the entire cosmos as the mute revelation of the spiritual unity of God. Human language, as the fallen form of that higher symbolic expression, still retains a flicker of the original divine spark. The power of words, therefore, lies not in their arbitrarily assigned meaning or rational content, as it does for the theorists of the Enlightenment, but in their supra-rational source, in their origin in God. Poetry has the power to return us, or at least to bring us closer again, to the origin from which we and language have fallen. In this theory of the essential nature of language, the pronouncing of the poetic word is seen as causing the speaker to enter magically into contact with our cosmic origin. As Friedrich says:

> As poetical word it immerses trivial things again into the secret of their metaphysical origin and sets the hidden analogies among the links of being into the light. [*FML*,52]

The magical power of language here rests in its ability, on the one hand, to afford us a glimpse of the cosmic unity from which we have fallen and, on the other hand, to bring us closer to that unity once again by the power of speech, which is understood as the participation of language in the essential nature of things. In contrast, the magical power of autonomous speech lies in the freeing of language from all origins and goals and, consequently, in the freeing of the imagination of speech from all outer and inner bondage to an entirely playful and self-absorbed creativity.

Friedrich's tendency, and the tendency of most who have adopted his view, whether fully or not, is to overlook the contradiction, disjunction, or at the very least tension that lies in the claim that the magical power of language, for Novalis, is due at once to its being an autonomous faculty, as the *Monolog* is understood to assert, and to its being an essential expression, as the theory of the Illuminati holds. Overlooking the distinctions between these views, the dictum that "every word is a word of incantation" is then cited as proof for Novalis's magical theory of language. But far from supporting this double-edged and self-contradictory interpretation, the fragment asserts a third position that is not identical with either the autonomous or the essential theory of language and is compatible only with the latter. For the complete aphorism reads:

> "❚Every word is a word of incantation. Which spirit[46] calls—such a one appears.❚" [II,523,#6][47]

Speech is here linked to spirit, specifically to the kind of spirit that does the calling. For this reason the statement, instead of proving the independence and autonomy of language as a "world for itself," supports the view that language is intimately tied to the nature of the speaker. The fragment thus shows Novalis holding an expressive theory of language, a view which can be supported further by the following notation from the *Logologische Fragmente*:

> Every human being has his own language. Language is expression of spirit. Individual languages. Genius of language. The ability to trans-

late into and from other languages. The richness and euphony of every language. The true expression constitutes the *clear* idea. As soon as one has the right names, one also grasps the ideas. Translucent, guiding expression. [II,560,#164]

The spirit of the speaker calls out in the words he pronounces and is answered by a kindred spirit. For the poet-magician this means that the magical power of his words ultimately resides neither in the autonomous power of language nor in its cosmic origin, but rather in his own soul.[48]

But whether the imagination is understood as independent from nature and from all outer stimuli, or as associated with chance, or as part of the active self-expression of the artist's soul, it is, in this view, always claimed to be free. If, in addition to being freed from all inner and external stimuli, the imagination is also thought of as freed from the rule-giving or order-imposing governance of the understanding, a lack of rule becomes the rule for the imagination. To support this assertion Vietta, for instance, points to the following phrase from the *Allgemeine Brouillon:*

Non-rule is the rule of fantasy—*arbitrary rule*—chance-rule—miracle-rule.

Yet Novalis continues the fragment by saying:

Rule—*direct* law—indirect (crooked) law = non-rule. Rule of the productive imagination—synthesis of direct and indirect law.
[III, 409,29–410, 2, #730]

Clearly, Novalis's position regarding the imagination's being subject to rule or not being subject to rule is quite a bit more intricate and subtle than those critics acknowledge who deny that rule-giving and order-imposing structures have any effect on it.

The assertion that Novalis freed the imagination from all "direct rule" leads to the conclusion that the work of art must necessarily be a "product of chance" for Novalis and that he, therefore, sees the imagination's very lack of intention in artistic making as its truly poetic creativity. Thus, for instance, Vietta says:

"Chance production" lies in the "intention" of Romantic poetics. "Intention" undertakes no controlling function, rather it sets into motion uncontrolled production. [*VSS*,29,2.3.6]

Intention, then, is considered to have no controlling function in the production of art for the Romantics in general and for Novalis in particular. But this claim is far more extreme than any assertion that the imagination is stimulated by some chance event or accidental pattern. For here the entire creative process is seen as being intentionally unintentional. The artist is thought to hold back or withdraw all intentionality from the creative enterprise and to allow mere chance alone to determine the shaping of the work of art.[49]

But quite the contrary must be true for Novalis. In fact, he suggests that our making has to be very narrowly guided if it is to be excellent:

> The greater the poet, the less liberty he permits himself, the more philosophical he is. He will content himself with the free choice of the first moment and will afterward only develop the predispositions of this germ—to its resolution. [II,581,6–9#242]

Why then the erroneous interpretation? The reasons seem to be twofold: on the one hand, reading back into Novalis the mood and stance of the Symbolists leads to a view of his fragments that leaves out of consideration those aspects of his thought the Symbolists overlooked or deliberately neglected and, on the other hand, dealing with Novalis's fragments in isolation from each other and in isolation from his fictional and poetical works can easily mislead the unwary reader. Take, for instance, fragment 953 of the *Allgemeine Brouillon:*

> The poet uses things and words like *keys,* and all of poetry is due to an active association of ideas—due to self-active, intended, ideal *chance production*—(Accidental—free *catenation.*) (Casuistry—fate. Casuation.) (*Game.*) [III,451,#953][50]

It is reasonable to assume that the mistaken interpretation rests on a misreading of the phrase "self-active, intended, ideal chance production." But in light of Novalis's view of the meaning of chance (which will be developed below) this phrase ought not be read as a declaration of the withdrawal of all intentionality from the creative process. Rather, the fragment points both to the near prophetic nature of poetic creation and to the poet's ability to infer, by a chain of events and ideas, the determinative moment of a life.[51] Indeed, rather than advocating any extraordinarily free or uncontrolled and intentionless activity of the imagination, Novalis suggests that only the first moment of any creative act is "intentionless" and that, far from being free, the good artist is bound to develop what is contained in that moment.

Novalis, then, appears to stand firmly within the classical tradition of creativity. He would, for instance, have agreed fully with da Vinci's suggestion that artistic creation is furthered by allowing chance to serve as a stimulus or impetus to the imagination, but he would not have thought that chance, and only chance, should produce the entire work. Nevertheless, intentionally unintentional or accidental and uncontrolled making are cited as the reason for the importance of dreams and fairy tales for Romantic poetry in general, and for Novalis in particular. Dreams, however, clearly are not the production of *intended* intentionlessness; they are merely unintentional creations, and fairy tales are not chance productions, though both rely on or make good use of the active association of ideas.[52] The tradition of Novalis interpretation that follows Friedrich is correct, though, in claiming the importance of "chance" for understanding the place fairy tales and dreams occupy in Novalis's theory of poetic language. But it is not chance defined as haphazard, unconnected, or meaningless occurrence—or *mere* chance—that plays a significant role in Novalis's theory of language and poetry.

CHAPTER TWO

Occasion, Chance, and Kairos-Time

NOVALIS'S RULE OF CHANCE AND HIS METHOD OF *RAISING*

In the introduction to his essay "The First Love,"[1] Kierkegaard discusses in an ironical and playful manner the serious question of the role of the occasion in artistic production, and why it is that some artists deny or overlook its importance while others become enamored of it. Does Kierkegaard's assertion that there is a "productivity that falls in love with the occasion" [*E/O*,232] have the same meaning as Novalis's aphorism that "the poet adores chance"? Or do *chance* and *occasion* name two different moments in the creative enterprise?

The German word for occasion is *Anlass.* In the sense of Anlass, occasion names what we have in mind when at retirements, birthdays, or anniversaries, for instance, we begin our after-dinner speeches with the remark: "On this occasion. . . ." Occasion here serves a trivial function and holds none of the mystery "chance" has for Novalis. We therefore must distinguish between occasion and chance, at least on the level on which occasion refers to a *merely* accidental occurrence or circumstance. But the paradox of the relation between chance and occasion is that the *merely* accidental occasion may contain in its folds the more than only accidental gifts of chance; with the occasion may come for the creative artist an opening of the heart by which inspiration may enter, and under such circumstances the occasion is of great importance indeed. Occasion, then, is an ambiguous concept—being at once the name for a merely trivial circumstance and for the opportunity that houses the gifts of chance.

Kierkegaard does not distinguish between chance and occasion, but rather subsumes the meaning of "chance" under "occasion." He says, for example, that in the creative enterprise

The occasion is always the accidental, and this is the tremendous paradox, that the accidental is just as absolutely necessary as the necessary. [*E/O*,232]

But whereas the occasion is accidental in the trivial sense of that word and, therefore, plays a minor role for the creative artist, the necessity it paradoxically appears to display to Kierkegaard is due not to its own paradoxical nature, but to the relationship it has to chance. Thus, the paradox is not that the accidental *is* the necessary, but that it may contain or house it!

The occasion, then, may be trivial or not, depending on whether chance offers its gifts with the occasion and inspiration takes hold of the creative impulse. But as Kierkegaard says:

Without the occasion precisely nothing at all happens, and yet the occasion has no part at all in what does happen. The occasion is the last category, the essential transitional category, from the sphere of the idea to actuality. [*E/O*,236]

The artist, however, who "sees everything in the occasion" [*E/O*,232], takes a chance that the occasion is indeed "the nothing from which everything comes" [*E/O*,234]—which it is only when, by chance, it occurs at that moment in which inspiration can break through the everyday and offer to the artist the vision of truth.

Novalis rarely considers the role of the occasion. The concept of *Zufall*, or "chance," on the contrary is of great importance to him, and its meaning is central to several of his main concerns. But how Novalis understands Zufall needs to be thought through carefully. Discussions of this concept's significance for Novalis usually are couched in the positive language of "freedom."[2] But it is not at all clear whether this reference to freedom intends Zufall to mean an uncaused event (bringing up the question of what "freedom" could possibly signify here) or an event that is the result of an unknown and unknowable, that is, irrational, cause (again raising the question what "freedom" might stand for in this connection) or whether, in fact, we are to have nothing more in mind than an act that was not willed, wished, or intended by the actor. But whatever the ambiguity and ambivalence toward the value and meaning of Novalis's concept of Zufall may be in this approach, it usually aims to praise the works of art that are productions of chance. In one estimation, for instance, it is held that:

> The very blurring of the contours of content belongs to the nature of
> Romantic poetry. The dynamics, for which fixed relations no longer
> are valid, are the "beautiful." . . . Chance production calls forth its
> own, new structure of work. [VSS,30,2.3.7.]

In other words, we are meant not to fault works of art that are products of
chance for lacking "clear contours of content" or "fixed relations between
events." But aside from the question whether this is really the nature of
the Romantic work of art in general and of Novalis's in particular—and I
would claim that it is certainly not true of Novalis's work—there seems
implied in such a defense a notion of "chance" as "*mere* chance": for a
lessening of some sort (rather than a heightening) of value in the product
seems to be acknowledged, even though we are told to understand this
lack as essential to Romantic poetry. But is Zufall for Novalis *mere* chance?
And can chance for Novalis ever be of lesser value?

"*Mere* chance" is a causal explanation that not only indicates the sheer
unpredictability of the effect, but also implies a lack of meaning in its
origin and consequently in the effect itself. As a result, the effect of *mere*
chance—be that effect a work of art or a specific event in a particular life—
cannot be integrated into a meaningful whole, that is, into a sequence of
events that taken together are a significant part of the greater whole that is
man's history. But "*mere* chance" is not the only way in which "chance"
can be understood and interpreted.

As fragment 953 of the *Allgemeine Brouillon* shows,[3] chance, for
Novalis, (as in the phrase "ideal chance production") stands in a nexus
with fate, with the subtle, moral questions raised by casuistry, and raises
them, in turn, in "casuation." It also stands in relation to game. In like
fashion a *Blüthenstaub* fragment speaks of chance and game as belonging
to the same universe of meaning:

> Ordinary life is full of similar chance occurrences. They constitute a
> game that, like all play, amounts to surprise and deception.
> [II,425, 6–8#27][4]

Yet "games" are not only the playful occupation of children (although
such occupation may be far more serious than is usually admitted), for
games are also those competitive engagements in which an agonistic
element determines the mood and significance of the undertaking.[5]
Games are competitive matches, and in some games life itself is at stake.
In the jousts of the knights, the war games of the Middle Ages, for
instance, a man literally gambled for and with his life. Similarly, nature
herself appears to Novalis to play with life:

▌Do not God and nature *play* as well? Theory of playing. *Holy games.*
pure game-theory—*common*—and *higher.* Applied game-theory.▐
[III,320,#418][6]

The German word *Spiel* covers the meanings of "play," "game," and
"gamble." The question, therefore, whether God and Nature do not play
as well—although it certainly and primarily points to the playfulness of
creativity—allows us also to wonder whether God and Nature do not
gamble. The idea of chance is thus associated with "Spiel" on two distinct
levels. Gambling, obviously an activity tied to luck or fortune—Fortuna—is indeed based on chance. But "play" also belongs under the
domain of chance, particularly since Friedrich Schiller in his *Aesthetic
Letters* tied "Spiel" to the creation of beautiful works of art:

> The drive to play would be directed at negating time in the temporal
> and at uniting becoming with absolute being as well as change with
> identity. . . . The drive to play in which both [the physical and the
> formal drive] work together shall make our formal and material
> nature, our perfection and happiness at once a matter of chance;
> precisely because it shall make both a matter of chance, and because
> along with necessity also chance shall disappear, the drive to play
> shall again sublate chance in both, thus bringing form into matter and
> reality into form. . . . Man shall only play with the beautiful and only
> with the beautiful shall he play. For to say it at once, man only plays
> when he is in the full sense of the word man, and he is man completely
> only when he plays.[7]

We can hear an echo of Schiller's letters in one of Novalis's fragments of
the year 1797:

> Rights of conversation—/absolute play./ True communication takes
> place only among those who are like-minded, like-thinking.
> [II, 559,#148][8]

Here Novalis once more ties the notion of "play" to the order of situations
of contest and competition. But now he is speaking of play as an aspect of
the universe of language and thought. Novalis in these fragments seems
to have anticipated Huizinga's understanding of man as *homo ludens.* And
Huizinga seems to agree with Novalis in particular about the rule-governed nature of play and games, for he says: "Play is based on the manipulation of certain images, on a certain 'imagination' of reality (i.e., its
conversion into images)." [*HHL*,4] It therefore permits a manipulation of
reality according to our own desires, provided we meticulously observe
the clearly defined rules of play as they are set out in the appropriate

game theory. It is in this connection that we must understand Novalis to speak of the work of art as a product of chance, and therefore of the poet as "adoring chance." [III,449,#490]

Most basically then, Novalis distinguishes between "raw" or "mere chance" and "organized chance"—where "organized" is meant to refer us to the organic or organlike function of chance, that is, to chance as a means to a determined end.[9] Similarly, Novalis also speaks of "developed" or "formed chance." He writes: "▌Raw chance—*formed* chance—Harmony./▌" [III,304,#354][10] He once more links "harmony" and "chance" in a fragment about the Atomists: "Strange harmony in the atomistic system of that which is by chance." [III,446,#928] But harmony is a sort of order, an aesthetic regularity, and so the statement that "chance, too, is not *without reason—it has its* regularity" [III,414,#752] is, on the one hand, a reiteration of the harmonious nature of chance but, on the other hand, goes beyond the claim of aesthetic harmony by asserting that chance is not unreasonable and is therefore rule-governed. That Novalis has this in mind can be seen in the following fragment:

> The laws of chance—the *laws of change in general*—the series of laws—the calculus of law. [III,425,#793]

For Novalis, then, there are not just harmonies and rules, but even laws of chance, and the latter are not understood as being statistical probabilities, but as being of a higher nature, as being divine laws.

Let me return now to the line from fragment 730 in the *Allgemeine Brouillon*:

> Non-rule is the rule of fantasy—*arbitrary rule*—chance-rule—miracle-rule. [III,409,29–410,2,#730]

Chance-rule here occurs in a series of expressions that are lined up in an ascending order and have a dialectical relationship to each other in such a fashion that the extreme terms of the order function as polar opposites. Novalis called such an arrangement an *Erhebung*, that is, a raising, or a *Potenzierung*, which means a setting to the second, third, etc. power. It is a systematic ordering of which Novalis is fond and to which he is committed. Serving to intensify a concept by changing the level of its meaning beyond its initial power and scope, Erhebung is a hierarchical principle of structure. In it each term is superseded by another of a qualitatively higher rank in such a manner that between the central terms a break or turn of valuation, a switch of qualitative status is produced. Erhebung thus unites polar opposites into one ascending order of expressions and so points to their mutual interdependence and relatedness while retaining the qualitative abyss that divides them. In the *Allgemeine Brouillon*, for example, Novalis writes:

> *Raising* is the most excellent means I know for escaping at once from awkward collisions. Thus, e.g., the general raising of all mankind to the status of nobility—the raising of all human beings to beings of *genius*—the raising of all phenomena to *miracles*—of matter to spirit—of human beings to God, of all time to the Golden Age, etc.
>
> [III,440, #894]

The elegance of this fragment is that it practices what it preaches: it is itself ordered in the manner of such a continuous Erhebung in which one of the "extreme terms" or polar opposites—"all mankind," naming man as the source and manifestation of history—is set in contrast to the extreme term "the Golden Age," which for Novalis denotes the cessation of all history. The qualitative break occurs here between the still historical and therefore temporal idea of "miracle" and the ahistorical and atemporal notion of "spirit."

Although Novalis does not explicitly draw our attention to the tonal and etymological kinship of *erheben* or *Erhebung* with *erhaben* or the *Erhabene*, that is, with the sublime, this association is doubtless at work in his process of raising. For in Erhebung the prosaic is made sublime and poetical. And Novalis finds raising for this reason *the* method by which to accomplish his fondest hope and project, namely the poetization of nature, life, and history.

In fragment 730 of the *Allgemeine Brouillon*, then, the method of Erhebung works as follows: after starting out with the assertion that "non-rule is the rule of phantasy" (a nicely paradoxical statement and therefore entirely appropriate for the form of the fragment, which, after all, means to invite the reader to just the sort of participatory rethinking that Fichte's notion of "self-activity" [*Selbstthätigkeit*] means for Novalis), the expression "non-rule" is raised by consecutive steps to an ever-increasing qualitative meaningfulness and importance. The thought that begins as a paradoxical statement about the nature of the rule of fantasy, namely that it is non-rule (*Unregel*), moves away from the rule of *mere* chance; by an importation of volitional whim, it raises non-rule in the direction of its opposite and so arrives at "arbitrary rule" (*Willkührregel*). This in turn is raised; a higher order of rule is now aspired to with the result that "chance rule" (*Zufallsregel*), in the sense of organized or formed chance, is arrived at and constitutes that term in which the

qualitative switch or turn becomes apparent. A further raising or intensifying in the direction of a still more meaningful order and rule begets
the last term in this series, "miracle-rule" (*Wunderregel*). Thus all the
terms of the rule that determines fantasy come to belong to the ordering
principle that Novalis calls "crooked" or "indirect law."[11] Chance, as
organized chance, then, stands somewhere between arbitrary rule and
miracle rule, but in its qualitative nature it is more closely aligned with
miracle rule, and more nearly opposed to arbitrary rule. Far from sug-
gesting a lack of rule for the imagination (as one might think at first
glance, and as is often claimed by the interpreters of Novalis), this line,
therefore, sets out one of the series of laws Novalis is asking about in
fragment 793 of the *Allgemeine Brouillon*.[12]

"Miracle" is a word that for us has lost some of the seriousness of its
meaning. Through its association with the sensational and with the world
of advertising it is now used more by barkers at a carnival and in commercials than by clergymen in the pulpit. But for Novalis it still held much of
its original and literal sense. A miracle for him is an event caused by
divine intervention. As a consequence, its causal nexus may be entirely
obscure to us, without implying that the event is either uncaused, or a
mere chance event which is irrational, that is, less than rational, since its
cause is essentially unknowable. When miracles are accepted among the
many possible sorts of events that can and do occur in this world, their
apparent nonrational nature is reduced to being simply a perspectival
problem: only to *our* limited powers of perception, only from *our* angle of
vision do they then appear to stand outside the meaningful series that is
constituted by everything that happens. For in a world that acknowledges miracles as reasonable explanations of events, all events occur for
the sake of an ultimate goal or *telos*. It is a world with a divine plan, and so
God, or the gods, or divine agents can at any time intervene to facilitate
the coming about of the desired and planned-for end. In fact, miracles are
then necessary complements to natural laws, rather than—as Hume, for
instance, put it—"violations of the laws of nature."[13] For Novalis, therefore, both miracles and natural laws are each fully comprehensible in
their own nature only in contrast to one another, and only together do
they constitute the entire effective evolution of the divine telos:

> Miracles alternate with the effects of natural laws—they limit one
> another mutually, and together form a whole. They are united by
> canceling one another. No miracle without a natural occurrence and
> vice versa. [II,416,#13][14]

The positioning of formed or organized "chance-rule" between "arbitrary rule" and "miracle rule," therefore, ascribes to the chance event as cause (and consequently to the rule of Zufall, whether it is or is not obscure to us, and despite its being extraordinary) both a reasonableness and a higher value than the effects and rule of more common or ordinary causes have. How close Zufall stands to miracle for Novalis can be seen from the following fragment:

> All *chance* is miraculous—the touch of a higher being—a problem *datum* of the active religious *sense*. (Metamorphosis into *chance*.) Miraculous *words*—and *formulas*. (Synthesis of the arbitrary and the *non-arbitrary*.) (Flame between nothing and something.) [III,441,#901]

The last line, "flame between nothing and something," refers to the union of nothing and something. Novalis uses "flame" equivalently and analogously to synthesis:

> About our ego—as the *flame* of the body in the *soul*. Similarity of the soul to oxygen. (Oxygen as an irritability process.) All synthesis is a *flame*—or spark—or an analog of them. [III,440,20–23]

In fire a transformation of the state or nature of that which is aflame occurs. Yet "flame" names not only the process of that change or becoming, but also the momentary union of the two—often antithetical—states: body and soul, being and non-being, something and nothing. The miraculous words and formulas are those that can, like the flame, synthesize nothing with something, or the arbitrary with the non-arbitrary, the latter being, for Novalis, an analogous expression of the former. Miraculous words are the creative words that bring something into being out of nothing, the creative word of God is their paradigm.

In the events of chance then, according to Novalis, God's direct interference in the universe is revealed to us. Novalis continues to the end of his life to think of chance in this light. In his diary entry of July 27, 1800, we read: "Everything that we call chance comes from God." [IV,55,6] Similarly, only when we understand Novalis to believe that chance contains a divine gift or immediate act designed to be of great meaning in the individual's life can we make any sense of his calling Sophie's death after her long illness a chance event. And when he writes to Caroline Just in his letter of March 27, 1797, "Even then when the chance that ended her beautiful life was so close" [IV,208,27–29] he obviously is thinking of Sophie's death as something already intended or planned for. But

Novalis is even more explicit in the use of the expression Zufall or chance when a few weeks later, on April 13, he writes to Friedrich von Schlegel:

> Of that much I solemnly assure you—that it is entirely clear to me what *heavenly chance* her death has been—a key to everything—a wonderfully fitting step. [IV,220,12–15]

Chance, then, for Novalis, is anything but a *merely* accidental occurrence or intentionless event. On the contrary, it is the happening in which the divine telos becomes apparent and requires of man that he cooperate with it.

SOME REMARKS ON THE HISTORY OF THE IDEA OF CHANCE

In order to understand the meaning "chance" and "occasion" have for Novalis, it will be helpful to appreciate more fully the historical development of their significance within the religious and cultural traditions to which Novalis was heir. I will, therefore, attempt to point out some dimensions of these ideas that may well have impressed Novalis.

As we have seen, *Zufall* is miraculous for Novalis, because it allows us to come into contact with a higher being. The idea of the divine breaking through into the commonplace of everyday life on certain occasions is an old one, and it is in some sense already implied in the word "Zufall" or "chance."

The German word "Zufall" is an expression borrowed and translated from the Latin *accidens*. Accidens is the participle of *accidere*, which is formed by adding the prefix *ad*, "to or toward," to the verb *cadere*, "to fall." Similarly, the English word "chance" derives from *cadere*, or rather from its noun *cadentia*, which means a falling, especially of the dice of fortune. Both Zufall and "chance," then, refer quite literally to that which falls to us (*uns zufällt*). But from where? And why? In the fall of the dice of fortune, we are given a hint. For fortune stands under the management of the goddess Fortuna (the Greek *Tyche*), goddess of the wheel of fortune, which derives its shape and meaning from the symbolic representation of the orbits of the stars and the zodiac.[15] The gifts of Fortuna, or Tyche, come to the lucky or unlucky recipient not because he is deserving of either reward or punishment, or because he simply asked to be given good fortune or luck, but because the circumstances are such that the giving is appropriate, indeed inevitable. In other words, it is the right time and place for whatever happens to happen. It is the proper opportunity, the favorable moment or fit time for an event—be it good, bad, or indifferent—to occur. For in the concept of *Tyche* (*Zufall* or chance) the temper of the moment is an active ingredient, and time is understood as a dynamic power. Such active time the Greeks called *kairos*.

Whereas *chronos*-time names the quantitative aspect of time as the linear progression of qualitatively undifferentiated moments that succeed each other, kairos-time refers to the qualitative nature of time. Meaning originally "due measure," "proportion," or "fitness," it has the sense of "critical time" or "season" when it names specific intervals that determine the possibilities of events occurring during its efficacy. Tyche and kairos appear in close proximity, often overlapping or cutting across each other. In concert with each other they bring about the will of God as the final Good or telos, to which in one view both are subservient. Thus, for example, Plato says in the *Laws:*

> One might be moved to say . . . that no law is ever made by man, and that human history is all an affair of chance (tyche) . . . and yet there is something else which also may be said with no less plausibility. . . . That God is all, while chance (tyche) and circumstance (kairos), under God, set the whole course of life for us, and yet we must allow for the presence of a third and more amenable partner, skill. [16]

While not identical with each other, kairos and tyche here nevertheless refer to the same unpredictability of the outcome of an action at a critical moment. But they approach that moment from two distinct points of view. Tyche names the uncertain nature of all human action and is therefore that which sets limits to human skill. It names the opacity of the future, which becomes translucent and reveals what it holds suddenly, only at the moment of its becoming presence, that is, in the execution of the act. Kairos, on the contrary, names the moment's qualitative nature as that factor that determines the only right or fitting action to take at the time.

Kairos, then, has two distinctive characteristics: First and foremost it refers to the quality of time as the "right time" for something to happen. So we speak, for instance, of ideas whose time has or has not come; or we hear wine commercials avowing that the vintner will "sell no wine before its time." Second, kairos points to the qualitative nature of time in a crisis or conflict. Here it either offers an occasion for creative action, that is, an opportunity for the individual to enter into the conflict and resolve it by a spontaneous and creative act; or, on the contrary, it presents a constellation of circumstances that leave our hands entirely bound: one act and one act only is right and appropriate, and we are required to recognize

this and act accordingly or lose the moment's possibility and opportunity.[17]

Kairos and tyche both refer to the experience of the fatedness in certain human events. But kairos, as the qualitative nature of time in general,
serves as grounds or condition for each one of the different aspects of
destiny: Moirai; Tyche; Potmos; or Daimon—all receive their ability to
influence events by being anchored securely in the qualitatively determining power of time. The sudden changing and shifting of constella-
tions that constitute the crisis moment are the manifestation of the kairotic character of time acting as Tyche. It is for this reason that Tyche
typically defines the uncertainty of the outcome of all combat and con-
tests, that is, of the *agon* in the widest sense. In the "Twelfth Olympian
Ode," for example, Pindar addresses Tyche as the goddess who stands at
the helm and guides all of man's struggles, those with nature, those of
war, and those in politics:

> Daughter of Zeus the Deliverer! thou saving goddess, Fortune! I pray
> thee to keep watch around mighty Himera; for, at thy bidding, swift
> ships are steered upon the sea, and speedy decisions of war and
> counsels of the people are guided on the land.[18]

But never is Tyche, in this sense, simply blind chance. As navigator she is
handmaiden to the telos and determines the outcome of all conflicts in
agreement with the divine will and plan.

As the goddess of the agon, Tyche is the decisive element in all battles,
including those battles fought with words. Language is an agonistic
realm. We are charged with words and meet the dangers of such a challenge with words. We fight rhetorical skirmishes in politics and in the
courtroom, and the poet is the single combatant who meets an opponent
with song.[19] Here the word becomes the missile which either hits its mark
or misses it, and so decides who emerges as victor.[20] But which contes-
tant wins, and which loses, is not decided by the skill of the warring
opponents alone. Tyche, and through her kairos, are ingredients in the
outcome of the contest.

But the agon in the realm of words is not only defined by the challenge
opponents present to each other. Poetry is understood as a conflict in
itself. The word is a weapon not only against an opponent one seeks to
overcome—as it always is in politics and in the courtroom—but it is also a
missile which either hits its target, when it says what it means to say, or
misses, when it fails to do so. The agon in language is the battle for the
right word, and the battle can be won only when chance is on one's side

and the time is right or favorable. It is for this reason that the poet prays to the muses.[21] They can inspire the proper word and can put the words that are needed into the singer's mouth.[22] But Tyche and kairos decide whether the moment is such that the poet may or may not succeed, even when praying—for, after all, prayers also require the right words and must be spoken at a moment when the muses are disposed to hear the petition.

THE CHANCE-KAIROS NEXUS IN NOVALIS'S METAPHYSICS AND POETICS

Pindar's providential notion of Tyche is echoed in Novalis's concept of Zufall.[23] Both contain the idea of the divine entering into the realm of human action. Although Novalis does not explicitly develop or discuss the idea of kairos-time at any length, he notes that everything has its time, and that we ought to be aware of the possibility of rushing time and guard against a prematurity in events: "Everything has its *time*. Precipitance." [II,562,#178] The notion of kairos-time is essential to Novalis's understanding of both poetry and history. It plays a decisive role for him in the relation of history to poetry and of the historian to the poet. Clearly, though, kairos-time is also of importance to people in general, since, as temporal beings, we—if we are to understand the meaning of our own lives, or of the world as a whole—must be able to sense, see, or read what are called in the Bible "the signs of the times." But, as even Jesus complained about his enemies, this unfortunately does not seem to be an ability man is abundantly blessed with.

Yet the poet, who in Novalis's eyes is the *true* historian, must be able to discern the meaning hidden in the obscurely present quality of particular times, for in this, above all else, the truth of history resides.[24] Born in times of an interim character, when both what furthers poetry and what hinders it are present and doing battle with each other, the poet has an enhanced ability to recognize and to respond to the meaning of time as it manifests itself in chance events.[25] For chance too is an interim moment of shifting quality in which prevailing conditions suddenly are changed and turned into their opposites, thus allowing us to glimpse the divine as it enters into and touches our daily lives. It is the poet's task to see behind the apparently arbitrary events and situations that are our life the higher order of meaning to which they conform and because of which our life is a meaningful whole rather than an irrational collection of unconnected bits and pieces of experience. The method of Erhebung is the tool that serves the poet in accomplishing this task. For Erhebung produces deliberately sudden breaks or shifts in quality, thus proliferating at will and artificially those moments in which the poet may have the chance to see the divine behind the flow of daily events.[26] Poetry, in turn, is able to interrupt the usual flow of our life and to present us with moments of shift or change in which we can see, like the glint of a will-o'-the-wisp, that which gives meaning to the direction of our life and therefore sustains us and renews our vitality.

★All poetry interrupts the usual state of affairs—the common life, almost, *like sleep,* in order to *renew*—and thus to keep *alert* our feeling for life. [II,568,#207]

But the reverse is also true. For whereas poetry interrupts the ordinary flow of events, every interruption, every break in the usual chain of happenings is especially poetical: "nothing is more *poetical* than all *transitions* and heterogeneous mixtures." [III,587, 17–18#221] And this, of course, describes chance and is precisely what chance is.

The ability to discern the meaning of the moment or to understand kairos-time is an ability of insight rather than of rationally discursive thought. As Paul Tillich says, "Awareness of a kairos is a matter of vision. It is not an object of analysis and calculation."[27] But if the awareness of the qualitative meaning of time depends on a visionary understanding of it, that is, on a sudden and complete presence of the meaning of the signs of the time to the observer's inner eye, then the imagination is the "sense organ" that as the "inner sense" or "wonderful sense" can deal with and know that meaning. Novalis accepts Kant's formulation of time as the form of the inner intuition that cannot be outwardly intuited. The poet, in writing poetry or history, must rely on the productive imagination for the visionary insight that allows him to see the higher order or meaning that manifests itself in the chance event and its kairotic nature. For Novalis, therefore, it is the imagination that furnishes the path to the truth. And it is the poet, with his highly skilled and developed imagination, who presents us with the truth when he sings about the events of the past, the present, or even the future.[28]

In May 1798, during his stay in Freiberg, Novalis wrote a lengthy fragment that dealt both with the role Zufall plays in determining our life and with the writer's task to grasp the unifying thread of one individual life-history within the mass of diverse situations. Starting with the example of an "absolute" event of chance determining the "excellent" individual at birth (such that the rest of his life is determined by and in fact contained in that absolute event of chance, as, for instance, Christ's life can be said to have been determined by or contained in the moment and event of his birth) Novalis moves on and sets the writer's task in near opposition to such an unfolding of events out of one all-important instance of chance. For the writer must take the unfolded variety of events and discover what unifies them and makes of them a meaningful whole: their *arché* and telos. He must link the many occurrences in a life to their origin in those moments of chance that determine the individual and are determined by him:

> That individual will be the most perfect, the *purely systematic*, who is individualized by one *single absolute chance event* alone—e.g., his birth. In this chance event all his other chances, the infinite series of his conditions, must be encased, or better yet, be determined as his chances, his conditions. Derivation of an individual life from one single chance event—from one single willful act.
>
> Analysis of one chance event—of one great act of willfulness into several—into infinitely many—by means of a gradual absorption— slow successive intrusion—happening.
>
> ★A novelist makes a kind of *bouts rimes*—which from a given number of chances and situations—arranges a well-ordered, lawful series—which guides one individual to one goal through all these chances, that he purposively [develops]. He must have one proper individual who determines the events, and is determined by them. This metamorphosis, or the changes of one individual—in a *continuous* series constitute the interesting content of a novel.
>
> [II,579, 30–580,13,#242]

Bouts-rimés are collections of given end-rhymes, or the poem constructed from them. In smithing a poem out of such an arbitrary group of words that have nothing to hold them together but the similar sound of their endings, meaning must be brought about by letting the given set of words suggest a content. In the bouts-rimés, then, intention does not find for itself its own appropriate words. Here, meaning is always due to the subsequent ordering of the given material since the words in which the sounds happen to inhere must determine the content. To compare the writer's art with this eighteenth-century parlor game played at genteel gatherings—without wishing the comparison to be a slur on the poet's craft—is to stress in the task of writing the element that seeks to make sense of, or find the unifying thread for, a given set of seemingly unconnected facts and events. In other words, it is pointing to the backward direction in which a writer, be he historian or poet, must proceed: from the given to the intended. For indirect-rule, in contrast to direct-rule, allows the inference of the cause from the effect. It is in the nature of non-rule, willful-rule, the rule of chance, and miracle rule that the event of which they are the cause reflects them and therefore reveals them and their meaning to the discerning eye.[29] But in reality this series of indirect laws functions like the series of direct laws. From an initial intention, individual lives and the world at large develop into the facts, events, and situations that give expression to that intention. And in the story of Heinrich von Ofterdingen's life, which is Novalis's attempt to write a *Lehr- und Wanderjahre* tale, this principle underlies all that occurs.

It is the man blessed with an abundance of spirit (*Geist*) who can best take advantage of the possibilities offered in the chance occurrence:

> In our lives all chance events are materials that we can fashion into what we will. He who has much spirit makes much of his life—For to him who is altogether spiritual—every acquaintance, every occurrence would be the first member of an infinite series—beginning of an infinite novel. [II,436,31–438,3,#65][30]

Yet the ability to act on what is hidden in the chance event as an offering or opportunity is not simply dependent on exercising our will. For although will is a necessary ingredient for shaping the gifts of chance into what is the flow of our life, we can will to act on the possibilities of the moment only after we have understood what they are. And it is "spirit" that allows us to see the options chance spreads before us even in secondary chance occurrences, that is, in chance events whose meaning to us is strictly symbolic:

> Whoever has the proper sense for chance can use everything that is by chance to determine an unknown chance event—he can look for destiny with equal luck in the formations of the stars, in grains of sand, the flight of birds, and in configurations. [III,687,#680]

The last two fragments quoted come respectively from Novalis's earliest published work, *Blüthenstaub*,[31] and from a manuscript written during October and November 1800; they, therefore, represent some of his earliest and latest thoughts on the subject. Plainly, his thinking on Zufall remained relatively unchanged and, if anything, it grew stronger toward his initial inclination to find in it a cosmic as well as a private meaning.

To be blessed with the spirit that understands the moment of crisis or conflict and to see in the folds of the future all the hidden opportunities for successful action is clearly a necessary ability for those who exercise political power and those who wield power in general. To assign to the poet an abundance of such spirit and to think him possessed of a particularly keen insight into the nature of kairos and tyche is to credit him with extraordinary potency and a privileged relation to power as such. Add to this the *daimonic* might or genius traditionally ascribed to the poet, and his power is elevated far beyond that of ordinary men. For the poet then stands in a direct and personally enhanced relation to two of the four aspects of fate and, through them, to the qualitative nature of time. According to Novalis this is in fact the case. The poet, by means of his insight into the meaning of chance, is the interpreter, translator, and visionary of the specific nature of the kairos. His knowledge of kairoi allows him to gain mastery over time, at least insofar as its qualitative nature is concerned. In addition, his powerful personal genius is not only the spirit who guides him, but is also the expression of an unusually strong life-force and creative ability which ties him firmly to the processes of natural renewal. Doubly privileged with respect to time, the genius of the poet is genius elevated to the second power, for, according to Novalis, genius is present in all men by degrees:

> Without genius none of us exist at all. Genius is necessary for everything. But that which we usually call genius—is the genius of genius.
> [II,420,10–12,]

On the one hand, Novalis here seems to follow an earlier established usage of the term *genius*. Addison, for instance, writes in *The Spectator* of a "person of ordinary genius" who will be less effective in the expression of ideas than a great writer.[32] On the other hand, when Novalis speaks of "the genius of genius" he does not have a simple and purely quantitative increase of the quality of genius in mind—as does Croce, for example, who holds that the difference between the genius and the common man is only a difference of degree. Rather, the expression "genius of genius" is equivalent to saying "genius to the second power" and so refers us to Novalis's method of raising, or Erhebung, which indicates, in addition to the quantitative increase, a qualitative intensification that brings about a jump to a new and different kind of genius ranked on a higher level. This qualitative change suggested by Novalis can also be traced in the very history of the term "genius."[33]

The etymological roots of "genius" refer to the generative powers of semen. In time, the individual's creative force in general came to be understood by the term. Genius became the projection of the inherent active ability of a man's vital force and character as an autonomous spirit guiding his life. When the Greek notion of *daimon* was translated into

Latin by the word genius, that term took on some of the specific meanings of daimon: the idea of "the effective force of a god," in Latin otherwise referred to as the *numen* of a god, was added to "the life force as destiny" notion of genius. This nexus of meaning easily permitted an expansion of the concept of genius to include the idea of an effective, creative force that is not only vital but also spontaneously inventive, and that expresses itself in various fields of human endeavor, acting with particular strength when man's spirit creatively shapes his place in the world through the sciences or arts. The vital and the spontaneously creative aspects of genius are the poet's effective powers. With them he holds the destructive force of time at bay. For even if he ultimately cannot overcome time, he succeeds in partially counteracting it. Novalis suggests accordingly that there is a natural ability that we call either instinct or genius and that expresses our relation to the "fullness of the future—the fullness of times in general."

> Should there not be an *ability* in us which plays here the same role as that *fortress* outside of us—*the ether*—that invisibly visible matter, the philosopher's stone—which is everywhere and nowhere, everything and nothing—we call it *instinct* or genius—it is everywhere *prior*. It is the *fullness of the future*—the *fullness of times* in general—in time, what the philospher's stone is in space—reason—fantasy—understanding and sense (*meaning 3–5 senses*) are only its *single function*.
>
> [III,462, #1036]

Genius thus has a double relation to time: as a creative ability it is itself temporal but counteracts and balances out time's destructive force. As a particular understanding of the fullness of time, or of future-time, it is the ability to enter into the qualitative nature of time as a rhythmic manifestation: "*Rhythmic sense* is genius." [III,310,1] The poet, who on the one hand both is and has genius, and on the other hand has a privileged relation to chance, thus possesses extraordinary powers in respect to the qualitative flux of time.[34] The poet's understanding of chance and his being a genius, or having a specific genius for creative expression, conspire to give him his extraordinary insight into the nature of the moment and with it into the significance of particular lives as histories or novels and into the meaning of life in general. It is for this reason that "only an artist can fathom the meaning of life." [II,562,#177]

In perceiving Zufall not as *mere* chance, Novalis stands, as I have shown, in an old tradition. The shift from one qualitative state to another in the moment of crisis breaks the usual chain of events. The individual suddenly stands at a threshold that allows both the divine to break into everyday life, and the individual, particularly the poet, to become aware of its presence and to have a presentiment of its ruling, governing, or steering influence over our destinies. The poet, having been born at such a crisis or threshold moment himself, becomes, according to Novalis, the translator of the brink, the mediator of all the opposite and conflicting elements that touch each other on this occasion. Having a fleeting vision of the swift meeting of the transcendent and the natural realm in that quick shifting of chance, the poet's task becomes that of giving voice to its truth. And it is his genius that allows him at once to sense the rhythm of that moment's quality and to express it spontaneously and creatively, that is, to translate it into verbal imagery. For Novalis, therefore, "translation" is a concept with a technical meaning that differs somewhat from its ordinary sense.

CHAPTER THREE

Translation as a Linguistic and Metaphysical Method of *Raising*

GRAMMATICAL AND TRANSFORMATIONAL TRANSLATION

"Translation" is a concept of broader significance for Novalis than the simple transposing of words and sentences from one language into another. Aspects of transformation and interpretation are included in its scope, and the highest form of translation, mythical translation, goes far beyond a merely accurate translation. In fragment 68 of the *Blüthenstaub* collection, Novalis calls translation in the usual sense "grammatical translation" and considers it to rely on "much scholarship" but to require only "discursive abilities." [II,439, 68, 20–22] In other words, in Novalis's view it requires little or no imagination.

The fact that translation in this sense does not demand extraordinary abilities of insight or gifted powers with which to overcome—or at least temporarily step outside—the sequential ordering of the flux of time puts it for Novalis on the lowest level of the several meanings of "translation." For such translation is an activity and accomplishment entirely caught up in the successive moments of the present. It has no need or inclination to reach beyond itself into either the past or future, nor does it attempt to reach above or behind itself to catch what lies beyond the information conveyed by the text. It settles for the surface content and renders it in another language. Its aim is to repeat the original as faithfully as possible, but repeat it in another language. It fulfills exactly Dr. Johnson's definition of "to translate," namely: "to change into another language retaining the sense."[1]

In contrast, "changing translation" (*verändernde Übersetzung*) is transformation or interpretation and requires the highest poetical spirit if it is not to become a travesty. Novalis therefore says:

> The true translator of this kind must, indeed, be the artist himself, he must be able to give the idea of the whole at will, either thus or thus. He must be the poet's poet and therefore must be able to let him speak, at once, according to his and the poet's own idea.
>
> [II,439,26–29]

No notion of literal faithfulness can be at work here; the word *verändernd* denies literalness. Changing or transformational translation, then, must require a different loyalty. Instead of fidelity to the text before him, the "true translator" must have an unwavering commitment and sensitivity to the idea that shines through it. Only in this manner will the "highest poetical spirit manifest itself." [II, 439, 23–26] For Novalis this seems to mean that the translator must be able to grasp in an act of empathetic understanding or sympathetic intuition the original creative idea and give it a new and independent expression in his own creative voice. As a result, transformational translation comes to express two interpretations of the creative idea at once. The true translator, serving them both, mediates between them and in so doing elevates the poetical expression to a higher rank. Yet there is reason to believe that for Novalis this ability to grasp the original idea by some sympathetic act is, at least in part, also due to the translator's understanding of the writer. In the *Vermischte Bemerkungen,* for instance, we can read:

> I demonstrate that I have understood a writer, only when I can act according to his spirit, and translate and change him variously without lessening his individuality. [II,424,#29]

By focusing on the work not as an autonomous and independent entity but as an expression of the writer's spirit—and thereby focusing ultimately on the writer himself—Novalis suggests in this fragment that the transformation to be accomplished is as much a transformation of the translator as it is of the work before him. The true translator must conform his spirit to that of the author he addresses, because it then becomes possible for him to "act in his [the author's] spirit" or to "change his [the author's] work" without doing violence in any real sense to "his [the author's] individuality." A translator who has so transformed himself and assimilated his spirit to the spirit that is the origin, life, and shape of the work's idea can then in a double sense be said to "be the artist himself." For now in a manner of speaking he thinks and feels both as the creator of the original work and as the artist who transforms that work into its new expression. But he can be the translator only because he succeeded in "becoming" the artist. And as the incarnation of such a dual being the translator is indeed "the poet's poet" who can "speak, at once, according to his and the poet's own idea." Yet care must be exercised here not to misunderstand Novalis. The true translator's ability to transform his own spirit and grasp the idea of the whole, as well as be faithful to that idea, must not be misread as the translator's attempt to be true to the poet's intention. For Novalis does not suggest that the true translator go outside the text before him to its author's aim or avowed purpose in the creation of the work of art.

As so many of Novalis's fragments, the *Blüthenstaub* fragment on translation, is short and frustratingly cryptic. It requires much reading between the lines and knowledge of Novalis's literary and metaphysical attitudes in general. Yet I think that for Novalis transformational translation demands a deeper penetration of the text, that is, a going into it rather than a going outside of it. Only by such an immersion in the text can the idea of its whole offer itself to the translator and the translator become able to assimilate himself to the spirit that formed the idea— thereby becoming capable of transforming it, of giving it an entirely changed expression in a new idiom.

In such an analysis of translation the idea of the work is clearly understood as transcending the particular expression it has been given. Therefore, in principle one expression can be changed or replaced by another without doing damage or violence to the idea. What is odd about this account of translation is that Novalis is not thinking of some factual or historical report, scientific theory, or philosophical tractatus in which the particular linguistic forms have rather little determinative effect on the thoughts they contain. Rather, Novalis has literary works in mind—works, that is, whose ideas we do not usually think of as being independent or relatively free of the expression in which they occur. Nor is Novalis's unusual view of the translatability of poetical works due to any general shift in historical perspective on this question. Herder, for example, who exerted some of the earliest influence on Novalis's thoughts on language and who again and again considered the role and value of translation, suggests, in contrast to Novalis, that the beauty of poetry is lost in translation:

> Poetry in its beauty is nearly not translatable, because here the melodious sound, the rhyme, the individual parts of speech, the composition of words, the form of expression, all present beauty.[2]

Clearly, the formalist's influence has been such that many today side with Herder rather than Novalis and often go further than he did, for they feel the justice of the Italian pun: *traduttore, traditore!* (translator, traitor!). Because the form of the expression in literary works is so often understood as an essential, if not *the* essential aspect of their being, changing or transforming the expression is considered to do damage or violence to the work's aesthetic being and creative idea. It is by no means then only a question of the insufficiency of translation, as expressed, for instance, by George Steiner when he says, "No literary translation will ever satisfy those intimate with the original."[3] Rather, there is a strong tendency to espouse a perception of translation as a positively malignant enterprise and the mood expressed in the following lines by Nabokov is, therefore, easily accepted: "What is translation? On a platter/ A poet's pale and glaring head,/ A parrot's screech, a monkey's chatter,/ And profanation of the dead."[4] Both Steiner and Nabokov must be felt to be right if the expectation is to compare not overall work with overall work, whole with whole, but original passage with passage in translation or, worse, original sentence with the "same" sentence in its new idiom or, altogether inappropriately, word-for-word original and translation. Under such circumstances the best one can hope for is precisely what Novalis calls "grammatical translation"—a more or less literal transposition of each phrase and word of the original into a new language. Beauty under such circumstances must be lost. But not only beauty! The very life and spirit of the original in its entirety is here made subordinate to the accurate equivalence of particulars. No way out of the dilemma exists as long as, on the one hand, a desire for scholarly accuracy either determines the translator's method entirely or is mixed in with his aesthetic considerations and, on the other hand, his aesthetic sensibility is, to the exclusion of all other considerations, formalistic. Novalis's preference for what he calls verändernde Übersetzung is the attempt to give to the essence of a literary work a new expression, where "essence" in no way means what is usually called content in contrast to form. For the essence of a literary work also involves its form. The problem is one of perspective. Focusing on a word or phrase, we may meet not only insurmountable differences in the associated meanings and the color of the contextual universe to which each word or phrase belongs in its respective language, but we may lose the work's harmonious unity and specific beauty, as well. If we focus instead on the work as a *whole,* Novalis suggests, translation becomes not only feasible, but entirely possible.[5]

TRANSFORMATIONAL TRANSLATION AND INTERPRETATION

The eighteenth century did not have our problems with translation because it still considered the work of art to be a well-ordered whole. But an aesthetic that is increasingly shaped, formulated, and structured in accordance with the nature of snapshots can no longer conceive, or anyway does not conceive, of the work as a whole—a unity with beginning, middle, and end between which determinate and non-interchangeable relations hold. Most modern views of art are atomistic, in part as a consequence of learning about art from reproductions in art books that produce enlarged details of works alongside representations of monumental pieces of art. The work of art has come to be looked at as if it presented its "message" in much the same way that a digital clock tells time: in more or less unconnected bits of expression, each of which in its own right has a weight, presence, life, and meaning. The eighteenth century, by contrast, still holding an Aristotelian view of art, saw the entire thrust of the work long before it was concerned with the work's parts, and never was it concerned with these in separation from their determinate and distinct relations to each other and to the whole. Then time was still told by the sweep of the hands around the face of the clock, which returned at day's end to their beginning position. This image is not an arbitrarily chosen one. For Novalis it was the determining perspective on life. For only with such cyclicality is the method of raising to higher potencies possible: it then occurs as a restructuring of the cycle into a spiral. So too in the case of a literary work of art, in which the whole has priority over its parts and in which the translator, having gathered in the idea of the whole in one sweeping vision, can begin to express the idea anew on a higher level.[6] Thus the whole—meaning the work's idea rather than its content—is translatable, as all ideas are that have been represented in a work of art. For the representation itself constitutes a translation. It is for this reason that Novalis can say "all poetry is translation." But if this is so, a translator's concern must be his fidelity not to the representation of the idea in some particular expression, but to the essential nature that lies beyond all expression.

Speaking about translation, James Grieve remarks:

> Magic is in the eye of the beholder. No flick of a trickster's wrist can turn tie-died clothes into a Union Jack. It's because it's impossible that we applaud when it's done. Too many Tommy Coopers of translation run their sabres through the sequined stooge inside the trunk. But even those whose tricks work must sometimes admit to being conjurors.[7]

The strength of Novalis's point of view is that it allows him to answer Grieve's accusation of the translator. For according to Novalis, if the translator is a conjuror, so too is the poet. And if there is artistry in one, so there is in the other. But in sheer panache it is the translator who outdoes the poet, for he must succeed in turning one trick into another, one bit of magic into another, adroitly exchanging one mask for another with "the flick of a wrist." Yet the translator must be careful to change only the outer form, the tricksterish appearance, and not the essence of the idea expressed. There is magic here in either case—in the poet's translations as well as in the translator's—and success for either is the pure gift of chance.

Insofar as transformational translation requires the translator to grasp not only the poet's words but the idea that lies behind them, it must be understood to be as much an act of interpretation as of translation. And since this interpretation is given a fully new poetic expression by the translator, transformational translation is for Novalis potentiated writing of poetry, that is, poetry raised to the second power, and the translator is therefore the poet's poet, whose art is *Nachdichtung*. This term became common coinage after the Schlegel/Tieck translation of Shakespeare's works.[8] It denotes a poetical rewriting of a text rather than its scholarly and literal transposition into another language. Far from harboring the puritanical suspicions with which scholarly translators might view such an undertaking today, Novalis, seeking a new expression for the work's idea and valuing aesthetic considerations a good deal more highly than scholarly accuracy, sees Nachdichtung not as a second-hand version of an original text but as its higher poetical form. Nachdichtung, therefore, rather than doing damage or violence to the original (in the sense of lessening its poetical expression and with it its poetical worth), actually enhances the original. Starting not with nature but with an already beautifully formed representation of it, transformational translation becomes the poetical raising of poetry, while poetry itself is understood as a translation of the raw, natural experience into poetical expression.[9]

On November 30, 1797, Novalis writes to August Wilhelm von Schlegel:

> [Your Shakespeare] is among translations what Wilhelm Meister is among novels. Is there as yet a similar one? Ever since we Germans have been translating, and however national this tendency for translation is, there being hardly any German writer of repute who has not done translations of which he is as truly proud as of his own original works, we nevertheless appear to be of nothing more ignorant than of

translation. With us Germans translations can become a scholarly enterprise or art. Your Shakespeare is a proper canon for the scholarly observer. . . . Poetical morality, sacrifice of one's own inclinations are required in order to undertake a true translation. One translates because of a genuine love of beauty and of one's own national literature. Translation is as much a writing of poetry, as the bringing about of one's own works is—and more difficult, rarer.

In the end all poetry is translation. I am convinced that the German Shakespeare is now better than the English. [IV,237,12–33]

It would be a mistake to believe that Novalis here intends only to flatter his friend, who was considered to be *the* translator of the day. For Schlegel's translation is for Novalis just what he says it is, and his evaluation of the German Shakespeare rendition is genuinely meant; it is not an expression of either a misapplied German nationalism or an unjustified overestimation of the worthiness of the German tongue.

Since human creation is generally understood not to be *ex nihilo* but always to be the transformation of a given material, the translator's enterprise is seen as a lesser task only because the material *he* reworks has already been fashioned into shape by a human mind, has already been "created," or wrested from the "natural" realm of "raw" experience. The translator's efforts are perceived as attempts to appropriate the labors of another and are therefore judged likely to be nefarious and certainly not entirely legitimate. Novalis inverts this evaluation and esteems the translator's work more highly precisely because it starts with a material that is not raw but already shaped into a higher level of organization. Thus the translator's work is seen as an opportunity to reach farther than other human creators can, since in his making he elevates what others before him have already ordered. In constrast to the usual Romantic view of the human artist as a Prometheus challenging the creative ability of God with the defiant cry "I too can bring forth!"[10] Novalis does not view man's creativity as being in competition with God. Rather, he sees man as cooperating with God. For through man, God shapes the raw materials of nature or natural experience into beautiful and poetic expressions. The translator as poet, working to transform such expressions, simply starts where the poet as translator of the raw reality ends. Novalis's conviction that "the German Shakespeare is now better than the English" rests on the principle that as Nachdichtung it is a potentiated poetical work and, therefore, an example of poetical expression raised to the second power.

Without going so far as to agree with Novalis that the Schlegel/Tieck version is better than the original Shakespeare, we can nevertheless see that there is something to the idea of transformational translation that rests on a true insight. For if poetical works were indeed entirely untranslatable in their essential literary nature, Schlegel's Shakespeare would not be Shakespeare at all, but Schlegel—and we should not be able to recognize *Romeo and Juliet,* for instance, in the Schlegel translation, as Shakespeare's play, but would have to believe it some other tale of star-crossed lovers. The bare facts of the plot do not suffice to furnish us with such recognition. Consider, for example, the many versions of the tale of Faust. Several agree with each other extensively in respect to the bare essentials of the legend's story. Nevertheless, we are able to recognize and distinguish, even in translation, passages that in plot diverge very little from one another, say in Marlowe's *Faust* and the folk-play.[11]

Furthermore, if nothing but the mere elements that advance the story were recognizable in translations, we could hardly speak of good, adequate, or bad translations. It is only because translations can catch the mood, expression, or general complexion of the original that we think some to be successful as translations whereas others fail because they do not retain something of the evanescent presence of the original. And this is why Novalis thinks that a gifted poet-translator can give, with his own voice and in his own language, new form and expression to the creative idea of a work—provided he sufficiently assimilates himself both to the spirit that shaped that idea and to the idea itself. But he will succeed in the translator's enterprise only by sacrificing his own inclinations, on the one hand, and by exercising what Novalis calls "poetic morality" and what I have called fidelity or faithfulness to the idea, on the other hand. Yet any such new expression of an idea will amount to an interpretation of the idea and therefore constitute in part the poet-translator's own creative thought.[12] In this manner the resulting work or Nachdichtung, according to Novalis, will come to represent a higher expression of the idea and will also speak with an authentic rather than a derivative voice. For this reason it will succeed in entering the mainstream of the cultural traditions of its new linguistic environment and will, in fact, broaden the horizon of that environment by its presence. In the translation that is a transformation, the true translator will present both the original work and his own intuitive insight into the creative idea behind it. This is why transformational translation can be said to add dimensions to the mother tongue that it did not have before and that have their roots and proper place in the language to which the text originally belonged.

Even Herder, who highly values the national characteristics of language, calling them "patronymic beauties" [*HSW*,II,44], is aware of the linguistic fruitfulness of translations when he writes: "We also consider this translation to be an original piece of work which can influence our literature more than ten originals." [HSW,I,274] And in *Stücke der umgearbeiteten zweiten Sammlung*, Herder remarks how much language changes in the course of a few hundred years and exhorts translators, therefore, to seek a middle ground between translations that are too free and those that are too narrowly exact. For in his opinion, only such well-balanced translations are able to awaken language to its fruitful possibilities:

> As easy as our workaday reviewers think it is to treat translators high-handedly, and to show them mistakes in their language, so do I think it the finest criticism to be able to show exactly the middle point, how a translator should not do injustice by a hair's breadth to either of his two languages, not to the one from which, and not to the one into which, he translates. A translation that is too lax and that our judges of art usually call free or unforced, sins against both: it does not do justice to the one and it does not bring the other to bear fruit. A translation that is altogether adapting, and which easy and lively souls scold for being too slavish, is much more difficult. It is eagerly concerned for both languages and is rarely as appreciated as it deserves to be. Its author must everywhere be experimenting, adapting, and daring, but our censors, with raised eyebrow, abuse him for three failed attempts, and take everything daring to be a mistake, and treat the samples of an artist as if they were the apprentice-pieces of a pupil. [HSW,I,107–8]

Even though Herder here chides what he calls "free" or "unforced" translations, I do not believe that we are to understand by these what Novalis defined as transformational translations. For Herder's "adapting" translations seem to involve just the sort of approach Novalis ascribed to translations that are *verändernd*, that is, transformational.

Early in this century, Walter Benjamin made a similar observation when, in his essay "The Task of the Translator," he quoted Panwitz as saying: "The basic error of the translator is that he preserves the state in which his own language happens to be instead of allowing his language to be powerfully affected by the foreign tongue. Particularly when translating from a language very remote from his own he must go back to the primal elements of language itself and penetrate to the point where work, image, and tone converge. He must expand and deepen his language by means of the foreign language. It is not generally realized to what extent this is possible, to what extent any language can be transformed."[13]

Novalis seemed to have something like Panwitz's suggestion in mind when he claimed in his letter to August Wilhelm Schlegel that "one translates because of a genuine *love of beauty* and of *one's own national literature"* [my emphasis]. For clearly both the beauty of the language and the national treasure of literature are expanded when translation proceeds as here suggested. But most importantly, what Panwitz calls the "deepening and expanding" of one's own language is precisely that sort of transformation of an expression and its language that Novalis thinks of as a raising or potentiating of language.

What Novalis calls transformational translation, then, may be able to give to language what no other poetical enterprise can, and the transforming translator thus renders a valuable service. Not only does he make the works of great men available to those who do not know the language they are written in and so cannot turn to the original texts,[14] but he also allows the works in their new expressions to open new horizons for themselves, to create their own new worlds and spheres of influence, and in so doing to change and widen the boundaries of their host language. Yet translation as transformation and interpretation holds only an intermediate position in Novalis's hierarchically-structured notion of translation, in which the highest form of translation is mythical.

MYTHICAL TRANSLATION

While transformational translation must attempt to reach beyond the words to the idea, mythical translation must try to reach even further and attempt to see the ideal behind the idea. As Novalis says, mythical translations "represent the pure excellent character of the individual work of art. But they do not give us the actual artwork, rather its ideal." [II,439, 11–13] Such translations, however, do not yet exist. They are themselves largely an ideal to be realized in the future. And although Novalis does not say so explicitly, he gives the impression that mythical translation is the form translation will have in the Golden Age. For while some "bright traces" (*helle Spuren*) of it can already be found "in the spirit of some reviews and descriptions of works of art," [II,439,14–15] mythical translation as a whole requires a mind "in which poetical and philosophical spirit have interpenetrated each other in their entire richness." [II,439,15–17]

The remarkable aspect of mythical translation is that it appears to belong to the realm of critique rather than to the poetical enterprise proper. But lest language deceive us here, let me add that this is neither a Platonic nor a Kantian move on Novalis's part: the ideal is not the sort of discursively rational form the late eighteenth and particularly the nineteenth century considered the Platonic idea to be—although it is a formal archetype—and the spirit of reviews or critiques is not the spirit of Kant's critical enterprise. For as examples of mythical translations that nearly succeed, Novalis names "the modern Madonna" and "Greek mythology," which he sees as translations of national religions. Nor is this move to criticism akin to Hegel's demand for a science of art and thus a sign for a diminished standing of poetry in general. The fact that Novalis calls this level of translation mythical and gives Greek mythology and the modern myth of the Madonna as instances of its nearly perfected form points to where, for him, the crux of the matter lies. As the fruit of the completed unification of the poetical and philosophical spirit, mythos is the highest symbolic expression possible; as poetized religion it is the iconic translation of the ideal.[15]

Finally, translation for Novalis does not pertain to literature alone. "Not only books, everything can be translated in these three ways." [II,441,3] And so he writes in the *Logologische Fragmente*:

> Laws of association./ The philosopher translates the real world into the realm of thought and vice versa, in order to give to both of them *understanding*. [II,561,#169]

At first glance, the term "translation" appears to be used metaphorically here. But for Novalis, translation as this sort of transformation is the heart of the translator's task. To translate a text from one language into another, therefore, does not differ essentially from translating objects of the real world into expressions of thought. The ability to move by means of translation—or transformation—from one field of endeavor to another is at the center of Novalis's world view. In religion, this view is anchored in the doctrine of transubstantiation; in philosophy, it relies on the nature of language, which is seen as paralleling the alchemist's model of transformation, that is, as being able to represent symbolically by a variety of expressions the same thought, as well as symbolizing several thoughts in one expression.[16] Interpretation, or hermeneutics, then, is the essential business of language, and this is most evident when the business of language is translation. Ultimately this means that things can either be taken literally, be interpreted in such a manner as to reveal the creative ideas underlying them, or be seen as symbolic translations of the ideal, which as yet lies hidden behind the screen of objective being.[17]

The result is that, for Novalis, the poet as translator is not free either of the subjective ideas of other poets or of the objects for which his poetic words are to be a translation. Most importantly though, the translator as poet stands in the service of the idea. In contrast, the poet as translator is bound by the moment of chance, in which it becomes possible for him to reach beyond the subjective word and idea to the ideal, and in which that ideal can beckon him to its translation.

Thus, art in relation to chance, far from being "free," is triply bound. First, the writer who must see *one* gathering meaning in the infinite variety of life's fortuitous events is bound by the truth he finds at once hidden and revealed there. Second, as a product of chance, he is himself an expression of the commonplace opening up and allowing the divine to enter, and so in his own person he darkly mirrors the presence of the order he serves. Last, the work that is thought to be a product of chance and hence thought not to follow any clear intention is—insofar as chance means the occasion or opportunity in which the divine finds a perceivable expression—an inspired work, and, therefore, a truer statement of the final intention, the telos, or the god's will, than any merely humanly willed work of art could ever hope to be. Insofar as the poet is the translator of the brink that manifests itself in chance, he is free neither of the object or content of what he speaks about, nor of the subject from whom he speaks, that is, of himself, since his own person is always an intimate part of the translation. Nor is he free of the subject to whom he speaks and for the sake of whose understanding he must choose the word that is not only the right word, insofar as it expresses or translates most faithfully what the vision has given to the poet, but also insofar as it most effectively touches or invites the reader or listener to the re-creative task of understanding.

The end of this excursion into the meaning of Zufall and the role it plays in Novalis's understanding of poetic creation, as both interpretation and translation, returns me to my starting point, Novalis's *Monolog,* which I will consider now against the background I have developed.

CHAPTER FOUR

Novalis's *Monolog*

THE *MONOLOG*'S PLACE IN NOVALIS'S VIEW OF LANGUAGE

As I have shown earlier, Novalis is often thought to hold—in addition to
the theory of the emancipation of language from objects and subjects
alike, which he is said to have developed in the *Monolog*—a view of
language as "essential expression." In the latter, the relationship between objects or states of affairs and the words that designate them is
thought to be more than conventional or arbitrary. In the *Lehrlinge zu Sais,*
for instance, Novalis describes the nature of such essential language and
considers it to have been the manner of speech of a more highly developed people, of whom modern man is but the degenerate descendant.

> Its pronunciation was a wonderful singing whose irresistible tones
> penetrated deeply into the inner nature of every being and unfolded
> it. Each of its names seemed to be a password to the soul of a natural
> object. With creative force its vibrations brought forth all the images of
> the phenomenal world and one could say of them with full justifica-
> tion that the life of the universe was an eternal, myriad-voiced conver-
> sation. For in their speaking, all the forces, all the different kinds of
> activity, seemed to be united in the most incomprehensible way.
>
> [I,106,30–107,3]

Something of the substantial nature of the world, something of its very
essence is here thought to be mirrored in the language that describes and
names it, that is, in the characteristic structures and sounds of words. For
human language, having been created in the image of God's spirit as man
himself was created in His likeness, reflects the essential being of the

world as it was established by God's world-creating word. If this is so, Novalis's theory of language must be admitted to be either self-contradictory and without any inner coherence—in which case it is hard to see why it became as influential as is claimed—or we must think Novalis to have undergone such a violent change of mind that in less than a year he came to believe the opposite of what he thought when he wrote the *Monolog*.

Those who believe the latter usually invoke the influence on Novalis of Jacob Boehme's mystical theory of language, or of the Illuminati's theory of language, or of the alchemical and theurgic tradition. But if one wants to claim that a development took place in Novalis that brought him from a more or less classical, rational view of language (as it was commonly held before and during the Enlightenment) to an entirely mystical perspective on this subject, then one has to believe that Novalis's development was circular, and took him past the ideas of the *Monolog* to a radicalization of the very position he began with. For Novalis started out with a theory of language that was traditionally religious. But such a circular view of his development must diminish the importance of the *Monolog* for Novalis's philosophy of language and make of its assertions nothing more than way stations Novalis left behind when he moved on to consider language as essential expression.

Yet if we understand Novalis's development differently, if we see it not as a circle returning to its beginnings but as a widening of and moving away from the views on language held by either Enlightenment or traditional religious theorists, and if we see in it, most of all, a synthetic undertaking that attempts to unite both these strains into a harmonious whole, we avoid having to consider Novalis as putting forth an incoherent theory of language or as developing toward his beginnings, with the *Monolog* being only a short side-trip or adventure of thought that ultimately held little meaning or importance for his view of language. And it is my contention that we are well justified in doing so.

Among the works of Novalis's youth—written between 1788 and 1790—is an essay entitled *Von der Begeisterung* (*About Inspiration.*) [II, 22, #9] Only a page or so in length, it alone of his youthful attempts can be considered to have been completed. Written under the influence of Herder, the essay deals with the origin of language and credits inspiration with being the source of man's speech. Novalis suggests that the experience of nature awakens in the young savage an inspired or enthusiastic idea of a higher being, which he lacks only the words to express. Not having words, he bends his knees and shows all the feelings that crowd in on his heart with a mute gesture. As language slowly begins to form and man no longer merely stutters in "natural tones," but still speaks with a voice that is more nearly emotion and is not as yet refined by abstract concepts and symbols, poetry is born:

> There poetry came to be, daughter of the most noble impetuosity of the most sublime and strongest sensations and passions, who, it is true, later, like a chameleon, changed herself according to the organi- zation of the various regions, times, and characters, but who in her original meaning, for her greatest strength, magic, and effect on the mind, still stands in need of her mother, sublime inspiration. But all I have said here is mainly valid only for the Orient, the proper home- land of mankind, language, poetry, and, therefore, also inspiration, from which, as from the original root, everything actually was propa- gated into and grafted onto the remaining regions and zones of the Earth. [II,23,3–15][1]

Inspiration and enthusiasm do not seem to be distinguished here altogether clearly, and one might be tempted to read *Begeisterung* as en- thusiasm were it not for the fact that the essay directly preceding *Von der Begeisterung* (*About Inspiration*) [II,22,#7] is entitled *Apologie der Schwär- merey* (*Apology of Enthusiasm*) [II,20,#8], and so gives some evidence that even the very young Novalis distinguished between enthusiasm and inspiration. It would appear, therefore, that the enthusiastic overtones are due to the fact that in the essay on the origin of language, inspiration is understood to be enthusiastic or, as the Greeks would have said, Diony- sian inspiration.

Thus, at the very beginning of his concern with language and poetry, Novalis believes that language arose out of experiencing nature as the expression and manifestation of a divine being to whom man feels him- self called to answer, first by mute gesture alone, but soon with emotional utterances that in time turn into poetry. To the very young von Harden- berg, then, language is a religious response: man finds language in order to pray; and prayer finds its proper form in inspired poetry. But man is himself a part of that very nature that first aroused in him the desire to raise his voice in poetic adoration. Prayer and poetry are, therefore, the enthusiastic expression of God's own nature in man and consequently are inspired speech.

Novalis expresses a similar view in a more developed and poetical form in his last work, *Heinrich von Ofterdingen*. When Heinrich sees all of God's creatures enter the magnificent cathedral of the universe through "wide gates" and hears them "plainly express their innermost nature in a simple petition and peculiar dialect," Novalis metaphorically asserts that man's very being is language as prayer. With the very word *Bitte* (peti-tion), in which each being expresses his innermost nature, Novalis points to prayer. For the tonal similarity of *bitten* (to petition) and *beten* (to pray) is not simply a happy coincidence but is due to the etymological kinship of these words: The Gothic *bida,* meaning prayer as well as petition, is related to the Gothic *baidjan,* with the sense to demand, command, or force, and to the Gothic *beidan,* which translates into waiting trustingly, or hoping for, and which is still apparent in the English *to bide.*[2] And when Novalis says that this prayer is spoken with "mighty tones that tremble in the silvery song" of the future, he claims this prayer to be poetry. Thus at the beginning of Novalis's thought about language, as well as at the end, he sees prayer and poetry to be the essential expression of man's speech and also finds in them the impetus to language in general.

Chronologically the *Monolog* stands between the essay *Von der Be-geisterung* and the novel *Heinrich von Ofterdingen.* The question that there-fore must be answered is whether in terms of its language theory it stands in contrast to them or forms a harmonious whole with them. In order to facilitate the interpretation of the *Monolog* let me first quote it in its entirety.

MONOLOG

Actually it is an odd thing about speaking and writing; proper conver-sation is a mere word-game. The ridiculous mistake people make when they think they speak for the sake of things—can only be mar-veled at. Nobody is aware of the most peculiar property of language, namely, that it is concerned only with itself. Because of this, language is such a wonderful and fruitful secret that when someone merely speaks in order to speak, he utters just the most glorious, most origi-nal truths. But when he means to speak about something specific, capricious language lets him say the most ridiculous and perverse stuff. From this, too, arises the hatred some serious people feel for language. They are aware of its mischievousness but are not aware that idle chatter is the infinitely serious aspect of language. If one could only make people understand that it is with language as it is with mathematical formulas—they constitute a world for themselves, they play only with themselves, express nothing but their own won-derful nature, and are for that very reason so expressive—for that very reason, too, the peculiar play of relations between things is mir-rored in them. Only because of their freedom are they links of nature, and only in their free movements does the world-soul express itself, and make of them a delicate standard and ground plan of things. Thus it is also with language—whoever is sensitive to its application, its measure, its musical spirit, whoever perceives in himself the delicate effects of its inner nature, and accordingly moves his tongue or hand, will be a prophet; in contrast, whoever knows, yet has not sufficient ear or sense, will write truths like these, but will be tricked by language herself and will be mocked by man, like Cassandra by the Trojans. If I believe I have given here a most accurate account of the essence and function of poetry, I nevertheless know that no one can understand it, and that I have said something entirely silly, because I intended to say it, and in this manner no poetry comes to be. But what if I had to speak? and this compulsion to speak were a sign of the inspiration of language, of the effectiveness of language in me? and what if my will also only wanted what I were compelled to do, then this could, without my knowing and believing it, be poetry after all, and could make a secret of language understandable? and so I would be called to be a writer, for what is a writer, but a man inspired by language?—[II,672,1]

As I pointed out earlier, it is generally thought that Novalis's *Monolog* accomplishes the final severance of poetic language from all imitative functions by breaking the link between word and object absolutely. The *Monolog* is said to free language into its own musical and poetic nature so that it no longer refers to anything but itself and therefore "essentially only exhibits *itself*."[3] What is not heard in such an interpretation are the fine tones of irony that sound in Novalis's essay. As a consequence its assertions are taken literally, and no inquiry is made into the purpose of the dissemblance. The oversight, though, is understandable: irony is a surprising literary device for Novalis. A perfectly usual form of expression for his friend Friedrich von Schlegel and other Romantic authors, it fits neither Novalis's character nor his artistic temperament. Yet this very fact makes the question of why he chose to write the *Monolog* from behind an ironically teasing mask interesting and indeed urgent.[4]

THE *MONOLOG*'S STRUCTURE AND MEANING

The *Monolog* begins with the assertion that there is something "odd about speaking and writing." The German for "odd" here is *närrisch*, a word that might be better translated as "foolish" were it not for the fact that "foolish" has lost some of its more powerful implications. Närrisch is the adjective of the noun *Narr*, meaning "fool." But "foolish" and närrisch do not say quite the same thing. For "foolish" has come to mean no more than "silly" or "stupid," while the German närrisch has retained its association with *Narr*, that is, jester or trickster, and madman. The Narr, as mad fool and trickster, is possessed of a spirit that purposefully misleads and tricks all who come into contact with him. His jokes are at the expense of his audience. Therefore, to begin the *Monolog* with the assertion that there is something närrisch about the acts of speaking and writing is to claim for them the pranksterish spirit of the jester. But if speaking and writing are said to be misleading or tricky, then who is being misled? Who is being tricked? Interestingly, Novalis does not have in mind those who are spoken to or who are doing the reading: he is not thinking of the audience. For according to Novalis, it is not the listener or reader who becomes the dupe of the act of speaking or writing, but the speaker or writer himself who, though, is not setting out to deceive either himself or others with his speech deliberately. In other words, speaking and writing are in themselves misleading. The consequence of such a view of language follows naturally: where speech is tricksterish, conversation—with oneself or with others—is merely a game with words, a "word game." As my earlier discussion of chance has shown, chance, game, trickery, and language are intimately connected for Novalis. Already in a *Blüthenstaub* fragment dealing with Goethe's art—of which Novalis says that it "entertains the imagination with a mysterious game,"—Novalis further remarks that Goethe

> discovered *one of nature's tricks* and learned from her a *neat knack.* Ordinary life is full of similar chance occurrences. They constitute a game which like everything of a gamelike nature results in *surprise* and *deception.* Several sayings of daily life are based on the observation of this *perverse connection;* thus, for instance, bad dreams forebode good luck; to speak of someone's death, long life; a hare that crosses one's path, bad luck. Almost all the superstitions of the common people rest on interpretations of this *game.* (The emphasis is mine.) [II,425,#27, 3–13]

Goethe's artistic and poetic trick is said by Novalis to be a "mysterious game" because, like everything that has a gamelike character, it surprises and deceives us. But Goethe supposedly has learned this poetic knack from nature herself. For in our ordinary daily life nature provides us with similarly mysterious and deceptive games, playing tricks on us that surprise and confront us with the unexpected. Indeed, ordinary people feel the chance occurrences of daily life to be the confidence games of nature, whose deceptive and startling character finds acknowledgment in their superstitious sayings. The general unpredictability of chance, thus, is thought to signify the perversity of fate or its tricksterish spirit. But what the *Blüthenstaub* fragment suggests Goethe learned from Nature and used in his art, the *Monolog* asserts is part also of the very nature of language herself.[5]

Not surprisingly, when language in its own nature is tricky, it is not suited for speaking seriously or purposively about particular objects.[6] It is then not a tool that can be used to speak "for the sake of things." That people are nevertheless under the impression that they are so using language is laughable. This is not only a judgment made by the author (who, it may be pointed out, as author, remains hidden behind the mask of irony and an entirely impersonal form of expression), it is also a natural consequence of the ironic situation. The dupe of a prank, the one having been fooled by a trick, becomes laughable. And here the ironic twist at work is threefold. First, there is language presenting itself as a serious, serviceable tool with which one is to speak about things, and so language ironically dissembles its own nature. Second, there is the author hiding behind the masks of impersonal and ironic expression and so appearing, at once, to be present and absent, hidden and revealed, truthful and false. And finally, there is his judgment that not the tricksterish nature of language is to be marveled at, but the mistake made about its true character.

The result of language's tricksterish nature is that its actual character remains hidden. No one knows that it is concerned only with itself, that it cares only for itself, except the author, who has succeeded in looking behind the mask and illusions language presents to the unwary. He has stopped its quicksilver changes, seen its true character, and therefore can tell us the fruitful secret of its nature: namely, that when it is spoken for its own sake—and in daily life that means spoken as idle chatter—language will yield the most wonderful and original truths. Presenting such conventional opposites as "idle chatter" and "truth" as united in the same sphere of meaning, indeed as identical in meaning, is a standard maneuver of ironical expression. It is used here partly for its shock value, to awaken us to the problem at hand, and partly to prepare us for the even more startling paradox that follows.

Whereas the author, so far, has remained an impersonal voice, language itself is now subjectivized. It is said to be *launisch*, a word that means capricious, moody, or ill-tempered. All these are attributes that properly fit a person but are inappropriate descriptions of a mere faculty. Language, therefore, is being treated here as an independent and separate figure. Indeed, a faculty is now ascribed to it, in turn, and we are told that it has *Muthwillen*, a form of mischievous will. It is to this Muthwillen that "serious people" react with hatred. Yet hate, too, is a form of aggressive emotion that we feel toward people or other living beings, and which we use metaphorically when we assert it about things. Looking back from this personification of language to the opening remarks of the *Monolog*, we can see in the objectively and impersonally expressed claim that there is something närrisch about speaking and writing a preparation for the emancipation of the faculty of speech. For only as an independent figure can it also be närrisch.

The tone throughout this first part of the *Monolog* is entirely ironical. All claims are at once put forth with the seductive accent of wit and taken back again, retrieved by the very tone of the voice that asserts them. We are left uncertain, as irony means us to be. But now the tone changes. A simple analogy is presented, in which language is said to resemble mathematical formulas.

The outstanding characteristic of mathematics for Novalis, as Käte Hamburger points out, is that "it contains laws that are self-explanatory by being self-legitimizing."[7] Language is like mathematics for Novalis, because its rules have their origin in language itself and find their justification and legitimization within the language system rather than outside of it. But this self-sufficiency of the language system says nothing about language's inability to function as a sign with which we point to things. On the contrary, the assertion is rather commonsensical, and the mentioning of mathematical formulas that constitute "a world for themselves" does not imply that they, or language which resembles them, express nothing about the world. Indeed, Novalis makes a point of saying that this very self-sufficiency of mathematical formulas not only makes them expressive but even allows the world-soul to make of them a "standard and ground plan of things." In addition, Novalis thinks mathematics proves "the sympathy and identity of nature and the soul,"[8] which is why mathematics says something not only about the world, but also about man's inner being. Language, paralleling mathematics, similarly mirrors not only the world, but human nature as well.[9] As a result, and contrary to the prevailing opinion, language for Novalis is rather far from "exhibiting essentially only itself."[10]

Yet, as with mathematics, if language is to be used "truly," a certain sensitivity to its nature is required. A fine ear for its musicality and a good sense for its structure will allow one to become "prophetic." Here the traditional relationship of the poet to the priest or seer—to which Novalis repeatedly makes reference—is touched on.[11] The comparison to mathematics points in a similar direction: language is shown to take up the same intermediate position between matters entirely human and matters entirely divine that Novalis, following the Platonic tradition, thought to be the natural home of numbers.[12] In its resemblance to numbers the liminal nature of language is asserted and becomes apparent, and with it language's essential kinship to the poet is established: for it now turns out that both the poet and the language of his song are spirits of the threshold, brothers to Hermes. Born of enthusiastic inspiration into the reality of its self-governing existence, language also resembles mathematics in that it points beyond itself. For mathematics, Novalis claims, is grounded in "the intimate coherence, the sympathy of the cosmos." [III,593,16–17] Being based on the relationships that obtain in the universe, mathematics represents them. "Numbers, like signs and words, are appearances, representations katexoxin." [III,593,18–19] To Novalis "pure mathematics is religion." [III,594,3] In connection with art, therefore, it functions as a mediating agency to the divine: "In music it appears formally, as revelation—as creative idealism. Here it legitimizes itself, as heavenly messenger, kat anthropon. [III,593,26–28] Language, being like mathematics, mirrors the world as well as man and serves them both as heavenly messenger. The claim that is made on behalf of mathematical formulas and that by analogy is applied to language—namely that mathematical formulas are "a world in themselves"—is, in light of Novalis's other remarks on the subject, far less extraordinary than some interpreters would have us believe. Without doubt, there exists for Novalis a sort of Platonic realm of ideal reality to which, in general, all abstractions belong, and of which mathematics and language are the foremost expressions. As members of this realm they do, indeed, exhibit first of all the characteristics of the systems they belong to. But these systems, in turn, reflect the condition of the world and link man to the domain of the divine.

Once this analogy of language to mathematics has been made, the tone of the *Monolog* changes again, and so does its perspective. Now the essay turns in on itself and considers the value of its own act of speech. The effect of this questioning of the essay's own speech-status, in conjunction with the raising of language to the position of an independent being, is not unlike the effect of the Saul Steinberg cartoon showing a draftsman's hand drawing scenery that includes a draftsman drawing a hand drawing scenery, and so on *ad infinitum*. But Steinberg seems to start where Novalis ends. One wants to ask, where does the first drawing hand originate? Or, who is the first draftsman? In contrast, language conceived as an autonomous being who inquires about the nature of her own speech-act raises the question about the last speaker. For if indeed the author speaks in the essay, but language speaks in the author, then who speaks in language? And if it is language herself, is it her utterances we hear in the author's voice? This question, like Saul Steinberg's, is not meant to be answered; it suffices, for the time being, that it is being asked.

By turning in on itself and applying its own dictum to itself, the *Monolog* returns to the ironic claim that only he who speaks for the sake of speaking—and not for the sake of things—will say "the most glorious, most original truths." Clearly the essay does not heed its own advice. Both in its ironical beginning and in its dictum on the nature of language, which compares language and mathematics, it sets out to speak for the sake of things, namely, for the sake of discovering the nature of language. In addition, the author, who so far has remained hidden behind the impersonal voice, now steps forward in the personal pronoun *I*, and inquiring into the character of his own undertaking, comes to judge it, in accordance with the ironical dictum, as faulty. The *Monolog* thus turns out to state a paradox.

But whereas the ironic mood of the first section of the *Monolog* belongs to the pranksterish spirit of the Narr, with this new turn we find ourselves in the grip of the demonic, in which meaningful speech is muted and the disclosing nature of language is closed off by the endless circling of self-contradiction. For the demonic, as Kierkegaard says,

> *is the sudden.* The sudden is a new expression for another aspect of inclosing reserve. When the content is reflected upon, the demonic is defined as inclosing reserve; when time is reflected upon, it is defined as the sudden. Inclosing reserve is the effect of the negative self-relation in the individuality. Inclosing reserve closes itself off more and more from communication. But communication is in turn the expression for continuity, and the negation of continuity is the sudden. . . . But the sudden knows no law. It does not belong among natural phenomena but is a psychical phenomenon—it is an expression of unfreedom. . . . In relation to the content of inclosing reserve, the sudden may signify the terrible, but the effect of the sudden may also appear to the observer as the comical.[13]

Applied to language, the interruption of continuity that the sudden or the demonic represents is a freezing of the flow of thought within language; the negative self-relation is the denial by the paradoxical assertion of the very claim made with the assertion. On both counts, therefore, self-contradiction is demonic. In addition, self-contradiction leaves the thinker-speaker unfree: stopped by the denial that lies hidden within the very assertion he makes, he has nowhere to turn, nowhere to go, and so becomes indeed a comical figure. While the irony of the prank-sterish spirit dissembles by denying what it asserts merely by the tone with which the assertion is made—and thus only leaves uncertainty in its wake—the comic of the demonic spirit denies its assertion explicitly by phrasing it as a self-contradiction—and leaves nothing in its wake. The demonic resolves the uncertainty negatively into an immobility of thought. The demonic spirit, therefore, is a raised or intensified prank-sterish spirit. The self-contradiction it presents to us in the *Monolog* concerns the *Monolog*'s own language. For if all intentional speech says "ridiculous and perverse stuff," the *Monolog*, being a bit of intentional speech, says ridiculous and perverse stuff. Its claim, therefore, that intentional speech says ridiculous and perverse stuff is false, and intentional speech is indeed true speech. But then the claims of this essay, being intentional speech, are correct, and all intentional speech is just what the *Monolog* claims it to be, namely, ridiculous and perverse stuff. And we are ready to start anew on the merry-go-round.

The immediate result of the paradox is that it binds us into a vicious circle from which (as is to be expected with the demonic) there is no escape. Only an ever-tighter inward spiraling into the paradox appears possible. In such a situation the only maneuver left us is one of evasion: we must turn to questioning as an activity of value for its own sake. Doomed not to find any certain answer, we must be satisfied to seek, without even the hope of finding what we search for. And so, in its fourth and final part, the *Monolog* strings together question after question for which neither the essay nor its author can give or find an answer. But the questions themselves point us in the direction in which we must seek. In the case of the *Monolog*, that direction is inspiration. Asking whether ultimately he has willed nothing, the author, the "I" of the essay, that is Novalis, muses whether the poet is inspired by language, or as the Greeks would have said, possessed by the muse.

The structure of the *Monolog* follows the method of Erhebung, or raising, and its confrontation of opposites. In this manner, arriving at his own dialectic,[14] Novalis moves from the ironic and pranksterish mode of the first part to a straightforward attempt in the second part, to describe the nature of language by an analogy to mathematics. The thesis of the essentially tricksterish and misleading nature of speaking and writing is opposed by the antithesis of language's true and ideal character, as it is given in the comparison to number understood in the Neo-Platonic and Pythagorean tradition. From here the *Monolog* returns once more to the ironic mode, only now intensifying or raising its effects by showing, in the third part, the prankster to be the demon he is and, consequently, by letting a paradox grow out of the text's dictum. Writer and reader alike are thus captured in the circularity of the vicious argument, and the only escape possible is into the essential uncertainty of the question as it occurs in the fourth part of the *Monolog*. Yet in the very act of questioning, the direction in which an answer may possibly present itself is found. The realm of the divine is pointed to as the source and home of the solution to the conundrum that confronts any speaker, but particularly the poet. This dialectical move, while it leaves us and the author uncertain about the author's own status, shows the pranksterish aspect of everyday language to be a lower manifestation of the demonic, of which the paradox is the raised or more highly intense expression. And whereas the pranksterish nature of language is adequately contrasted with the opposite claim of its mathematical nature and truth, the higher demonic expression, the paradox of its self-reflexivity, finds resolution in the questioning assertion that language might be inspired speech. Synthesis is finally achieved in the suggestion that language is a manifestation of the divine.

LINGUISTIC DEMONS AND THE GAMES THEY PLAY

In addition to serving as the first moment in the dialectical raising of language to the divine realm, the assertion that there is something pranksterish about it also allows Novalis to allude to the transformational character of language. For the trickster or Narr is the mythic representation of the shape-changer. Paul Radin, in his study of the trickster, says of him that "he possesses no well-defined and fixed form."[15] He plays his tricks on the unsuspecting not so much by any deliberate attempt as by the very nature of his being. As a mythological figure he is a *"speculum mentis* wherein is depicted man's struggle with himself and with a world into which he had been thrust without his volition and consent." [*PRT*,xxiv] In the figure of the trickster we project our reaction to our thrownness outward and thus use irony as the weapon with which we attempt, against all odds, to gain a measure of control over destiny by distancing us from ourselves. And so "laughter, humor, and irony permeate everything Trickster does." [*PRT*,xxiv] In the trickster's sudden and inexplicable changes of form, the ultimate opacity of man's destiny and future are given expression. The shape-changer is a trickster to us precisely because the shape of things to come is never "well-defined and fixed."

Like the trickster, language, and particularly poetry, "the daughter of

inspiration," resembles "a chameleon."[16] For Novalis shape-changing is
as essential an aspect of language as it is of the trickster.[17] Language,
especially as poetic speech, is Protean, fluid, and without fully congealed
or definite form. In a letter to August Wilhelm Schlegel Novalis writes on
January 12, 1798:

> Therefore true to the essential laws of its nature—it [poetry] becomes,
> as it were, an organic being—whose entire structure betrays its rise
> from the fluid element, its original elastic nature, its unlimitedness, its
> omnipotence. [IV,246,25–29]

Similarly, in the prophetic dream image Heinrich has of his own con-
secration to poetry in *Heinrich von Ofterdingen*, we can read of the poet's
baptism in the cave of the cool, blue fountain of poetic language. The
imagery is remarkable not only for ascribing to poetry liquidity and fluid-
ity, but also for the clear shape-changing it thinks poetry capable of:

> He dipped his hand into the fountain and wet his lips. It was as if a
> breath of spirit poured into him and he felt himself deeply strength-
> ened and refreshed. An irresistible longing to bathe seized him, he
> undressed and stepped into the fountain. He felt as if a glowing cloud
> of sunset flowed around him; a heavenly feeling swept over his inner-
> most being; innumerable thoughts within him drove ardently and
> voluptuously to intertwine; new and never-seen images came into
> being and also flowed into each other and became visible beings and
> every wave of the lovely element clung to him like a tender bosom.
> The stream appeared to be a thawed flow of charming girls who,
> touching the young man, momentarily congealed into bodies.
>
> [I, 196,32–197,7]

Faced with this chameleonlike nature of language, how is the poet ever to
recognize her true face, her true form? How is he to catch her and make
her stand still long enough to shape her according to his will? As his
weapon in this struggle he chooses irony. With irony's negativity he
confronts the infinite changeability of language as indirectly as Perseus
confronted the Medusa—and just as successfully stops language dead in
her tracks. But that is the problem: the negative will, asserting itself in this
act, is the final negation of the possibility of poetry, which is a making,
not an unmaking.

Having caught language—poetry—in his ironic net, the poet finds
himself caught with her. Irony is the proper tool for the critic, but not for
the poet. Its vacillating nature leads to a separation or analysis of everything it holds frozen in its gaze. Poetry by contrast is synthetic. For

Novalis considers poetry to be that agency by means of which knowing as a doing and as a making can grasp the universe in its infinity and form in one visionary insight a union with the whole.[18] But in ironic speech poetry is mute. The poet speaking in the ironic mode silences poetry. And so the poet's dilemma is the paradox that, he must either force language by means of irony to take the shape he wills her to have but then lose the very thing he seeks, namely the poetic voice; or he must abandon along with the ironic mode his desire to control his own talent fully, and accept his lack of power to will his destiny as poet. He must cultivate a mood of receptive stillness and acquiesce to accept the words of the higher power that may speak through him. The poet's paradox, then, is that silence is his proper mode. In silence the voice of the muse, or of language herself, defined as the independent figure of the *Monolog* who belongs to the realm that spans the world of man and the kingdom of the gods, can be heard. As heavenly messenger, language sings in the poet only when the poet himself is silent and therefore "wills nothing, but what he must."[19]

In this his silence the muse's voice comes to the poet as the gift of chance. The *Monolog* describes and is itself an example of the process by which the poet comes to hear the call of the divine in the interstices that the occasion opens up for him. And Zufall then is that which falls to the poet, which accrues to him with this his calling.

We can, therefore, now conclude that the tradition that sees Novalis as belonging to the first modern thinkers about language and poetry is correct.[20] But the tradition errs in associating Novalis with the school of thought that proclaims the autonomy of language and regards all assertions of inspiration with suspicion. For if Novalis is to be understood as an eighteenth-century precursor of twentieth-century thought about poetry and language, he must be seen as preparing Heidegger's way to language, even though Heidegger himself would probably have denied this. In a 1959 lecture, Heidegger takes Novalis's *Monolog* as the starting point for his own thinking, but he comes to the conclusion that whereas language *is* indeed monologue, it is so not in the sense Novalis suggests: "Novalis understands language dialectically, in terms of subjectivity, that is, within the horizon of absolute idealism."[21] Heidegger, on the contrary, although he agrees that language is monologue, thinks it is so because "it is language *alone* which speaks authentically; and language speaks *lonesomely*." Heidegger then explicates this and comes to the conclusion that:

> Man is capable of speaking only insofar as he belongs to Saying, listens to Saying, so that in re-saying it he may be able to say a word.

For as Heidegger asserts:

> In order to be who we are, we human beings remain committed to and
> within the being of language, and can never step out of it and look at it
> from somewhere else. Thus we always see the nature of language only
> to the extent to which language itself has us in view, has appropriated
> us to itself. . . . Saying will not let itself be captured in any statement.
> It demands of us that we achieve by silence the appropriating initiat-
> ing movement within the being of language—and do so without talk-
> ing about silence.[22]

But if I am right, this is exactly what the *Monolog* not only claims but
demonstrates in its own structure and being. Heidegger's essay, by contrast, makes the claim but is not itself a demonstration or example of it.[23]
Heidegger, then, as the philosopher thinking and writing about language, can at best state what is true about it, while Novalis, as the poet
considering language, is able to speak its truth and make an icon of it,
thus far more faithfully fulfilling Heidegger's demand than Heidegger
himself. For the icon speaks a silent language. In it that "appropriating
initiating movement within the being of language," which we "achieve
by silence . . . without talking about silence," is present. Novalis has
given us in the *Monolog* a statement about language that is a representation of language and therefore succeeds in capturing "Saying," but does
so only insofar as it is icon rather than statement.

This conclusion, resting in part on the iconic character of language,
now raises that character as an issue to be addressed. I will in part two,
therefore, turn to consider the role of the image or icon in Novalis's
thoughts on language.

PART II

The Philosopher and the Earth

CHAPTER FIVE

Introductory Remarks on Language, Herder, Fichte, and Novalis

Novalis's abiding interest in the origin and nature of language found its first youthful expression, as we have seen, in the essay *Von der Begeisterung*.[1] It was written under the influence of Herder's prize-winning *Abhandlung vom ursprung der Sprache (On the Origin of Language)*,[2] which in turn was indebted to Condillac.[3] Novalis became familiar with Fichte's *Von der Sprachfähigkeit und vom Ursprung der Sprache (On Language Capacity and on the Origin of Language)*[4] some years later when, in the course of the years 1795–97, while living and working in Tennstedt and Weissenfels, he studied Fichte's works thoroughly in his free time.

Several years intervened between Novalis's first acquaintance with Herder's treatise and his reading of Fichte's tractatus on the origin of language. But more than time separates the two essays: they approach the question of language from very different points of view.[5] Yet despite their many differences, both address the following four questions of particular interest for an understanding of Novalis's work on the nature of language:

1. Does language have a human or a superhuman origin?
2. Does language have its source in the emotions or in reason?
3. Is the relationship of a sign to the object for which it stands arbitrary, conventional, or essential?
4. Which is the primary sense in the formation and development of language—the sense of hearing or the sense of sight?

On none of these issues does Novalis simply follow either Herder or Fichte. He uses bits and pieces of their ideas as take-off points for his own thinking. But as always when he is faced with a set of contradictory traditions and theories, his response is basically syncretic: Insofar as Novalis considers the origin of language to be divine as well as human, and in its human origin to be tied to the emotions, his theory of language resembles Herder's. But insofar as he is acutely aware of the ties language has to rational thought, he gives greater credence to Fichte's theory. Yet Novalis's view of the relationship that holds between a sign or word and its object is more complex and many-layered in its structure than either Fichte's or Herder's. For Novalis sees language in some respects as a freely created and freely chosen system of representations, that is, as both arbitrary and conventional in its representational functions; but in other respects he finds that a deeply meaningful relationship exists between a word and what it names. Novalis's most strikingly synthetic response, however, occurs in his approach to the question whether language is ultimately rooted in man's visual abilities or in his sense of hearing. The question whether the origin of language is tied more essentially to man's ability to represent the world and his experience of it by means of images, or by means of acoustic signs, occupied Novalis extensively. We may assume, therefore, that he considered it to be a question about the most basic characteristics of language. Rather than take up each of these four issues in turn, I will focus primarily on the fact that the origin of language, for Novalis, is tied to both the sense of sight and the sense of hearing, and that depending on what language is used for, either the one root or the other is apt to show itself more prominently. Only a proper understanding of Novalis's position on this point will enable us to evaluate his thinking on language correctly and to do justice to his poetical, philosophical, and religious convictions.

Most interpreters of Novalis's theory of language attempt to reconstruct his thinking on this subject by turning to the fragments and to the notes of his philosophical studies. For in addition to his remarks in the *Monolog,* the fragments and notes contain most of what is explicitly concerned with language. Although I, too, will rely a good deal on the fragments, I will pay closer attention to the fictional works, since what particularly interests me is frequently implied in their structure and content rather than explicitly stated in Novalis's more theoretical writings.

Like Herder and Fichte, Novalis sees language as originating with man and considers it, in one of the *Logologische Fragmente,* to be the result of man's organic makeup and nature:

> Language, too, is a product of the organic formative impulse. As this impulse forms everywhere *the same,* under the most diverse circum-

stances, so also language forms itself in accordance with both culture and an ascending development and animation into the profound expression of the idea of organization, into the *system of philosophy.*

Language in its entirety is a *postulate.* It has a positive and free origin. One had to agree to think of certain objects when certain signs were used, to deliberately construct within oneself something specific. [II,558,#141]

But despite the free and positive origin of language, and despite the necessity to agree to associate particular objects with particular signs, and despite the fact that the specific thought at the sight or sound of a specific sign is a deliberate undertaking, the relation holding between the sign and what it signifies, for Novalis, is not arbitrary. In a fragment of the *Allgemeine Brouillon* in which he asserts the human origin of language, Novalis also claims the original language to have been "truly scientific" (*wissenschaftlich*). Deriving this term from Fichte, Novalis uses it to mean at once transcendental and possessed of knowledge. But if a kind of knowing resides within language itself, then the sign must in some essential manner mirror the nature of what it stands for and cannot be merely arbitrary:

Synthesis is a *chronic triangle.* / *Language* and the *signs of language* arose a priori from human nature, and the original *language was truly scientific*—to recover it is the purpose of the grammarian. [III,461,#1034]

Novalis thus agrees with both Herder and Fichte that the origin of language lies in man. But whereas for Fichte it is man's essentially rational and social character that combines with his representational nature to eventually bring forth language proper,[6] and whereas for Herder it is man's *Besonnenheit,* or reflective circumspection, that works together with his emotions to produce a voiced response to the world, even if that voice is heard only in the human heart,[7] for Novalis language is the result of man's religious impulse and desire to pray. In contrast to Fichte and in agreement with Herder, therefore, Novalis believes that human emotions played a major role in bringing about language: overwhelmed by a feeling of adoration for the being who made him and the world, man bends his knees in a silent gesture of prayer. In *Von der Begeisterung* (*About Inspiration*), which, as we have seen, represents Novalis's earliest thinking on the nature of language, he does not appear to consider this silent and nearly involuntary behavior to be language.[8] For he says:

The first wind, the first breeze that rustled through the crown of the oak tree and was heard by the ear of the savage, must certainly have produced in his young, uneducated bosom, which was still open to all outer impressions, an emotion, a thought of the existence of a powerful being, that was very close to enthusiasm and for which he lacked nothing but the words with which to express his overflowing feeling and in some manner to share it with the inanimate objects of his surroundings. For now *without language* and surely involuntarily he sank to his knees and in a mute gesture betrayed that feelings upon feelings crowded in on his heart. (My emphasis.) [II,22,22–31]

The expression "without language" (*ohne Sprache*) is ambiguous; it may simply refer to the earlier wordless state (*ohne Worte*). But to say that as a consequence the young savage "betrayed" (*verriet*) that feelings crowded in on his heart seems to indicate that this communication is not only involuntary and nearly accidental, but also that it is as communication incomplete. A well-developed *language* of gestures does not "betray" what it means, but clearly communicates its specific intention. Although Novalis, in this early piece, then, considers mute gesturing to be pre-linguistic behavior—even when it communicates something about the emotional and cognitive state of the gesturer—he nevertheless sees this speechless act as a precursor of language. For man gestures silently in response to a feeling and thought that would find more adequate expression in language. Novalis's view on this issue seems to be shared in this century by Martin Buber, who in *I and Thou* expresses a similar thought when he says that in the third sphere in which the world of relations with spiritual beings arises,

> relation is wrapped in a cloud but reveals itself, it lacks but creates language. We hear no You and yet feel addressed; we answer—creating, thinking, acting: with our being we speak the basic word, unable to say You with our mouth.[9]

In later remarks, too, Novalis does not consider gestures to be a form of language, although he does think that what at the dawn of man's development is merely prelinguistic behavior eventually will evolve into a language:

> Are gestures really meant to be grammatically symbolic, or expressive? I do not believe that they are (meant to be)—but they will be—when they are, in the ideal sense, natural products of the ideal association of the inner and outer bodily members—They belong to the domain of *dance*. [III,570,#102]

In other words, only when gestures become ideal outward expressions of ideal inner states will they become grammatically symbolic or grammatically expressive, that is, part of a language. Novalis does not deny then, the expressiveness of gestures or their ability to communicate meaning, but neither of these qualities suffices to make of gestures linguistic signs. Only after a grammar or formal structural system of gestures has developed can they be thought of as a language. Novalis, however, does not think that such a formalization of their abstract or general order as yet exists or is possible. But this does not mean that the horizon of language is as narrow for him as it is for Fichte. In fact, it is wider than even Herder's. For ultimately, language can and will encompass not only man's expressive behavior, but all of nature as well:

> GRAMMAR. Man does not speak alone—the universe *speaks*, also — everything speaks—infinite languages./ Doctrine of signatures.
>
> [III,267,35–268,2]

For Novalis, the universe speaks because every object of it *is* the uttered word of God. The doctrine of signatures functions like a sort of grammar that can guide us to distinguish between the outer appearance (what in a spoken language would be the sound or, more appropriately, in a written text the graphic representation) and the inner meaning of that utterance. With such a perspective any material object on earth, and indeed the earth itself, becomes a decipherable hieroglyph.

CHAPTER SIX

The Figurative Language of Earth

THE LANGUAGE OF STONES AND FOSSILS

In Novalis's tendency to think of nature as having a language, we again recognize his indebtedness to Herder, for whom even the plucked string does its natural duty when it calls to another for an echo, and for whom nature decreed that the world let its emotions sound. [*HSW*,V,5–6][1] But for Herder this music of nature, or natural poetry, although a form of language, is not related to human speech and is also not the source of human poetry or song. In other words, Herder distinguishes rather sharply between the language of nature and that of man. Novalis, in contrast, sees a continuum of languages that begins with the silent presence of inorganic nature and progresses through the sounding speech of man to the creative word of God. Everything that is capable of revealing a feeling, a thought, an idea, or an ideal, and does so in ways that can be thought to have a formal structure, either has language or is a communication (*Mittheilung*), or linguistic expression. In the *Logologische Fragmente* Novalis notes:

> Everything we come to know is a *communication*. Thus the world is indeed a *communication*—revelation of the spirit. [II,594,#316]

And so Novalis muses whether the mechanical motions of physical bodies do not constitute a form of conversation between them:

> Perhaps all *mechanical motion* is only nature's *language*. One body addresses the other mechanically—the latter answers mechanically—

for both, though, the mechanical motion is secondary and merely a means—an occasion for inner change and the result thereof.

[III,427,10–13,#804][2]

But not because such mechanical motion produces sounds is it language for Novalis. He is not thinking of a bell ringing when hit by its clapper or a thundering rock-slide produced by boulders tumbling each against the other. For neither the sounding of bronze nor the crashing of stones interprets their meaning. Rather, the language of physical bodies is contained in their shapes and results from a translation of their qualitative nature and quantitative aspects:

/About the language of the world of bodies by means of *figure*. The translation of quality into quantity and vice versa.

[III,449,12–13,#938]

In contrast to Herder, who thinks of the language of nature as a sounding and tonal language, for Novalis the language of the inorganic world is silent, both as figure and as mechanical interaction or physical change of quality and quantity. For mechanical interaction is a language produced by touch and resulting not in sound but in spatial relations: moving bodies inscribe patterns in the physical history of the world. The mechanical motions of bodies, therefore, are language insofar as the paths they traverse constitute figures whose qualitative nature can be translated into a quantitative expression. How much, for Novalis, these natural processes resemble language—or rather *are* language—is astonishing. In a fragment of the *Allgemeine Brouillon* he goes so far as to find grammatical names for physical phenomena:

Could it be that the *bodies* and *figures* are nouns—the forces, verbs— and natural philosophy—the art of deciphering. [III,443,#913]

It would appear, then, that Novalis speaks of the language of nature not merely metaphorically. As a mining official, part of his daily work involved seeking in the rocks and stones of the region for evidence of the metals or salts they might contain.[3] An interpretation of such evidence as a "message" or "communication" of nature is not so very far-fetched. For the metaphor of the "book of nature" facilitates the tendency to interpret the phenomena of nature as communications. Nor is such a "reading" of nature peculiar to Novalis. In a letter to Johann Heinrich Merck, Goethe, for instance, wrote:

Since once and for all I cannot learn anything from books, only now, after having turned the mile-long pages of our regions, do I begin to study also the experiences of others and to make use of them.[4]

In addition, Novalis's interest in history as a source of knowledge for the sciences, religion, and poetry, led him to be fascinated early on by fossils and by the petrification of life. The change that turns a living organism into stone became for him an example of nature's own symbolic representation of the qualitative shift that is an aspect of chance, understood as a kairotic moment. Similarly, the fossil's petrified life appears to be an embodiment of Novalis's method of Erhebung, in which the overcoming as well as the maintaining of the opposition of qualitative states and the shift that overcomes the opposition are not only prominent features, but are seen as presenting the most poetical or Romantic moment of both life and poetry. And so, in a discussion of the Laocoön sculpture, Novalis ponders whether the task of the sculptor ought not be to catch that moment in which life, when it is at its greatest intensity, turns into the frozen form of its own petrified symbol or sign:

> Could we not think of a more comprehensive, in short more intense moment in the Laocontic drama—perhaps the one in which the greatest pain turns into intoxication—resistance into surrender—the highest life into stone. (Ought the sculptor not *always* grasp the moment of *petrification*—and single it out—and depict it—and also be able to represent only it?) The greatest works of art are generally *not pleasing*—They are ideals that can only—and *ought to* only—approximate pleasing us—aesthetic imperatives. [III,412,33–413,4,#745][5]

The suggestion of this fragment is that the work of the sculptor in stone is not unlike—or ought to be not unlike—the work nature does in stone. Both the fossil and the statue are perceived as silent and solid signs, as representations of life at its moment of greatest intensity turning into its opposite, a petrified form—which, however, still speaks of its former state and, therefore, still represents in its inorganic state and mute image the story and essence of life.

It is a peculiarity of stones and earth that, despite their apparent lifelessness, they have served man as symbols of his own beginning and end throughout history. Thus, in the myth of Deucalion, for instance, it is said that after the great flood had wiped out mankind, the goddess Themis instructed Deucalion and his wife Pyrrha to throw the bones of their mother over their shoulders in order to renew the human race. Since they had different mothers, Deucalion and his wife took Themis to mean not their human mothers, but mother Earth, whose stones they thought were her bones. And so, throwing stones over their shoulders, they once more engendered the human race. Although an ancient Greek myth, this tale continued to serve the scientific community as parable and metaphor well into the Baroque Enlightenment. Interpreting it in a manner meant to criticize the usual practices of the alchemists, who sought to transform and rejuvenate not only metals but also man, Roger Bacon, for instance, writes:

> This fable [the Deucalion myth] seems to disclose a secret of nature, and to correct an error which is familiar to the human mind. For man in his ignorance concludes that the renewal and restoration of things may be effected by means of their own corruption and remains; as the Phoenix rises out of her own ashes; which is not so: for matters of this kind have already reached the end of their course and can give no further help towards the first stages of it: so we must go back to a more common principle.[6]

But not only in Greek mythology do earth- and stone-born men and women play a role. In the Judeo-Christian tradition, as well, man is said to have been fashioned from the clay of the ground by God, who breathed life into him. And even when stones or earth were not directly images or symbols of man's origin, they yet served to connect man to the realm beyond, to the holy. Thus altars were originally made of stone or clay because they were thought to resemble most the nature of the divine. In fact, Earth herself, personified as Gea or Tellus, was a goddess. The cults of the great mother goddesses—Isis, Ishtar, Astarte, or Danaä, for instance—were all based on a personification of earth and nature as a woman.

The alchemical tradition, on the one hand, continued this archetypal symbolism, but on the other hand gave it a new twist. The *Corpus Hermeticum*, for example, sees the Earth in the shape of a woman and thinks of the various parts of the Earth (as Deucalion and Pyrrha did when they decided the bones of their mother were the stones of the earth) in analogy to the members of the human body, and then extends the analogy to the spirit of Earth, of Nature, and thinks of it as resembling the human spirit. When the philosopher of Romanticism, Schelling, in the introduction to his *Ideas to a Philosophy of Nature* (1797), claims a kinship between the spirits of man and nature, he continues an ancient tradition:

> We do not want that nature only accidentally correspond to the principles of our spirit (for example by mediation through some third thing), but rather that she herself not only necessarily and originally express the principles of our spirit, but herself realize them, that only insofar as she does so, she be nature and be called so. Nature shall be the visible spirit, and spirit the invisible nature.[7]

Although Novalis's interpretation of the symbolism of Nature, Earth, and stone is entirely molded by his own particular world view, he nevertheless stands in this old tradition. For his thorough acquaintance with the ancient Greek authors and with the texts of the alchemical tradition made him well aware of the symbolic significance of stones and earth. In agreement then with Schelling, Novalis identifies earth with nature and adds in *Die Lehrlinge zu Sais* the idea of history as part of their analogy:

> Everything divine has a history, and should not nature, this singular whole with which man can compare himself, be involved, just like man, in a history or, which is the same, have spirit? Nature would not be nature if she had no spirit, if she were not this singular counterimage of mankind, if she were not the indispensable answer to this mysterious question or the question to this infinite answer.
>
> [I,99,17–23]

In other words, the sort of mutual representation or *Wechselrepräsentation* Novalis considered to be an essential mark of all representational relationships is for him also an important aspect of the symbolism of Nature, Earth, and stone. Although Novalis usually finds himself in agreement with Goethe's philosophy of nature, he seems to have differed with him sharply on this point. For Goethe has his own alchemist, Faust, mocked when he suggests that he resembles the Earth spirit. When Faust conjures up, the spirit of Earth, he finds that there are limits to their kinship:

FAUST. Swift spirit, you whose projects have no end,/ How near akin our natures seem to be!

SPIRIT. You match the spirit that you comprehend,/ Not me. (He vanishes.)

FAUST (filled with dismay). Not you!/ Whom then?/ I, made in God's own image,/ And not with you compare![8]

But Goethe was interested not only in the ancient symbolic systems in which stones and earth were held to be of great significance for an understanding of origins. In Novalis's own time the controversy between the Neptunists and the Volcanists, that is, between those who thought stones and mountains had come into being as the result of processes of sedimentation, and those who credited volcanic activity with their formation, was in full swing. Both Werner, Novalis's teacher at the mining academy in Freiberg, and Goethe, whose *Wilhelm Meister* and *Märchen* greatly influenced Novalis, were deeply involved in the controversy. Novalis himself notes in the *Paralipomena* to *Die Lehrlinge zu Sais*:

> The geognostic quarrel between the Volcanists and the Neptunists is actually the quarrel whether the debut of the earth was sthenic or asthenic. [I,110,#1]

In addition, Goethe, who wrote that granite is "the oldest eternal altar built immediately over the abyss of creation," made frequent use of the idea of granite as a symbol of the eternal order, in contrast to the volcanic basalt which he considered to be a negative, not originary, and destructively revolutionary rock formation.[9] Goethe, however, does not only use granite and basalt as specific symbols of order and chaotic violence, but also makes use of the imagery of subterranean caves and inner earth caverns as, for instance, in *Faust*, *Wilhelm Meister*, and the *Märchen*, where whole worlds exist in such deep chambers of the interior of the earth. But whereas for Goethe the power of this imagery is altogether allegorical and metaphorical, it is for Novalis of metaphysical and religious significance. For Novalis finds the imagery of nature, earth, and stones compelling because of its ability to literally—not metaphorically—express ideas.

But if in this fashion, stones can quite literally incorporate ideas, it must be possible to order them hierarchically according to the degree of meaning they contain. The mystical tradition of the philosopher's stone becomes the highest example of such a possibility for Novalis, and calls forth ideas of similarly ideal stones:

> MINERALOGY. Stones raised to higher powers—specifically different fossils—stones differing in degree. If we have a philosopher's stone, then surely we also have a mathematician's stone and an artist's stone? etc. [III,258,#96]

The apparent problem with this fragment is that Novalis moves freely, and seemingly without the slightest hesitation or discomfort, between stones that are ideal or mystical representations and stones that are concrete physical presences, as if he were speaking of items of a similar nature. He can do so because, for him, they belong to a continuum ordered according to increasing levels of ideal content and value: inorganic matter, organic matter, speech, language, and thought. Clearly such a continuum constitutes a sequence of phenomena ordered by the method of Erhebung. Here the opposites are inorganic matter and thought, while organic matter, speech, and language constitute phenomena that are a mixture of the physical and the ideal. They differ from each other by belonging respectively to the realm of matter—as organic matter obviously does—or to the realm of ideas, as thought does. The qualitative shift occurs, therefore, between the two intermediate terms.

In this fragment of the *Allgemeine Brouillon*, the Erhebung is thought in connection with the world of fossils and stones: in rocks that are not the petrified forms of past life the material aspect is so weighty a presence that it nearly obliterates all ideal content. But in fossils, despite the fact that material nature is a formidable component of them, the ideal content is obscurely present and presenting itself in ciphers, in coded form. Yet fossils vary in the degree to which they partake of the ideal, and they give their messages, therefore, with differing clarity. In the mystical stone of the philosophers, finally, the ideal prevails, and matter is represented only darkly. In a world in which meaning is hidden and revealed in such diverse ways, some rules are clearly needed for decoding and translating the infinite variety of messages nature holds for man.

Since stones, even in their nonmystical form, contain meaning for Novalis, the amount of ideal value they possess can vary. In fact, viewed as manifestations of the various levels of ideal valuation, stones or fossils can reach up to and achieve philosophical significance:

> NATURAL HISTORY. As all the sciences converge more or less in a common—*philosophical science*—and can be ordered accordingly, so one might also order fossils according to a *philosophical fossil*—the outer descriptions of this philosophical fossil would be the present preparatory part.
> Double outer classification of fossils.
> Ideal—complete outer fossil—*simple* outer fossil. *Formal—real* fossil. Double, formal fossil. (Likewise also with the sciences.)
> [III,364,#564]

Novalis uses the adjective "philosophical" to express the fact that something is indirectly autotelic.[10] The philosophical fossil is, therefore, to be understood as serving no end outside its own being or outside the purposes and the sphere of fossils. It can function, then, as the rule-giving and order-imposing principle of fossil-rocks. The structure Novalis provides here might be considered a grammar of the language of stones. Armed with such an analysis of the double nature—physical and ideal— of the world of stones and fossils, the natural philosopher can translate into discursive human language not only the various physical characteristics of fossil stones, that is, give us a description of simple actual fossils, but can also raise that description to such levels of completeness that it becomes an ideal description of the outer or physical phenomenon of the fossil rock, much as Goethe's *Urpflanze* (original plant) gives us a paradigmatic description of all flora. Similarly, the formal structure of the fossil can be given in a simple structural model or, alternatively, can be raised to such ideal perfection that it becomes a formal paradigm.

The ideal phenomenal and the ideal formal description are both of an archetypal nature. They resemble what Plato would have called the form or idea of an object. For both Plato and Novalis, this ideal description possesses a particular value as well as a cognitive content or meaning. But for Novalis, in contrast to Plato, this archetypal fossil does not stand at the beginning and is not somehow a causal agent of all "fossilness." On the contrary, the archetypal fossil is that toward which a fossil (and also our understanding of it) develops. Novalis thus agrees with Fichte that the most basic form of language is hieroglyphic in nature and therefore imagistic rather than tonal. But in contrast to Fichte, Novalis considers these primary hieroglyphs to be neither mimetic in character, nor to be a form of human language. Rather, he considers them to be the developing ideal forms of the universe itself.

But since arché and telos in the ideal form are interdependent notions, and since the beginning holds within itself the promise of the end, the end can be inferred from the beginning. The scientist or natural philosopher's task, therefore, parallels that of the poet. But while the poet infers the entire history of an individual from one decisive event, the scientist discovers the final paradigm in the original, primitive form or structure. Whereas the poet is thus concerned mostly with the development of a given phenomenon over time, that is, with its history and the meaning that resides in it, the scientist deals with the shapes and structures of natural objects, with their spatial manifestations. As a consequence, understanding the figures of nature is a good deal more like deciphering a written text than understanding a spoken language, which explains why the natural philosopher is said to study the *book* of nature. Reading this book, though, is made more difficult by the fact that its text is written in a script of hieroglyphic representations to which man has all but lost the key:

> Once everything was appearance of spirits. Now we see nothing but dead repetition which we do not understand. The meaning of the hieroglyph is missing. We still live off the fruit of better times.
>
> [II,545,#104]

Or as Novalis put it in the *Logologische Fragmente:*

> The time when we understood the spirit of God is no longer. The meaning of the world has been lost. We have stopped at the letter. We

have lost that which appears for the sake of the appearance. Formular-being. [II,594,#316]

If man is to decipher the messages of the hieroglyphs, he may find in the doctrine of signatures a basic principle by which to understand them. Novalis probably first came across the notion of "signatures" in connection with his reading of medical texts. Sophie's illness, and later his own, awakened an interest in medicine in Novalis. Among the medical handbooks he owned, Sprengel's *History of Medicine* gave an account of Paracelsus's reintroduction of the concept of signature into the discourse of medicine.[11] For Paracelsus, "signature" signified any outer, physical characteristic that reveals an inner, nonphysical force or ideal reality. Thus, the shape of an herb, for instance, is the signature of its healing power, as in the case of thistles, whose needlelike leaves indicate that they are good for curing inner stitches, or as in the case of man, where face and body are the signature of the soul and character to whom they belong. But Paracelsus speaks of signatures also when signification is not natural. He includes such man-made, freely chosen, and arbitrary signs as the particular color of an item of clothing that identifies the wearer's race, profession, or allegiance to one army rather than another. However, Novalis's use of the term "signature" rather resembles Boehme's, as it is explicated in *De Signatura Rerum*.[12] Boehme says:

> "All that is said, written, or taught about God without the knowledge of signature is mute and without reason; it is the result therefore only of a historical illusion from someone's mouth in which the spirit without knowledge is mute. But when the spirit reveals the signature then we understand the other's mouth and understand further how the spirit out of its essence has revealed itself by means of the *principium* in the sound of the voice. . . . [chap. 1, sec. 1]
>
> There is nothing in nature that was created or born and that does not reveal its inner figure (*Gestalt*) also outwardly, for whatever is inward works to reveal itself outwardly. . . . [chap. 1, sec. 15]
>
> The signature, therefore, is the greatest means of understanding by which man (as the image of the greatest virtue) not only comes to know himself, but also the Being of all beings in the outer figurity (*Gestaltnis*) of all creatures. In their drive and desire, as well as in their outpouring sound, voice, and language, we recognize the hidden spirit; for nature gave each thing its language according to its essence and figurity; for from the essence originates the language or sound, and the *fiat* of this essence forms the quality of this essence in the outpouring sound or energy of what is alive in the sound, of what is

essential in the smell, energy, and figurity: every thing has its mouth for the purpose of revelation.

And that is the natural language in which each thing speaks from its nature and reveals itself and represents itself. . . .

[chap. 1, secs. 16–17]

The entire visible world with all its beings is a sign or figure of the inner, spiritual realm. Whatever a thing's inwardness and effectiveness is, that also is its outer character: as if the spirit of each creature represented and revealed its inner birth-figurity (*Geburts-Gestaltnis*) with its body; so also the eternal Being. [chap. 9, sec. 1]

With the movement of all figures, with this visible world [God's] word has revealed itself as in a visible likeness so that the spiritual Being would stand revealed in a comprehensible bodily one. Since the desire of the inner figure externalized itself, and the inner is given in the outer, the inner holds the outer before itself as a mirror in which it watches itself in its capacity to give birth to all outer figures: the outer is its signature.

Thus everything born of what is inward has its signature."

[chap. 9, secs. 3–4]

The doctrine of signatures, then, asserts that the phenomenal reality of the world—the figure or shape of every stone, plant, animal, or man— expresses its inner essence as it was created by God, and that this expression of the inner essence is, in turn, the outer expression of God's own inner spirit. The world, therefore, is God's outer signature. It is God's body, and its meaning is His spirit. But not only the outer physical shapes of things are the signatures and expression of their own and their maker's essence; each being's natural voice is also such an outer representation of its essential nature, it is its signature. Language, therefore, when truly spoken, is an externalization of a being's inner spirit; and the origin of language is found in each being's desire and drive to give outer expression to its inner truth. The relation between words and what they stand for, then, is anything but arbitrary.[13]

THE NATURAL PHILOSOPHER'S RELATION TO TIME AND SPACE

Despite the predominantly spatial character of the hieroglyphs of nature, time and space are interdependent aspects of *one* reality. As a consequence, if we are to have any true knowledge of the universe, we must understand time and space to be interconnected. In fragment 809 of the *Allgemeine Brouillon*, Novalis writes:

Time and space come into being simultaneously and therefore are probably one, like subject and object. Space is persisting time—time fluid, variable space—space—the basis of all that persists—time—the basis of all that is changeable. Space is the schema—time the concept—the act (genesis) of this schema. (To every moment I must think a moment that came before and one that comes after.)

[III,427,#809]

And similarly in fragment 1011:

Space devolves into time as the body devolves into the soul. Simultaneous engendering process of one *side*. [III,458,#1011]

Since, as we have seen, it is the poet's task to be the interpreter and translator of the nature of time, and since it has now become apparent that it is the natural philosopher's task to decipher, interpret, and translate the figural meaning of space, the relationship of the philosopher-scientist to the poet can be said to be like that of the body to the soul, or of space to time: one passes into the other, and together they form one reality without any clear-cut separation, yet each remains distinct from the other in his own nature. Similarly, as the notion of a subject is a meaningless idea unless it can be set against and conjoined to the notion of an object (or, as we have seen earlier, the idea of natural laws, for Novalis, is a meaningful idea only in conjunction with and in opposition to a rule of miracles), so also the idea of the natural philosopher is a useful and meaningful idea only if it is thought in connection with and in contrast to the idea of the poet. The idea of the natural philosopher as the translator of the hieroglyphic truths of nature—that is, of the meaning contained in and expressed by spatial configurations—finds completion in the idea of the poet as the translator of visionary insights into the constitution and meaning of the quality of time, into the kairos.

The task of both the philosopher and the poet, then, is to put what is given them in complete images into discursive form. Each translates what speaks to him either in the visual language of nature or in the visionary revelations of the gods into the successive structure of human speech. What is remarkable about this view is that for Novalis both space, which necessarily orders by juxtaposition, and time, which necessarily orders by succession, express their basic truths—or speak—in terms that are nonsuccessive but extended. Notwithstanding the importance of music and a musical ear for the task of the poet, the most basic characteristic of language, for Novalis, turns out to be predominantly spatial. Primordial language, for both the poet and the philosopher, is a language of imagery!

Yet Novalis not only considers time and space to pass one into the other—time becoming space, and space becoming time—but also thinks that the parts of time—past, present, and future—pass one into the other in such a way that what has been in the past will return again in the future, and what has not as yet come to be and still is held in the secret being of all tomorrows has already been once before.[14] The consequence of such a view of time is that the value of the finds of archeology and mineralogy are essentially epistemological and ontological in nature, rather than historical or scientific. That this is, in fact, true for Novalis can be seen in the following fragment of the *Allgemeine Brouillon,* in which he looks at archeology from a double perspective: first he considers what the excavated artifacts and bodies mean to mankind; then he attempts to evaluate the very same finds in their relation to and meaning for nature.

> ARCHEOLOGY. Galvanism of antiquities, their *matter*—revivification of antiquity.
> Miraculous *religion* which hovers about it—Its history—the philosophy of sculpture—gems—human petrifications—painting—portraiture—landscapes—man always expresses the symbolic philosophy of his being in his works and in what he does and does not do—He proclaims himself and his gospel to nature. He is the Messiah of nature—Antiquities are at once the *products* of the *future and of former times.* [III,248,12–20#52]

Commonly, the development of our lives does not present us with instances in which the products of the past are also products of the future. We, therefore, either must understand Novalis to be speaking in dark and mystical tones in this fragment or must interpret the last lines to be entirely metaphorical, claiming nothing more than that what is now still buried in the earth cannot be, for us, a present product of the past. Therefore, objects made in former times that are still in the ground waiting to be brought to light again are, in their status as objects for us (and only in respect to us can they be objects at all) products of both the past and the future.

But I would like to suggest a third alternative: It is in relation to spatial symbolism that time loses its forward-pointing "arrow." The formal structure of space, which is juxtaposition, allows no other symbolization of the successive states of time than as juxtaposed extensions. But whether we move in space from left to right, downward and upward, or forward and backward is an arbitrary and voluntary matter. Space, therefore, as a symbolic medium representing the various parts of time all at once, leaves it up to us in what direction—or succession—we read them off. Conversely, any symbolization of space in a temporal medium must represent what is all at once as successive moments. The significance of this state of affairs for the nature of language is that—depending on what the poet or the philosopher attempts to decode—his translation is always also a transformation of what is temporal into spatial form or, conversely, of what is spatial into temporal form. Successive historical states represented in space must appear to be simultaneous and so can be read in any order we choose. The artifact or fossil as visual record of past events presents temporal developments in nontemporal symbols and therefore allows no direct temporal distinctions to be made, but, at best, only indirect temporal inferences. The consequence is that past and future, when represented by iconic signs, cannot maintain their unidirectional relation to each other.

But space and time for Novalis are conjoined not only as abstract principles and general phenomena. Their specific manifestations interact and pass over into one another. The relation of "passing over into" or "becoming the other" denotes a causal link; primarily spatial and primarily temporal phenomena therefore can, and do, causally affect each other. Tonal sequences, for instance, shape patterns in the sand atop a metal sheet vibrating with their sound, thus turning temporal manifestations into spatial phenomena and furnishing in this way an example of just how closely the ciphers in the book of nature can resemble the letters of the alphabet.[15] For the shapes and figures drawn in the sand by the vibrations of sound are visual signs representing acoustic phenomena just as the written letters standing for spoken words are visual representations of acoustic events. Novalis explores this theme in a rather lengthy fragment of the *Allgemeine Brouillon:*

> PHYSICS AND GRAMMAR. We think a muffled tone that is close by to be *far* away./ Lateral motion of the air in case of sound. Figured motion of sound resembling *letters.* (Could letters originally have been *acoustic figures.* Letters a priori?) Lateral and figured motion of light and heat. Color-*images* are light-figures. The light ray is the stroke of the violin's bow. What might here take the place of sand? We actually (force) the sound to *make a print* of itself—to *encipher* itself—to bring itself onto a *copper plate.* Further application of this idea. (The strewing of a plate with phosphoric powder—which would take on the colors of *different light,* or which, with a slight *warming* of differently shaped and variously touched bodies would burn in extraordinary figures—and would shine—preparation of such a powder.)

> Reflection, refraction, and *inflection of sound.*/ The *painful noise*—
> scratching a plate etc. A sharp tone./ About the speech of *starlings.*
> Natural, mimetic, pictorial language—artful, accidental, voluntary
> language.
>
> (The concept of causality, for instance, is an *arbitrary sign* [a tran-
> scendental sign] of a certain relation.) Transcendental logic./ Every
> word should be an acoustic formula of its construction, of its pronun-
> ciation—pronunciation itself is a higher *mimetic sign* of a higher pro-
> nunciation—the *construction of meaning* of the word. All this depends
> on the laws of *association.* The so-called arbitrary signs in the end
> might not be as arbitrary as they appear—but rather stand in a certain
> nexus of reality with what they signify." [III,305,#362]

For Novalis, as we have seen, nature in its primitive and basic manifestations does not speak with sounds and has no tonal language but expresses itself in ciphers and hieroglyphs, that is, in visual signs. Clearly,
though, there are natural sounds: wind rustles through the leaves of
trees, brooks and springs murmur and splash, landslides and falling
rocks thunder toward the valley, and thunder itself claps, exploding
across the sky. But all these sounds are made by the interaction of natural
objects whose non-sounding presence exists prior to the tones produced.
Therefore, insofar as nature in fact does have sounds, Novalis understands these to be the *actions* of nature—verbs. When nature's verbs and
nouns combine to form a natural expression, that is, when the acts or
forces of nature interfere with nature's objects—whether these forces be
tonal vibrations, magnetic fields, or scales of differing light rays—all in
turn impress or shape some object into a hieroglyphic sign or cipher of
their effective presence. And so even the active temporal processes come
to be represented by visual, that is, nonactive and spatial signs.

As a result, the most basic word of the language of inorganic nature,
for Novalis, appears to be the phenomenal object, which he considers to
be nature's noun rather than her verb. But this primacy of the "nouns" of
inorganic nature over the "verbs" is not to be understood as a temporal
priority. Thus one of the fragments of the *Allgemeine Brouillon* reads:

> The doctrine of relations is a part of algebra—or of the natural history
> of quantity.
>
> (The *verbs* are the actual forces of words—the so-called *nouns* came
> into being from *verbs*—and the verbs from nouns. Motion and rest—
> changeable—constant x. All rest is *figure.*) [III,400,#691]

As always in Novalis's philosophy, opposites imply and condition each
other. The signs of passivity and rest, nouns, are conditioned by verbs,

the signs of activity and motion, and vice versa. Yet this interdependent conditioning does not deny the possibility of one holding a more basic position as functioning symbol than the other. The final line, therefore, asserts the figural nature of rest. At rest—as object rather than force, as noun rather than verb—nature constitutes those figures that are the symbolic hieroglyphs with which she speaks to us.

For Novalis this primacy of nouns over verbs in the language of inorganic nature is due to the logical and ontological priority of space. Space and time are contemporaneous, but the schema of space is the formal possibility of being. Time, however, is the concept of this schema, or rather the act of its conceptual genesis. As such, time is not only the formal structure underlying all our discursive thought, it is also the form of the self as the unity of all our experiences.[16] Novalis is here in agreement with Kant's formulation of time as "nothing but the form of inner sense, that is, of the intuition of ourselves and of our inner state."[17] Yet whereas Novalis at first finds himself in agreement with Kant's analysis of the nature of space and time and their relation to each other, he eventually pushes the Kantian position beyond its boundaries. For he finds that it can accommodate neither the kind of turning over into one another he envisons for space and time nor the mutual representation he finds to hold between them. Novalis, therefore, rephrases and expands Kant's view to better suit his own purposes. He calls time the inner space and space the outer time and thereby stresses their mutuality without eliminating their difference.[18] With this move Novalis comes to resemble that pupil of Heraclitus who, to defend his master's philosophy, asserted that we cannot step into the same river even once, thus making of the philosopher of flux and change a Parmenidean monist. We clearly cannot expand Kant in this way and retain what is essential to his thought. But Novalis is only doing here what he usually does with the philosophy of his predecessors—using it simply as a take-off point for his own thinking without concern for what his elaborations do to the coherence of the system of the thinkers who impelled him toward his own project.

Our most ordinary and daily experience with language teaches us that physical, visually present objects can be and are symbolized by tonal representations, namely by spoken words. Likewise our experience with the written word teaches us that acoustic phenomena can be and are symbolized by visual representations, namely by written letters. Novalis's fragment 305 of the *Allgemeine Brouillon* points out that a similar situation holds for the language of nature: acoustic symbols can represent visual objects and visual signs can stand for tonal phenomena.

This state of affairs leads Novalis to proclaim that in all relations of representation a mutuality is at work (*Wechselrepräsentation*). Not only space and time in general turn into one another, but so do specific spatial and temporal manifestations. Images and sounds are interrelated.[19] And so Novalis not only sees sounds as creating patterns in the sand, which leads him to wonder whether letters originally might have been acoustic figures; he also thinks that light rays might possibly act like the bow of a fiddle. Yet whereas the tonally arranged sand is an actual physical phenomenon, speaking of light rays as the tone-provoking bow of a fiddle appears, at first glance, to be no more than a metaphor. But is that so? Without necessarily accepting the validity of Novalis's position we can nevertheless find examples that support his view. In antiquity, for instance, the statue of Memnon was said to sing with the rising sun, whose warmth caused the air inside the statue to expand and exit through cracks in the brass, producing a flutelike tone.[20] Novalis surely was aware of this ancient tradition, even though he does ask what, in the case of the bow of light rays, may take the place of sand. Clearly one of the answers is "air!"[21]

Once we accept the perspective of Novalis's thought, in which objects are understood as signs, the question is whether things have to become as complicated as all that. Is it not sufficient evidence that objects which we are primarily aware of because we see them, such as a violin and its bow, can and do produce sounds when they interact? And could Novalis not have maintained with equal justification that the sad song of any passing gypsy and his violin is an acoustic sign of the bow and strings that are the instruments of its production, as much as an expression of the gypsy's mood, or an example of the musical tradition of his people? In fact, does the doctrine of mutual representation (*Wechselrepräsentationslehre*) not imply—indeed, demand—that all sounds be the acoustic signs of what produces them, just as the instruments of sound production, whatever else they might be, must be the visual representations of their acoustic effects?[22] Ultimately, then, in the doctrine's most abstract formulation it is cause and effect that are said by Novalis to mutually represent each other.

And thus, what at first seems an unmotivated interruption of and intrusion into a fragment on the nature of sound and its visual representation—namely the remark that the concept of causality is an arbitrary and transcendental sign of a certain relation—is indeed an integral part of the theme under discussion. For Novalis holds that in the realm of representations or signs, causes can stand for and be symbols of their effects, just

as effects can be signs for their causes. And this is so because in the realm
of representation the ruling law is the law of the association of ideas.
Clearly, the idea of a cause, any cause, calls forth the idea of its effect, or is
associated with the idea of its effect, as the idea of any effect also will, by
the mere association of thought, call forth the idea of its cause. But since
Novalis's understanding of the relation of cause and effect is in the Kantian tradition, it naturally follows for him that the sign and that which it
signifies stand in a more than merely conventional and arbitrary relation
to each other. Nor are they conjoined by only habitual associations of
thought. On the contrary, and in contrast to Hume's use of this phrase,
the law of association that rules the relation of thoughts denotes a real or
essential connection.

The possibility of symbolizing in space events that occur in time takes
on an ever-greater importance for Novalis. Peculiarly, therefore, in the
enterprise of understanding human utterances, the speech of inanimate
nature becomes of far greater interest than the language of animate
nature, although man's speech shares with the latter the characteristic of
being a sounding expression rather than a silently visual one. It is not
surprising, then, that Novalis says little about the sounds of animals or
plant life, or that, when he does mention them, it is mostly in poetical
expressions in which trees are metaphorically said to speak to each other,
as for instance in *Heinrich von Ofterdingen*, in which we find the following
description of an early morning:

> The sun was just beginning to gild the crowns of the old trees, which
> moved with gentle whispers as if they meant to awaken each other
> from the dreams of night in order to greet the sun together.
>
> [I,219,24–27]

In this and similar passages the language of animate nature is a traditional
poetic convention and nothing more.

But the situation appears to be quite different in the lines of fragment
362 in which Novalis mentions the speech of starlings. After a slash
mark—which for Novalis always indicates the beginning of a new association of thought—he writes:

> The *painful noise*—scratching a plate, etc. A sharp tone. /About the
> speech of *starlings*. /Natural, mimetic, pictorial language—artful, acci-
> dental, voluntary language. [III,305,#362][23]

Starlings, although they are counted among the songbirds, have a singularly screeching voice, so here the obvious association of the speech of
starlings is to the sharp and unpleasant tones Novalis has been consider-

ing in the preceding lines. In addition, due to what one encyclopedia of birds calls their "gift for language," starlings used to be made into household pets in rural areas, thus the very next thought Novalis jots down deals with the status of various forms of linguistic expression. In other words, the fact that starlings, not unlike parrots, are thought to be able to learn how to "speak," raises for Novalis the question of the varying levels of speech. He begins his enumeration with "natural language," which is not to be confused with the language of nature. It denotes, rather, the kind of sound-making that is the natural expression of a given species or speaker, such as human speech is for man. In contrast to such naturally given speech there is the merely mimicking language of the starlings. And finally, in contrast to both these tonal forms of expression, there is the pictorial language of inorganic nature. With these first three terms, then, Novalis gives a hierarchical series of some of the levels on which language occurs. In the three terms that follow, he gives to each level an opposite that not only is in contrast to it, but also stands above it. Without working out the intermediate steps of a methodical Erhebung, Novalis is content here simply to note the higher polar opposites. Thus natural human speech, raised to its highest potential, becomes the language of art.[24] The meaningless chatter of starlings, with its mimicked phrases, becomes—when raised to its highest power—the language of chance, such as it was for the ancients, who heard the voice of fate in the apparently accidental cries of birds, as they did in the rustling of leaves or the murmuring of a brook. And finally, the pictorial language of inorganic objects, since it is an entirely involuntary communication, becomes, when raised to its highest level, a voluntary language, an expression chosen by will—*willkührlich*.

But because the pictorial language of inorganic nature is not as yet a voluntary expression, the meaning of its message is not immediately self-evident. Even though the relation between the natural object as sign and the message it communicates is anything but arbitrary, that message is still not easily understood. In other words, despite the fact that an essential relation holds between a sign and what it signifies, the specific character of that relation is not always readily apparent. Indeed, because it is often entirely elusive, a particular expertise is needed for discerning it, for translating it into more readily accessible forms. Insofar as the understanding of natural phenomena is concerned, this expertise belongs to the natural philosopher. He, more than anyone else, is capable of decoding and deciphering the phenomenal language of nature. For what nature has to tell us at once presents itself to us in her objects and also withdraws

into these objects, leaving them to appear as mere things of our surroundings whose symbolic character remains at least partially secret and mostly
inaccessible to us. Here again, therefore, Novalis points to the similarity
between the task of the natural philosopher deciphering the code of
nature and that of the poet translating the qualitative turns of time.

But whereas the poet with his privileged relation to time finds himself
uttering the truths of the heavens or heavenly powers, that is, finds
himself singing with a divinely inspired voice, the natural philosopher's
dialogue is with the Earth, whose spatial constitution expresses itself in
the silent language of her phenomenal objects: in images. Let us then
discuss the spirit that is necessary to decipher the hidden truths of the
hieroglyphs and signatures of the earth, and let us consider the role that
images and symbols of earth, as well as inner earth caverns, shafts, and
worlds play for Novalis.

THE MINER: PRIEST AND INTERPRETER OF THE EARTH

As we have seen, of the many of Novalis's fragments dealing with the
language of nature, by far the greater number are concerned with the
language of the inorganic world. In part this is due to Novalis's work as a
mining engineer, which involved him much more immediately with metals, rocks, and crystals than with plants and animals. But another factor is
that Napoleon's return from his campaign of 1798–99 with ancient Egyptian artifacts that inspired wonder and admiration everywhere and made
Egyptian art the dominant influence on the style and taste of the Empire,
also rekindled the curiosity about the meaning and function of Egyptian
hieroglyphs.[25] Found alongside other Egyptian oddities buried in the
desert sand or proclaiming the splendor of the past on ancient monu-
ments, they seemed particularly enigmatic. As the most literary and philosophical puzzle inherited from medieval alchemy, hieroglyphs had occupied the attention of writers and thinkers even during the Baroque
Enlightenment. But now their mysterious imagery and exotic origin spur-
red the mystical inclinations of the early Romantics. Indeed, the significance of archeological finds in general now captured the imagination and
interest of the public, and as Greek finds had done in the Renaissance, or
the excavations of Pompeii and Herculaneum earlier in the century, so
now Egyptian antiques showed, once more, that ancient knowledge and
ancient treasures lay hidden and buried in the earth.[26]

Yet even more important for Novalis is the fact that the world beneath
the light of day, the world of caves and mining shafts, this world of the

interior of the earth—whose outer layers are so familiar to us and on which we feel ourselves at home—is a strange and secret world. Its appeal for Novalis lay in the aesthetic and poetic quality of its imagery and in the psychological, religious, and philosophical possibilities of its symbolism. To Novalis this inner earth is as foreign to us as our own inner self is a mystery.

> Fantasy imagines the coming world in relation to us either as above or as below or as in metempsychosis. We dream of traveling through the universe: is not the universe in us? We do not know the depth of our spirit—Inward leads the mysterious way. In us or nowhere is eternity with its worlds, the past and the future. The outer world is the shadow-world, it casts its shadow into the realm of light. It now seems inwardly indeed so dark, lonely, shapeless, but how differently will it appear to us, when this darkening has passed and the shadow-body has been removed. We will rejoice more than ever, for our spirit was deprived. [II,417,30–419,4,#16]

It is our inner world that, for Novalis, is most essentially the self, and so the inner earth is also most essentially the earth for him. It, therefore, suits Novalis to use the earth as an allegory or metaphor of life, particularly of the inner life of man. The inward journey and all its mystery is expressed in images of mining and archeology.[27] And so, for instance, the old *Bergmann* or miner in *Heinrich von Ofterdingen* speaks for Novalis when he says:

> Truly the man who first taught mankind the noble art of mining and who buried in the womb of rocks this earnest symbol of human life must have been divine. Here the vein is easy to mine, but of poor quality, there the rock crushes it into a miserably thin layer, yet here it is that the noblest strokes of chance break in. [I,246,9–15]

In the English rendering of this passage I translate *verborgen*, which literally means concealed, as "buried." Both words derive from a common root: the German *Berg* and the English "barrow," as well as "bury," originally refer to grave mounds.[28] In the German text the word "verborgen" ties the Bergmann or miner closely to what is verborgen, that is, buried or concealed, since in the word's infinitive—*verbergen*—the same root syllable (*-berg-*) associates the miner with what is buried and thus implies that it is both the Bergmann's task and special ability to uncover what is verborgen or buried. In addition, as the derivation from the notion of a burial mound suggests, that which is buried is not only hidden, but also precious; it is not only concealed in the grave, but also kept

safe. Yet the sense in which things are kept safe in the earth, and therefore also in the grave, is ambiguous. On the one hand, they are thought to
be safely locked up in the earth as, for instance, the spirits of the dead
who otherwise might return as ghosts to haunt the living,[29] but on the
other hand, these spirits are also safeguarded from harm and sheltered in
the earth until they will rise again on judgment day. An essential tension
at the base of the idea of the sheltering earth, then, accompanies most of
the earth symbolism as it can be found in chthonic religions, alchemical
traditions, and folk superstitions. It is also present in Novalis's approach
to the symbolic significance of the earth. In the German *bergen* (to bring to
safety or shelter) the positive sense of the meaning of safekeeping in the
earth is still alive, and since verbergen seems to contain bergen, this
meaning is alluded to as well. What is said by Novalis in the cited passage
to be verborgen or buried "in the womb of rocks" is "the earnest symbol
of human life." The meaning of our life is therefore not only concealed in
the inner earth, but is also sheltered there in the care of the earth. At once
hidden and protected, it remains for all future generations a veiled but
inexhaustible source for our self-knowledge.[30]

The religious and philosophical associations Novalis attaches to the
profession of the Bergmann are given in a folksong-like *Lied* that the old
miner sings in *Heinrich von Ofterdingen:*

He is the lord of earth	Der ist der Herr der Erde
Who measures well her depth	Wer ihre Tiefen misst,
And all that burdens him	Und jeglicher Beschwerde
Within her womb forgets.	In ihrem Schooss vergisst.
And who can understand	Wer ihrer Felsenglieder
Her rock-limbs' secret build,	Geheimen Bau versteht,
And unvexed does descend	Und unverdrossen nieder
Into her workshop deep.	Zu ihrer Werkstatt geht.
With her he is allied	Er ist mit ihr verbündet,
And fully intimate	Und inniglich vertraut,
By her he is inflamed	Und wird von ihr entzündet,
As if she were his bride.	Als wär' sie seine Braut.
He watches her each day	Er sieht ihr alle Tage
With newly kindled love	Mit neuer Liebe zu
And shuns not toil or trouble,	Und scheut nicht Fleiss and
As rest she gives him not.	Plage,
	Sie lässt ihm keine Ruh.
The mighty histories	Die mächtigen Geschichten
Of times long since gone by,	Der längst verflossnen Zeit,

She happily is willing
To him now to supply.

Ist sie ihm zu berichten
Mit Freundlichkeit bereit.

The past world's holy airs
Waft round his countenance,
And in the night of mines
Shines forth eternal light.

Der Vorwelt heilge Lüfte
Umwehn sein Angesicht,
Und in der Nacht der Klüfte
Strahlt ihm ein ewges Licht.

He meets on all his paths
A well familiar land,
And she is glad to help
The workings of his hand.

Er trift auf allen Wegen
Ein wohlbekanntes Land,
Und gern kommt sie entgegen
Den Werken seiner Hand.

The waters follow him
Helpfully mounting high,
And all the rock-built castles
Their treasures open wide.

Ihm folgen die Gewässer
Hülfreich den Berg hinauf;
Und alle Felsenschlösser,
Thun ihre Schätz' ihm auf.

He guides the flow of gold
Into his King's abode
And tiaras he adorns
With precious gems and stones.

Er führt des Goldes Ströme
In seines Königs Haus,
Und schmückt die Diademe
Mit edlen Steinen aus.

Though he gives faithfully
The king his luck-blessed arm,
He asks of him for little
Remaining gladly poor.

Zwar reicht er treu dem König
Den glückbegabten Arm,
Doch frägt er nach ihm wenig
Und bleibt mit Freuden arm.

They may go on and murder
Down there for coin and goods;
He stays atop the mountains
The joyful lord of earth.

Sie mögen sich erwürgen
Am Fuss um Gut and Geld;
Er bleibt auf den Gebirgen
Der frohe Herr der Welt.
[I,247–48][31]

The multivalence of associations in this song is particularly dense. Most striking are the mystical overtones in Novalis's depiction of the Bergmann's relation to the earth. For the metaphor of the groom and bride is not primarily a symbol of erotic involvement. Rather, the erotic imagery points to a basically religious meaning of the ideas of love and union.[32] And so the Bergmann, even though the fruit of his labor is given to the king, must be understood as a priest in the service of Earth.[33] What is significant in this distinction is a difference in attitude. As priest of the earth the miner not only toils on behalf of the earth—rather than for the king's profit—but does so without greed and self-interest. He enters the mine with a pure and childlike heart eager to serve and to learn from the earth, but with no intention or desire to exploit her. Goethe's alchemist, Faust, expresses a similar attitude when he says:

> That I may see with vision clear,
> What makes the inner earth cohere.
> To grasp creative force and seed,
> And have of words no further need.[34]

Alchemists and miners share this reverence for the earth since both stand in the old tradition of the metal-working guilds whose superstitions and codes of behavior are based in ancient religious practices and doctrines that regulated the work of all miners, smelters, and smiths.[35] Working in the mine shafts and caverns of the earth, that is in her womb, the miner, as the priest of the earth, forgets all the burdens of his life and finds the treasures of an ecstatic, mystically erotic happiness as well as its opposite—an all-embracing calm of mind, peace of heart, and rest for his soul.[36] Here then a second symbolic tension is associated with the idea of earth: for both the high emotional excitement of an ecstatic happiness and the emotional calm of a trancelike rest are ascribed to it. Novalis thus finds within the idea of earth both of those qualities that Nietzsche in *The Birth of Tragedy* came to distinguish and to symbolize respectively as Dionysian intoxication and beautiful Apollonian dream or illusion. Yet even in Nietzsche's definition, the Dionysian harbors within itself elements of peaceful harmony as well as ecstatic frenzy or intoxicated abandon.[37]

In addition, the Bergmann serves Novalis as a symbol of man. For just as the miner finds both ecstatic pleasure and calm peace in the earth, so man in his grave, according to Novalis, finds not only the well-deserved rest from his life's troubles, but also the fulfillment and completion of all the promises of his fate. The grave, therefore, despite its association with death, or rather because of it, is not a negative symbol. It is as much doorway to a new beginning as it is end and final resting place. As a result, because the passageways of the mine and the night of its caverns resemble the grave, they are also the source of eternal light, which here is a metaphor for salvation as well as knowledge.[38] For Novalis conceives of the earth as literally houseing within her depths the mighty stories and histories of times long past as they are contained in and told by fossils or archeological finds; the earth thus shelters knowledge and wisdom while she also serves as an image of salvation. Working within the earth, the miner becomes the recipient of all her various treasures: of the gold and jewels he mines and passes on to others; of the knowledge and understanding he brings to light when he discovers fossils or the artifacts of bygone days; and most important, of the wisdom and blessing earth bestows on him as a promise and foretaste of eternal salvaltion.[39]

As priest of the earth the Bergmann discovers and uncovers her treasures. He acts as the interpreter of her oracular patterns by understanding them as her symbolic expressions. Consequently, the work of the miner serves Novalis as an analog for the philosopher of nature. In fact, only when the natural philosopher proceeds like the miner is he, in Novalis's eyes, a true teacher of nature and not merely a limited analytical chemist or manipulator of her various parts. Only when the natural philosopher stands before nature with a spirit that resembles the miner's as he enters the earth, will he be able, like the miner, to probe the depth of nature in order to bring to light or uncover—that is, decode—what lies hidden in the womb of space. But since what the miner discovers in the inner world of the earth is history, the philosopher in the depth of space will find time.

THE LANGUAGE OF EARTH AND *THE NOVICES OF SAIS*

Heinrich von Ofterdingen, in which the figure of the *Bergmann* appears, is Novalis's last literary product. He was still working on it when he died. The significance of its earth imagery, however, developed out of the notion of nature as it was presented in Novalis's first fictional work *Die Lehrlinge zu Sais*. Novalis first mentions this fragmentary story in his letter of Febrary 24, 1798 to August Wilhelm Schlegel, written to accompany Novalis's manuscript of the fragment collection *Blüthenstaub*. Novalis writes: "I further have . . . a beginning, with the title *der Lehrling zu Sais*—likewise of fragments—only all in respect to nature." [IV,251,26–29#116] But by the end of the year Novalis speaks of a *novel* in Sedez, which usually is thought to refer to *Die Lehrlinge zu Sais*. As late as January 31, 1800, Novalis has still not finished *Der Lehrling* (singular), but hopes to get to it as soon as he completes *Heinrich von Afterdingen*. [sic] [IV,318,3–8#149] And on February 23, 1800, he writes to Tieck that he is glad as yet not to have finished *Die Lehrlinge* (plural!), since now that he has read Jacob Boehme he means to make of it "a genuinely symbolic novel of nature." [IV,323,2–5#152] What Novalis wanted to change we do not know, but even in the form that has come down to us, *Die Lehrlinge zu Sais* is a highly symbolic account consisting of three distinct parts, all of which were probably written during 1798. The first part, called *Der Lehrling*, was written early in the year, the wonder tale of "Rosenblüthe und Hyacinth" probably during the summer, and the second part, *Die Natur* (Nature), could not have been written much before the end of the year.[40] The philosophical importance of this fragmentary story lies in its idea of nature and in the connection this idea has to language. Since earth, as we have seen, is an analog of and symbol for man, and since the language of earth is the primordial language of nature, and since man responds to nature and to the spirit of God he finds manifest in it by raising his voice in prayer—that is, by speaking—a pattern emerges for Novalis that ties nature as earth, man, and language into one interconnected universe of ideas and symbols. Novalis begins *Die Lehrlinge zu Sais* by describing the most important features of the language of nature and of the character of the philosopher who learns to understand it and who, having discerned its meaning, sees hidden in its myriad forms the ultimate unity of Being. It is this unity on which the meaningful connection between all symbols or signs and that for which they stand is based. Novalis begins the novel by saying:

> Many are the paths we travel. Whoever observes and compares them will see marvelous figures emerge; figures that appear to belong to the great cipher-script we see everywhere: on wings and eggshells, in clouds, in the snow, in crystals and in the formation of rocks, in freezing waters, on the inside and outside of mountains, of plants, of animals and of human beings, in the lights of the heavens, on panes of pitch and glass when stroked or struck,[41] in the filings around a magnet and in the strange conjunctions of chance. In these we find a presentiment of the key, of the grammar of this miracle-script. But alas the presentiment will not shape itself into a fixed form, it appears not to want to become a higher key. An alcahest[42] seems to have been spilled over the senses of mankind. Their desires and thoughts seem to congeal only momentarily. Thus their presentiments arise; yet after a short while everything is as before, swimming again before their eyes.
>
> From afar I heard it said: incomprehensibility is merely a consequence of not understanding; the latter seeks what it already has and, therefore, never can find anything futher. We do not understand language because language does not understand itself, does not want to understand itself. The true sanskrit speaks for the sake of speaking, because to speak is her pleasure and her nature.
>
> Not long afterwards someone said: Holy Scripture needs no explanation. He who speaks truly is full of the eternal life and his writing appears to us marvelously akin to the true mysteries, for it is a chord from the symphony of the universe.
>
> Surely the voice spoke of our teacher. For he knows how to gather the features that are everywhere scattered. A strange light kindles in his eyes when the high runic letter lies before us and he looks into our eyes to see whether the star that allows figures to become visible and

understandable has risen in us as well. If he sees us sad because the night will not give way, he consoles us and promises to the industrious, faithful observer future good fortune. He told us often how as a child the impulse to exercise his senses, to keep them occupied, and to fulfill them gave him no peace. He watched the stars and imitated their orbits and positions in the sand. He looked into the sea of air without rest and did not tire of observing its clarity, its motions, its clouds, and its lights. He collected for himself stones, flowers, beetles of all kinds and laid them into rows in many ways. He paid attention to human beings and animals, he sat by the seashore, he sought shells. He listened carefully to his thoughts and to his heart. He did not know where his longing was taking him. As he grew up he traveled far and looked at other countries, other seas, new airs, foreign stars, unknown plants, animals, people. He entered caves, saw how in shelves and colorful layers the structure of the earth was carried out, and pressed clay into strange images of rock. Now everywhere he found what was familiar, only wonderfully mixed and paired. Similarly, even in himself strange things ordered themselves. He began to be aware of the link between everything, of encounters, of concurrences. Soon he saw nothing anymore in isolation.—The perceptions of his senses were pressed into large colorful images: he listened, saw, touched, and thought all at once. He took pleasure in bringing strangers together. Sometimes the stars were people for him, sometimes people stars, the stones animals, the clouds plants. He played with the forces and phenomena and knew where and how to find this and that and to let it appear. And so he himself struck the strings for tones and passages. [I,79,1–80,23]

With the very first sentence Novalis sets the mood of the story he means to write and which he calls a novel. Yet we may not wish to call it that. Generally in a novel, events and developments described pertain to the growth and change of human characters and lives, which we are meant to take as real—whether they are fictional or not. But here, with the first few words, Novalis gives us a hint that no ordinary account of human destiny is to follow. For although Novalis usually reserves the term "figure" for the expressions of inorganic nature, *Die Lehrlinge zu Sais* begins with the statement that human lives—human stories or histories—describe "marvelous figures." For the temporal succession of events that constitute our lives to be called "figures," conditions must prevail that set this "novel" beyond the scope of what we ordinarily think of us acceptable fare for the genre. When time is spatialized and space temporalized so completely that either can be fully expressed by the other, the redemption of corruption, the resurrection of the earth is either being prepared or has already taken place, and we are in the newly born Golden Age. While excerpting from Murhard's *Grössenlehre*,[43] Novalis, as an aside to himself, notes in parentheses:

> (Words and figures determine each other in constant alternation—the audible and visible words are really word-figures. The word-figures are the ideal figures of the other figures—all figures, etc., shall become word or language-figures—they shall all become inner images—just like the *figure-words*—the inner images, etc., are the ideal words of the other thoughts or words.
>
> Therefore, the predicate genius belongs especially to fantasy, which forms the *figure-words*.
>
> This shall be the Golden Age when all words—shall be *figure-words*—myths—and all figures—shall be language-figures—hieroglyphs—and when we learn to speak and write figures—and to plasticize words completely and to make them music.
>
> Both arts belong together, are inseparably connected, and will be completed simultaneously.) [III,123,25–124,3]

The perspective of *Die Lehrlinge zu Sais* has this Golden Age in view: the successive constitution of audible, spoken words is to be understood as juxtaposed imagery, since ultimately that is what it is to become. Similarly, our primarily spatial understanding of nature is to be transformed, and we are to understand her as having "a history just like man or, which is the same, as having spirit." [I,99,18–20][44] Man's life, conversely, which usually is considered to be a history, is grasped as a shape drawn into space. In other words, here the essentially temporal character of human life is seen in its spatial form as figure. But the many ways man walks are not like lines drawn into space, arbitrarily beginning in one place and arbitrarily ending somewhere else. In speaking of them as figures, Novalis has something more like the figures in ice-skating in mind, where the skated figures describe deliberately designed and executed patterns drawn on the ice, in other words, shapes that have a recognizable order and organization.[45] Furthermore, as with the patterns in figure-skating, Novalis sees the figures of human lives as having a kind of closure, and not just the closure of death. The patterns we live lead to completion, and what is not completed here will be completed elsewhere and at another time. As Novalis observes in his diary entry of June 14, 1797, a few months after Sophie's death, when he was chronicling his resolve to follow her:

The engagement was not for this world. I shall not be perfected here—All talents shall only be touched on and shall be quickened.

[IV,46,5–7][46]

Die Lehrlinge zu Sais is thus a mystical natural history in poetical form. The adept of Sais or the teacher of nature may approach his subject in various ways, and as the tale develops the reader is led to an ever more spiritual view of nature.

From the beginning, though, the close interconnection of nature and space is evident. For in describing the natural philosopher's relation to nature and nature's language, Novalis uses verbs and nouns pertaining to the sense of sight twice as often as he uses words pertaining to the sense of hearing. As far as the natural philosopher is concerned, the universal symphony is, therefore, primarily to be seen rather than heard. The teacher, the man of natural science, has learned the language of nature because he was eager to observe, to watch, to see and look tirelessly. Even his relation to his students is governed by the superior use of his eyes: he understands the progress a student has made—or failed to make—by looking into his eyes, by seeing whether a new light of understanding has risen in them. But this is so mainly because the language of nature is a written rather than spoken language, a high runic letter. The eyes are of such importance only because nature communicates her many meanings in figures, in ciphers, and in the miracle-*script* of creation.

Having given in the first paragraph of *Die Lehrlinge zu Sais* a description of the figural character of nature's language and of man's inability to understand it, Novalis moves on, in the second paragraph, to consider why it may be that man cannot grasp the natural script of figures. He comes to the conclusion that man lacks the ability to translate or transform them properly. Imprisoned in the narrowness of his practical concerns, man seeks in the cipher-script only what he already has: he is interested in the objects of nature only for the sake of their practical and objective usefulness. Instead of looking at them as signs signifying something other than themselves, namely the spirit of nature that expresses itself in them, man perceives them only as things. But in some respects man is himself such a natural object and therefore a cipher of nature: "man—metaphor." [II,561,#174] But we do not understand this, indeed, do not want to understand it. As natural objects which are the language of the spirit of nature, we—who refuse to see this—are ourselves language not wanting to understand itself. The task to comprehend the language of nature, therefore, becomes the project to understand oneself. To help man in this pursuit of himself, Novalis now offers the hint that "the true Sanskrit speaks for the sake of speaking because to speak is her pleasure and her being." Sanskrit, for Novalis, means the perfect, the truly ordered language.[47] Yet the perfect language is the original language or creative word of God. But for Novalis the divine word *is* divine creation; in God thought, speech, and act are one:

> GRAMMAR AND LOGIC. Thinking is speaking. Speaking and doing or making are One merely modified operation. God spoke let there be light, and it was. [III,297,319]

In the pefect language, then, the sign and what it stands for are identical; in the "true Sanskrit," expression and being are one. Novalis can therefore say that *to speak* is the pleasure of the true Sanskrit as well as her *being*. But this pronouncement could have been reversed and Novalis might have said with equal justification that *to be* is the pleasure of the true Sanskrit and is her *language*. The words of the true Sanskrit are the objects of nature; their being *is* their language and their language, therefore, is their pleasure. They are for no other purpose than to be. And insofar as what they are is also what they mean, they can be said to speak for the sake of speaking.[48]

In such a view of language several distinctions that we usually make have been cancelled, or rather *aufgehoben* in the Hegelian sense, and language here has been raised to occupy the place of God. When divine thought, word, and act are considered to be *one*, and God is thought to express His being in them, in fact to *be* His operations, the distinction between either speaker and speech or between word and object is no longer decisive. As long as language is merely a means of communication, a tool to serve a speaker's purposes, there is no danger that the word can be taken to be, in some essential sense, either the speaker or that which it signifies. The danger here is rather that the word's serviceability will be seen as far less than perfect. The latter is a problem with which modern man, particularly the modern poet, seems to be afflicted and which, as a consequence, he variously expresses in literary form. Faulkner, for instance, has Addie Bundren say:

> That was when I learned that words are no good; that words dont ever fit even what they are trying to say at. When he was born I knew that motherhood was invented by someone who had to have a word for it because the ones that had the children didn't care whether there was a word for it or not. I knew that fear was invented by someone that had never had the fear; pride, who never had the pride. I knew that it had

been, not that they had dirty noses, but that we had to use one another by words like spiders dangling by their mouths from a beam, swinging and twisting and never touching, and that only through the blows of the switch could my blood and their blood flow like one stream. . . . And so when Cora Tull would tell me I was not a true mother, I would think how words go straight up in a thin line, quick and harmless, and how terribly doing goes along the earth, clinging to it, so that after a while the two lines are too far apart for the same person to straddle from one to the other; and that sin and love and fear are just sounds that people who never sinned nor loved nor feared have for what they never had and cannot have until they forget the words. Like Cora who could never even cook.[49]

For Addie Bundren the world of objects and deeds, on the one hand, and the world of the words that name them, on the other hand, are drifting apart until ultimately they not only do not coincide but have no relation to each other at all. Tending in opposite directions, it is the world of words that grows unreal and pales and ceases to mean anything, while the dark and silent reality of doing and things grows rich in significance:

I would lie by him in the dark, hearing the dark land talking of God's love and His beauty and His sin; hearing the dark voicelessness in which the words are the deeds, and the other words that are not deeds, that are just the gaps in peoples' lacks, coming down like the cries of the geese out of the wild darkness in the old terrible nights, fumbling at the deeds like orphans to whom are pointed out in a crowd two faces and told, That is your father, your mother.[50]

Addie feels that physical reality overwhelms all attempts to name it truly. The experiences life and nature present cannot be adequately expressed by speech. Human language fails the person who is seized by the wondrous reality of the natural world, as Hofmannsthal's Lord Chandos says:

Rhetoric, which is good for women and the House of Commons, whose power, however, so overrated by our time, is not sufficient to penetrate into the core of things.[51]

For Lord Chandos this recognition leads to an inability to use language at all. But Lord Chandos did not always feel this way. The loss of language for him is a new development and is the result of the greater loss: that of understanding and seeing the unity that makes of the many objects, deeds, and events a universe.

In those days [before his loss of language] I, in a state of continuous intoxication, conceived the whole existence as one great unit: the spiritual and physical worlds seemed to form no contrast, as little as did courtly and bestial conduct, art and barbarism, solitude and society: in everything I felt the presence of Nature, in the aberrations of insanity as much as in the utmost refinement of the Spanish ceremonial; in the boorishness of young peasants no less than in the most delicate of allegories; and in all expressions of Nature I felt myself.[52]

The disintegration of this unity into parts brings with it an experience of language and discursive thought as merely empty sound and word. But Novalis's point of view is still one of unity. He is not beset by doubt about either the unifying spirit of God that manifests itself in nature or the perfect adequacy of language to express that spirit. What Novalis regrets, and even mourns, is the loss in this age of a general awareness of the unity of all things. But while he sees this loss affecting others, he himself does not suffer from it and, therefore, seems to feel himself standing at a distance from his own time. Clearly, though, an awareness of the disintegration of a unified world understanding in others must carry with it an assault upon one's own world view. That Novalis speaks out on behalf of unity is, therefore, as much due to a desire to defend his point of view as it is an attempt at healing the wounds of the age. The proclamation of the nature of the true Sanskrit, then, serves to remind mankind of the oneness that underlies all reality and makes of the manifold a universe. The loss of clear-cut distinctions such unity requires is seen not only as the price to be paid for its continued effectiveness, but as a superior form of being, since it overcomes the strife of opposites by harmony and love. Language is raised onto the throne of God as a result of the unity of all being. As God's word, it is at once divine and sits in the place of God. The speaker and his word, being one, become interchangeable, and the word as creative word becomes what it names, *is* what it signifies. For as it is written in the Gospel according to St. John: "In the beginning was the word and the word was with God, and the word was God." Yet when language thus *is* God, and in time comes to *replace* Him, then the priest is not only also poet, but the poet becomes the true priest. And insofar as the divine word is thought to have created, as well as to *be* the natural world, the miner (and by analogy therefore also the natural philosopher) must, in order to be the priest of the earth, also be a poet of sorts.

Furthermore, since in the Christian tradition the word in Christ became flesh, Novalis can speculate that

If God could become man, he can also become stone, plant, animal, or element and maybe there is in this manner a continual redemption in nature. [III,664,#603]

For all these reasons, then, the spirit of nature, according to Novalis, speaks in nature's objects and through them to us, thereby expressing itself. If we were to take Novalis's hint and understand the natural phenomena as signs, we would seek in the objects of nature for her spirit and thus would indeed go further than merely seeing them as potentially useful raw materials. But since our attempts to understand nature are directed mainly at analyzing and categorizing her objects for the purpose of making use of them, Novalis can say that we seek only what we already have: namely, the objectness of the object.

Novalis elaborates this point further when, in the second part of *Die Lehrlinge zu Sais*, entitled *Die Natur*, he suggests that until now only the poets have understood and sung about nature's unified and unifying soul and spirit, while the scientists, bent on controlling nature, have in their research by and large either ignored or even killed that spirit:

> What these [the poets] gathered whole and erected in great, organized masses, those [the scientists] made use of for the human heart's daily nourishment and necessity by splintering and shaping unfathomable nature into manifold small, pleasing natures. When these [the poets] pursued with a light touch what is flowing and ephemeral, those [the scientists] sought to explore with the sharp cut of a knife the inner structure and relation of her members. . . . In their hands friendly nature died, and only dead and twitching remains were left. . . . Whoever wants to come to know her spirit well must seek for her in the company of poets, there she is open and pours out her marvelous heart. But whoever does not love her from the bottom of his heart and only admires and attempts to know this and that about her must conscientiously visit her sickbed, her charnel house.
> [I,84,17–36]

This passage as well as the one quoted below bring Mephisto's lines in Goethe's *Faust* to mind:

> To docket living things past any doubt
> You cancel first the living spirit out:
> The parts lie in the hollow of your hand,
> You only lack the living link you banned.
> This sweet self-irony, in learned thesis,
> The chemists call naturae encheiresis.[53]

When the natural philosopher attempts to understand nature in the manner the modern scientist frequently does, not by contemplating her living spirit, but by dissecting her various members—and that means her living creatures![54]—Novalis would not compare him to the miner, or think of him as a *true* philosopher of nature. Such a scientist lacks the proper attitude of reverence and love, which alone can lead us to approach nature with the receptive attitude that allows us to see and understand the messages of her spirit in her objects:

> How odd it is that just the most sacred and enchanting phenomena of nature are in the hands of such dead people as analytic chemists usually are! They awaken the creative sense of nature with force when it should be only the secret of lovers and the mystery of a higher mankind. Instead, it is called forth shamelessly and senselessly by crude minds that never will know what miracles their flasks enclose.
> [I,105,5–11]

In contrast, the true adept of nature is more like the poet, whose deep longing for nature makes him sensitive to her spirit. The miner or the true natural philosopher deals with nature by attempting to be her sensitive tool in the effecting of her own secret and mysterious activities. Resembling the poet or enraptured lover in their ardent commitment to nature (rather than the merely curious and selfish analytic scientist) the true adepts are "poeticized" scientists attempting to understand or to interpret the meaning of the whole without first needing to analyze the structure of the parts. The true philosopher of nature approaches his subject synthetically rather than analytically. For only in this fashion can the meaning of the whole, which is its spirit, be grasped. Understanding the whole before he knows the parts, the true philosopher of nature understands the parts properly: he knows their relation to the whole as well as to each other and, therefore, can fully appreciate the role they play and the significance they have. Clearly, Novalis is influenced here by Spinoza's conception of intuitive knowledge, which "proceeds from an adequate idea of certain attributes of God to an adequate knowledge of the essence of things."[55] But in contrast to Spinoza, who does not think the imagination capable of perceiving wholes or grasping the unity of all natural phenomena because it tends to lose itself in details, Novalis ties such holistic intuition of the meaning of nature primarily to the imagination.

The true adept of nature, such as the teacher in *Die Lehrlinge zu Sais,* must come to see the unity of nature and to understand the language of the true Sanskrit as a readable script. As holy Scripture the world needs no interpretation, it simply *is* the word of God. And whoever understands it as such and replies with simple truthfulness, that is, with his whole being, is in possession of eternal life, is already on the way to the Golden Age or indeed a member of it. Such an individual can then "play with the forces and phenomena" and will know how to let this and that appear; how to strike for himself "the strings for tones and passages." His language will be "akin to the true mysteries" of nature and therefore will itself be "a chord from the symphony of the universe." He will know how to make the spatial language of nature sing; and having understood the harmony of nature that is her unity, he will compose his own chords on her instrument. But still these chords will be visual patterns, or even mathematical relations, rather than tonal compositions. For even such a man, such a teacher or philosopher of nature, has not achieved the highest level of understanding. This belongs to that man alone who not only can decipher her hieroglyphs and grasp the unity of their meaning, but can also see their historical character:

> The authentic knower of ciphers will perhaps be capable of prompting several of nature's forces at once to set splendid and useful phenomena into motion, he will fantasize on nature as on a great instrument. And yet he will not understand nature. This is the gift of the natural historian, of the visionary of times, who, well versed in the history of nature, and familiar with the world, this higher theater of natural history, grasps her significance and prophesying reveals it.
>
> [I,99,4–12]

Such a man has accomplished the raising of his soul to a high level of visionary insight. For, as Novalis believes—in true mystical tradition— the raising of our souls is accomplished by the various strivings of individuals. Not all of us succeed at the same rate. Some of us may already have reached spiritual levels still denied to others. And thus the many roads on which man travels not only inscribe many different figures, but also find their completion at many different moments in time. The historian of nature combines the poet's privileged relation to time with the natural philosopher's understanding of space. As *Zeitenseher* he finds— inscribed in nature's figures, in her rocks and metals, her crystals and fossils—the meaning of times. As the miner in the womb of earth finds history, so he in the heart of space finds time. But since all of time is enciphered in space by the juxtapositions of patterns and figures, the historian of nature, being able to decode these ciphers, can see all of time at once and so becomes nature's prophet, able to predict her future as well as unearth her past.

CHAPTER SEVEN

Isis, the Great Mother-Goddess of Nature and the Mystical Earth

THE TRADITION OF THE ISIS MYTH AND SCHILLER

The truth hidden in and by the earth found a powerful symbolic representation in the image of nature personified as the goddess Isis wearing a veil.[1] Making a note for *Die Lehrlinge zu Sais*, Novalis plans to make use of this image:

> / Mysticism of nature. Isis—virgin—veil—mysterious treatment of the natural sciences./ [III,423,27–29#788]

Novalis's view of nature and her language has to be understood, therefore, against the background of the tradition of the myth of Isis, the mother-goddess of Earth. Novalis was particularly well-acquainted with the tradition of this myth, since not only the classics, but also Rosicrucian and Medieval alchemical texts, which he studied while in Freiberg, abound in references to Isis and contain a conception of nature founded in and derived from the ancient fertility religions.[2] An illustration from Athanasius Kircher's alchemical text *Oedipus aegyptus* depicting the goddess without a veil enumerates, in the column at her left, the many other mythic names by which nature as the great sheltering and concealing mother is known.[3] Kircher's authority for these names was Apuleius's *Golden Ass*, in which the protagonist, Lucius, invokes the Goddess of Heaven as follows:

> Blessed Queen of Heaven, whether you are pleased to be known as Ceres, the original harvest mother; . . . or whether as celestial Venus now adored at sea-girt Paphos; . . . or whether as Artemis; . . . or

whether as dread Proserpine to whom the owl cries at night, whose triple face is potent against the malice of ghosts, keeping them imprisoned below earth; . . . you . . . whose misty radiance nurses the happy seed under the soil . . . I beseech you, by what ever name, in what ever aspect . . . have mercy on me.

Having hardly closed his eyes after this prayer, Lucius sees an apparition of a woman rise from the center of the sea:

First her head, then her whole shiny body gradually emerged and stood before me poised on the surface of the waves. . . .

Just above her brow shone a round disc, like a mirror, or like the bright face of the moon, which told me who she was. . . . Her many-coloured robe was of finest linen; part was glistening white, part crocus-yellow, part glowing red and along the entire hem a woven bordure of flowers and fruit clung swaying in the breeze. But what caught and held my eye more than anything else was the deep black lustre of her mantle. She wore it slung across her body from the right hip to the left shoulder, where it was caught in a knot resembling the boss of a shield; but part of it hung in innumerable folds, the tasselled fringe quivering. It was embroidered with glittering stars on the hem and everywhere else, and in the middle beamed a full and fiery moon.

This magnificent Queen of the Night addresses Lucius, telling him who she is:

I am Nature, the universal Mother, mistress of all the elements, primordial child of time, sovereign of all things spiritual, queen of the dead, queen also of the immortals, the single manifestation of all gods and goddesses that are. My nod governs the shining heights of Heaven, the wholesome sea-breezes, the lamentable silences of the world below. Though I am worshipped in many aspects, known by countless names, and propitiated with all manner of different rites, yet the whole round earth venerates me. The primeval Phrygians call me Pessinuntica, Mother of the gods; the Athenians, sprung from their own soil, call me Cecropian Artemis; for the islanders of Cyprus I am Paphian Aphrodite; for the archers of Crete I am Dictynna; for the trilingual Sicilians, Stygian Proserpine; and for the Eleusinians their ancient Mother of the Corn.

Some know me as Juno, some as Bellona of the Battles; others as Hecate, others again as Rhamnubia, but both races of Aethiopians, whose land the morning sun first shines upon, and the Egyptians who excel in ancient learning and worship me with ceremonies proper to my godhead, call me by my true name, namely, Queen Isis.[4]

The prominence given here to the description of Isis's robe and man-tle—although other aspects of her beauty are also discussed—leads one easily to think of her not only as clothed, but also as both revealed and hidden by her garments, since they on the one hand cover her naked truth, but on the other hand give a sign of it in the imagery that adorns them.

For the alchemists, that which was expressed in the symbol of the veil could also be expressed by nature's Protean character, since in part it is nature's shape-changing that—due both to time and the forces of mat-ter—conceals and reveals the mysterious truths she has to offer. Thus, for instance, Francis Bacon, standing at the threshold of modern science, says:

> And whereas it is added in the fable that Proteus was a prophet and knew the three times; this agrees well with the nature of matter; for if a man knew the conditions, affections, and processes of matter, he would certainly comprehend the sum and general issue (for I do not say that his knowledge would extend to the parts and singularities) of all things past, present, and to come. Most excellently therefore did the ancients represent Proteus, him of the many shapes, to be likewise a prophet triply great; as knowing the future, the past, and the secrets of the present. For he who knows the universal passions of matter and thereby knows what is possible to be cannot help knowing likewise what has been, what is, and what will be, according to the sum of things. Therefore the best hope and security for the study of celestial bodies I place in physical reasons.
>
> The sense of this fable relates, it would seem, to the secrets of nature and the conditions of matter. For under the person of Proteus, matter—the most ancient of all things next to God—is meant to be represented.[5]

Since the earthly element is thus both Protean and of the body or veil of the Goddess, the earth-mother, Isis, must be understood to be a shape-changing demon or spirit. In this respect then, she resembles that other great shape-changer and trickster, the spirit of language. But since earth, as we have seen, is also for Novalis a symbol of man, an analogical trinity of sorts emerges in which man, language, and earth, particularly the inner earth, are conjoined in one interwoven universe of symbolic signification.[6]

But although the tradition of Isis is much discussed in the classics and in the Medieval alchemical texts Novalis read, his immediate acquain-tance with this imagery probably came from a source nearer in time if not in spirit: Schiller, who discusses Isis and her cult in several of his works.[7] For Schiller, Isis is the symbolic representation of the universal spirit of nature and its truth. The most widely known of his several writings on this subject is the poem "The Veiled Image at Sais."[8] His earliest treatment of it is the essay "The Mission of Moses."[9] In this work, Schiller sees intertwined in the mythic symbolism of the Isis mysteries issues pertaining to hieroglyphic representation, to revelation and concealment of truth, and to the importance of imagery for the initiation into wisdom. The following excerpt from the essay sheds light on Novalis's treatment of this subject: it shows us how much he stands, on the one hand, within the tradition of his own time and how, on the other hand, he entirely opposes it.[10] Schiller writes:

> The Historian Philo says that Moses was initiated by the Egyptian priests into the philosophy of symbols and hieroglyphs, as well as into the mysteries of the holy animals. There are many to corroborate this evidence, and if one takes a look at what were called the Egyptian mysteries and at what Moses later did and prescribed, a remarkable resemblance will emerge. . . .
>
> The idea of a general connection between things unavoidably had to lead to the conception of one single highest mind. Where was this idea to germinate first if not in the head of a priest? And since Egypt was the first civilized nation known to history, and since the oldest mysteries originated in Egypt, it was most likely also here that the first idea of the unity of the highest Being was first conceived of by a human mind. . . .
>
> But it was thought best to make this new dangerous truth the sole possession of a small secret society and to select from the crowd those who showed the necessary capacity of understanding and to accept them into the society, but to wrap the truth itself, so that it might remain hidden from undeserving eyes, in a mysterious cloak that could be withdrawn only by someone who had been prepared to do so by the members themselves.
>
> For this purpose the hieroglyphs were chosen. They were a telling, pictographic script which concealed general concepts in a combination of sensuous signs. It was based on a few arbitrary rules that had been agreed upon. Since from the practices of idol-worship these enlightened men still knew how deeply one could affect the heart of the young by means of the imagination and the senses, they did not hesitate to use this trick of deception also in the service of truth. Thus they taught the new conception with a certain sensuous solemnity. By means of various ceremonies appropriate for this purpose, they put the soul of their apprentice first into a passionate state meant to render

him receptive to the new truth. Of this kind were the purifications the initiate had to undergo: the washing and sprinkling, the wrapping in linen garments, the foregoing of all sensual pleasures, the tensing and uplifting of the soul by song, a significant silence, the alternation of darkness and light, and more.

The ceremonies in combination with the mysterious images and hieroglyphs and the hidden truths which they concealed and for which these customs were a preparation were conceived together in the name *mysteries*. They had their seat in the temple of Isis and Serapis and served as model for the mysteries at Eleusis and Samothrace and, in more recent times, for the Brotherhod of Freemasons.

It appears to be without doubt that the content of the very oldest mysteries in Heliopolis and Memphis, before they were corrupted, was the unity of God and the refutation of paganism and that the immortality of the soul was pronounced in them. Those to whom these important revelations had been imparted called themselves beholders (*Anschauer*) or *Epoptes* because the recognition of a previously hidden truth can be compared to a passage from darkness to light, and perhaps also because they really and truly looked at the newly discovered truths in sensuous images.

But they could not come to this beholding all at once, for the spirit had to be cleansed first of all sorts of errors and had to go through several preparations before it could bear the full light of the truth. There were, therefore, steps or degrees, and only in the inner sanctuary did the blanket fall off the eyes completely.

The Epoptes recognized one single, highest cause of all things, one original power of nature, the Being of all beings, which was the same as the demiurge of Greek thinkers. Nothing is more sublime than the simple greatness with which they spoke of the creator of the universe. In order to honor him extraordinarily, they did not give him any name. "A name," they said, "is a necessity only for distinction; he who is alone needs no name, for there is no one with whom he can be confounded." At the base of an old statue of Isis one read the words: "I am what there is." And on a pyramid at Sais the remarkable ancient inscription was found: "I am all, what is, what was, what shall be; no mortal has lifted my veil." No one was permitted to enter the temple of Serapis who did not bear on his chest or forehead the name Joa—or I-ha-ho—a name resembling in sound the Hebraic Jehova and probably also having the same meaning. In Egypt no name was pronounced with greater respect than this name Joa. In the hymn that the hierophant or the overseer of the sanctuary sang for the initiate the first revelation made about the name of the godhead was: "He is alone and of himself and to him alone all things owe their existence."

In the temple the initiate came upon several sacred implements which expressed a secret meaning. Among these was a holy tabernacle which was called the sarcophagus of Serapis and which in its origin was perhaps meant to symbolize the hidden wisdom. But later, when the institution became corrupt, it served the priests in their games of secret machinations and miserable practices. To carry this tabernacle was the prerogative of the priests or of a special class of servants in the sanctuary who, as a consequence, were also called *kistophores* (box-bearers). No one but the hierophant was allowed to open this chest, or even merely to touch it. One who had the audacity to uncover it was said to have suddenly gone mad. . . .

The mysterious figures for which no one but the Epoptes had the key gave to the mysteries an air of sensuous appearance that deceived the common people and even resembled idol worship. . . .

But finally the key for the hieroglyphs and mysterious figures was lost, and they were taken to be the truth itself, which in the beginning they were meant only to cloak.[11]

Although Schiller sees that the hieroglyphs are not "the truth itself" but merely a "cloak" for it, he still stands in the tradition that prevailed before the Rosetta stone allowed a proper reading of them as a straightforward pictographic script. This interpretation of the mysteries of Isis, therefore, mixes into one interconnected set of concerns all those elements—a cipher-script, symbolic imagery, secrecy, initiation, and the wisdom of nature tied to the earth and to death—that Novalis, too, thought to be of great meaning and symbolic importance.

THE SECRET LANGUAGE OF ISIS: CONCEALMENT AND REVELATION

The idea of a secret language, a language understood only by those initiated into its world, served Novalis as a metaphor by which to speak about the language of nature. But he also uses the idea and its function as described by Schiller for a more general application and draws the distinction between a secrecy achieved by tonal variations and one constructed by means of images. In the first of the aphorisms, used as motto at the beginning of *Glauben und Liebe* (Faith and Love),[12] Novalis says that:

If in a large, mixed social gathering one desires to speak in secret with only a few, and one is not seated next to one another, one has to speak in a particular language. This particular language may be a foreign language either in *tone* or in *images*. The latter will be a language of tropes and riddles. [II,485,#1]

For Novalis, as we have seen, nature speaks in just such a secret language of riddles and tropes. And in the large, mixed company that constitutes humanity, only those few who have learned her language well will understand her. But on second thought Novalis wonders whether mysteries do not protect their secrets naturally, just as nature does and, therefore, need no deliberately coded language to conceal their truths:

> Many thought we should speak of fragile and vulnerable things in a learned language, for instance, write in Latin of such matters.[13] It would depend on an experiment whether we could not in ordinary language speak in such a manner that only *he* could understand who should. Every true mystery must exclude the profane spontaneously. Whoever understands is, as a matter of course and justifiably, an *initiate*. [II,485,#2][14]

Spinning this thought out further, Novalis comes to the conclusion that a deliberately mysterious expression at best only adds spice or interest but nothing essentially new to the thought it expresses.

> The mystifying expression is an added excitation to thought. All truth is as old as the ages. The allure of newness lies only in the variations of expression. The richer the appearance is in contrast, the greater is the pleasure of recognition. [II,485,#3]

Here Novalis turns the thought that began by questioning the necessity and possibility of a coded conversation into a discussion of the effect such ciphered language has on the truth contained in the secret expression. He finds that the effect is of aesthetic consequence, but is not significant in adding to or subtracting from the idea it gives voice to. As a result we can now say that the ciphers of nature with their mysterious forms and figures also have a primarily aesthetic allure to which the poet is obviously more likely to respond fully than the philosopher.

But Novalis's kinship with Schiller goes both further and deeper than a merely shared interest in the possibility of a coded language would suggest. For Schiller believes this secret language of riddles and tropes was used not only in the service of Isis; he also places it at the beginning of the Judeo-Christian tradition, claiming that Moses was instructed by the Egyptian priests in "the philosophy of symbols and hieroglyphs." In other words, hieroglyphic language serves not only in the mysteries of nature, but also in those of the spirit. It does so for two reasons: first, because Moses, the religious founder, was instructed in it; and second, because nature, as celebrated in the personification of Isis and her cult, *is* an expression of spirit. If she is "what there is" and "all, what is, what was, what shall be," then that is only because she herself is the hiero-glyphic expression of that nameless being, the Being of all beings, the spirit that is the unity of the universe. In *Die Lehrlinge zu Sais,* the teacher has learned to see this unity that links the many objects of nature, and he is guiding his students toward seeing it as well. For this reason he is deeply moved when the slow and particularly clumsy novice who usually cannot find anything one day brings home the central pebble. Having gone out in a sad mood to gather what nature has to offer, the student fails to return by nightfall. In the morning his happy voice is heard from a small wood:

> He sang a high, cheerful song; we were all surprised; the teacher looked toward morning with a glance I shall probably never see again. The novice soon stepped into our midst and with unspeakable happiness in his face brought a plain little stone of peculiar shape. The teacher took it in his hand and gave the novice a long kiss, then he looked at us with moist eyes and set the little stone down in an empty place amongst other stones, exactly where many rows touched like rays.
>
> I will never forget this moment. We felt as if in passing we had had a bright presentiment of this wonderful world in our souls.
>
> [I,81,12–22][15]

The "wonderful world" the novices had a momentary presentiment of is that of the unity of all being. The central pebble demonstrates this unity visually. Being the nodal point, the point of convergence of so many rows of stones, it functions as a symbol and sign of unity. And the diverse objects of nature—all her stones and stars, flowers and animals, and even mankind—are, because of the pebble's symbolic power, suddenly perceived as hieroglyphic representations of that unity. The double character of all natural phenomena is thus made evident: everything is both symbol and sign of something other than itself and also simply itself as natural object.

In order to gain a well-founded understanding or even just a presentiment of this unity, Novalis thinks the philosopher of nature must exercise his observational powers. The pebble could not have served as meaningful symbol of nature's unity if a painstaking observation of nature's regularity and serial progression had not preceded the lucky find. Indeed without such observations the pebble could not have been found, or if found, its significance would not have been recognized or understood. Similarly, Schiller emphasizes the role of the sense of sight in the recognition of the truths of nature. The Epoptes are Anschauer, or beholders, men who have *seen* the truth. As Schiller suggests, this may be understood not only metaphorically because a "recognition of a previously hidden truth can be compared to a passage from darkness to light," but may also be taken literally, since the beholders "*truly looked* at the newly discovered truths in sensuous images." Such sensuous images must have resembled the sight the novices beheld when the central pebble was set in its pivotal place. It is a relatively small step from Schiller's suggestion of a pictorial representation of the truth to an understanding of natural objects themselves as such sensuous images of it. And clearly this is precisely the step Novalis takes: for thinking nature herself to be the hieroglyphic expression of spirit, he takes all of her phenomena to be visual symbols of that spirit.

In Schiller's essay, as well as in his poem, this hieroglyphic cloak is the veil under which the spirit that is the truth of nature is hidden. Since we speak of the "naked truth" and of "veiled remarks," the ideas of truth concealment and revelation have been metaphorically linked to cloth and clothing. Oddly, though, the textile metaphor seems to have been used traditionally to denote both a revelation of truth—such as Isis presents with the figures adorning her robe—as well as a concealment of truth— such as occurs in her wearing a veil. But not only the wearing of clothes, also the making of cloth is metaphorically tied to the ideas of revelation and concealment. Thus we speak for instance of weaving a web of lies or of spinning a tale, and talk of a good yarn—possibly in analogy to the Moirai, who weave the fabric and spin the thread of man's life and at the end cut it short. That cloth as a veil or cloak is used metaphorically to express a concealing or hiding seems at first less surprising than its opposite use in metaphors of revelation. Yet a covering cloak or veil always also points out and draws attention to what is covered, while the patterns woven into the fabric simply are pictorial signs that are meant to reveal a truth about either the weaver or wearer or both. As in the case of Philomela: raped by her sister's husband, Tereus, who to ensure that his crime would not be discovered imprisoned Philomela and cut her tongue out, she weaves the tale of her woe. For while her "speechless lips can give no token of her wrongs. . . . She hangs a Thracian web on her loom, and skillfully weaving purple signs on a white background, she thus tells the story of her wrongs." Having finished the fabric, she sends it to Procne, who "unrolls the cloth, reads the pitiable fate of her sister, and (a miracle that she could!) says not a word." But takes revenge![16]

What unites Isis and Philomela is that both make silent matter tell a tale. Nor is it accidental that both are women. Denied active participation

in the political realm, the marketplace of speech, women have traditionally expressed themselves silently in the crafts they have produced.
In fact, even a woman's body may silently disclose her story. Tereus
imprisons Philomela because cutting her tongue out is not sufficient to
ensure his safety. The repeated acts of rape may result in pregnancy, and
then Philomela's very body would speak of her outrage. In general, therefore, the weaving of cloth and the wearing of clothes, cloaks, or veils is
done as much to cover up the revealing body as it is done to uncover its
meaning to make a telling sign of the truth. This is shown by the example
of Adam and Eve, who felt the need to cover the silent nakedness of their
bodies only after eating of the tree of knowledge, thus making of the fig
leaf both a sign of their guilt and a covering beneath which they hoped to
hide their shame and the truth.

The goddess's veil—in both Schiller's poem and in his essay—similarly serves both functions: it conceals, and by concealing, it draws attention
to and points out what it covers. Yet the unveiling, the uncovering is to be
done by no one other than the goddess herself. Only nature herself will
and ought to raise her own veil and reveal the truth she shelters. The
novice's task is to ready himself to receive whatever she may want to
reveal. The preparation for this reception takes place under the guiding
and watchful eye of the beholders, or Epoptes, who seek to purify the
heart of the novice. Thus neither the seeking nor the finding of nature's
deepest truths must ever be a capricious or willful act. In Novalis's *Die
Lehrlinge zu Sais*, it is therefore the clumsy, innocent student who brings
home the small stone that completes the unity of the pattern. When in
Schiller's poem, on the contrary, a student willfully and without the
proper purity of heart—but driven by curiosity—lifts the veil of Isis in
opposition to the injunction, he is overwhelmed and struck unconscious
by the light of the truth he finds shining forth from under it. Not having
been properly prepared for the truth, he never recovers from its impact
and lives out his few remaining days in the darkness of gloom:

> Unhappy man, what do you plan to do?
> So calls a faithful voice within his heart.
> Do you thus plan to tempt what is most holy?
> No mortal, said the oracle, removes
> This veil, except if I raise it myself.
> But then did not the same voice also add:
> Whoever lifts this veil shall see the truth?
> "Let there be under it what may. I'll raise
> This veil—" He shouts out loud— "and I shall see!"

Shall see!
Shouts back sarcastic'ly an echo.
He speaks it and then raises up the veil.
What, you may ask, saw he beneath it?
I do not know. The priests, they found him there
By the next day, unconscious and so pale
He lay prone at the statue's pedestal.
What he had seen and what he learned
He never said. The gladness of his life
Had left his side for ever
And to an early grave took him despair.
"Woe unto him," this was his warning word,
When urging questioners pressed him to say,
"Woe unto him, who guiltily comes to the truth;
It will not bring him joy."

Not so Novalis's apprentice. He is not harmed by his daring deed. On the contrary, it brings him a beneficial enlightenment, for he comes to recognize a revelation of himself beneath the veil:

One succeeded—he raised the veil of the goddess at Sais—But what did he see? he saw—miracle of miracles—himself. [II,584,#250]

As thoroughly as this fragment stands in opposition to Schiller's essay and poem, Schiller still must be seen as having set the stage for Novalis's novice. For the student in Schiller's poem, coming suddenly and unexpectedly upon the veiled image of the goddess, asks the hierophant accompanying him what consequences would befall him if he were to disregard the injunction and remove the veil. He receives this answer:

"That you have to settle with the godhead," said
The hierophant. "No mortal," she proclaims,
"Removes this veil, except if I raise it myself.
And who with uninitiated, guilty hand
Lifts in advance what's holy and forbidden,
He, the godhead says—"Well?—He shall see the truth!"[17]

Such a prohibition comes close to being an invitation. The seeker after truth must want to lift that veil after a threat that is so much like a promise. And if he is a Romantic mystic who feels man's spiritual kinship with the godhead, then, barring selfish and greedy interests as motives, man in his essence is naturally an initiate and, therefore, at the very least is not acting with unclean hands and heart.

Nature, according to Novalis, can provide such a revelation of the self for several reasons: to begin with, as we have already discussed, man in some aspects of his being is a part of the natural world, and as such nature reveals man to himself when she presents him with the truth about herself. Next, where nature as earth-mother and inner earth stands in a relation of mutual representation (Wechselrepräsentation) with man, the true being of nature and the true being of man are analogous, and one, therefore, can indeed reveal the truth of the other. Last, insofar as the many things are linked by the One unifying spirit that underlies them all, the spirit that expresses itself in nature and is hidden beneath nature's veil is also the spirit that animates man. The mysterious journey inward, then, is a journey beneath and beyond the veil of Isis. And the "universe in us" and the worlds of "the past and future" are the worlds of the "depth of our spirit."[18] Thus Isis—of whom, according to Schiller, the ancients said that she is "all, what is, what was, and what shall be"— becomes a symbolic representation of that inner universe in which time and eternity are conjoined in a coincidence of opposites. And the Delphic exhortation "Know thyself!" can be rephrased to read "Raise the veil of Isis!" In the ending of the fragmentary part of his work Novalis suggests that this is indeed what the true novice at Sais must do:

> Rather he [the teacher] wants us to follow our own path. For every new path goes through new territory, but finally returns to these dwellings, to this sacred homeland. So I, too, will describe my figure, and if no mortal, according to that inscription there, raises the veil, then we must attempt to become immortals; whoever does not want to raise the veil is no true novice of Sais. [I,82,17–23]

The true homeland to which we return, the sacred dwelling, is our inner self. For Novalis follows the Christian tradition that man, and particularly his body, is the only temple, the only sacred dwelling of the godhead.[19]

> There is but One temple in the world and that is the human body. Nothing is more holy than this high figure. The bowing before people is rendering homage to this revelation in the flesh. (Divine veneration of the Lingam, of the bosom—of statues.) [III,565,#75]

Returning from one's travels to this homeland, then, is a returning home to the self from traversing the world. It is the turn inward after an outward-bound observation of the world. And so in a poem written in Freiberg on May 11, 1799, the year Novalis also wrote most of *Die Lehrlinge zu Sais*, he addresses the Delphic exhortation as follows:

Only *one thing* there is for which man has sought at all times
    Everywhere, now on the heights, now in the depth of the world–
Under various names—in vain—it kept itself hidden always,
    Always he still felt its presence—yet grasp it he never did.
There was a man long ago, in friendly myths he gave to the children
    The way and the key to what in the castle lay hidden.
Few did interpret the easy cipher of the solution,
    But just these few became the masters now of the goal.
Long were the ages that passed—and error sharpened the senses—
    So that the myth itself no longer concealed the truth.
Happy is he who wisely no longer ponders the world,
    Who of himself demands the stone of eternal wisdom.
Truly an adept is only the man of reason—he transforms
    Everything into life, into gold—and no longer has need of elixirs.
In him steams the sacred flask—the king is in him—
    And Delphi too, and he it is who finally grasps: *Know thyself!*
                                                                    [I,403–404]

This poem interprets the undertaking of alchemy as a project in psychology. It intertwines standard alchemical imagery with the ancient classical
dictum of Delphi for the sake of making it clear that only through a
journey inward can man begin to grasp his own nature and with it the
truth. For it is hidden in man himself. We ourselves are the cipher, the
myth concealing from our own eyes the truth that is our salvation. Both
the poem "Know Thyself" and the last paragraph of the first chapter of
Die Lehrlinge zu Sais make this point. The true adept, therefore, in his
search for the truth, must dare to seek himself, to face himself. For the
king is in him. In alchemical symbolism the king stands for the sun, which
in turn is the symbol and sign for enlightenment. Thus, only he who
knows that he must demand of himself the philosopher's stone or stone
of wisdom has understood that no elixir, no outside means, no mere
observation of the world can reveal the ultimate truth. In lifting the veil of
Isis man grasps that he and nature are one insofar as neither is more than
a cipher. Both are merely a symbol and sign of the spirit that lives in them.
But man is the more perfect sign of that spirit. His ideality is greater than
nature's and so he symbolizes spirit more truly than nature does.

> What is man? A perfect trope of spirit. All true communication there-
> fore is symbolic. [II,564,#197]

To understand what is symbolized and to interpret the hieroglyph correctly is consequently to perceive the truth without its cloak, that is,

naked.[20] The exhortation to lift the veil of Isis, therefore, is the demand to undertake the journey inward and to have the strength to accept the awesome truth found there, to dare to live with the spirit of God.

NOVALIS'S REVALUATION OF THE ISIS SYMBOLISM

This turning of the traditional injunction against the lifting of the veil into its opposite—a command to raise it—is for Novalis, I believe, closely tied to Sophie von Kühn's death. Particularly his experience at her graveside leads Novalis to reevaluate some of the traditional meaning of symbols. In addition, Schiller's suggestion that the ancients thought the coffin of Serapis to contain "hidden wisdom" or to be a symbolic representation of it must have struck a responsive chord in Novalis, who after Sophie's death found that the grave and the coffin within it held all that was good and meaningful to him: his love and the wisdom of the ages. For from the beginning of his acquaintance with Sophie, Novalis had taken her name to be no mere accidental designation, but believed *nomen* in this case to be indeed *omen*. He took "Sophie" to mean wisdom, literally, and saw the girl as its incarnation. In the diary of the weeks after Sophie's death, when Novalis formed the plan to follow her into death, to make a sacrifice of himself, he chronicles his resolve, as we have seen, in a matter-of-fact tone. In a similarly detached voice he also reports on the occurrence at Sophie's grave. Novalis's account of the unusual experience of May 13, 1797—that was to have such far-reaching and lasting consequences for him—is embedded in the casual and even banal happenings of the day:

> Arose in the morning at 5. The weather was very good. The morning passed without my doing much. Captain Rockenthien and his sister-in-law and children came. I got a letter from Schlegel with the 1st part of the new Shakespeare translation. After lunch I went for a walk—then coffee—the weather became overcast—first a thunder squall then cloudy and stormy—very lustful—started to read Shakespeare—read myself quite into it. In the evening I went to Sophie. There I was indescribably cheerful—flashing moments of enthusiasm—I blew the grave like dust before me—centuries were like moments—I could feel her nearness—I believed she would step forward any moment—when I came home I was moved several times while talking with Machere. Otherwise I was cheerful all day long. Niebekker was here in the afternoon. In the evening I had several good ideas. Shakespeare made me think a lot. [IV,35,23–36,7,#56]

The mystical experience at Sophie's grave found its poetic reflection in the third of the *Hymnen an die Nacht* (*Hymns to the Night*), which Heinz Ritter in his interpretation calls the *Urhymne* (original hymn).[21] The edited version of the hymn as it was published in the *Atheneum* journal was probably not written before 1800. And even though the manuscript that has come down to us is dated only a year earlier, 1799, it appears to be a close copy of Novalis's original conception of the hymns in 1797, and is, therefore, likely to be a more accurate representation of Novalis's mood and reaction immediately following the event at the graveside. I will quote from the manuscript. It differs significantly from the published hymns in only a few lines:

> Once as I was shedding bitter tears, as my hope dissolved into pain vanished, and I stood alone at the barren mound that in narrow, dark space buried the figure of my life, I, lonely as no one was lonely before, driven by unutterable fear, powerless, only a thought of suffering still—when I then looked for help, not able to go forward, not backward—and clung to the fleeing, extinguished life with infinite longing—there came from the blue distance, from the height of my old happiness, a twilight shudder—and at once the cord of birth, the fetters of light broke—away sped the splendor of the earth and with it my mourning. My sadness fused into a new unfathomable world—you, enthusiasm of night, slumber of heaven, overtook me. The country gently raised itself upward—above it my delivered, newly born spirit hovered unchained. The mound became a cloud of dust, and through the cloud I saw the transfigured features of my beloved—In her eyes rested eternity—I grasped her hands and the tears became a glittering, unbreakable bond. Millennia passed downward into the distance like thunderstorms—At her neck I cried enchanting tears to the new life. This was the first dream in you. It passed, but its reflection, the eternal unshakable faith in the heaven of night and its sun, the beloved, remained. [I,134,170–196]

In the *Atheneum* version the last lines read:

> It was the first singular dream—and only since then do I feel eternal, unalterable faith in the heaven of night and its light the beloved.
>
> [I,135,25–27]

The *Atheneum* edition replaces the more erotic and more mystical expression that his vision is "the first dream *in you*" [emphasis mine] with the more detached and impersonal phrase "the first singular dream." It

then distances the last line even further from the immediacy of the underlying experience by deleting the expression of regret that such an
ecstatic vision is after all a fleeting, a merely momentary presence, that it
"passes" and that only "its reflection" remains. Nor is the affirmation of
faith in the beloved beyond the darkness of death nearly as strong in the
Atheneum version. For only by following the observation that the
"dream in you" passed does the mere reflection of the beloved's presence take on the power that allows it to become an article of faith and an
everlasting source of consolation.

Formerly it was thought that the changes in the *Atheneum* version
were due to Schlegel's editing. The terser rhythms as well as the altered
punctuation were thought to be his addition. But according to Ritter they
are most likely Novalis's own revisions. Ritter thinks that most of the first
four hymns and part of the fifth were composed soon after the experience
at Sophie's grave in 1797, then copied by Novalis himself in 1799, and
finally revised by him for publication in the *Atheneum* early in 1800. Basing
his opinion on an analysis of both the manuscript pages and Novalis's
handwriting, Ritter comes to the conclusion that the first line of the third
hymn as well as its last few phrases were not part of the original hymn, or
Urhymne, but were added to it in 1799. In the copying of the original
composition and in the editing for publication, Novalis made changes
that are clearly the result only of aesthetic concerns. But there are other
alterations as well, and for these we must seek an explanation that considers Novalis's emotional state and his philosophical or religious
convictions.

It seems likely that the addition of the first line, "Once when I was
shedding bitter tears," two years after the event at the graveside, is, on
the one hand, no more than an attempt to join an existing literary convention and, on the other hand, an acknowledgment of the time that
had elapsed. In addition, it seems to hint that a quite different mood has
now taken hold of the author. By 1800 this must in fact have been the case,
for Novalis had met, fallen in love with, and become engaged to Julie von
Charpentier. But placing the occurrence thus historically in the past, the
line neither denies nor undermines the validity of the event. Its addition
therefore seems to have a relatively simple explanation. The addition of
the last few lines, in contrast, strikes me as both less simple and more
meaningful. For why should Novalis delete or significantly alter in the
published version of 1800 what he had just added in the 1799 copy? If we
assume that Ritter is right and the line "this was the first dream in you"

was added in 1799 and then edited out again prior to publication, it seems likely that other such dreams "in you" followed the first one—for why call a dream "the first" if it was, as the published version claims, a "singular" one? Clearly there are two possibilities: either other dreams followed the first, and then even as late as 1800 the emotional intensity connected to the experiences expressed in this line must have been great and would not have permitted Novalis to make a public confession of them (since publicizing such a deeply private truth would have felt like the desecration of a holy mystery). Or, on the contrary, the alteration of the published hymn was undertaken simply as a correction, precisely in order to avoid giving the false impression that there was more than one such dream. Obviously there can be no clear-cut answer.[22] Yet I incline toward the first explanation. The published version remains ambiguous. It calls the dream both "first" and "singular," thus apparently denying as much as asserting that there was only one dream. But considering how Sophie became for Novalis much more than merely a lost love or dead beloved, it seems likely that other strongly felt presences of her must have followed upon the first experience at the grave. For how else would she have become for Novalis the mediator of the spiritual realm—his own saint—who in his diary he associates with the savior: "Christ and Sophie."[23]

Novalis, whose method of Erhebung is based on finding intermediate levels by which we can proceed from any given point to ever higher levels until we finally reach the opposite of what we started out with, not surprisingly also conceives of our relation to God as mediated by objects or beings who we either believe rank higher than we ourselves do, or who actually do so. The level of the particular mediation a man chooses describes that man's spiritual development. The more primitive a man is, the lower his choice of the mediating agency will be:

> Nothing is more indispensable for true religiosity than a mediating link that joins us to the Godhead. Without mediation man can by no means stand in relation to it. In the choice of this mediating link man must be entirely free. The least constraint in this does damage to his religion. The choice is characteristic, and, therefore, well-educated people will choose rather similar mediating links, whereas the uneducated will be determined in this by accident. But since so very few people are at all capable of a free choice, some mediating links will become more general; be that by mere accident, by association, or because of their particular appropriateness. In this manner national religions come to be. The more independent man becomes, the more the quantity of the mediating link diminishes and the more its quality

becomes refined and man's relations to it become more manifold and more highly developed: fetishes, stars, animals, heroes, idols, gods, a godman. We soon see how relative these choices are and inadvertently are driven to the idea that the essence of a religion is not dependent on the nature of the mediator but merely on the view we have of him and the relations we have to him. [II,441,30–443,18,#74][24]

For Novalis, Sophie becomes such a mediating link after her death. He can say "Christ and Sophie" because both fulfill for him in equal measure that mediating function without which Novalis thinks no religiosity is possible at all. Thus even after he meets and falls in love with Julie von Charpentier, Sophie remains that ideal figure through whom he finds entrance into the realm of the divine, the realm of spirit:

> Toward Söfchen I feel religion—not love. Absolute love, independent of the heart, based in faith, is religion! [II,395,#56]

This fragment now also illuminates the last lines of the third hymn: the "unshakable faith in the heaven of night and its sun, the beloved," speaks of a faith that is possible only because the beloved is dead. While Sophie was still of this earth, this life, Novalis felt love for Sophie, indeed was in love with her. But for the dead Sophie his emotions have undergone a transformation. He is not simply mourning his lost love as he was doing before the experience at her grave. Now his love for the dead beloved turns into a faith for a loved and revered immortal spirit. The solace of this experience is that she now becomes an ever-present companion who is his mediating link to the godhead and, therefore, and, only therefore, also his muse.

This transformation of Sophie into a mediating religious figure is for Novalis partly the result of an act of will:

> Love, by means of absolute will, can become religion. We become worthy of the highest Being only through death./ Death of atonement./ [II,395,#57]

But it is also due, at least in part, to the impression Sophie made on Novalis—and on others as well—while she was still alive. Something about her, particularly her eyes, made this uneducated, childlike and childish young girl an ephemeral figure to whom people responded with their *Gemüth*, their soul. The images we have of her (a cut-out silhouette and the miniature of her on Novalis's engagement ring) give us no real idea what her aura must have been. Nevertheless Novalis reports in his letter to Caroline Just of March 24, 1797:

My mother said when she saw her [Sophie's] silhouette for the first time—I like her face indescribably much—she looks so devout, so quiet—as if she were not in her place in this world.

[IV,210,9–12,#92][25]

There is some question as to just what Novalis's relation to Sophie was while she was still alive. When they first met she was twelve; four months later—by then Sophie was thirteen—they secretly became engaged; nine months after that she fell ill with the sickness that fifteen months later killed her. All in all, then, she was part of Novalis's life for less than two and a half years. During this time Novalis wrote a remarkably unemotional and distanced account of some of her traits. The fragment is entitled *Klarisse*. [IV,24–25] The character that emerges is that of a child, a precocious child, but a child nonetheless. Among the many observations Novalis makes are the following: *"Her behavior toward me.* Her anxiety about the marriage." [IV,24,20] And further: "She does not want to be disturbed by my love. My love often oppresses her. She is *cool* throughout." [IV,25,5–6] This hardly allows us to think the relation to have been an ardent love affair. Whatever bound Novalis to Sophie, it was not passionate sexuality. Something else about her fascinated him. And maybe the remark in *Klarisse* that "she *does not desire to be anything*—she *is* something" [IV,24,13] can give us an inkling of what it was Novalis loved about her. A girl of thirteen who does not want to be something, to become something, who has no desire for something she still lacks in her person, who is no project to herself, clearly is not an erotic character. She is not driven to fulfill herself, to find whatever she yet lacks. And when we in addition hear that at thirteen "she *is* something," then the nonerotic ideality of her nature becomes evident. And so in a letter to Karl Woltmann, written on April 14, 1797, shortly after Sophie's death, Novalis observes:

—It certainly is not passion—I feel it too incontrovertibly, too coolly, too much with my whole soul that she was one of the noblest, most ideal figures who ever were or will be on this earth. The most beautiful of mankind must have resembled her. A painting by Raphael has in the physiognomy the most striking resemblance to her I have so far found. [IV,222,22–27][26]

Even if we disregard the slightly exaggerated tone and recognize in it the tendency to see only the positive and good in the dead beloved, there still remains enough of a description for us to assume that it was Sophie's ideality that mattered to Novalis. The child-woman, the "eternal virgin," can be his muse, his religious mediator in a way that a fully grown and sexually mature woman could not have been.[27] For such a woman—as Julie von Charpentier doubtless was—would have resisted all psychological efforts to incorporate her into his own psyche.[28] Being her own project, Julie could not have become part of his. The independent reality of her own being would have asserted itself over and over again. Sophie's already remarkable ideality was further facilitated by her death. No longer a living presence, her personality could not assert itself at all anymore, and so nothing stood in the way of her complete idealization. She was present now only to Novalis's mind, soul, and heart, and took on the shape he needed her to have, thus becoming the "figure of *his* life." Kierkegaard gives a remarkable description of just such an idealization of an unfulfilled love:

> A young lad falls in love with a princess. . . . Yet the relation is such that it cannot possibly be realized, cannot possibly be translated from ideality into reality . . . he does not give up the love, not for all the glories of the world. He is no fool. First of all, he assures himself that it actually is the substance of his life, and his soul is too healthy and too proud to waste the least of it in an intoxication. He is not cowardly; he is not afraid to let it steal into his most secret, his most remote thoughts, to let it twist and entwine itself intricately around every ligament of his consciousness—if his love comes to grief, he will never be able to wrench himself out of it. . . .
>
> His love for that princess would become for him the expression of an eternal love, would assume a religious character, would be transfigured into a love of the eternal being, which true enough denied the fulfillment but nevertheless did reconcile him once more in the eternal consciousness of its validity in an eternal form that no actuality can take away from him. . . . The desire that would lead him out into actuality but has been stranded on impossibility is now turned inward, but it is not therefore lost, nor is it forgotten. Sometimes it is the vague emotions of desire in him that awaken recollection; sometimes he awakens it himself, for he is too proud to be willing to let the whole substance of his life turn out to have been an affair of the fleeting moment. He keeps his love young, and it grows along with him in years and in beauty. But he needs no finite occasion for its growth. From the moment he has made the movement, the princess is lost. He does not need the erotic titillation of seeing the beloved etc., nor does he in the finite sense continually need to be bidding her farewell, because in the eternal sense he recollects her, and he knows very well that the lovers who are so bent on seeing each other for the last time in

order to say farewell once again are justified in their eagerness, justified in thinking it to be the last time, for they forget each other very quickly. He has grasped the deep secret that even in loving another person one ought to be sufficient to oneself. He is no longer finitely concerned about what the princess does, and precisely this proves that he has made the movement infinitely.[29]

In the third of Novalis's *Geistliche Lieder* the same idea is expressed as follows:

> What you have lost
> was found by him;
> with him you meet,
> what you have loved:
> And bound to you
> remains forever
> what his hand
> has returned to you. [I,163,33–36]

But while Novalis certainly idealized Sophie, he was not like Kierkegaard, who gave up Regina Olsen by choice. On the contrary, Novalis's relationship to life was psychologically a sturdy one. And so he had no hesitation to again fall in love and to again become engaged. It was his friends who regretted that he did so and would rather have seen him mourn Sophie forever. But Novalis managed to split his love into an earthly one for Julie and a heavenly or religious one for Sophie.

With the complete idealization of Sophie it becomes possible for Novalis to connect her symbolically to the other female ideals that illuminate his soul. And while it is not entirely clear whether she was aligned with them or they with her, the latter seems more likely. The Virgin Mary and Isis both come to be symbolic representations of Sophie. And Novalis's complete identification with Sophie—and of Sophie with him—finds expression in the tale of "Rosenblüthe und Hyacinth" in *Die Lehrlinge zu Sais*. At the story's end Hyacinth finds the temple of Isis, for which he has been searching, blissfully falls asleep in it, and dreams that he is led into the inner sanctuary:

> Everything appeared so familiar and yet in never seen splendor, and then even the last wordly tinge waned, as if consumed by the air, and he stood before the heavenly virgin. He raised the thin shiny veil, and Rosenblüthchen fell into his arms. [I,95,4–7]

As the dream at the graveside mystically united Novalis and Sophie, so the dream in the temple of Isis unites Hyacinth and Rosenblüthe. Under

the veil of the goddess Isis, described as "heavenly virgin"—an appelation more appropriate for the mother of Christ—the novice not only finds
himself, but as Hyacinth he also finds his beloved. Therefore, to find
oneself and to find the beloved amount to the same. In the union of two
lovers the true act of self-recognition takes place. The earth-mother of the
seasons, the moon-goddess of the night, as well as Sophie—Novalis's
own goddess of heavenly love and wisdom—are one and the same and
are what Novalis finds on his journey inward. They are part of *his* soul
and are the key and the way to the "know thyself" given to man long ago
in myths.

Novalis speaks of the same need for self-sufficiency in matters of ideal
or religious love as Kierkegaard, but he claims for it a world-originating
power.

★We seek the *plan* for the world—this plan we are ourselves—What
are we? personified *omnipotent* points. But the execution, as image of
the plan, must also be equal to its freedom of action and its reflex-
ivity—and vice versa. Life or the nature of spirit thus consists in
begetting, giving birth to, and educating one's own kind. Thus, only
insofar as man leads a happy marriage with himself—and constitutes
a beautiful family, is he at all capable of marriage and of having a
family. The act of self-embracing.

One must never admit to oneself that one loves oneself—The
secret of this admission is the life-principle of the only true, eternal
love. The first kiss according to this understanding is the principle of
philosophy—the origin of a new world—the beginning of the absolute era—the execution of an infinitely growing self-union.

Who would not like a philosophy whose seed is a first kiss?

Love popularizes personality—it allows individualities to be
communicable and to be *understandable*. (Understanding of love.)

[II,541,#74]

As we have seen, the novice of Sais is given the task of raising the veil of
Isis because under that veil he will find a revelation of himself. Yet when
in the tale Hyacinth raises the goddess's veil, he does not find himself
but Rosenblüthe, who sinks into his arms while far-off music accompanies the union of the lovers. We, therefore, came to the conclusion
that for Novalis true self-recognition occurs in the union with the beloved. But since the exhortation to raise the veil is followed by the recol-
lection that no mortal may do so, Novalis suggests that if mortals cannot
do so we must become immortals. It, thus, appears that the ultimate
union of Hyacinth and Rosenblüthe, as of all lovers, is a union after

death. Novalis's vision of Sophie in the grave, therefore, is merely a presentiment of his union with her after death. Since Isis, like all great mother-goddesses, is the giver of death as much as of life, the act of embracing the beloved found under the veil of Isis is the act of self-embracing in death. And thus self-recognition in the act of self-embracing for Novalis is the start or the "seed" of philosophy. But this is so only because

> The true philosophical act is self-annihilation; this is the real beginning of all philosophy, toward this end tend all needs of the philosophical apostle, and only this act fulfills all the conditions and characteristics of the transcendental deed. [II,395,#54][30]

For Novalis, then, death is not the end of life. On the contrary, life is the beginning of death and, as such, part of the education that will be concluded only after death.

> Life is the beginning of death. Life is for the sake of death. Death is ending, and beginning at once—separation from and closer union with one's self at once. By means of death the reduction is completed. [II,416,#15]

Life for Novalis is thus not the beginning of death, in the sense in which Faulkner's Addie Bundren in *As I Lay Dying* quotes her father's opinion that "the reason for living was to get ready to stay dead a long time."[31] Here a despair at the meaninglessness of all action, rooted in the lack of meaning of death, is expressed. This clearly is not the case for Novalis. Sophie, as Novalis tells us in the essay *Klarisse*, believed in rebirth, not in the Christian resurrection of the flesh, and after her death Novalis seems to have brought both of these beliefs together. He obviously offers a symbolic representation of the rounds of rebirth when he has Heinrich von Ofterdingen find a history book that depicts his own figure in the costumes of different ages. In saying that the book's ending is missing, however, Novalis suggests that the rounds of recurrence are as yet not complete and cannot be completed before the return of the Golden Age, thus clearly alluding to the Christian idea of the second coming of Christ. Death for Novalis is the divide through which an individual must pass if he is to reach his higher self. And in that sense death becomes a victory, namely over the lower self.

> Death is a victory over oneself—which like all self-surmounting, brings about a new, easier existence./ [II,414,#11]

For Novalis, the Isis symbolism thus retains the traditional duality of life and death, but reverses their customary valuation. For it is death that leads to new rounds of births and affords man the opportunity to raise his soul to ever higher levels, until man finally begins the life eternal. In an inversion of the voice of Faulkner's Addie Bundren we could say, then, that for Novalis "the reason for dying was to get ready to stay alive a long time." Death is the gate to the Golden Age where the ultimate union of the lovers will take place, where the other will be the self, as much as the self the other, in an eternal and infinite conjunction of opposites: darkness and light, death and life, the body and the soul, time and space or heaven and earth.

THE EARTH IN NOVALIS AND HEIDEGGER

The preceding discussion in this chapter and chapter 6 has shown that what is usually thought of as Novalis's "metaphysics of night" or "darkness" is for him intimately tied to a philosophy of earth and nature. Yet Novalis is by no means the only thinker who appreciates the philosophical importance of the idea of earth. In this century it is most obviously Heidegger who has made this turn toward the earth and who, as we have already seen, has other points of contact with Novalis's thought as well; let me, therefore, consider briefly what unites and what separates their understanding of the concept earth.

When Heidegger in *The Origin of the Work of Art*[32] expounds the meaning of "earth," he gives two distinct images as illustration: the Greek temple and van Gogh's painting of a pair of peasant shoes. In these two examples, several different aspects of the concept earth are presented. First, there is the earth as material, exemplified in the stones with which the temple is built. But these stones are not merely some "stuff" the temple happens to be made of. Rather they are so much part of its nature that the architectural work depends for its specific character on the particular kind of stone (or material) used. This notion of earth as *humus* Heidegger first presented in the *Cura* fable of *Being and Time*.[33] Humus is the clay out of which Care forms the body of man, making it so essentially part of the earth that after death it returns to earth—dust to dust and ashes to ashes. In the work of art this material aspect of earth is brought to our attention: "the material, not being used up by the work, shines forth." [*PLT*,46] In the case of instruments and tools, by contrast, Heidegger suggests that their material nature recedes into their usefulness as object and withdraws from our awareness. Concentrating on how well a tool serves our purpose, we remain unaware of its particular materiality.

Nothing in Novalis's work corresponds to this distinction. He is simply not aware of any difference between our experience of matter as mediated by the work of art and our experience of matter as it occurs in the used object. When Novalis considers usefulness at all, it is not in terms of its phenomenological, but its moral nature. His concern is that we should not be using any matter, and certainly not living creatures, only for the sake of our own purposes and goals, that is, only as means. For in all matter, insofar as it is part of nature, spirit manifests itself. For Novalis, then, in works of art as in instruments or tools, matter primarily serves the intention of its human re-shaper and thus is an expression, sign, or symbol of the human spirit and its enterprises. Man's nature being such that we are concerned equally with our body, mind, and soul or spirit, the distinction between a tool and a work of art as sign or symbol of the spirit that made them is for Novalis a distinction of focus in the human project. As far as he is concerned, it has no effect on how the medium of that project is perceived.

According to Novalis, earth, as the matter of the physical presence of any object, is always the expression of the divine spirit. Human re-shaping of matter has no effect whatsoever on this. The stones used for building the temple and the ore smelted and cast into a hammer or sword remain, insofar as they are stone or metal, hieroglyph and cipher of their maker. Only insofar as they are temple, hammer, or sword, that is, objects of a human project and, therefore, part of the human world—and that means precisely not in their materiality—do they express man's spirit. Yet Novalis might still have agreed partially with Heidegger: since earth as matter is always a coded or hieroglyphic expression of spirit, what separates different configurations and makes one harder to decipher than another would be simply a question of degree. And so Novalis could have, and probably would have, considered the work of art to be a partial key or deciphering code that helps man read the material hieroglyph. But Heidegger's belief that the work of art allows matter to shine forth as *itself*, in its *own nature*, Novalis would have found harder to accept. The earth as matter, whether it appears in the re-shaped form of art or tool, is for him first and foremost an expression of the universal spirit and therefore always stands primarily for something other than itself.

Second, when the stones of the earth are not the ashlars out of which man builds his temples, they are, for Heidegger, the rocks on which the temple is built and which support it. They represent the earth as that which carries man's life and world and serves as anchor and shelter for his existence. Here we find that aspect of earth which in the *Cura* fable appears as *Tellus,* the *terra mater* giving of herself by bearing fruit in the summer and denying herself in the bare winter months. It is the earth of vegetation cults and fertility rites. It is the sacred womb, which gives birth not only to beings but to life itself, and which is also the grave to which at the end of life all beings must return. Therefore, it is also the place that harbors death. Heidegger sees it in the van Gogh painting expressed by the shoes of the peasant woman, which, he says, call forth thoughts of tilled fields and ripening grain, of fallow desolation, of child-bearing, and of the menace of death. [*PLT,*34]

Clearly this conception of earth developed out of the notion of nature. Yet nature for Heidegger sets limits to the world of man. It is the border at which the world or that which is open to man's understanding ends and in fact ceases to be world. In this sense earth is that which does not allow man to penetrate it. It remains closed off from our understanding and becomes present to us only insofar as it is permitted to "remain undisclosed and unexplained." [*PLT,*47] In other words, earth here stands for the sheer opacity and final mystery of the natural processes, for the ultimate reticence of the universe to disclose itself to us.

Obviously this conception of earth is in its origin the same as Novalis's. Earth as mother of both life and death, as shelter and caretaker of man as well as his grave, is the primary notion of earth in Novalis's thinking. But while Heidegger and Novalis here start out with very much the same general idea, they come to rather different conclusions. Both agree on the mystery surrounding the natural processes, on the secretiveness and concealing character of earth and nature; both are acutely aware of the religious aura associated with this idea and tradition. But whereas Heidegger focuses on the limits nature sets on the human enterprise of knowledge and understanding and considers these limits an insurmountable part of the human condition, Novalis is firmly convinced that they can be overcome and, therefore, focuses his attention on the means by which man can and ought to try to break through them.[34]

In *The Birth of Tragedy,* speaking about Lessing, Nietzsche remarks:

> The most honest theoretical man [Lessing] dared to announce that he cared more for the search after truth than for truth itself—and thus revealed the fundamental secret of science [*Wissenschaft*], to the astonishment, and indeed the anger, of the scientific community [*der Wissenschaftlichen*]. Beside this isolated insight, born of an excess of honesty if not of exuberance, there is, to be sure, a profound *illusion* that first saw the light of the world in the person of Socrates: the

unshakable faith that thought, using the thread of causality, can penetrate the deepest abysses of being, and that thought is capable not
only of knowing being but even of *correcting* it. This sublime metaphysical illusion accompanies science [*Wissenschaft*] as an instinct and
leads science again and again to its limits, at which it must turn into
art—which is really the aim of its mechanisms.[35]

Novalis would agree with Nietzsche that science in its unpoetized form
suffers from an illusion when it believes itself able to penetrate the deepest secrets of being. But he would also think that art is eminently capable
of doing so. The poet—particularly the poet as priest of both the earth
and the heavens—can, by an act of inspired insight, grasp the meaning of
the universe and understand the spirit that manifests itself in it. For
Novalis, however, the poet is a man who differs from other men only in
that he precedes them in his development. He is ahead of the rest of us.
But we will one day follow him, and all mankind will eventually reach the
poet's level of spiritual evolution. Then the Golden Age, the Second
Coming of Christ, or Paradise will indeed be at hand again. Clearly
Heidegger would not want to go that far. No such optimism is at the base
of his thought—and probably cannot and ought not be at the base of
anyone's thought in this century. But this notwithstanding, is Heidegger
in fact not closer to Novalis than he appears to be when we concentrate
our attention only on the difference in their understanding of the limits
nature sets for man? Does not Heidegger as well see in the poet both the
predecessor and successor to the priest?

It is the poet, for Heidegger, who illuminates our world and prepares
the way:

> *All art*, as the letting happen of the advent of the truth of what is, is, as
> such, *essentially poetry*. . . . Nevertheless, the linguistic work, the
> poem in the narrower sense, has a privileged position in the domain of
> art. To see this, only the right concept of language is needed . . .
> language alone brings what is, as something that is, into the Open for
> the first time. Where there is no language, as in the being of stone,
> plant, and animal, there is also no openness of what is. . . . Lan-
> guage, by naming beings for the first time, brings beings to word and
> to appearance. Only this naming nominates beings *to* their being *from
> out of* their being. Such saying is a projecting of the clearing, in which
> announcement is made of what it is that beings come into the Open
> *as*. . . . Projective saying is poetry: the saying of world and earth, the
> saying of the arena of their conflict and thus of the place of all nearness
> and remoteness of the gods. Poetry is the saying of the unconcealed-

ness of what is. Actual language at any given moment is the happening of this saying, in which a people's world historically arises for it and the earth is preserved as that which remains closed. [*PLT*,72–74]

Novalis and Heidegger, thus, agree that the poet brings the earth into the openness of our awareness, that he speaks its truth. They disagree as to the way in which this bringing-into-the-Open occurs. For Heidegger it is the poet who raises all objects out of an indistinct background of undifferentiated being into their distinct presences, who brings to expression the difference between world and things. In the case of stone, plant, and animal, the poet primarily names their muteness, their silence, their incapacity for a full sounding language. Speaking of Trakl's poem "*Ein Winterabend*" (a winter evening), Heidegger says:

> No. This naming does not hand out titles, it does not apply terms, but it calls into the word. The naming calls. Calling brings closer what it calls. . . . [*PTL*,198]
>
> *Language speaks as the peal of stillness.* Stillness stills by the carrying out, the bearing and enduring, of world and things in their presence. The carrying out of world and thing in the manner of stilling is the appropriative taking place of the dif-ference. Language, the peal of stillness, is, inasmuch as the dif-ference takes place. Language goes on as the taking place or occurring of the dif-ference for world and things.
>
> The peal of stillness is not anything human. But on the contrary, the human is indeed in its nature given to speech—it is linguistic. [*PTL*,207]

The sounding speech of man is in response to the silent peal of language. But such language can also be heard in what Heidegger speaks of as the silent call of the earth, and that also means things. Man speaks insofar as he knows to listen to that peal of silence, that is, to things as being part of the earth.

> Mortals speak insofar as they listen. They heed the bidding call of the stillness of the dif-ference even when they do not know that call. Their listening draws from the command of the dif-ference what it brings out as sounding word. This speaking that listens and accepts is responding. [*PTL*,209]

Thus, for Heidegger, the poet must bring into view both the silent peal and the opacity of things, that is, both their silent language and the limits of our understanding of it. For Novalis that is only the poet's first step, upon which must follow the translation and transformation of that silence into sound and of that opacity into the translucency of poetic know-ing. Heidegger and Novalis, then, are very close in their view of this point, but also distinct. For Novalis does not set limits on the poet's ultimate ability to translate everything, even the silence of his listening. It is in this silence that he hears and sees the signs of the times, the revela-tions of chance and of the earth.

Third, earth is for Heidegger that ground on which a historical people develops as a nation. This—in contrast to a conception of the earth as man's sheltering home, or in accordance with the *Cura* fable, as essen-tially our mother—is the earth as father, as fatherland. This earth as homeland does not mean an area a people merely happen to inhabit. In an interpretation of Hölderlin's poetry Heidegger thus says:

> The national (*das Vaterländische*, literally, the father-landish) desig-nates the country in regard to the father as the highest God, it means that life-giving "relation" in which, having a destiny, man stands. Similarly the "national" (*Das Nationelle*) means the country of birth (*nasci, natura*), which as beginning determines what lasts.[36]

Here the earth is a decisive element in the history of nations and their individuals. Having originated in *Being and Time* as *Umweltnatur* (environ-ing nature), this conception of earth becomes increasingly more mystical for Heidegger. In the *Rektoratsrede* he speaks of the "earth and blood forces" of a people, meaning the emotional strength a people derives from both its racial inheritance as it is tied to the earth upon which it makes its home, and its relation to a particular landscape as the ground for its cultural development and identity.[37] Ultimately personifying this aspect of the concept earth, Heidegger writes in *Remembrance of the Poet*:

> This space is given by the immaculate earth. The earth houses the people in its historical space. The earth serenifies "the house." And the earth which thus serenifies is the first angel "of the house."[38]

Although the meanings of "earth" I have outlined here are separate and distinct for Heidegger, they are also interrelated and indeed part of *one* conception. One cannot think of the earth as man's sheltering home and support for his world, as the fertile soil of fields, and as the place of man's grave without also thinking of its materiality. No moreso can one make sense of the earth as historical ground without the meanings developed in the concept of earth as it derives from the original notion of nature.

It is in this last conception of the earth as national ground that Heideg-ger and Novalis have the greatest kinship. In *Heinrich von Ofterdingen*, Heinrich and a small group of merchants with whom he is traveling, along with some farmers from the village where they have stopped for the night, are led by the old Bergmann in the moonlight up the mountain to a large cave. Novalis thus conjoins several of the earth-mother symbols in one image: the night-time darkness illuminated by the moon-goddess; the inner earth cavern; and as guide to this *raised* inner-earth—for this is a cave, or rather a series of caves, as high up on a mountain as Zarathustra's—the miner, the priest of earth. When this small expedition arrives at the cave's mouth the farmers are not very eager to enter, and when near the entrance a great many ancient bones of animals are found, they decide to turn back and descend again to the valley. The farmer, as the man whose life is spent in the service of the upper earth, who never penetrates it any deeper than his plough can cut, remains behind, as is proper for the meaning he represents, while the miner leads the rest of the small troupe farther down into the cave. As the bones of by-gone ages indicate, this cave is to be understood as housing history. In contrast to the ever-recurring seasonal cycles to which the farmer is subject and which determine his life, these bones are part of a linear historical development. In the first cave, history, represented by the find of ancient bones, is the past, gone now and leaving as traces of its life only the dead remains of animals.

As Theseus used the thread of Ariadne to find his way out of the maze of death, so the miner now uses these dead remains of the past to mark the opening by which the small group advances farther into the second cave, thus using the past in the present as guide for the future. Here the life of the upper earth recedes even more, and Heinrich has a presentiment of the spiritually powerful figures (*geistesgewaltigen Gestalten*) of the earth. Newly made human tracks are discovered, and from beneath the floor of the cave the troupe hears, much to their surprise, a voice singing a song at once of lament and of thanksgiving.

Glad I dwell beneath the
        [mountains
Smiling in the darkest night;
Here of love are many fountains
Flowing daily free and bright.

And her holy waters lift me
With my thirsting soul on high,
Where, though still in life, I drift
        [me
Drunken, heaven's portal nigh.

Gern verweil' ich noch im Thale
Lächelnd in der tiefen Nacht,
Denn der Liebe volle Schaale
Wird mir täglich dargebracht.

Ihre heilgen Tropfen heben
Meine Seele hoch empor,
Und ich steh in diesem Leben
Trunken an des Himmels Thor.

Cradled there in adoration
Never dread can smite my soul;
Mother queen of every nation,
Make my heart all pure and
[whole.

Years by sorrow sped and craven,
Glorified this humble clay
And thereon a seal have graven,
Whence eternity alway.

Now the tale of years I've tarried
Seems the twinkling of an eye;
When one day from her[e] I'm
[carried,
I'll look backward gratefully.[39]

Eingewiegt in seelges Schauen
Ängstigt mein Gemüth kein
[Schmerz.
O! die Königinn der Frauen
Giebt mir ihr getreues Herz.

Bangverweinte Jahre haben
Diesen schlechten Thon verklärt,
Und ein Bild ihm eingegraben,
Das ihm Ewigkeit gewährt.

Jene lange Zahl von Tagen
Dünkt mir nur ein Augenblick;
Werd ich einst von hier getragen
Schau ich dankbar noch zurück.
[I, 254–55]

The song is a song of passage. Its singer is preparing himself to leave this "vale of tears" in which he now still dwells. What makes his waiting bearable is love's full cup, offered to him daily by the woman who is—like Isis, Mary, or Sophie—queen among women and in whose contemplation the singer's soul is cradled. At this point, in the second cave, the text of the song functions as a secret key. The singer, awaiting the moment when he will leave his present situation behind, describes with his song the similarly expectant attitude of his listeners, who are on their way farther down into the cave-world of the earth and thus metaphorically also into their own souls. In this middle cave, then, the history and life of the upper earth are left behind, and we are turned toward a different life, a life for which this second cave is the symbolic conduit.

Following the voice deeper into the earth, the miner takes the small group of explorers to the third cave. Here they are met by the majestic figure of a man whose meditations on a higher life have led him into the depth of the inner earth and into himself. On a sarcophagus that serves this noble hermit as a table, Heinrich discovers the supine, full-sized figures of a man and a woman carved into the stone. They are grasping a wreath of lilies and roses, and Heinrich recognizes the man as the hermit. This peculiar table is covered with many chronicles and books of history, and on its sides the following legend is inscribed:

ON THIS SPOT
FRIEDRICH AND MARIE VON HOHENZOLLERN
RETURNED TO THEIR FATHERLAND
[I, 257, 13–14]

While Heinrich is preoccupied with the sarcophagus that carries history within it as well as on top of it, the miner and the hermit are discussing the meaning of history, emphasizing the secret bond that links past and future. But this talk about history is peculiar. It does not have the ring of the usual historical observations people are apt to make. Here, in the third cave, this is appropriate, for time in its straightforward linear nature is bracketed here. The third cave is a symbolic stopping place on the way to the Golden Age in which all time is at once. Deep in the earth and yet also raised on a mountain, the third cave allows a representation of time only by juxtaposition, and thus presents a raised representation of time, an image in which time's nature resembles eternity. To plainly mark this the count of Hohenzollern declares that

> the church is the dwelling of history, the quiet courtyard its symbolic garden of flowers. [I,258,15–16]

And finally the conversation about history reaches the conclusion that fables and stories of poets have more sense for the meaning of history, that more "truth is told in a wonder tale than in the most scholarly chronicle." [I,259,23–24]

While the count of Hohenzollern now takes the others for a tour of the caves, Heinrich remains behind to read in the hermit's books. He is particularly taken by a manuscript that depicts with beautiful illustrations that are "incarnations of words" [I,264,4] everyone who is present in the cave: the count of Hohenzollern; the miner; the merchants; and most important, himself. As in a magic mirror, it shows Heinrich the history of his own previous lives. As he reads on in this book the depictions of himself appear to become nobler and greater. Unfortunately the ending of the book is missing. But the count of Hohenzollern, returning with the others, tells Heinrich that he brought the book back with him from Jerusalem and that it is a novel about the marvelous destinies of a poet. [I,265,22–25] Now bidding his visitors goodbye, he says:

> How long will it be when we shall see one another again and smile about today's conversations? A heavenly day will embrace us and we will be glad to have greeted each other in these valleys of trials and to have been inspired by the same opinions and the same presentiments. These are the angels who here guide us safely. If your eyes are turned steadfastly toward heaven, you shall not lose the way to your homeland. [I,266,4–10]

This journey into the ever deeper caves of the earth is a reversal, then, of Plato's ascent from the cave to the light of truth. For Novalis truth is found in the descent into the earth, into the self, and away from the light of reason to the imaginative accounts of fables and wonder tales. But not only does this account reverse Plato's imagery and with it the traditions of

Western philosophy, it also is a paraphrasing of the Kyffhäuser legend of Barbarossa, or rather Friedrich II. Novalis's story ties the inner-earth truth to the myth of historical hope of the German nation. The belief that some beloved and powerful national hero is biding his time in the cave of a mountain until he is needed again by his people, or that he is beneficial to his nation even while buried in the earth, is widely held. Oedipus, for example, is careful in his choice of burial site. He knows his grave will be a source of national strength, and desiring to deny this power to Thebes, he asks for the right to be buried near Athens. Similarly, King Arthur is said to wait inside a mountain for the time when England needs him again. In Sweden it is King Olaf who is thought to wait, and in Germany Friedrich II. In all these cases a sanctification of the national ground is involved; a national power is ascribed to the earth. For Novalis this power of the earth is intimately bound up with religion and love. For while the individual finds in the dead beloved the mediator to the spiritual realm, the nation finds the same spiritual hope—at least symbolically—in the person of the king, whose spiritual mediator is the queen.[40] The individual's destiny is thus, in some respects, only the specific instance of his people's destiny. The one cannot be thought in isolation from the other. Thus Isis, as the queen-goddess of the earth, becomes a nation's spiritual mediator to the homeland of the father, who is God. In this conception, then, Heidegger and Novalis are indeed very close. For both, a people's destiny is tied to the earth as mediating agency for the divine.

But Heidegger and Novalis differ in their views of how clearly the earth-force can reveal itself. For Heidegger, precisely because history is intertwined with a fateful but silent earth, our understanding of it must remain obscure. For Novalis, on the contrary, because the earth has a language of its own that can be learned, deciphered, and translated, the historical destiny of individuals, as well as nations, can be divined. But because the language of the earth is a language of imagery, an iconic language, it becomes essential for Novalis to develop imagistic and iconic powers in the language of man, as well. And since the earth as metaphor also stands for the irrational powers of love, life, and death through which man is most essentially tied to the qualitative nature of time, Novalis must find the iconic power of language in a genre of literature removed as far as possible from the rational forms of discourse and their successive character or bond to chronos-time. To this end the fairy tale or *Märchen* becomes an important poetic expression for Novalis, and dreams, as a highly imagistic product of the nonrational power of the human mind and soul, serve him as models in this undertaking.

CHAPTER EIGHT

Toward a Metaphysics of Märchen

THE MÄRCHEN AND OTHER NARRATIVE FORMS

Although Novalis's poetic theory of fairy tales is very much his own, it may nevertheless be instructive to consider first the significance of wonder tales in general. Whereas "fairy tale" or "wonder tale" are the usual English translations of the German term *Märchen*, they are both different enough in their connotations—as will become apparent further on in the discussion—that I will mainly use the German word Märchen to designate both the *Kunstmärchen* (literary or artistic tales) of Novalis and the wonder tales of folk tradition. Long before the narrative became a written art with different literary forms, oral folk tradition developed several distinct types of stories. Since the Märchen will figure prominently in this chapter, it may be helpful to distinguish it from these other related narrative forms.

At the greatest remove from the Märchen stands the *fable*, which like the Märchen deals with matters that transcend the possibilities of everyday experience: animals talk with human voices and even inanimate objects come to life, act, and become personified. But in contrast to the Märchen, the fable has a frankly heuristic utility. It is created for no other purpose than to illustrate a moral point. The audience or reader is fully aware of this deliberate limitation and so never takes a fable's characters to be anything more than schemata from which to gather the lesson they were invented to teach. Where the fable chooses for its characters beings from a realm below man (animals, plants, and inanimate objects), the myth is a tale that deals with the realm above man.

The *myth*'s significant figures are gods who, even if they appear in the shape of animals or men, never leave any doubt about their divine status. The realm the myth addresses lies beyond human powers, beyond the human world and human order of history. And so the events of the myth take place in a region beyond space and time and deal with the actions, passions, and sufferings of the gods. For this reason the myth is not only tied closely to religious cult and ritual, but also offers in its stories and characters archetypes of human experience and so serves man as a mirror in which to recognize himself. The prototype of the myth can be said to be the cosmogonic myth or myth of origin. In connection with cult and ritual it sets up a world that demands and expects, as Eliade has shown, ritual reenactment. In contrast to the relative playfulness of the Märchen, the myth means to be taken seriously. Yet the Märchen, in some sense, is a secularized myth, which not infrequently serves the myth as graveyard. Thus Propp, for instance, observes:

> It turns out that the forms which, for one reason or another, are defined as basic are linked with religious concepts of the remote past. We can formulate the following premise: if the same form occurs both in a religious monument and in a fairy tale, the religious form is primary and the fairy tale form is secondary. This is particularly true of archaic religions.[1]

As religious beliefs and practices die, then, they leave an echo or shadow of themselves in the popular tales of the day. And so Märchen preserve the central ideas of myths, although often in hardly recognizable form. For the Märchen always reshapes what it incorporates into itself in order to have it serve its own purposes and ends.

In contrast to the myth, the *legend* deals with the histories not of gods but of men, yet of men who rank higher than most mortals. It tells their stories and shows how they came to be elevated beyond ordinary human status as a reward for their extraordinary devotion and commitment to an idea or task. Starting with a definite and often religious perspective, the legend is hagiography and as such recounts feats of superhuman endurance and miracle-working powers of national heroes, saints, and other holy or highly revered personages. Beginning its history with a time before the hero achieved his more than mortal status, the legend, on the one hand, means to inspire us and to invite us to emulate its hero and his life, and, on the other hand, suggests that our own life is redeemed by its hero's extraordinary feats and faithfulness.

Similarly, the *saga* deals with what purport to be historically true events. But in contrast to the legend, its events frequently include supernatural occurrences. And while fairylike characters may be the center of its tale, teller and audience alike take the saga to be the report of an actual happening. Sagas deal with both the extraordinary in relation to man and the extraordinary in general, and so tell of ghosts and spirits, of giants and dwarfs, of wood sprites and water nymphs, of desert ogres and mountain demons, of plant fairies and animal spirits, of witches and magicians. In other words, the saga deals with beings that have something of the otherworldly about them. As a result, the saga circles around the secretive and numinous, and a good deal of its interest lies in the nature of these liminal figures that populate it. In the saga, the presence of the numinous or otherworldly is at once treated reverently and accepted as belonging to the historical world. It is considered to be a dimension of reality, but one that is more powerful and more essential than the passage of everyday life. Thus the saga commands reverence and respect for the liminal beings it treats of, while in the Märchen the same magical characters are quite simply taken for granted.

The *fairy tale* is a saga that has lost, with time, much of its numinous aura and has joined the Märchen in its matter-of-fact and profane mood and tone. Frequently, therefore, it is not distinguished from the Märchen and—as I have pointed out—indeed made to serve as the Märchen's English translation. Recently, however, the happier expression *wonder tale* has become the more acceptable translation for Märchen. And fairy tale now generally is used to designate the sort of story that, in contrast to the Märchen, deals exclusively with the lives of elves and fairies, and so is a good deal more narrow in what it encompasses.

In contrast, the *folktale,* although it closely resembles the Märchen and shares with the fairy tale its entirely matter-of-fact and profane tone, is drawn wider than either, and so includes in its sphere comic tales, farces, narrative riddles, jokes, and anecdotes of every variety. Any good and entertaining story that grows out of the oral traditions of a people and is told and told again ultimately is a folktale. And so the Märchen, too, is a folktale, but not all folktales are Märchen.

In many ways, the *Märchen* most closely resembles the saga. But where the saga focuses on the numinous nature of its figures, the Märchen is primarily interested in the simple plot it tells. "And then what happens?" is the form of its narrative mood. Nor does the Märchen pay any attention to the extraordinary status of the marvelous. People and gnomes or elves and giants and talking trees meet and deal with each other as if such interaction were the most normal occurrence in the world.

For in the Märchen the feeling for the sublime is missing. The threshold figures of the in-between realm, of that region between the divine and the worldly, appear and act on behalf of human beings or interact with them without this causing a moment's wonder or pause for either audience or tale-teller. We hear of miraculous and magical deeds and events so matter-of-factly that it never occurs to us to consider them exceptional or extraordinary. They are mentioned easily and are taken lightly and, in fact, for granted.

Whereas the saga contrasts the world of the profane with the world of the numinous, highlights their differences, and deliberately points to the distance between them, the Märchen denies that distance and difference in the very tone of the tale it tells. For in the Märchen no tension exists between the ordinary and the marvelous. They are perceived as a natural continuum along which easy passage is possible. Where the saga is bound emotionally, ethically, temporally, and spatially, the Märchen freely and playfully skips from station to station of the tale it tells and, therefore, in contrast to the saga's historical nature, has a poetical dimension that all but invites us to take it up as a proper literary form. In the words of Grimm: the Märchen "is far more poetical, while the saga is historical."

Thus the Märchen shares with the saga otherworldly motifs but is distinguished from the saga by the attitude it exhibits toward these motifs. Yet the Märchen's playful and light-hearted treatment of the magical and miraculous must not deceive us into believing that it, therefore, means only to entertain and amuse. On the contrary, in the very playfulness of the Märchen is contained its more serious and meaningful purpose. For it is in its matter-of-fact lightheartedness that the Märchen asserts the possibility for man, any man, to join the liminal characters of its plot in that threshold region, that borderland, where the ordinary and the extraordinary, the divine and the profane meet. It invites the audience to become part of that moment and place in which man can interact with and grasp the reality that lies hidden behind the world of everyday appearances. Märchen, thus, are tales with a "simple plot of mythic or moral import with archetypal figures, set in an unspecified time and place."[2]

Because of both these dimensions, their achetypal and timeless character, as well as their genesis from folk tradions, theorists of the Märchen have claimed that language comes to poetic flowering in them as if of its own accord. Andre Jolles, for instance, writes that in the Märchen occur "simple forms which, so to speak, without the efforts of a poet, take place within language itself and work themselves out by themselves." According to this view, Märchen are a form of natural poetry that makes and shapes itself. Kurt Ranke similarly suggests that "Märchen are basic powers of creativity which fashion the simple forms or archetypes of human expression."[3] But Ranke and Jolles can come to hold such views about the Märchen only because, as a tale, it gives us the feeling that its imagery is deeply significant, while at the same time it is possessed of an extraordinary iconic endurance.

In the Märchen the same iconic constancy is at work that impressed the Greeks in their myths and made them ascribe to the myths not only an archaic nature, but also, and most important, a deeper insight into truth. And as in the case of the myths, so also in the Märchen: their great durability is taken as proof of both the essential veracity of their meaning, and also as the reason for their wide dispersion. A tale may travel unchanged in its metaphysical core elements from Asia to Europe, from northern Africa to the Far East, and lose nothing of either its powers of expression or its basic content. Despite its transition from culture to culture and from age to age, the Märchen preserves its essential nature. Only the culture-specific social and historical details change, but for the meaning of the tale, these are no more than the particulars of the beauty of its wrappings.[4]

Thus while some aspects of the Märchen change in accordance with certain developments of the society that tells them, the Märchen's metaphysical core meaning is essentially undated and undatable and meant to be so. Its iconic constancy is the very sign of its basically nonhistoric nature. In addition, the "once upon a time" of its opening phrase, like its ending "and they lived happily ever after," is a denial of the effectiveness of time for the tale's most basic meaning. But whereas the opening "once upon a time" leads us into the Märchen's timeless presence, the closing "and they lived happily ever after" dismisses us from it and returns us to the normal flow of time and events. The standard beginning and ending, then, bracket the Märchen. Like a pair of gates they shut out the usual flux of time. It is for this reason that the Märchen in contrast to the saga, for instance, is never claimed to be part of a chronicle, even if it is embedded in, or framed by, observations that appear to be of historical significance. But the impossibility of locating the Märchen's central significance historically or of finding for it a meaning that lies outside its own boundaries— far from being a shortcoming—is the condition on which the Märchen's claim of greater worth and significance rests. The independence of its truth from any framework of historical reference upholds the eternity or archetypal validity of its meaning, while its tendency to endure and to maintain its iconic description is experienced as an assurance of its veracity. For it is an ancient and widespread belief that memory protects from corruption and oblivion only that which is true and eternally significant.

Because the claims for both the Märchen's autonomous validity and its well-remembered significance ultimately rest on the tale's iconic constancy, the question arises, from what is this constancy of its core meaning derived? Wherein lies its origin? Such interpreters of the Märchen as Marie-Louise von Franz or Bruno Bettelheim, for instance, have replied that its origin lies in the fundamental patterns of our psyche. While this may be perfectly true, this answer leaves us feeling decidedly dissatisfied, since the question is precisely how the Märchen comes to possess forms of such an archetypal psychological—or rather metaphysical, and also religious—nature in the first place.

TIME AND THE PHENOMENOLOGY OF MÄRCHEN

Clearly the Märchen's ability to survive the vagaries of time and place, of taste and cultural difference, does not rest with its having been recorded faithfully or preserved dutifully in written form. Quite on the contrary, one is rather reminded of Plato's dictum in the *Phaedrus* that the art of writing, far from enhancing memory, will tend to impoverish it. The folk tale, whose claim to enduring value is based at least in part on its being well remembered, is not enhanced by being recorded. But even if we do not share Plato's pessimistic view of records and record keeping and are, therefore, perfectly willing to see in its preservation in written form a partial explanation of the Märchen's constancy, the mere writing down of the tale cannot be the source of its endurance. For endurance here cannot refer simply to its survival, but must signify its continued meaning for us.

Märchen, like myths or sagas, are the result of a long oral tradition. Somewhere in this oral genesis, therefore, we must seek the roots of their peculiar staying power, on the one hand, and, on the other hand, of their apparent autonomy, which Schelling called their "ability to intrude themselves into existence." With this formulation Schelling suggests that the nature of their archetypal form is such that it is hard for us to imagine that any one person, no matter how gifted, could have been able alone to invent them.

Let us, then, for a moment, consider what distinguishes the oral tradition from the written one. We readily assume that the recording of an oral tradition serves to save that tradition for posterity.[5] And insofar as traditions have come to a point in their existence in which they no longer are alive or viable concerns of the people, this assumption is quite correct. Yet having a text can be the source of corruption as easily as it may be of constancy. Not only may careless recorders make mistakes, which subsequent copiers faithfully carry on, but when a tale's ancient icons or folk traditions are no longer readily understood by the recorder, a misinterpretation of their meaning can become canonized. Since such variations are the consequence of simple and arbitrary mistakes, they do not stand in a meaningful relation to the tale's significance and, therefore, in contrast to any deliberately chosen variation, constitute a corruption of the basic form or archetypal icon which is the tale's strength and reason of being. But if, on the contrary, one should like to make some changes in order to suit the tale more adequately to the situation in which it is being told, one will find that such deliberate and meaningful variations become harder to incorporate into the tradition, since all deviations from the "text" take on an air of inauthenticity in comparison to the written version's established wording.[6] In fact, having a written version often gives to the text such an inflexibility that all deviations and variations come to be perceived as assaults on its authority. The written version turns into the authoritative rendition, and all subsequent tellings of it are judged in comparison to it. Thus arises the scholarly and academic preoccupation with the origin of the written text, and the earlier or earliest version tends to be considered the most authentic, least corrupted and, therefore, also the truest. Truth, as a consequence, comes to be aligned more often than not with origin. And the true meaning of the tale is thought to reside in its beginning, even if the original recorders of the tale neither intended their recording to have this effect nor themselves viewed the written version of a tale in this light.

In contrast, the oral tradition easily and nearly unnoticeably substitutes the new for the old. Variations of a text are easily incorporated into it; they simply take the place of what they supersede and allow that which is superseded to drift out of memory, out of the remembered tradition, out of the tale to be told. The new version becomes the authoritative tale. It *is* the tale. There is no other. Thus the period in which there is as yet no written version serves as the spawning ground of the tale. In the countless tellings of it, and in the audience's reactions to it— which prompt the singer to adjust and fiddle with the tale to suit it better to his listeners, to make it more effective, to ensure for it an enthusiastic reception—the tale emerges. It is this period that tests and retests the content and the imagery of the tale for its effectiveness. Here the simple form, which Schelling thought no one person could be author of, is slowly whittled from the oral history of the tale. And so Schelling is right: the simple form and archetypal icon that is the basis of the tale's constancy and durability is not the result of any one person's inventive genius. Rather it is the result of centuries of cooperation between audience and singer, between the teller of the tale and his listeners.[7] But the tale, or rather its simple impressive and meaningful form, did not thus "intrude itself into existence by itself." Instead, it came to be by the agency of countless generations who carried the tale within their memories and hearts, let it ripen there, and gave it in each telling a more polished, terser shape. Thus the oral tradition builds itself out of the interdependence of audience and performer or bard. The tale thrives as a new turn finds favor with the audience and, therefore, is incorporated into subsequent renditions. Here, then, variation and deviation do not constitute corruption or inauthenticity, but the evolution of the tale into its most effective form—provided that the teller knows his craft, and both teller and audience belong to an oral tradition that is still fully viable. For an oral tradition that has lost its vitality will no longer understand its own tales or will misunderstand elements of them and tell weaker versions of its own stories. But when an oral tradition is hale and well and its teller possessed of some talent, then truth and meaning reside not in the beginning or the origin, but are end products and the outcome of centuries of cooperative labor.

The difference between the oral and written tradition, therefore, is that the former is teleological while the latter is not. It is the oral tradition that orients itself at least toward the immediate future; its truth and meaning reside in the present and are meant to endure in the future. The written tradition looks to the past. Truth resides for the one in what has been and for the other in what is and shall be. As a consequence, a Märchen tradition that no longer lives in the people who do the telling, but lives only in the books that record and preserve the Märchen, in many ways resembles our relation to the works of art of the past in general, when these works are removed from the living matrix of our life and from their own surrounding. The Gothic church in which the congregation each Sunday holds its services, the Baroque manger in which the farmer each morning milks his cows, are living aspects of the past in the present. But the Greek sculpture, Romanesque mural, or even Art Nouveau artifact that we admire in a museum are no longer living elements of our life. We take time out to visit them. Our interest in them is no longer existential; it is now scholarly, historical, or aesthetic.

The Märchen, not living in the nursery between parent or grand-parent and child, or in a gray winter evening between the teller of tales and his gathered audience by the fireplace, is a dead tale, an artifact of the past that is being kept safe in a book from the ravages and corruptions of time. We can still appreciate its beauty and its interest, as we appreciate the beauty and interest of art objects of the past that we do not live with or use in our daily rounds of activities. Opening a book of Märchen, there-fore, resembles a visit to the museum. There is still much pleasure to be found here, but as time passes, the meaning residing in the tale de-creases, while its historical or anthropological interest increases. It be-comes a subject for study and ceases to be an object of contemplation. But what, then, is the unique gift of the Märchen when it is a living presence in our lives?

It is the relation to the marvelous in the Märchen that sets it apart from any other story dealing with human actions. Take, for example, the tale of *Cinderella*.[8] Reduced to its simplest point, it appears to illustrate a moral rule: namely, that suffering endured with forbearance eventually is re-warded. Yet reduced in this fashion, the point is not only trite, but false. Not all suffering is eventually rewarded, and not all rewards are preceded by suffering. Surely, then, if that were all the story had to give us, it would not have endured. It would not have traveled the long route from China, where it most likely originated as a tale concerned with the bene-fits of footbinding: the smaller the foot, the greater the sexual and societal reward, so that the pain accompanying the tight bandaging of the feet was well worth suffering! When the original tale is so reduced, it states a simple and commonsensical historical fact. But if that were all the tale contained, it would not have successfully undergone its metamorphosis: a concern with the rewards following upon the pains of footbinding could not have turned into a concern with the rewards following upon the patient endurance of the arbitrary injustices of a stepmother who ban-ishes an orphaned girl to the kitchen to perform difficult—no, impossi-ble—tasks. What a ludicrous transformation is involved in the moment of reward taking place at a ball! The Chinese girl whose feet were bound so they would grow to no more than two or three inches could not properly walk, let alone dance; at best, she could barely hobble around the house. As Cinderella, she can dance, and dance with a prince at the ball! The story makes this shift easily and incorporates the dance into its plot. For, ultimately, it is unimportant whether the tale is about footbinding or about an orphan's difficult tasks. The ball, the slipper, indeed, even the suffering and final reward for her endurance, are merely superficial embellishments. For all Märchen have finally one, and only one, basic and essential theme: they depict man as having a casual relation to the extraordinary and the miraculous. What matters in the story of Cinderella is not *that* her suffering ends and is rewarded, but *how* it is brought about that she becomes the prince's bride. In the different versions different magical agencies are at work. In some it is a fairy-godmother who intervenes,[9] in others the spirit of the tree growing on the grave of Cinderella's mother, or a bird nesting in it. But always it is inexorable, inexplicable, unpredictable interference with natural events that drives the tale to its conclusion. Nor is this inexplicable intervention a deserved answer to prayer or the result of a bargain. It is always a quite accidental occurrence, or rather a gift of chance. And that, I contend, is the point of the Märchen: it matter-of-factly assumes and then proceeds to illustrate the sudden and inexplicable intervention of chance in the orderly affairs of man and nature.

The Märchen, or wonder tale, is that product of man's creative ability in which our relation to chance and our insight into its qualitative nature are presented in one imaginative tableau. The Märchen, whatever else it is, is an icon of the qualitative nature of time and its effect on man.[10] Chronos-time is banished from the essential meaning of the tale, underscoring that we are primarily dealing not with time's historical, successively ordering characteristics, that is, its quantitative aspects, but with its qualitative and fateful functions. The archetypal character of this icon of the quality of time is due to its being a symbol of man's relation to fate. The liminal beings who bring about the sudden changes of fate, and with whom man interacts so casually, are the promise of the hope that the qualitative nature of time need not be entirely beyond man's grasp. As magical beings of the threshold, the characters who act on behalf of the tale's hero are the adequate and appropriate symbol of the divine telos breaking into the everyday. If we also remember that Märchen traditionally were told at the day's end, when the strong light of the sun begins to withdraw from the world and night has not yet settled in, and dusk hangs over the earth, then we should feel how very strong the power of the icon must have been. For dusk, too, is liminal; it is the threshold time when nymphs, dwarfs, and elves awaken and can be glimpsed, or caught, or talked to. At the moment when day changes into night, the universe offers itself as a meaningful image of the shift or change that is at the heart of fate and chance. The power of the Märchen told at dusk is increased by the symbolic force of the cosmic icon, and man listening to the tale in a contemplative mood will feel himself to be part of what its imagery asserts.

The Märchen's relation to time is thus twofold: on the one hand, it is itself subject to a forthright linear development or evolution in which the tale's ultimate truth is unfolded in ever more succinct forms by a dialectic of successive tellings and listenings and retellings. On the other hand, the story, while on one level advancing its own plot by means of the passing of time, on another level denies the meaningfulness and effectiveness of just such a linear passage of time; it asserts time's qualitative nature to be its most important and ultimately meaningful aspect for man. As a result, a tension arises in the Märchen's relation to time. Alternating between asserting and denying the essential characteristics of both the qualitative and quantitative aspects of time, the Märchen, even in this contradictory attitude toward the nature of time, mirrors and resembles man's tension-laden and contradictory relation to his own temporality. For we, too, grow and age and change in our form and have the incontrovertible proof of it every morning in our mirrors. Yet we, as the content of our own feelings and thoughts, as our own inner continuous self, are not aware of time's passage, nor does it affect our essential self-experience even if empirical observations prompt us to acknowledge its reality. To ourselves, to our inner feeling of self, we remain unchanged by time's passage and do not feel ourselves limited by its unidirectional flux. What is past can, and often does, become present as memory or as emotional reaction, and we just as easily project ourselves forward into times that have not yet arrived as we travel backward and feel ourselves to be present in the past. What matters to us here is time's qualitative nature. It impresses us with its unpredictability when we encounter it as a particular mood of the times, as our destiny, or as chance event. Our inner consciousness of self remains outside any temporal measures; here we are ageless and eternal and entirely free of the relentless hurrying of time. The Märchen's temporal duality is an icon of our own relation to time. At once subject to the passage of time and to the changes wrought by the successive nature of time, but also impervious to them, and sensitive only to the qualitative structures or shifts and turns of time, both we and the Märchen are an ongoing exhibition and representation of the tension residing within the nature of time itself.

In addition, insofar as the Märchen is an icon of chance and of its sudden and inexorable shifts and changes, that is, of misleading appearances and unpredictable transformations, it is also a representation of the spirit of the trickster. In its twofold relation to time the Märchen hovers between the uncertainties and qualitative moods of time, on the one hand, and time's quantitative measures, on the other hand. Its never quite belonging to either, while being able to forgo neither, enhances the

Märchen's association with the trickster and the tricksterish characteristics of life. For this reason the trickster, whose origin can be traced to several ancient mythological traditions, has been taken over by the Märchen without any significant changes and is now one of the most frequently appearing characters in the repertory of Märchen personages. Insofar as the trickster has become one of the Märchen's most active and popular figures, the icon of chance in the Märchen often takes on the shape of the fool or Narr. This connection to the tricksterish element ties the Märchen to chance and fate, to the playful and mischievous dimension of man's life. For some of the Romantics and certainly for Novalis, this dimension, therefore, also binds the Märchen to the tricksterish nature of language. Whether this association, which in the Romantic tradition became an explicit and conscious concern, has always been an element in the Märchen's meaning and reception, even if only an unconscious one, can at this point no longer be affirmed or denied with any certainty. But, because Märchen frequently use and incorporate the playful and tricksterish linguistic game of the riddle, I would like to suggest that there is a good possibility, at least, that this is so. Little wonder, then, that the Märchen held particular fascination for Novalis.

THE ROMANTIC NOVEL AND THE MÄRCHEN

Novalis's preoccupation with, and high esteem for, the literary genre of the Märchen is not only well documented but has for many years been a central focus of much of the interpretation of his work. Taking the Märchen to be primarily of importance for understanding Novalis's poetic productions and theories or his Romantic fascination with magic, scholars have done little to understand its metaphysical significance. But even when Novalis's interest in Märchen has been considered from a philosophical point of view, only those tales that Novalis himself called Märchen have usually been included in the analysis; these are the "Rosenblüthe und Hyacinth" and the "Klingsohr" tales. The larger stories in which these tales appear Novalis called novels. As far as I know, this categorization has not been challenged, although frequently the "Arion" and "Atlantis" tales in *Heinrich von Ofterdingen* are also considered Märchen and are included in accounts dealings with Novali's Märchen.

Obviously, Novalis's poetic stories are not folktales. They do not arise out of an oral tradition, but are the literary and artistic creations of one man. They are called Märchen because they attempt to catch that tone, mood, and iconic worth that is the mark of the true folktale. The tendency on the part of the Romantics to think of the folktale as having a collective author allowed them to appreciate fully the communal effort that was involved in the tales' genesis; unfortunately, it also often obscured for them the difference between Märchen that were literary creations and Märchen that were the product of folk traditions. In order to distinguish the poetic work from the folk tale, therefore, the convention arose of calling the latter a *Volksmärchen* and the former a *Kunstmärchen*, that is, an artistic or literary wonder tale. Instead of being the product of a collective oral-poetic creativity over an extended period of time, the Kunstmärchen is the imaginative creation of one writer. But calling poetic tales "Kunstmärchen" is not in any way meant to indicate a higher artistic value for them. Rather, it is meant simply to differentiate the poetic invention from the folk tradition. Not surprisingly, though, for Novalis the poetic tale or artistic Märchen is a raised form of the folktale. Just as he understands the translation of literary works to constitute a raising of their poetical worth to a higher power, so he also believes that the reworking of the icons of proper folktales into Kunstmärchen is an *Erhebung* of their value to true poetic potency. Therefore, when Novalis makes a note to himself that he "should write a Märchen, "he does not plan to transcribe or record traditional folklore but to invent a poetic wonder tale, a Kunstmärchen.[11] The question is, first, what Novalis considered the nature of Märchen to be; second, whether the tales Novalis thought of as his Märchen really are Märchen; and third, whether they are his only literary products that are to be understood as Märchen.

In her article "Novel, Tale, Romance," Mary McCarthy remarks on how lacking the German literary tradition is in novels and how richly it is blessed with tales.

> If the tale is native to northern countries—I think not only of the German-language Romantics sprung from *Des Knaben Wunderhorn* but of the Danish Isak Dinesen in our own day and her predecessor J. P. Jacobsen, originally a botanist—the novel, on the contrary, is a foreigner. It is remarkable how few German examples there were in the nineteenth century—the great period of the novel elsewhere. . . . Even today German writers of fiction persist in the traditions of the tale and the romance. . . . The German tale, unlike those of other languages, has found it hard to separate from the fairy story, especially the *Märchen*.[12]

Whether one considers McCarthy's judgment to contain some truth or not depends in part on how one defines the novel. No other literary genre has consistently defied definition and been so recalcitrant in allowing itself to be delimited. In addition to having successfully eluded agreement about its scope, that which in English is called a novel is in German a *Roman*, and so in the genesis of the respective terms a further reason for disagreement is concealed. Anthony Burgess's etymological approach might, therefore, be helpful:

> To dig out the Greek *tragos*, meaning "he-goat," from the word "tragedy" will not enable us to use that term with any greater accuracy. But with "novel" things are a little different. We use the word as an adjective meaning "new; recently introduced," and, though novels have been in existence for a long time now, there is, in comparison with the traditional forms of literature, still a sort of upstart quality about them. There are people who despite the high example set by Cervantes, and Flaubert and Henry James, insist on regarding the novelist as the lowest kind of literary practitioner: the novelist is more concerned with entertainment than with poetic or epic uplift; he does not ennoble the world but presents it as it is, with all its meanness, dirt and sexuality. . . . In other words, he does not stand in robed dignity like Homer or Sophocles, speaking fire; he identifies himself with the men and women of ordinary homes, streets, pubs, schools, prisons, using all kinds of language, flinching at no situation. Moreover the novelist admits that he wants to give pleasure, while the poets and epic dramatists talk more about spiritual exaltation. Where the novel is "new," it is "new" in the sense that it seems to strike at certain traditional values—reticence, modesty, decency, dignity.[13]

According to Burgess, then, the novelist does not write of what is true ideally, but of what is apparently real, and if it is not a factual historical account than it has, at least, the air of such an account—it could be real and is to be taken by us as if it were real.

The etymological root of the German *Roman*, however, does not focus on the novelty of the tale told but on the language the tale is told in. The term "Roman" came into use in twelfth century France, where it referred to any text written in the language of the people—the *lingua romana*, in contrast to scholarly texts, which were written in the *lingua latina*.[14] By the end of the thirteenth century only a work of prose was called a "Roman," and from the seventeenth century on only a prose work of a fictional nature and with a grand design or format was considered a "Roman" and thus was distinguished from the equally broadly conceived epic, out of which, in fact, it had developed. In accordance with his evolutionary philosophy, Novalis perceives this development as a raising:

┃The Poem of the savages is an account without beginning, middle and end—the pleasure it gives them is merely pathological—simple occupation, merely dynamic animation of the representational function.
The epic poem is the ennobled primitive poem. In its essentials entirely the same.
The novel stands already much higher—the epic poem endures, the novel continues to grow—progression in the former is arithmetical, in the novel geometrical.┃ [II,534,#34]

It is interesting that Novalis, who considered speaking in prose a very much lower activity than singing in verse, should here evaluate the prose novel to rank higher than the epic, which was almost always written in verse. Possibly he was prompted to do so because the novel is obviously a work of the imagination and thus a product of man's free creative ability, whereas the epic claims to chronicle real, and not fictional, events. Furthermore, while the archetypal hero of the epic pursued his well-established goals by unfolding a wide variety of well-determined events against a background of a public and coherent social, temporal, and spatial world order, the protagonist of the Roman lives in a far more private world. As Novalis observes:

The more personal, the more local, the more temporal, the more specific a poem is, the closer it is to the center of poetry. A poem must be entirely *inexhaustible,* like a human being and a good proverb.
What was the parallelism of oriental poetry?
What is said above of the poem, also applies to the novel.
[III,664,27–31,#603]

As a result of this greater personal specificity and therefore greater possibility of inwardness, the hero of a novel, though, is caught in the private dilemma and agony of free choice and has to act against the background of a fluid and not publicly determined world structure. The development of his character is thus a matter not only of highly individual growth, but is fraught with the tensions, insecurities, and dangers that accompany the recognition of the discrepancy between our private, ideal hopes and goals, our realistic possibilities, and our actual accomplishments in the world.

Initially the designation "Roman," then, grew from primarily formal distinctions; in contrast, the term "novel" indicated the sort of content a tale presented. But, as even this short description makes plain, "Roman" soon enough was used to distinguish kinds of content, as well, and "novel" was used to acknowledge formal differentiations, also. And yet, some of the initial focus of either term still hovers about the discussions concerning their respective theoretical definitions.

In order to make the term "Roman" a more useful tool for the theorist of literature, Wolfgang Kayser, building on already existing traditions, suggests we ought to differentiate between three distinct and over-arching types: first, the *Geschehnisroman* (or novel of events) in which the structure of the text is primarily determined by the dynamics of the plot, by what happens next to the hero—the adventure tale, the detective mystery, and the love story are examples of this type. Second, Kayser distinguishes the *Figurenroman* (or character novel) in which the formal structure of the work is determined not by outer events but by inner occurrences, by the psychological and spiritual changes, growth, and development of the main protagonist—the *Bildungsroman* (or novel of education and tutelage), for instance, belongs as a subspecies to this group, and so do most autobiographies. Kayser proposes the category of the *Raumroman* (or novel of place) in which "the myriad aspects" of the world are presented in a "kaleidoscopic mosaic" of places, people, and events that form a loose aggregate. The structure of this type of Roman is most problematic since it has no inner principle of completion driving it towards its conclusion. Precisely because it is an open-ended representation of an arbitrary slice of the world—and an entirely personal and individualistically experienced slice at that—the Raumroman's formal structure remains similarly incomplete. In Kayser's typology, then, it is mainly content that determines structure, and as a result, the distinction between novel and Roman loses most of its significance, which is entirely acceptable for the modern work of literature.

In fact, already the Romantic novel, although it is to be differentiated from the modern novel in other ways, cannot meaningfully distinguish between the novel and the Roman, and that despite the fact that the term "Romantic" refers back to that which was written in the *lingua romana*. Ignoring the differences between the romance and the Roman—"The Roman is to be understood entirely as a romance," [III,687,#681] says Novalis—Roman-ticism with its very name indicates its admiration for what it thinks of as the Roman of the Middle Ages: the romance of knightly exploits, honor, and chivalric love. The Romantics' definition of the novel, though, is troublesome not because of its disregard for the distinction between the novel and the romance, but because it is conceived so broadly, and has such a wide scope that it practically loses all value as a categorizing tool. Novalis, for instance, suggestively asks whether the novel, from the point of view of form, should not be all inclusive:

> ROMANTIK. Should the novel not contain every species of style in a series that is variously bound by a common spirit? [III,271,#169]

But not only the form, the novel's content should also be similarly limitless, according to Novalis:

> The novel deals with life—depicts *life*. It would be a mime only in respect of the poet. It frequently contains events of a masquerade—a masked event among masked people. Remove the masks—there are well-known events—well-known people. The novel, as such, contains no determined result—it is not image and fact of one *sentence* (*eines Satzes*). It is a graphic execution—a realization of an idea. But an idea cannot be contained in a sentence (*Satz*). An idea is *an infinite series* of sentences (*von Sätzen*)—an *irrational quantity—not positable* (*unsetzbar*) (musical)—incommensurable.[15] (Should all irrationality be relative?)
> The law of its progression, though, can be formulated—and in accordance with it a novel is to be criticized. [II,570,#212]

Despite its impracticability, the Romantics' broad definition of the novel is of considerable interest. On the one hand, it shows the problem Romanticism has with all limitations and boundaries and, on the other hand, it makes apparent the effect this problem has on keeping life and art distinct. Several of the Novalis fragments I have cited here have already pointed to this difficulty. It comes to our attention once more when Novalis, speaking of chance events in *life*, continues the thought without so much as a moment's hesitation by speaking of *literature:*

> All chance events of our lives are materials from which we can fashion what we will. He who has much spirit makes much of his life—For him who is altogether spiritual, every acquaintance, every occurrence would be—the first member of an infinite series—beginning of an infinite novel. [II,436,31–438,3,#66]

In analogy to thinking of the physical world as the book of nature, the assimilation of literary art to life becomes explicitly part of the Romantic understanding of both life and the poetic work:

> Nothing is more romantic, than what is usually called world and fate—We live in a colossal (in *what is great* and *small*) novel. Observation of the events around us. Romantic orientation, judgment and treatment of a human life. [III,434,#853]

The thought, then, is elaborated and reversed: not only do we live in a novel—and a colossal one at that—but life is a text, and the text a life. As a result the very definition of the Romantic novel now turns on the idea of the equivalence of life and book:

> A novel is a *life* as book.
> Every life has a motto—a title—a publisher—a preface—introduction—text—*notes*—etc. or can have it. [II,599,#341]

Where the Renaissance thought of all the world as a stage, the Romantics see life as a book, as a novel, and so move from a metaphor of an acted out life to one of reading and writing a life. In this manner they remove themselves from the outer world to the inner life of the mind, of the spirit, and of the soul. It is not surprising, therefore, that Novalis wants to write but *one* such book all his life long. In a letter written to Caroline Schlegel on February 27, 1799, he comments on Friedrich Schlegel's novel *Lucinde*, which Caroline had just sent him, by pointing out how palpably he felt the presence of the inner self in Schlegel's representation of it:

> Possibly there exist only few more individualistic books. One sees before oneself clearly and wonderfully the drive of his [Schlegel's] inner being (*Seines Innern*), like the play of the chemical forces in a solution in a glass of sugar. A thousand manifold dark-light representations stream toward us and we lose ourselves in a dizziness that makes of the thinking human being a mere drive—a natural force—and involves us in the lustful existence of instinct. [IV,279,20–26]

After a few critical comments about some too youthful or immature aspects of Schlegel's novel and a number of rather lively speculations about the reactions critics were likely to have, Novalis continues:

> Above all the idealization of vegetation interested me. The highest love effected the two of us remarkably differently. With me everything was composed in the style of a church—or in the style of a Doric temple. With him [Schlegel] everything is Corinthian. Now it is bourgeois architecture with me. I am so close to the noon hour that the shadows have the size of the objects—and thus the formations of my fantasy fairly correspond to the real world.
> That much I see: our first novels will be worlds apart. Mine will probably be completed this summer in Toeplitz or Carlsbad. That is, when I say completed—I mean the first volume—for I feel like giving my whole life to One novel—which by itself shall constitute a whole library—perhaps contain years of education (*Lehrjahre*) for a *nation*. The phrase *years of education* is wrong—it expresses a definite *where-to*.

Yet with me it shall mean nothing but years of *transition* from the infinite to the finite. I hope thus to satisfy my historical and my philosophical yearning at the same time. [IV,281,1–18]

It is not easy to see what may have prompted Novalis to think of *Heinrich von Ofterdingen* either as a work of a bourgeois character or as corresponding to the real world. Very little about it seems to fit any such mundane description—which is not surprising with a work that means to trace the apotheosis of a poet. But if we take Novalis at his word and accept the appelation "novel" for *Heinrich von Ofterdingen*, then Wolfgang Kayser's category of the Raumroman comes closest to doing the work justice. For *Heinrich von Ofterdingen* presents indeed a "kaleidoscopic mosaic" of places, events, and people and has just that open enededness about it that makes its fragmentary nature appear to be less the result of Novalis's early death than of the novel's own structure and of its author's desire to give his life over to writing only one novel, which by itself alone is to constitute a whole library, is to be an infinite novel. Clearly, such an undertaking, while it may be ended, cannot be completed. Where the novel is conceived as such an infinite undertaking, a new approach must be found to its various parts. For if these as well were to be infinite, not only could the novel not be completed, it could not even be begun. And so Novalis gives the following prescription for the Romantic novelist:

The written form of the novel must not be a *continuum*—it must be a structure that in each of its periods is well articulated. Each small piece must be something separate—delimited—a proper whole. [III,562,#45]

Limit, boundary, and well-articulated wholeness then are acceptable, even to the Romantics, provided that they are the subordinate parts of an infinite larger continuum. Plainly this is so because in this, too, the novel is to resemble the physical world. Of course Novalis is right. If the novel is to be not a whole in the sense of a completed entity but an infinite aggregate of a book that by itself is a whole library, then it must be structured in just the way he suggests. And this, indeed, is how *Heinrich von Ofterdingen* is structured, which is why the description of a Raumroman appears to suit it better than that of a Bildungsroman—although the latter is what Novalis considered it to be.

But ultimately *Heinrich von Ofterdingen* does not really fit even the very broadest of Kayser's descriptions of the Roman. For whatever its problems of closure, and no matter how personally and privately experienced "a slice of world" the Raumroman presents, it still deals with *this* world.

Yet neither *Heinrich von Ofterdingen* nor, in fact, *Die Lehrlinge zu Sais* deal with what can be called the world. On the contrary, both deliberately go beyond this world, burst the confines of its prosaic nature and deal with what Anthony Burgess claims the novel and novelist do not deal with, namely, "spiritual exaltation" and "poetic uplift." Novalis not only had an all inclusive view of the novel but he also thought it to be magical, that is, a Märchen-like product of the imagination:

> ROMANTIK. All novels in which true love occurs are *Märchen—magical occurrences,*" [III,255,#80]

Yet in what novel does "true love" not occur? And so now we may once more take up Mary McCarthy's assertion that "the German tale has found it hard to separate from the fairy story, especially the Märchen." Without accepting the sweeping manner of her statement—for surely both the nineteenth and the twentieth centuries have produced a good number of proper novels and novelists, even in Germany—Theodor Fontane's *Effi Briest*, Thomas Mann's *Buddenbrooks*, and Alfred Döblin's *Berlin Alexanderplatz* are all examples of works that separate without difficulty from the Märchen—we can still see some justice in her remarks if we think of such earlier prose literature as *Heinrich von Ofterdingen* or *Die Lehlinge zu Sais*, neither of which separates from it at all, nor do I think that they ought to, for in my estimation they are, despite their resemblance to novels in some respects, not novels at all but a species of Kunstmärchen.

Both works lack many of the most basic characteristics indispensable to the nature of the novel yet have what is required to make of them the sort of tale called a Kunstmärchen. What has confused interpreters and reviewers alike, particularly in the case of *Heinrich von Ofterdingen*, is on the one hand its length and on the other hand its having been conceived explicitly as a Bildungsroman, or novel of tutelage, modeled after Goethe's *Wilhelm Meisters Lehrjahre*. But while Novalis wrote this tale in response to Goethe's *Meister*, he also meant to overcome the prosaic nature of the latter and have his *Heinrich von Ofterdingen* be a *Wilhelm Meister* raised to a higher poetic plane. As a result of his goal to poeticize it, to romanticize it, that is, to make it a magical work, Novalis excluded from *Heinrich von Ofterdingen* what is the most commonly agreed upon characteristic of the novel: its aim to present us with credible events and people. The novel achieves an air of reality not only because it sets its characters in recognizable social situations, geographical locations, and historical circumstances, but most importantly, because it deals with particular evolving life histories. Even if the novel is a Raumroman it must still present and evoke some genuine interest in the psychological reality of its protagonist and must, therefore, chronicle some emotional and mental growth or change which can be gathered most strikingly from the changing relationships the hero—or heroine—has with others. Yet Heinrich has little, if any, such psychological dimension. He in fact rather reminds us of the epic's archetypal hero. Thus where the novel presents us with an alternate world which, though it is fictitious, we are meant to recognize, and in fact accept as if it were both real and true, Novalis's *Ofterdingen* offers not an alternate world but a transcendent one. Mary McCarthy's definition of the novel—just like Anthony Burgess's and Wolgang Kayser's—stresses that the novel must present us with a this-worldly and apparent reality. Even though such a definition excludes some of the more experimental fictional works of the twentieth century that we tend to classify as novels and that we would be hard-pressed to categorize otherwise (for example the writings of Alain Robbe-Grillet or James Joyce), it is an admirably straightforward statement of what we most often and in general mean by the term novel.

> The novel, after all, is the literary form dedicated to the representation of our common world, i.e., not merely the common ordinary world but the world we have in common. The faculty for apprehending it— this world conterminous with each of our separate life experiences and independent sensibilities, this world that lies between us—is, of course, common sense, the faculty we need to serve on juries, assess job offers, judge the character of strangers. . . . Common sense, also known as the reality principle, rules the novel, commanding the reader to recognize only events and personalities that do not defy it. . . . Common sense tells you the way things *are*, rather than the way your covetous ego or prehensile will would like them to be. [*NTR*, 54]

But Novalis's *Heinrich von Ofterdingen*, whatever else it does, neither gives us a deepening insight into its hero's growing and changing character, nor tells us much about the way things are. On the contrary, it describes "what our covetous ego" and "prehensile will would like them to be," and what we hope and even pray they will eventually turn out to be. Therefore, the works Novalis spoke of as his novels, and that by and large were accepted as such, are in fact Kunstmärchen; the tales told in their framework and which Novalis considered his Märchen more nearly resemble symbolic allegories and are thus a species of verbal emblems.

The hope Novalis expresses in these Kunstmärchen, tales, parables, and allegories is that the second Golden Age, in which love triumphs and the poet is not only the true priest of the divinity, but is himself of divine status, will become the reality of existence. *Heinrich von Ofterdingen*, as the account of the poet's apotheosis, deliberately turns its back on reality and on the common sense with which we live in reality. Instead, it chronicles a journey inward to that uncommon private world each of us has within himself: the soul. Since however, for Novalis, the universal spirit dwells at the depth of each individual soul, this journey inward leads to a higher commonality for which a higher common sense is required. For the aspiring poet Heinrich, this journey becomes an affirmation of the religious role and status of art in general and of poetry in particular. All Märchen, and specifically the Kunstmärchen *Heinrich von Ofterdingen*, are then the gospel of this belief and hope. How closely Märchen and the Bible resemble each other for Novalis can be seen in a fragment from his last years:

> The resemblance of our sacred history to *Märchen* is most peculiar—To begin with an enchantment—then the miraculous atonement—etc. The fulfillment of the conditions of the enchantment—Insanity and enchantment are very similar. The magician is an artist of insanity. [III,639,#508]

Novalis seems to suggest, then, a parallel between the enchantment in wonder tales and the Fall, between the miraculous atonement and the incarnation of Christ, and between the fulfillment of the conditions of the enchantment and the Second Coming or final Paradise. The association of the miraculous atonement with the incarnation is not as farfetched in German as it is in English, for the word *Versöhnung* (atonement) seems to contain the word *Sohn* (son) while the prefix *ver-* appears to belong to that series of its meanings that indicates "taking the place of" such as in *vertreten* (substitute) or *Verweser* (administrator). In folk etymology Versöhnung can therefore be understood to mean "taking the place of the son" or "becoming the son," a phrase that metaphorically asserts forgiveness or resolution of the evil enchantment.[16] In *Heinrich von Ofterdingen* the intertwining of the religious with the magical enchantment of Märchen centers on the Märchen's relation to time and on the magical redemption from the Fall into time that occurs with the poet's transcendence of time.

THE NATURE OF DREAMS AND THEIR RELATION TO MÄRCHEN

Novalis constructs the tale of *Heinrich von Ofterdingen* in such a manner that the shape of the future is divined, then telescoped and projected backward into the past; at the same time this process is reversed when Heinrich finds in the cave of the Graf von Hohenzollern a picture book of bygone days that contains images of times that are yet to come. Novalis on the one hand brackets the ordinary flux of time in *Heinrich von Ofterdingen*, just as Märchen do, and on the other hand raises such bracketing to a thematic concern. Yet Novalis's poetic creation, instead of beginning with the standard "once upon a time," opens with Heinrich's long, intricate, and prophetic dream, which alerts us to suspend our usual temporal perception and assumptions and to take the story as belonging to the realm of magical reality. A dream can serve as substitute opening for Novalis's literary Märchen because in dreams, as in Märchen, the uncanny and marvelous are tied to a disregard for the orderly passage of successive moments. As Novalis points out, the easy interchangeability of past and future that holds sway in dreams is due to the dream's being structured according to the rules of association:

> Dreams are often meaningful and prophetic because they are natural effects of the soul—and are *thus* based on the order of association. They are meaningful like poetry—but for that reason also irregularly meaningful—*absolutely free.* [III,452,#959]

Because, as we have seen, the laws of association are not bound by the temporal order of cause and effect, but allow a reversal of that order, dreams permit us to move with absolute freedom through the temporal flux. As a result, it is the quality of time, rather than its unidirectional flow or quantitative and quantifiable aspect, that matters in both the Märchen and the dream.

Novalis's most sustained discussion of dreams occurs in *Heinrich von Ofterdingen*, when Heinrich and his father hold widely disparate positions. It would appear, though, that in the voice of the young Heinrich we hear both the Romantics' and Novalis's own view on the nature and meaning of dreams, for several fragments in the *Allgemeine Brouillon* show Novalis to take a similar approach to this subject. In contrast, Heinrich's father speaks for the Enlightenment's rational distrust of all products of the imagination, and certainly of dreams. When he reprimands his son for oversleeping because of an extraordinary, strangely beautiful, and prophetic dream of a blue flower, his skeptical attitude toward dreams is plainly expressed:

> Dreams are spindrift, whatever your learned men may think of them; and you will do well to turn your mind away from such useless and harmful reflection. The times are past when divine apparitions ap-

peared in dreams, and we cannot and will not fathom the state of mind of those chosen men the Bible speaks of. The nature of dreams as well as of the world of man must have been different in those days. [I, 198, 12–19][17]

By confining the possibility of a positive nature of dreams to the past, Heinrich's father easily escapes the need of having to take them seriously and of having to give an explanation for our capacity to be impressed by them. The reference to the Bible's different world and time notwithstanding, a book of the Apocrypha actually exhorts against trusting dreams in a fashion that rather resembles the views of Heinrich's father:

The hopes of man void of understanding are vain and false: and dreams lift up fools.
Whoso regardeth dreams is like him that catcheth at a shadow, and followeth after the wind.
The vision of dreams is the resemblance of one thing to another, even as the likeness of a face to a face.
Of an unclean thing what can be cleansed? and from that thing which is false what truth can come?
Divinations and soothsayings, and dreams, are vain: and the heart fancieth, as a woman's heart in travail.
If they be not sent from the most High in thy visitation, set not thy heart upon them.
For dreams have deceived many, and they have failed that put their trust in them. [Ecclesiastes 34:1–7]

When Heinrich responds to his fathers's deprecating view of dreams with his own glowing description of them, Novalis is not only challenging the truth of the Enlightenment's perspective but also the authority of a rational theology. He opposes both with his own deeply mystical, nonrational, and poetic explanation of dreams and their role in our life. In a passage that is at once remarkably modern, psychologically insightful, and very beautiful, he sets out the Romantic's view of the power and meaning of the unconscious and nonrational forces of our inner life:

But my dear father, what makes you so opposed to dreams? Their strange transformations and their lightsome and tender nature certainly do promote our meditations. Is not every dream, even the most confused one, a remarkable phenomenon, which apart from any notion of its being sent from God is a significant rent in the mysterious curtain that hangs a thousandfold about our inner life? In the wisest books we find countless authentic stories of dreams, and just call to mind the dream the venerable chaplain told us lately; it seemed remarkable even to you.

But even without these stories, if you had a dream for the first time in your life, how astonished you would be, and you certainly would not let anyone talk you out of the miraculous nature of this happening which has merely become commonplace to us. Dreams seem to me to be a defense against the regularity and routine of life, a playground where the hobbled imagination is freed and revived and where it jumbles together all the pictures of life and interrupts the constant soberness of grownups by means of a merry child's play. Without dreams we should certainly grow old sooner; and so we can regard dreams, if not as directly sent from heaven above, at least as divine gifts, as friendly companions on our pilgrimage to the holy sepulcher. Certainly the dream I dreamed last night will not have been an ineffectual accident in my life, for I feel that it reaches into my soul as into a giant wheel, impelling it onward with a mighty swing.

[I,198,30–199,19][18]

Dreams for Novalis, as for Heinrich, play the same role as poetry: they interrupt the ordinary flow of everyday life and are the tear in the curtain of consciousness behind which lies concealed our innermost self, as behind the veil of Isis lies hidden the truth. Through this rent in the common mode of consciousness the divine enters our awareness by means of the dream in a revelation of chance. And so the giant wheel that impels Heinrich's soul onward with a mighty swing is the wheel of Fortuna, the goddess of chance. While we sleep, the dream functions as that opening or gateway to the realm beyond that in our normal state of waking consciousness is opened to us by poetry. Since sleep, though, has anciently been thought of as the younger brother of death, passage through the gates of dreams will lead us deeper and farther into the unknown and veiled depth of our inner self than any road we can travel in our waking mode of awareness. But because the dream is an involuntary, free creation, it is the lesser gate. Poetry, in contrast, being a deliberate and free creation, offers a higher level of entry. Due to their communal genesis, which guards against any too conscious and deliberate or too rational structuring and, therefore, rather encourages the darker forces of our nature to enter the creative process, Märchen exhibit the same unconscious and involuntary harmony that occurs in our dreams:

A Märchen is actually like a dream-image—without coherence—an *assemblage* of miraculous things and events—for instance a *musical phantasy*—the harmonious sequences of an aeolean harp—*nature herself.* [III,454,#986]

With the image of the aeolian harp, Novalis points to the order of chance that is the ruling order in the free play of nature's creativity, as well. But where nature is a playful creative force, it is also, much like our imagination, governed by the law of the association of ideas:

> A play of clouds—a *natural play* exceedingly poetical. Nature is an aeolian harp—she is a musical instrument—whose tones are in turn the keys of higher strings in us. (*Association of ideas.*) [III,452,#966]

But if the principle order of nature's playful and, therefore, free creativity is the association of ideas, then there exists a link between the workings of nature and dreams; and since dreams in turn share with Märchen the rule of the association of ideas, a similarity arises in the creativity of all three domains. Since, in addition, the association of ideas is also active in us, in the free play of our imagination and fantasy, dreams, Märchen, and nature call forth from us a similar response, a response in kind.

Whereas the first part of Novalis's unfinished and incomplete "novel" *Heinrich von Ofterdingen* thus replaces the standard opening of Märchen with the recounting and discussion of dreams, it ends with the telling of the allegory of the magician Klingsohr, which depicts the end of time and the beginning of the Golden Age and, therefore, functions much like a dream:

> FUTURE DOCTRINE OF LIFE. Our life *is* not a dream—but it shall, and maybe will, become one. [III,281,#237]

Both the dream opening and the Golden Age ending of *Heinrich von Ofterdingen*'s first part symbolically signify the overcoming of time. The first and only finished part of Novalis's unfinished and incomplete "novel" therefore resembles in its structure a Märchen for several reasons: first, because it is weak in character development or psychology and in the suspenseful succession of events, which are the strong points of the novel; second, because it is rich in suggestions of the miraculous, the marvelous, and the uncanny, all of which are the Märchen's usual fare; third, because social rank, historical dates, and geographical places, all of which serve the novel to achieve an air of reality, are used in *Heinrich von Ofterdingen* only as framework within which to embed an entirely implausible and magical tale; and last and most important, because in its relation to time it resembles the Märchen in that it brackets the flow of time. But as a Kunstmärchen, that is a raised Volksmärchen, it achieves the bracketing by means of a dream of transcendence and an allegory of the Golden Age, which is the age of an atemporal, paradisical eternity. Both the dream and the allegory thus function as the raised forms of the expressions "once upon a time" and "happily ever after." Furthermore, since for Novalis the Märchen is the canon of poetry,[19] *Heinrich von Ofter-dingen* can best fulfill Novalis's goals, on the one hand, to overcome the prosaic nature of Goethe's *Wilhelm Meister* and, on the other hand, to be entirely Romantic and poetic, if it is a Märchen, and specifically a Kunst-märchen. Thus, despite its length, ambitious plan, digressions into sub-tales, and genesis from the medieval and supposedly historical chronicle of Thuringia that inspired it, *Heinrich von Ofterdingen* is a Kunstmärchen and not a novel.

The "Klingsohr" story, however, which traditionally has been accept-ed as a Märchen (as have the stories of "Rosenblüthe und Hyacinth," "Arion," and "Atlantis"), is an allegorical fable. In a fragment that actu-ally could be taken to give us a definition of the Kunstmärchen, Novalis considers the structure and nature of Märchen and remarks that they must be free of any programmatic intent:

> Nothing is more against the spirit of Märchen—than a moralistic fate—a lawful coherence. In the Märchen a true anarchy of nature is present. Abstract world—dream world—inference from the abstrac-tion etc. to the condition after death. [III,438,#883]

But none of the stories that Novalis himself—or the tradition of Novalis interpretation—considers a Märchen is without just such lawful co-herence or moralistic determination. As a result they are not Märchen but the parables and symbolic allegories of the gospel of poetry that Novalis intends his *Heinrich von Ofterdingen* to be.

TRUTH, MIRROR REFLECTIONS, AND MÄRCHEN

The similarity of the holy stories and histories of the Bible with Märchen (which Novalis points out in fragment 508 above) rest in part on a direct likeness between them and in part on the relation that holds between opposites. The resemblance caused by their opposite natures is due to the mirrorlike reversal that images have in relation to what they repre-sent. History, as it is given in the Bible, is the flux of events driving forward to their ultimate goal, the redemption of time. Before the Fall with which man's history begins, life was lived in the eternal present of the Garden of Eden, where time had an entirely qualitative character. With the Fall, time's quantitative directional flux becomes man's fate. But when on Judgment Day history comes to an end, man will again enter the eternal and qualitative present of Paradise. The Bible can, therefore, be said to be a history that is bracketed by time's qualitative and eternal present. Märchen, on the contrary, as we have seen, are tales of time's qualitative present that is bracketed by the successive flux of events. Märchen thus are the mirror images of Biblical history. In a fragment of the early Fichte studies dealing with the relation of being and image or the "I" and representation, Novalis notes:

> The analytical I alternates in turn with itself—as the I in general—in the representation—image and being alternate. The image is always the reverse of being. What is right in a person is left in the image. [II,142,14–17]

Images generally do not in fact reverse the spatial arrangement of what they depict. Only reflections or mirror images do so. But since Novalis's theory of representation is a theory of Wechselrepräsentation or mutual and alternating representation, with particular application to the mutual representation of opposites (the outer as a representation or signature of the inner, and the inner of the outer, for instance), he conceives of iconic representation in general as reversing or inverting the order of what it reflects or represents. The consequence of this view for Novalis's aesthetic theory is that art is mimetic, but not simply a copy of reality. Rather, the re-presentation of the world and of nature that occurs in art reflects reality in an inverted and reversed fashion. Art is the mirror image of reality. While thus accepting the Platonic definition of art as imitation, Novalis revaluates its status. What Plato considered to be art's metaphysical and epistemological deficiency—namely its being unlike Being because it is a reflection of Being thrice removed—Novalis redefines as its ability to represent Being authentically. As he says in the *Monolog*:

> It is with language as with mathematical formulas—they constitute a world for themselves, they play only with themselves, express nothing but their own wonderful nature, and are for that very reason so expressive—for that very reason, too, the peculiar play of relations between things is *mirrored* in them. Only because of their freedom are they links of nature, and only in their free movements does the world-soul express itself, and make of them a delicate standard and ground plan of things. [My emphasis.] [II,672,14–22]

Art or language—and for Novalis that means essentially poetry—present, in their mirrorlike reflections, a true image of reality. Art, language, or mathematics—in fact any representational system that has a formal structure—thus is a world in itself: as mirror image it is other than what it mirrors because it is a reversal of it. This reversal, on the one hand, constitutes the representation's freedom from reality; yet, on the other hand, it also explains why as a ground plan of things, it is an authentic expression of the world-soul. Insofar as we ourselves are representations of the world-soul or are created in God's image, we must then be in every respect the inverse and opposite of the divine attributes: we are limited in our power, our knowledge, and our relation to time, and are, therefore, subject to its flux. But by means of the imagination we can overcome this limitation and fashion a representation that deliberately reverses the reversal, thus giving a direct rather than an indirect presentation of the truth by actively raising the beauty and truth of the representation. While the world, human history, and nature with its natural laws represent the divine spirit in mirrorlike reversal, man's representation of these representations depicts them raised to a straightforward image. The artist replaces a mere copy with a freely and actively created one; acting not only on the impressions he receives but also creating free expressions of spirit, he expresses himself, as well. In a fragment comparing the relative freedom and active expressiveness of the arts of painting and music, Novalis says:

> ★As the painter sees the visible objects with eyes entirely different from the common human being's—so also the poet experiences the events of the inner and outer world in a very different manner. . . . Visible nature seems to prepare the way for the painter everywhere— to be entirely his unattainable model—but actually the art of the painter is as independent, as a priori in its origin as the art of the musician. The painter only uses an infinitely more difficult *sign-language* than the musician's—the painter really paints with the eye—his art is the art to see harmoniously and beautifully. Seeing is here entirely active— actually forming activity. His picture is only his cipher—his expression—his tool of reproduction. . . . Almost every human being is to some degree already an artist—he sees indeed outward and not inward—he feels outward and not inward. The main difference is this: the artist has activated the seed of the self-forming life in his organs, he has heightened their sensitivity *for the spirit* and as a consequence is able to bring forth ideas at will—without solicitation to use them as tools for the modification, *at will*, of the world—
>
> [II,573,25–574,26]

An imaginative or willfully modified representation of the flux of time, then, would have to reverse its temporal order. The past must be depicted as following upon the present and the present upon the future. In Märchen—or as I have pointed out earlier, in the witch's kitchen of imagination in Goethe's *Faust*, for instance—such a reversal of the temporal flux is the order of the day: effects can and do precede their causes. If the representation is to be of time as a whole, however, rather than merely of the order of its parts, it has to present what is successive as being all at once and *vice versa*. As a consequence, if human history in the Bible is represented as embedded in the eternal present of the divine realm, then an imaginative icon of this embeddedness would be a presentation of the eternal present embedded in the historical flux. And as we have seen, this is exactly what Märchen offer.

In a fragment of the *Allgemeine Brouillon,* Novalis remarks on the relation of history, time, and Märchen as follows:

> ROMANTIC ETC. Märchen. Nessir and Zulima. Romantization of *Aline. Novellas. A Thousand And One Nights.* Ginnistan. La Belle et la Bète. Musaeus Volksmärchen. The Romantic spirit of the newer novels. Meister. Werther. Greek Volksmärchen. Indian Märchen. New original Märchen. In a true Märchen everything must be miraculous— mysterious and incoherent—everything animated. Each in a different way. All of nature must be intertwined in a miraculous manner with the entire world of spirits. The time of a general anarchy—lawlessness—freedom—the *natural state (Stand) of nature*—the time before the *world* (state [*Staat*].) This time before the world furnishes, as it were, the scattered characteristics of the *time after the world*—like the natural state is a *peculiar image* of the Eternal Realm. The world of the Märchen is the world *absolutely in contrast* to the world of truth (history)—and just for this reason *resembling it throughout*—like the *chaos* resembles the *completed creation*. (About *the idyll*.)
>
> In the world *to come* everything is like it was in the *former* world— *yet entirely different.* The world *to come* is the *rational* chaos—the chaos that penetrated itself—is within itself and outside itself—*chaos²* [to the second power] or ∞.
>
> The *genuine Märchen* must be at once *prophetic depiction*—ideal depiction—absolute necessary depiction. The genuine poet of Märchen is a *seer of the future.*
>
> Confessions of a true, synthetic *child*—of an ideal child. (A child is far more intelligent and wiser than an adult—the child must be a thoroughly *ironic* child.) The games of the child—*imitation* of the adults. (In time history must become a Märchen—it will become again, how it was in the beginning). [III,280–81,#234]

In its games the child imitates, that is, mirrors the adults and thus presents an inverse and reversed image of them. The greater wisdom of the child, then, is due to its being a reversal of God's reversed image: man. In the child God's nature is presented more directly. Similarly, if man is to reverse history's reversal of true Being, history must become a Märchen. Yet even though Märchen are a more authentic representation of Being than history is, they still reflect it imperfectly since they more nearly resemble the initial chaos than the raised chaos that is the future world. *Heinrich von Ofterdingen* is an account of history as a Märchen, but as Kunstmärchen it is a raised or higher Märchen. Therefore, despite the tone, mood, and structure of a Märchen, which requires that no "lawful coherence" be at work, *Heinrich von Ofterdingen* succeeds in being a coherently significant account of the raising of history to the status of Märchen. If history is to be raised, then it does not suffice for the historian to remain a faithful record keeper or even artful proclaimer of the past.

> Frequently the historian in his presentation must become a rhetorician—after all he presents *Gospels,* for all of history is Gospel. [III,586,12–13]

But the rhetorician of history is not its priest or prophet—merely its preacher. In the raising of history to the status of Kunstmärchen, the historian is required to change his nature too, he must be raised to the status of poet. Thus whereas the historian, at best, is history's preacher, the poet is its prophet and possibly also its author or originator. But even though—or, in fact, because—history can and shall be raised to the status of Märchen, the Märchen itself must not exhibit any historical sequencing, that is, it must not have a story:

> If a story is brought into the Märchen it is already a forcing interference—A series of pretty, amusing experiments—a dialogue—a Redoute are Märchen. It becomes a higher Märchen if without driving out the spirit of Märchen some reason—(coherence, significance, etc.) is imported into it. A Märchen could even become useful.
> The tone of mere Märchen is varying—but it also can be simple. /Constitutive elements of Märchen [III,454,32–455,7,#986]

Rational coherence or significance in Märchen, then, is not to be due to any story the Märchen tells but to the law of association that rules both Märchen and dreams. As a result, it is, in fact, the Kunstmärchen, as a raised Märchen—Novalis calls it here a "higher Märchen"—that represents Being authentically. For it is truly like the chaos that penetrated itself: a rationally anarchic representation.

For Novalis the marvelous in Märchen is the Märchen's link to the miraculous in the sacred stories and histories of the Bible. As the true significance of Biblical history is most apparent in the miracles it presents, so, too, the marvelous in Märchen best exhibits their meaning for

Novalis. The Märchen's usefulness, therefore, is that it reveals the higher order of chance that on the one hand underlies the order of nature and on the other hand is in opposition to it. But although the miraculous is thus the opposite of nature, it is also nature's true representation, as conversely nature is the true hieroglyph of the miraculous. The Märchen, therefore, as mirror image is both the true representation of the natural realm and of the realm beyond; it can express and stand for everything: "POETICS. *Everything* is a Märchen." [III,377,#620][20]

THE ICONIC CHARACTER OF MÄRCHEN AND DREAMS

Most of the words we use to designate a story—tale, account, *Erzählung*, etc.—etymologically have their root in the notion of counting. To *tell* derives from the Old English *tellan* "to count." We still speak of bank *tellers*, and not only tell tales but also make *tally* sheets. Similarly, to "talk" is akin to *tellan*. And so are the Low German dialect's *tellen* and *vertellen* which in High German are *erzählen* (to tell) or in the noun form *Erzählung* (story). The latter are all associated with the notion of counting: *zählen* (to count), *zahlen* (to pay), *Zahl* (number). Like these, the English *tale* also derives from the original Germanic *talo* (notch in a twig or piece of wood). Etymologically the connection between the notion of counting and of telling stories or of giving a narrative account thus lies in the runic script. Formally, this connection points to the structure of early narrative, in which, much like in a Raumroman, events are strung together in an account that ideally is open-ended and therefore can be stopped but not completed.[21] In contrast, the root of the word "Märchen" refers not to the amassing of elements, but rather to something remarkable or great; in the later developments of this idea, it comes to mean news or a report of some extraordinary thing or event—thus resembling in its genesis the evolution of the term "novel!" While the ordinary tale proceeds by a steady counting off of events, the Märchen seems more like a *tableau* exhibiting a wondrous or remarkable event, person, or thing. Novalis nowhere explicitly remarks on this non-tallying nature of the Märchen; yet his preference for this literary form rests in no small degree on the iconic character that results from it and, therefore, allows the Märchen effectively to bracket the flux of time.

While traditional aesthetic theory since Horace's pronouncement that "a poem is like a picture," or Simonides' clever remark that "painting is silent poetry and poetry a speaking painting," sees the poet's and the painter's projects in close association and therefore draws no clear distinctions between the greater temporality of poetry and the greater spatiality of painting, Lessing in his *Laocoön* objects to such a view and attempts to set limits to both the art of poetry and the visual arts:

There are paintable and unpaintable facts, and the historian can relate the most paintable ones just as unpicturesquely as the poet is able to present the most unpaintable ones in a picturesque way.

To see it differently would be permitting ourselves to be misled by the ambiguity of the word "picture." A poetic picture is not necessarily something that can be converted into a material painting; but every detail, every combination of details by which the poet makes his subject so palpable to us that we become more conscious of the subject than of his words, is picturesque, is a picture. This holds true because it brings us closer to that degree of illusion which the material painting is especially qualified to produce, and which for us can best and most easily be drawn from the material picture. . . .

I reason thus: if it is true that in its imitations painting uses completely different means or signs than does poetry, namely figures and colors in space rather than articulated sounds in time, and if these signs must indisputably bear a suitable relation to the thing signified, then signs existing in space can express only objects whose wholes or parts coexist, while signs that follow one another can express only objects whose wholes or parts are consecutive.

Objects or parts of objects which exist in space are called bodies. Accordingly, bodies with their visible properties are the true subjects of painting.

Objects or parts of objects which follow one another are called actions. Accordingly, actions are the true subjects of poetry.

However, bodies do not exist in space only, but also in time. They persist in time, and in each moment of their duration they may assume a different appearance or stand in a different combination. Each of these momentary appearances and combinations is the result of a preceding one and can be the cause of a subsequent one, which means that it can be, as it were, the center of an action. Consequently, painting too can imitate actions, but only by suggestion through bodies.

On the other hand, actions cannot exist independently, but must be joined to certain beings or things. Insofar as these beings or things are bodies, or are treated as such, poetry also depicts bodies, but only by suggestion through actions.

Painting can use only a single moment of an action in its coexisting compositions and must therefore choose the one which is most suggestive and from which the preceding and succeeding actions are most easily comprehensible.

Similarly, poetry in its progressive imitations can use only one single property of a body. It must therefore choose that one which awakens the most vivid image of the body, looked at from the point of view under which poetry can best use it. From this comes the rule concerning the harmony of descriptive adjectives and economy in description of physical objects.[22]

Since Novalis's predominant drive is toward synthesis rather than analysis, such a clear-cut separation of the two art forms does not suit either his temperament or his world view. As his philosophy of nature begins with just such a distinction of the realm of space from the realm of time, only to conclude with a synthesis of the two dimensions in a coincidence of opposites in the Golden Age, so also his theory of art and representation in general seeks synthesis. Not simply content to wait for the ultimate resolution of all strife and opposition in the Golden Age, Novalis seeks aesthetic and formal moments that on the one hand will prepare the way for the final harmony of all beings, and on the other hand already foreshadow it now. In the doctrine of mutual representation Novalis believes to have found such a formal moment, and it is my contention that his aesthetics of the Märchen is another, for the Märchen is a verbal icon. Yet this does not mean that Novalis simply returns to the earlier notion of poetry as voiced painting or painting as silent poetry.

An understanding of poetry as voiced painting makes of poetry primarily metaphoric speech. But metaphors are part of a text, although a part which because of its indirect expression is capable of, and sometimes even in need of, further linguistic unfolding. In some sense, therefore, metaphors, because they lend themselves to verbal interpretation, are simply a form of condensed speech that generates further linguistic expression. Their use of imagery thus is primarily a linguistic rather than a pictorial device. The metaphor, in other words, although it relies on images and is imagistic speech, is more closely bound to the nature of language than to the nature of visual representation. If Novalis, therefore, is to succeed with his synthetic program, the metaphor will not fully satisfy his intention, even though in a series of Erhebung it would without doubt be one of the intermediate moments in the process of raising language to true imagistic speech, as nature's hieroglyphs and fossils or the artistic emblem also are intermediate steps toward a voiced or speaking image. In fact metaphor and emblem seem to hold equivalent positions in their respective series of Erhebung.

The true image, though, is neither like an emblem (and therefore not a discursive idea illustrated by an image designed to express it, yet still in need of a caption), nor like a metaphor (and therefore not condensed speech which to a large extent can be unfolded discursively), but is so essentially iconic that it resists discursive translation and interpretation; it is the presentation of a nondiscursive idea. If Novalis is to find the aesthetic equivalent of the formal moment of Wechselrepräsentation or mutual representation he must look for a verbal image with all the characteristics of the true icon. The Märchen is such a verbal icon. Therefore, if an interpretation or translation of its iconic nature is nevertheless attempted, it will either fail completely or transform the iconic nature of the image by taking it to be metaphoric speech or symbolic expression.

Märchen seem frustratingly to elude the grasp of discursive thought. And if we succeed in giving a discursive interpretation of them (as for instance Bettelheim has done), it is only because elements of the imagery are taken to be symbols or metaphors that can be translated or unfolded into discursively structured meaning. The result of such translations is often interesting and enriching. In other words, I do not in the least mean to question the possibility or even usefulness of such an approach, as long as we are aware that it either destroys outright something of the Märchen's most essential nature, or at the very least leaves it out of consideration by focusing on particular details rather than on the Märchen as a whole. But the most basic appeal of the wonder tale lies precisely in its iconic character or that aspect of its nature that need not be and should not be translated or transformed into a discursive mode, that need not have and should not have a textual hermeneutic.

My insistence on the necessity of keeping the iconic character of the Märchen intact does not contradict Novalis's theory of translation, which asserts a universal translatability. For at its deepest level that theory is a theory of transformation, and I am not denying the possibility or even worthiness of text-icon or icon-text transformations. I am insisting, however, that the iconic nature of the wonder tale makes it among all literary products most like the Greek myths and the story of the Madonna, both of which Novalis speaks of admiringly as nearly successful mythic translations. In order fully to appreciate the effect and impact of Märchen, therefore, we must behold them or contemplate them as we would an image. For even though we become familiar with wonder tales by hearing them told, they act on us unlike any other text or account, for they do not essentially have a successive nature and do not properly form a story—or history—but an image. When allowed to remain iconic, Märchen function like simple meditative devices: living with Märchen, and letting them affect us and work on us without attempting to explain them discursively, removes us from the ordinary, commonsensical mode of consciousness, in which we experience ourselves and our own meaning as being subject only to the succession and inexorable and one-directional flux of time. Engaged in the contemplation of Märchen we become aware instead of time's qualitative nature. As the canon of poetry, the Märchen is the icon of chance and of our relation to it, and according to Novalis it is in Kunstmärchen that this icon finds its highest poetic expression.

Whereas the archetypal character of Volksmärchen, that is of Märchen that have arisen out of a communal creative effort, easily convinces us of their iconic nature, the Kunstmärchen's literary origin seems to give it a far more discursive character. It is, therefore, not really described adequately as a verbal icon. In the case of *Heinrich von Ofterdingen* its open-ended and essentially fragmentary structure further works against our viewing it in any such holistic and contemplative manner. Indeed, if we think of it in imagistic terms at all, it rather seems to suggest an album of snapshots. But oddly enough, *Heinrich von Ofterdingen* nevertheless affects us, in part, as icon. Since the work is undeniably also structured to accommodate the open-endedness Novalis called an infinite book, it, at the same time, undermines its own iconic presence as well. As a result, we find ourselves caught in a contradictory and paradoxical response.

Since the work was not finished, there is no telling what Novalis, who just a few days before his death spoke of entirely reworking *Heinrich von Ofterdingen*, would have done to change and remedy this situation. But even if we doubt that he would have, or could have, done much, the partial failure of a particular work does not necessarily call into question the theory on which it is based—a theory that in Novalis's case is deeply anchored in his life.

The most decisive experience for Novalis's artistic and religious development is his vision at Sophie's grave, an experience of iconic rather than tale-like nature. On that day the coincidence of time and eternity and of earth and spirit presented itself to Novalis in *one* visionary image, in an icon of all space and of all time, all at once. The consequence of this presentiment of all meaning for his philosophy of cognitive and aesthetic representation is Novalis's search for synthetic moments. The road of this search leads Novalis, on the one hand, to an exploration of time and chance as poetic and heaven-inspired rifts in our everyday consciousness and, on the other hand, to an investigation of space and its earthly hieroglyphs as significant symbols of the spirit that animates the universe. In the sounding word, the former finds its adequate expression; in the image or icon, the latter; a synthesis of both is, therefore, the only true or complete representation of meaning. The Märchen as a verbal icon constitutes for Novalis such a synthesis, and the Kunstmärchen is its raised or complete form. In contrast, the dream is an iconic text, or tale. Märchen and dream, therefore, are complementary opposites and are at once united and divided, as all opposites are, by both their similarities and their differences. Where the Märchen presents a contemplative or meditative image in verbal form, the dream gives us, no matter how freely assembled, successively ordered imagery and, therefore, a storylike, talelike, or accountlike representation. The dream, in contrast to the Märchen, demands an interpretation or textual hermeneutic. While the wonder tale and the dream, thus, are both free products of the imagination structured according to the laws of association, only the Märchen is a deliberately created work, giving full expression to an idea. The dream, as an entirely unintentional product, is raised to its full possibilities of representation only when translated or interpreted.

Among all the various products of the imagination, therefore, only the Märchen, because of its essentially iconic nature, comes close to the level of translation that Novalis thought had not been truly attained as yet, namely mythic translation, or translation into archetypal icons. True mythos, thus, is the highest form of representation because it is archetypal in character.

The German for mythos is *Fabel*. This is also the name of the main character in the "Klingsohr" allegory, with which the first part of the *Heinrich von Ofterdingen* tale ends. Fabel, the illegitimate daughter of the nursemaid Ginnistan—a personification of the imagination—and of the personified senses, together with her half-brother Eros—whose mother is the Isis-like symbol of the heart or of man's natural being—brings about the end of this world and the beginning of the Golden Age. Yet as important as the role of Eros is in this transformation, it pales in comparison with the role Fabel plays. For Eros, to come fully into his own nature, must mature into young manhood. But Fabel remains a quick and lively child, is eternally a child. And for Novalis it is true that "where Children are there is a Golden Age." [II,457,#97] Thus it is Fabel who finally is the agency by which the Golden Age is brought about. As the personification of mythos, as the daughter of both the imagination and the senses, she is the child predestined to be midwife to the age of mythos, the Golden Age in which all partiality is overcome:

★Language to the second power. Mythos, for instance, is the expression of a whole idea—and belongs to the hieroglyphistic to the second power—to the *sound and written pictorial language*[2] [raised to the second power]. It has poetical worth and is not *rhetorical*—subordinate—when it is a perfect expression—when it is *euphonic*[2]—correct and precise—when it is, so to speak, an *expression for* the sake of expression—when at the very least it does not appear as means—but is in itself a perfect production of the *higher language ability.*

[*II,588,12–19,#264*]

The Kunstmärchen *Heinrich von Ofterdingen* is a raised mythos or fable containing within itself subfables. As such it is to be an infinite expression and, therefore, it is to be more than any simple fable can be. Through his synthetic approach, Novalis hopes to achieve the paradox of an infinite completeness of expression. Theoretically the Kunstmärchen for Novalis is that literary form which can achieve the paradoxical goal of an infinite as well as complete representation. But whether the tale *Heinrich von Ofterdingen*, in fact, succeeds at what it attempts is another question.

Conclusion

In the introduction I raised the question whether Novalis's belief that the creation of art required inspiration by a transcendent force was a genuinely held belief based on experiences in his life, or whether it was a poetic conceit, a nostalgic hope, and the attempt to deny the felt distance from the realm beyond by idealizing hopes and wishes into theoretical assertions. I also asked whether Novalis's reversal of the traditional relationship of art and religion—in which art is thought to be the handmaiden of religion—into an understanding of religion as subservient to art is not a sign of his belatedness and therefore also a measure of his alienation from the very sources of inspiration he asserts. I suggested that the answer to these questions was closely tied to our understanding of Novalis's philosophical temperament, his metaphysical position, and the role that Sophie von Kühn and her death played in his life. I then proposed that an investigation of Novalis's theory of language would yield the answers we were seeking, since language, for Novalis, is not only a tool of expression and a vehicle of communication, but, in fact, the very manifestation of beauty, knowledge, and faith.

In the course of my explorations I found that Novalis's synthetic impulse strongly determined the formulation of his theories. As a result, his aesthetics combines aspects of the major views of art as they developed over the centuries: art is mimetic, for Novalis, insofar as it is a sign or symbol with a semantic function. Yet this semantic function also means that art is expressive, since it is a sign and symbol both of the nature of the artist who expresses himself in the creation of his works and of the spirit that inspires the artist and gives him his voice. Novalis attempts to overcome the tension that is the consequence of combining both these views in one theory by assigning responsibility for art's mimetic character primarily to the craft of the artist, to the development of his skills, while he attributes art's expressive capabilities to the artist's willingness to serve as conduit, as voice to the spirit that inspires him. Yet Novalis's synthetic enterprise does not end here: since art in addition is to awaken the *Selbst-thätigkeit* (self-activation) of the observer in determinate ways, it also has the function to impress or call forth certain moods or thoughts, and in general to elicit particular responses that edify, purge, entertain, entice, or exalt its beholder. Finally, Novalis considers art to be for art's sake, to constitute a world in itself insofar as it presents a reversed or inverted image of the real. While this does not make art fully autotelic, it does make it autonomous and give it a syntactic function. As expression, art is a monologue; as an impulse to awaken the self to activity, it is directed at human beings and is therefore dialogical in nature. As the former it is epiphany of the divine, as the latter a vehicle of communication. Despite his synthetic approach, however, Novalis's aesthetic theory is mainly a theory of revelation and, therefore, an ontological theory of art. For art, according to Novalis, parallels in its structure the nature of language, and is, indeed, itself a form of language in all its various expressions: as poetry; as music; as painting; and as sculpture. Yet language, as we have seen in the analysis of the *Monolog*, belongs for Novalis to the mediating realm and is a divine messenger.

Since for Novalis all true understanding and knowledge is dependent on our ability to express something, and since the ability to express amounts to the ability to make, we know what we are able readily and in manifold ways to produce, to execute. Knowledge, for Novalis, accordingly, is inseparably tied to the artistic enterprise. The revelation that occurs in art is the revelation of truth, and in acquiring the skills needed for the craft of art, man not only teaches himself the language that can reveal and be an epiphany of the divine, but also learns to read the road maps that can guide him on his way inward. The turn into the inner labyrinth of the self and its darker nonrational aspects is Novalis's turn from a metaphysics of light to a metaphysics of night, which is essentially determined by an understanding of time as qualitative presence rather than quantitative succession, with its parts—past, present, and future.

With this turn inward and into the night, Novalis turns also toward the earth as metaphor of both inwardness and the denial of the flux of time. In relation to the earth as natural ground, man's nature finds its definition as much as it does in his need to measure himself against the heavenly vault, or the divine. In his art, this turn inward and away from a metaphysics of the rational is a turn toward the wonder tale or Märchen and toward the dream as natural model of a magical form of thought production. Novalis's love for Sophie von Kühn and his reaction to her death, which culminated in the mystical and visionary experience at her grave, were instrumental in his turn toward the earth. For it was in his experience at the grave site that Novalis gained the unshakable belief that man's union with the beloved ultimately is meant to be not sexual but religious, and that through such a loving union the oneness and tranquil harmony of all things is not only made evident but brought about. Novalis thus interprets the embrace to be the raising of knowing or making to its greatest potency, to its highest level: in the embrace the lovers are united, and the discovery of the self takes place and becomes a revelation of the unity of the uni-verse.

We are now in a position to answer the questions raised in the introduction by saying that Novalis's belief in a transcendent force that inspires the artist was indeed a genuine stance and not a poetic conceit. Although, as I have pointed out, consideration of Novalis's religious convictions is greatly curtailed in this essay, we nevertheless can conclude with some conviction that his religious talent was his greatest gift and entirely determined his outlook on life—and for him that also meant his outlook on art. It is more difficult to state with equally unhesitating clarity whether Novalis's reversal of the relationship of art's subserviency to religion is a sign of a late age, and specifically a sign of his belonging to the Romantics, who had an aesthetic view of religion. At this point we cannot be certain whether, for Novalis, such a reversal indeed took place, or if it did, to what degree. Since the tale of *Heinrich von Ofterdingen* is meant to be an account of the apotheosis of the poet, it is tempting simply to answer the question affirmatively. But we ought to remember that it is as priest, as maker of revelatory signs of the transcendent truth, that the poet is so exalted. It, therefore, becomes possible to argue that his apotheosis is precisely the result of, and reward for, his service to the divine. Yet it is my conviction that Novalis is ambivalent on this point, and that his stronger inclination is toward the service of art to the truth, to the divine, and that for this reason his truly religious poems, the *Geistliche Lieder*, are his most successful poetic work, while his *Heinrich von Ofterdingen* fails (certainly as a novel, but also even as a tale), because it does not heed Novalis's true inner voice. If I am right, we are justified to see in the ascendance of the aesthetic over the religious (particularly in the form of the interesting) the sign of a late age, as well as a perversion of

Novalis's own natural tendency and gift by the age he lived in, a perversion that possibly was brought about by his friendship with Friedrich von Schlegel.

All that remains for me to point out is that Novalis bridges the chasm that divides the rational approach philosophy took before and during the Enlightenment from the philosophy of the irrational that emerged in the nineteenth century. Novalis's indebtedness to Plato and neo-Platonic traditions as well as to Kant, particularly to the latter's *Critique of Judgement*, is counterbalanced by his foreshadowing of both Hegel's phenomenological dialectic and Schopenhauer's views of art in *The World as Will and Representation*. Even Novalis's literary and aphoristic style found successors, as did his conviction that poetry and philosophy finally not only address the same basic human concerns but must be understood in relation to each other. One only has to think of Nietzsche and Heidegger. Novalis thus stands firmly rooted in the past as he points the way to the future.

Fichte's Theory of Language

Fichte begins his essay "Von der Sprachfähigkeit und vom Ursprung der Sprache" with the assertion that it is not sufficient to show how language might have been "invented," but that one ought to show how "this invention follows necessarily" from the very "nature of human reason." [*FSW*,VIII,301] Defining language as the "*expression of our thoughts by arbitrary signs*," Fichte distinguishes what we may know of another's thinking through his actions from what we know of him because of his intentional use of signs.[1] He denies the former to be any sort of language at all, since in "what is to be called *language*, under no circumstances is more intended than the designation of the thought; for outside of such designation language has absolutely no purpose." [*FSW*,VIII,302] The crux of this distinction lies in the idea that in action the communication of any thought content is only an accidental by-product. When, for example, we strike a person in anger, the slap will communicate our hostility. But this bit of information is not part of the purpose of the act. In action the intention is only to *execute* or act on the thought, not to give a sign of it. The intention of language, on the contrary, is only to designate, or express the thought, not to execute it. [*FSW*,VIII,308] Language, for Fichte, is thus strictly distinct from doing.

Nevertheless, Fichte acknowledges that we can deduce from a man's actions what he thinks. But whatever a person's behavior may communicate to us has nothing to do with linguistic expression, is not language. Fichte, therefore, would have understood neither such primary and simple modes of communication as beckoning, begging, or pointing to and pointing out, nor what we call "body language," as language at all. For behavior of this sort is not arbitrarily defined and not voluntarily chosen. When we beckon, beg, or point, the meaning of the gesture is so directly linked to the motion we execute and is such an inherent part of that motion itself that we cannot arbitrarily assign a different or new meaning to it without doing violence to its communicative nature. As human beings we cannot help following the pointing finger to what it points out. Even infants, not yet able to sit up by themselves, will automatically follow the pointing gesture to the object pointed at.[2] Similarly, we seem to understand the meaning of a beckoning gesture or begging hand without having to learn it and, indeed, feel as if we were born with this knowledge. That this, in fact, may not be the case has little impact on how we perceive it. It seems entirely natural, and that suffices to make us think that the meaning of primary communicative behavior is not arbitrarily assigned. In addition, information communicated through body language is frequently neither voluntary nor intended. The attitudes or feelings we so express—or are perceived as expressing—are often the very attitudes and feelings we wish to hide. Indeed, not infrequently we labor mightily and nervously to give explicit expression in direct contradiction to what our body language is thought to divulge. The capacity of body language to convey the speaker-actor's feelings or beliefs is, therefore, not part of the communicative intention of the speaker. But when language is defined as the purposeful designation of thought, and stress is laid on voluntary and arbitrarily defined signs—"signs, I say, and not behavior" [FSW,VIII,302]—then neither voluntary nor involuntary gestures, even if they communicate something about our emotional or cognitive state, qualify as language.

But not only bodily gestures are denied linguistic status by Fichte. He also does not consider natural cries or such exclamations as "ouch!" to belong to language proper. For any such sounds made at the sudden rush of feeling joy or sorrow and pleasure or pain are not voluntary. And "the involuntary outbursts of sensations are not language." [FSW,VIII,303] The reasons Fichte has for thinking such voicings not a part of language appear similar to those of Beardsley, who says that in such exclamations "the speaker does not necessarily intend to communicate information about himself," but is "merely giving vent to his feelings."[3] For Fichte, then, language is a narrowly defined concept. It is applicable only to a system of arbitrary signs used voluntarily and symbolizing particular thought contents in a manner that allows a separation of the sign from the body making it. Drawn hieroglyphs or written letters clearly fall under this definition, as do spoken words, since they are sent forth into the world to stand independently of the speaker. As a result, language not only is a far more distanced response than are actions or reactions with their immediacy, but it is also peculiarly removed from any essential interaction with the sphere of doing, that is, from life. Such a formulation makes of language a privileged tool for aesthetic purposes, since the distancing that Kant claims for the nature of art is here seen to be an aspect of the very character of the medium or tool of poetry, namely of language itself.

But not only is there, according to Fichte, no strong interrelationship between speech and doing, the relationship holding between speech-signs and the objects they represent is also weak. For Fichte thinks that it matters little whether the sign has any "natural likeness" to or affinity with what it designates, and this despite the fact that he believes the origin of language to lie in the use of hieroglyphic representations that obviously are, and have to be, like what they stand for. But Fichte considers a certain kinship between a word and the object it names as the mark of only the early stages of the development of primitive language. And so he defines language and language capacity proper—or the faculty of language—as "the ability to designate one's thoughts *arbitrarily*," that is, as a free exercise of the will. [*FSW*, VIII, 303] In other words, denying any essential similarity between a sign and the object it signifies, Fichte claims a habitual and conventional nature for the relationship holding between them and suggests that it came about either accidentally or by an act of choice.

Man, according to Fichte, is a "representing creature" who cannot help representing things as they are to himself. [*FSW*, VIII, 306] Possessing in addition a reason that has all the characteristics of a drive and that prompts him to seek for reasonableness outside of himself [*FSW*, VIII, 307], Fichte proposes that as soon as man entered into a relationship of "reciprocal exchange" (Wechselwirkung) with other beings of his own kind, "a desire arose in him to indicate his thoughts to them and to receive from them clear communications in return." [*FSW*, VIII, 308] Anchored in the nature of man, this general drive to find "rationality (*Vernunftmässigkeit*) outside himself" contains "the specific drive to realize a language; the necessity to gratify this drive occurs when reasonable beings enter into reciprocal exchange with each other." [*FSW*, VIII, 309] Man thus comes to use language in part as a result of his social nature. Yet this social nature, in turn, is the consequence of man's need to find an echo of reason outside himself in the world, which, in turn, is possible only because of the essentially representational character of man's nature. In this manner, for Fichte, language, reason, the faculty of representation, and social behavior are joined into one hermeneutic circle.

Up to this point there is nothing particularly extraordinary or odd about Fichte's theory on the origin of language. Other Enlightenment thinkers also saw language arise as a result of human reason and community and similarity thought the relationship between sign and signified object to be either arbitrary or conventional or contractual in nature. But Fichte now makes the curious claim that although language arising under such circumstances is usually thought to consist only of "signs for hearing" (*Zeichen fürs Gehör*), he, Fichte, means to exclude *no* signs whatsoever, since in the "primordial language" (*Ursprache*) surely none were excluded either. [*FSW,*VIII,309] Giving a sketch of the evolution of signs, Fichte suggests that the "first signs for things" in any original language were mimetic representations, since they "were taken from the effects of nature, and were nothing more than imitations of them." [*FSW,*VIII,310] Man expressed the idea of a lion by roaring like that animal, or the idea of wind by imitating its rustling whir. As a result of this mimetic genesis, things that made themselves known to man through the sense of hearing were expressed by sounds, while the things man became aware of through the sense of sight were referred to by drawing a silhouette of them into the sand. [*FSW,*VIII,310]

Surprisingly, Fichte does not make the point that we know far fewer things by their sounds than we know by their particular configurations. Yet clearly, even most of those things that have distinctive sounds are also possessed of particular shapes: the lion that roars, the snake that hisses, the cow that lows—all have clearly defined body shapes and are as easily identified by these as they are by their voices. It is true, we do not see the wind—at best, we see only its effects—and we have no image of thunder. But the things we know because of only their sounding presence are very few and, by and large, constitute the exception. The peculiar consequence of Fichte's theory, therefore, is that speaking and writing—or a primitive form of it—are, at the very least, coeval in the development of human language. That this is true for Fichte becomes evident in his calling man's first language not only a "primordial language" (*Ursprache*), but also a "hieroglyphic language" (*Hieroglyphensprache*).

Fichte has two main reasons for holding visual representation to be man's original signs. First, basing his assertion on the fact that the affective exclamations are not a voluntary but an involuntary voicing, he dismisses all emotive expressions because they are neither language proper nor the source from which language arose. Cries of pain or joy, therefore, constitute immediate vocal aspects of the emotions involved, but are not linguistic expressions of them. [*FSW,*VIII,303] In other words, for the purpose of linguistic categorizing, emotive exclamations are a species of physical behavior rather than linguistic symbolization. Second, since a far greater faculty of abstraction is implied in the ability to fashion arbitrary tonal signs for given visual objects, Fichte thinks it likely that oral language developed much later than hieroglyphic expression. [*FSW,*VIII,318] He muses, "Who knows how many thousands of years went by before primordial language became a language for hearing?" [*FSW,*VIII,313] Thus, even though it is doubtful whether Fichte himself thought of hieroglyphic sign language as a form of writing, we are entitled to conclude that writing, for him, insofar as it is hieroglyphic mimesis, is not only coeval with speaking, but in fact precedes it. Man draws signs before he speaks words. And with the temporal priority of the visual representation, its logical primacy goes hand in hand. For the imagination, which serves as the ground of representation, is, according to Fichte, the organ that has ontological primacy.

That language eventually changed and became a purely oral expression is, Fichte thinks, due to the greater economy of vocal communication. We can hear—or be heard—when we are not looking at the speaker—or are not being looked at by the listener. As a result we can speak—or listen—to someone whose back is turned to us, and can make ourselves understood—as well as understand others—in the dark. [*FSW*,VIII,311–312] In other words, the primordial hieroglyphic language cannot arouse the other's attention; it presumes that attention in the enterprise of communication. Along with the greater effectiveness of oral language for calling attention to the speaker (as Fichte says, "hearing involuntarily prompts and guides the eyes" [*FSW*,VIII,311]), the development toward oral expression also brought a greater voluntary character to language. According to Fichte's model, then, the use of hieroglyphic signs was a matter of choice even for primitive man—he could choose either to "speak," that is, to draw or write, or to remain "silent," that is, to refrain from drawing or writing—but no choice existed for him in selecting the sort of signs he used, for all signs were determined by the natural objects they imitated. In contrast, the tonal signs of spoken language do not imitate what they signify and are, therefore, entirely voluntary and arbitrary representations.

Yet this greater freedom and sophistication of oral language in no way diminishes or undermines Fichte's belief in and commitment to the priority of the visual sign grounded in the primacy of the imagination. Thus, Fichte argues in a footnote to his discussion of what sort of signs primordial language might have been using: "I am not proving here that man cannot think without language, that without it he cannot have general concepts. For, indeed, he can, by means of the images his fantasy devices. I am convinced that language has been vastly overestimated, in the belief that without it no reasoning would have taken place." [*FSW*,VIII,309] Thinking and speaking, as a result, are not necessarily interdependent. Man thinks even without spoken language. Picturing, therefore, is a tool as valuable for thought as abstract words are, and it is indeed more fundamental.

Fichte seems ambivalent in his evaluation of primordial language. He never clearly and explicitly distinguishes between the linguistic status he assigns to hieroglyphic expression and to language proper, that is, to spoken words. Yet at times it appears that, despite the fact that he speaks of Ursprache or primordial *language*, and of Hieroglyphensprache or hieroglyphic *language*, he thinks of these forms of communication as a mere preliminary step on the way to language proper, which consists of "arbitrary signs." As a result, only our daily, spoken conversations, that is, ordinary words and phrases constructed of arbitrary signs, deserve to be called a language. Yet if the voluntary communication of ideas, rather than the involuntary expression of emotions or the merely accidental imparting of information within the framework of specific affective acts, constitutes proper language, then primordial, mimetic sounds and hieroglyphic signs must also be defined as language. Similarly, Fichte seems to be unaware, if not unwilling to recognize, that the hieroglyphic signs of his primordial language are a form of writing. He thought, for instance, that the silhouette of a fish drawn in the sand was equivalent to the request or suggestion to go fishing together. But the hieroglyphs, thus, not only are visible signs for particular objects (a state of affairs that might be judged the result of a mere drive to imitate) but are able to invite others to communal action. They are therefore representations of ideas in a fixed form; they are written linguistic signs very much like the pictograms of Far Eastern languages, which obviously are a form of writing.

Vacillating in his understanding of the linguistic status of hieroglyphic writing as writing, Fichte suggests that a language is far more prone to change when a people cannot yet write in alphabetic representation, but only speak. "The original tone of a sign, once lost, cannot be retrieved. But where there is writing, the tone will be fixed, and again and again it can be determined how a word ought to be pronounced. The invention of letters, therefore, very much stabilized language." [*FSW*,VIII,313][4] Aside from whether such an assertion is correct or even plausible, it presents a view of the development of writing that understands the hieroglyph as the representation of a whole idea, complete thought, or entire concept, yet it sees the letter not as an integral part of a word but as an atomistic particle of speech, as an individual sound bit, or rather its written representation. The opinion expressed in the quotation above also offers a view of the evolution of writing that, on the one hand, parallels, and on the other hand, moves in the opposite direction of Fichte's idea of the development of the spoken word. Fichte himself, though, seems not to be aware of this. The written letter, as the abstract and atomistic image or sign of a tone, stands to the imitative, concretely representative, and holistic sign of the hieroglyph as the abstract and arbitrary word sound does to the imitative sign of the primal language, be that a hieroglyphic archetype of sight or onomatopoeic prototype of sound. In other words, in both instances development takes place in the direction of abstraction: the representational symbol—initially at once a communicative sign of discourse and a written mimetic hieroglyph of an entire idea—loses its concretely imitative nature with the invention of the alphabet and changes into an arbitrary sign that bears no resemblance to what it represents. Clearly, the same holds true for the development of onomatopoeic tones into word sounds. In contrast to the evolution of writing, though, in which the letters of the modern alphabet not only have an arbitrary relationship to what they stand for, but also are the atomistic particles out of which written representations are constructed, the evolution of the spoken language is not in the direction of atomistic simplification. On the contrary, for Fichte, to whom words rather than phonemes are the smallest building blocks of meaning, the spoken word can in no way represent a simplification of sound structures. In fact, the reverse must be true, even though Fichte thought that the letters of the alphabet were capable of representing sounds perfectly. For onomatopoeic imitations are relatively simple tonal compositions in comparison with the sound complexities of abstract words. The evolution of spoken and written language, according to Fichte, therefore, takes place in opposite directions as far as the simplicity of the signs is concerned, but moves in the same direction with respect to abstraction. Yet such abstraction, both of sound and sight, ultimately is meaningful only because it is grounded in "concretely" imitative representation, that is, in the imagination.

Herder's Theory of Language

Very little in Herder's philosophy of language agrees with Fichte's point of view. In some sense Herder can even be said to represent an antithesis to Fichte's thinking on language, with the exception of their common opinion on the crucial point that language is rooted in the nature of man and has its origin in man. Yet they come even to this agreement by different routes and for different reasons. Fichte is mainly interested in showing that the imagination is ultimately the world-constituting organ and, therefore, also the home of language. Herder, in contrast, strives to demonstrate that the claim of a divine origin of language is nonsensical, because everything about language shows it to be a human tool, fitted for human use and exhibiting with it human weaknesses and strengths.[1]

Yet it is precisely in this human genesis of language that, for Herder, God is glorified and His plan made evident. Since the proponents of the divine nature and origin of language usually support their claim with an appeal to the Bible, Herder reminds us that the First Book of Moses says "the Lord God formed every beast of the field and every fowl of the air; and brought them unto Adam to see what he would call them: and whatsoever Adam called every living creature that was the name thereof."[2] The point of this passage, for Herder, is that "a higher origin has nothing to recommend it, not even the evidence of the oriental Scripture on which it is based: for, obviously, Scripture gives to language a human origin in the naming of the animals." Finally Herder concludes that "the higher origin, apparently so pious, is quite profane: it dwarfs God step by step with the lowest, most imperfect anthropomorphisms. The human origin of language exhibits God in the brightest light: His work, a human soul, by itself creating and developing a language, because it is His work—a human soul. As a creative entity, as an image of His Being, it constructs for itself this sense of reason. Therefore, the origin of language is honorably divine only if it is human." [*HSW*,V,146] Herder's claim of the human origin of language, then, contains nothing that would make it incompatible with an inspired view of language. For even if God is not the inventor of human language, His voice can still be discerned in human speech. Indeed, in an indirect manner human speech is the very manifestation of God's creative will. For not only has God given to man the ability and right to name His creatures, but He has given in that ability a simile of His own creative power: man's creation of language is an analog of God's creation of the universe, for with this naming man establishes his world.

Similarly, Herder and Fichte appear to agree that the emotional outbursts of joy and sorrow, or pleasure and pain, cannot be considered to constitute the roots of human speech or origins of human language. But Herder, in contrast to Fichte, distinguishes between language proper and the language of nature. The latter, man shares with the animals, as well as with inanimate objects. For not only do "all the strong passions of the soul express themselves immediately in cries, in sounds, in wild and inarticulate tones" [*HSW*,V,5], that is, not only do animals and man alike moan with pain, even when they are alone and cannot hope with this expression to summon either help or sympathy, but similarly, "the plucked string does its natural duty: it sounds! It calls to another of a like mood for an echo, even when no other is present, even when it itself does not hope or wait to be answered." [*HSW*,V,5–6] According to Herder, therefore, nature decreed to the world the law: "Do not sense for yourself alone, but let your emotions sound." [*HSW*,V,6] The sounds produced by these natural tendencies are characteristic of a given species, serving to bind its members to each other. [*HSW*,V,7] And these natural sighs or tones Herder calls language, although he also says that it would be folly "to seek the origins of human speech in these emotional cries." [*HSW*, V,17]

To Herder, then, it seems foolish to look for the roots of human language in the passionate cries of animals, because he thinks that man and animals differ from each other not only in degree, but also in kind. [*HSW*,V,27] Man does not simply have greater powers or a wider variety of capacities; rather, the manner in which he uses them is different: for man has a disposition toward reason, which, according to Herder, is not a separate and additional, specifically human faculty, but is the direction of all man's powers and abilities. [*HSW*,V,29–30] This disposition to reasoning Herder calls "reflective circumspection" (*Besonnenheit*). And when man for the first time used this characteristic of his freely, he invented language. It is as natural for man to speak as it is for him to be human, for with Besonnenheit man singles out from the "ocean of sensations in his soul one particular wave" and "stops it, turns his attention toward it and becomes conscious of his attending to it . . . and if he not only becomes aware of its properties, but can recognize them as distinguishing marks (*Merkmale*), this first act of recognition yields a clear concept, a judgment in his soul . . . and this first mark of reflection is a word of the soul! With it human language is invented." [*HSW*,V,34–35] The identifying mark (*Merkmal*) isolated by the human soul as a token by which to recognize that for which it comes to stand—the bleating of a sheep, for instance, or the rustling of leaves—also serves to name that for which it is a token of recognition. The first word, therefore, is an "inner *identifying word*" (*ein innerliches Merkwort*) [*HSW*,V,36], and language as a whole is constructed of many such distinguishing or identifying marks that have become names. For "what is human language, if not a collection of such words?" [*HSW*,V,37] In contrast to Fichte, Herder believes that this first word was *uttered*. It was a *spoken* word, a word of *sound*, even if it was not pronounced out loud but only whispered in the soul or thought in the heart. Therefore, even the silently thought word is, for Herder, intoned in the mind. It is formed along the structures of sound rather than according to the structures of sight. Indeed, its very designation as *"silent* word" points in the direction of the essentially tonal nature of language.

Both the language of nature and human language, for Herder, are languages of sound, languages for hearing. And although human speech cannot reasonably be thought to have its origin in the language of nature, man nevertheless relies on nature to learn language, for "many-toned and divine," she is his instructor and his muse. [*HSW*,V,50] Thus, following nature, man learns language by means of his ability to hear. The first distinguishing marks that sounded as the first word in man's soul were not prompted by the recognition of particular properties of the visual appearance of things, but were a recording of the sounding aspects of their nature: the tree was differentiated from its surrounding vegetation by the rustling of its leaves, and the sheep by its bleating voice. As a result, the first naming was not an assigning of specific nouns to particular objects. Man's relationship to things was not first and foremost determined by a knowing through the sense of sight, that is, by a merely passively beheld presence of similarly passively present objects. Rather, man actively responded to the objects of his environment, which in turn actively addressed him through the sense of hearing. Man and object were united in one *event* in which both participated, the one actively sounding and the other equally actively listening and marking the distinguishing sound. "The thought of the thing itself still hovered between the doer and the deed; the tone had to designate the object, as the object gave the tone." [*HSW*,V,52] Man's first words, therefore, signified events or actions and so were verbs, rather than nouns. [*HSW*,V,52–53] In contrast to Fichte, then, language for Herder is most intimately bound up with doing. It is, in fact, a form of human behavior which, though it does not have its origin in the sounding behavior of nature, still takes the cues for its own development from nature.

To Herder, sound is a sounding, a tonal event, and language proper begins where the sounding tones of nature end. Because of his reflective circumspection, the manner and direction of man's speech is entirely different in kind from the ringing voices of nature, the sounding of which is a natural music, a natural song. Nevertheless, because man takes nature for his teacher and his muse, because he apprentices himself to her, he learns to speak poetry before he learns to speak prose: "For what was the first language, but a collection of the elements of poetry?" [*HSW*,V,56] But although man learns from nature, he does not imitate her. Man's voice is poetic without attempting to copy any of the natural songs. Man's music is not an "aping" of the warbling of the lark or nightingale. For mere imitation does not allow any thought to accompany the imitated tones. [*HSW*,V,37] Yet man as the intrinsically reflective and circumspective being utters thought when he utters sound. From the first, then, his song is his own, and his poetry an expression of the musical measure and reflective thought in his own heart. Thus, learning from nature without imitating her, man, by means of his reflective circumspection and understanding, "has condensed (*gedichtet*) the natural languages of all creatures into sounds, into images of action, into passions, into a living and effective influence."[3] [*HSW*,V,56] As a consequence, a dictionary is formed in the soul that is, at once, "mythology and marvelous *epopoeia* of the deeds and speeches of all beings! And therefore, a lasting fable and poem of passion and interest!" [*HSW*,V,56–57]

A comparison of Fichte and Herder now yields the surprising result that, for Fichte, who believed speech to begin as an imitation of natural sounds and shapes, the imitation of sounds counts for so little that ultimately speech must be thought to begin as imaginative hieroglyph, or written sign. Herder, however, who considered speech to be intimately tied to hearing, nevertheless believed that it did not simply imitate the voices of nature—although he was, in contrast to Fichte, perfectly willing to call these voices a language. The origin of human speech, then, for Herder, is not at all imitative, but lies in the human characteristic of reflective circumspection, in a thoughtfulness that is fairly independent of sense altogether, but that, if at all, has greater affinity to sight than to hearing. Yet he also thinks that this rather sight-oriented thoughtfulness allows man, by means of the sense of hearing, to distinguish the objects in his environment according to their tonal qualities, and to form, on the basis of these acoustic distinctions, the first word within his soul.

Herder's greater emphasis upon the sense of hearing permits him to connect speech to poetry, not only because nature herself is understood to produce with her voices a sort of natural music or song, but also because Herder considers the sense of hearing, despite its close connection to the passions, to be a median sense, halfway between distance and nearness, between outside and inside, and between reason and passion. Sight, in contrast, according to Herder, "is the coldest sense," distant and distancing and directed entirely outward. And although Besonnenheit, that specifically human characteristic responsible for language, has greater affinity to sight than sound, the sense of sight by itself could not have given man language; for however clear and distinct our sense of sight, we cannot fashion an audible form from what we see. [HSW,V,62] On the other side of the scale, the sense of feeling is so utterly indistinct and obscure that with its completely inner-directed warmth, density, and immediacy of impressions, it allows, because of the overlapping of emotions, no distinct and clear differentiations and, therefore, could not have been the sense by means of which man invented the word. [HSW,V,63]

Hearing is directed outward as well as inward: we listen to others with our outer-directed sense of hearing and hearken unto ourselves, to the word we think in our soul, when we listen inward. Herder also thinks that hearing holds a median position with respect to clarity and distinctness and to liveliness and quickness. For he believes hearing perceives less clearly than the eye, but with greater distinctness than feeling, and reacts less quickly than the eye, but with greater swiftness than feeling. Conversely, it appears to him to be a sense of greater passion than seeing, but of less lively emotionality than feeling. [HSW,V,65]

Most important, though, the sense of hearing is, for Herder, the sense best equipped to handle time. For sight gives us everything all at once, arranging everything in space as a tableau of juxtaposed items. Feeling, similarly atemporal, in contrast, overwhelms us with the strongest explosions of emotions which, moving us suddenly, have no lasting duration. Only hearing gives us a distinct experience of succession. It allows, in fact, it requires us to hear one tone after the other and so is the only sense that could have given us speech. For, according to Herder, language, like man, has a progressive nature; it is an event taking place in time, taking time in its production as well as in its reception. [HSW,V,66–67]

Finally, Herder considers hearing to be the median sense because it can form not only impressions, but also expressions. The ear and the tongue work in cooperation, and we hear both what is being said to us and what we ourselves are saying. Similarly, hearing is the median sense in the course of man's development: for even as an embryo man feels—and is awakened to his own nature from this most rudimentary state of life—only when the sounds that ring and echo silently in his soul form the first word with which he marks his environment. Therefore, hearing follows feeling in man's evolution, yet precedes seeing, which develops later, when by means of his either silently thought or soundingly pronounced words, man's world has already taken shape. [*HSW,*V,67–68]

As noted earlier, for Herder, despite this median position, hearing has a rather greater affinity with feeling than with seeing. Thus he writes that "feeling is very close to hearing" [*HSW,*V,63], a fact which, he believes, on the one hand, enhances our ability to express our feelings and passions in words, and, on the other hand, furthers the poetic nature of speech. Herder takes this kinship of hearing and feeling to be particularly apparent in the older, original languages of the Orient, in which the rich tones of emotions still vibrate in the roots of words. Here feeling had to become sound. But man's soul, ultimately being inadequate to the task of fashioning as wide a variety of words as there are emotions, and not yet having learned to speak of experiences in abstract modes, turned to the use of strong and daring metaphors in order to express what he felt. [*HSW,*V,71–72] Imagistic language, then, for both Herder and Fichte, has a primitive origin. But whereas for Fichte it is quite free of any particular emotional nexus and, indeed, is *the* originary form of rational linguistic expression, it is for Herder closely and essentially connected to man's passionate nature, while it is at the same time the result of a shortcoming in the human faculty of speech.

It is somewhat surprising that Herder should have had such a relatively negative view of the relationship of language to images, for he frequently approached questions holistically rather than analytically. It would seem that such a tendency is greatly facilitated by the all-at-once characteristic of imagery and far less well-served by the more purely progressive or successive nature of speech, particularly when that speech is not imagistic or metaphoric but simply discursive or, worse, abstract. Indeed, Herder himself seems to be making just this point. In the opening pages of his *Treatise on the Origin of Language* he says that the natural tones of expression rely for their content nearly entirely on the nature of the situation they occur in, and that, cut off from this context, which is not just background but an interconnected set of circumstances, they cannot be properly understood. Deep despair, for instance, and the gentle surrender of love both come to sound in a faint "ah." The determination of what this "ah" means can be made only by taking into account the "larger *picture,*" by *looking* at all the conditions that give rise to it (the emphasis is mine). Herder, speaking in this connection of the voice of nature, says that it is a "painted letter made available for free choice," (*"gemalter, verwillkührter Buchstabe"*), [*HSW,*V,8–9] showing thereby quite plainly that his own language, despite his great emphasis on the importance of sound and tone for human speech, readily turns toward imagery and metaphor when the issue is not one for analysis, but on the contrary, deals with some sort of totality or completeness.

Although Herder calls the voice of nature a "painted letter made available for free choice," it is highly questionable whether he, in fact, held the view that the relationship between word and object is an arbitrarily willed or conventional one. In the *Treatise on the Origin of Language,* Herder does not explicitly address this issue, but we may deduce, from the fact that he considers man to have been the apprentice of nature in the matter of inventing speech, that he must lean in the direction of a more essential connection. For the sounds of the language of nature are always an expression of the essential characteristics of the sounding entity and, therefore, can serve to bind the members of its species together. In a passage alluding to the naming of the animals in Genesis, Herder says: "She [nature] leads all creatures past him: each carries its own name on its tongue, and pledges itself as vassal and servant to this concealed visible God. It delivers its identifying word (*Merkwort*) like a tribute into the book of his mastery, so that with this name he will in the future remember it, call it, and enjoy it." [*HSW*,V,50] Novalis's suggestion that in the cathedral of the universe each creature reveals its own inner nature in a petition is, therefore, a strong echoing of Herder.

In addition, Herder considers language and thought to be so intimately interrelated that neither has priority over the other. The first silently thought word of the soul is the prime example of this contemporality and equality of language and thought. The result of an inner activity that is not necessarily rational (*"Folge der Besinnung"*) [*HSW*,V,99], but always already reflectively circumspect (*"Folge der Besonnenheit"*) [*HSW*,V,99], this inner word cannot be an arbitrary or conventional naming, for it is far too closely tied not only to the nature of that which it names, but also to the very nature of man himself. Yet it is this inner word that is the root and origin of human speech: "Just as the first rational state of man could not have become real without the words of the soul, so all the states of reflective circumspection come to language. Man's chain of thoughts becomes a chain of words." [*HSW*,V,99] For Herder, therefore, man's language can be arbitrary or voluntary only insofar as man may choose to speak or to remain silent, or because, as a free being, man may will to say what he thinks.

German Text of Novalis Quotations from Volume I

Die Lehrlinge zu Sais

[I,79,1–80,23] "Mannichfache Wege gehen die Menschen. Wer sie verfolgt und vergleicht, wird wunderliche Figuren entstehen sehn; Figuren, die zu jener grossen Chiffernschrift zu gehören scheinen, die man überall, auf Flügeln, Eierschalen, in Wolken, im Schnee, in Krystallen und in Steinbildungen, auf gefrierenden Wassern, im Innern und Äussern der Gebirge, der Pflanzen, der Thiere, der Menschen, in den Lichtern des Himmels, auf berührten und gestrichenen Scheiben von Pech und Glas, in den Feilspänen um den Magnet her, und sonderbaren Conjincturen des Zufalls, erblickt. In ihnen ahndet man den Schlüssel dieser Wunderschrift, die Sprachlehre derselben; allein die Ahndung will sich selbst in keine feste Formen fügen, und scheint kein höherer Schlüssel werden zu wollen. Ein Alcahest scheint über die Sinne der Menschen ausgegossen zu seyn. Nur augenblicklich scheinen ihre Wünsche, ihre Gedanken sich zu verdichten. So entstehen ihre Ahndungen, aber nach kurzen Zeiten schwimmt alles wieder, wie vorher, vor ihren Blicken.

"Von weitem hört' ich sagen: die Unverständlichkeit sey Folge nur des Unverstandes; dieser suche, was er habe, und also niemals weiter finden könnte. Man verstehe die Sprache nicht, weil sich die Sprache selber nicht verstehe, nicht verstehen wolle; die ächte Sanscrit spräche, um zu sprechen, weil Sprechen ihre Lust und ihr Wesen sey.

"Nicht lange darauf sprach einer: Keiner Erklärung bedarf die heilige Schrift. Wer wahrhaft spricht, ist des ewigen Lebens voll, und wunderbar verwandt mit ächten Geheimnissen dünkt uns seine Schrift, denn sie ist ein Accord aus des Weltalls Symphonie.

"Von unserm Lehrer sprach gewiss die Stimme, denn er versteht die

Züge zu versammeln, die überall zerstreut sind. Ein eignes Licht ent-
zündet sich in seinen Blicken, wenn vor uns nun die hohe Rune liegt,
und er in unsern Augen späht, ob auch in uns aufgegangen ist das Ge-
stirn, das die Figur sichtbar und verständlich macht. Sieht er uns traurig,
dass die Nacht nicht weicht, so tröstet er uns, und verheisst dem äm-
sigen, treuen Seher künftiges Glück. Oft hat er uns erzählt, wie ihm als
Kind der Trieb die Sinne zu üben, zu beschäftigen und zu erfüllen, keine
Ruhe liess. Den Sternen sah er zu und ahmte ihre Züge, ihre Stellungen
im Sande nach. In's Luftmeer sah er ohne Rast, und ward nicht müde
seine Klarheit, seine Bewegungen, seine Wolken, seine Lichter zu betrachten. Er sammelte sich Steine, Blumen, Käfer aller Art, und legte sie
auf mannichfache Weise sich in Reihen. Auf Menschen und auf Thiere
gab er Acht, am Strande des Meeres sass er, suchte Muscheln. Auf sein
Gemüth und seine Gedanken lauschte er sorgsam. Er wusste nicht,
wohin ihn seine Sehnsucht trieb. Wie er grösser ward, strich er umher,
besah sich andre Länder, andre Meere, neue Lüfte, fremde Sterne, unbekannte Pflanzen, Thiere, Menschen, stieg in Höhlen, sah wie in Bänk-
en und in bunten Schichten der Erde Bau vollführt war, und drückte
Thon in sonderbare Felsenbilder. Nun fand er überall Bekanntes wieder,
nur wunderlich gemischt, gepaart, und also ordneten sich selbst in ihm
oft seltsame Dinge. Er merkte bald auf die Verbindungen in allem, auf
Begegnungen, Zusammentreffungen. Nun sah er bald nichts mehr allein.—In grosse bunte Bilder drängten sich die Wahrnehmungen seiner
Sinne: er hörte, sah, tastete und dachte zugleich. Er freute sich, Fremd-
linge zusammen zu bringen. Bald waren ihm die Sterne Menschen, bald
die Menschen Sterne, die Steine Thiere, die Wolken Pflanzen, er spielte
mit den Kräften und Erscheinungen, er wusste wo und wie er dies und
jenes finden, und erscheinen lassen konnte, und griff so selbst in den
Saiten nach Tönen und Gängen umher."
[I,81,12–22] "Er sang ein hohes, frohes Lied; wir wunderten uns alle; der
Lehrer sah mit einem Blick nach Morgen, wie ich ihn wohl nie wieder
sehen werde. In unsre Mitte trat er bald, und brachte, mit unaussprech-
licher Seligkeit im Antlitz, ein unscheinbares Steinchen von seltsamer
Gestalt. Der Lehrer nahm es in die Hand, und küsste ihn lange, dann sah
er uns mit nassen Augen an und legte dieses Steinchen auf einen leeren
Platz, der mitten unter andern Steinen lag, gerade wo wie Strahlen viele
Reihen sich berührten.

"Ich werde diesen Augenblick nie fortan vergessen. Uns war, als
hätten wir im Vorübergehn eine helle Ahndung dieser wunderbaren
Welt in unsern Seelen gehabt."
[I,82,17–23] "Vielmehr will er, dass wir den eignen Weg verfolgen, weil
jeder neue Weg durch neue Länder geht, und jeder endlich zu diesen

Wohnungen, zu dieser heiligen Heimath wieder führet. Auch ich will also meine Figur beschreiben, und wenn kein Sterblicher, nach jener Inschrift dort, den Schleyer hebt, so müssen wir Unsterbliche zu werden suchen; wer ihn nicht heben will, ist kein ächter Lehrling zu Sais."

[I,84,17–36] "Was jene im Ganzen sammelten und in grossen, geordneten Massen aufstellten, haben diese für menschliche Herzen zur täglichen Nahrung und Nothdurft verarbeitet, und jene unermessliche Natur zu mannichfaltigen, kleinen, gefälligen Naturen zersplittert und gebildet. . . . Unter ihren Händen starb die freundliche Natur, und liess nur todte, zuckende Reste zurück, . . . Wer also ihr Gemüth recht kennen will, muss sie in der Gesellschaft der Dichter suchen, dort ist sie offen und ergiesst ihr wundersames Herz. Wer sie aber nicht aus Herzensgrunde liebt, und dies und jenes nur an ihr bewundert, und zu erfahren strebt, muss ihre Krankenstube, ihr Beinhaus fleissig besuchen."

[I,95,4–7] "Es dünkte ihm alles so bekannt und doch in niegesehener Herrlichkeit, da schwand auch der letzte irdische Anflug, wie in Luft verzehrt, und er stand vor der himmlischen Jungfrau, da hob er den leichten, glänzenden Schleyer, und Rosenblüthchen sank in seine Arme."

[I,99,4–12] "Der eigentliche Chiffrirer wird vielleicht dahin kommen, mehrere Naturkräfte zugleich zu Hervorbringung herrlicher und nützlicher Erscheinungen in Bewegung zu setzen, er wird auf der Natur, wie auf einem grossen Instrument fantasiren können, und doch wird er die Natur nicht verstehn. Dies ist die Gabe des Naturhistorikers, des Zeitensehers, der vertraut mit der Geschichte der Natur, und bekannt mit der Welt, diesem höhern Schauplatz der Naturgeschichte, ihre Bedeutungen wahrnimmt und weissagend verkündigt."

[I,99,17–23] "Alles Göttliche hat eine Geschichte und die Natur, dieses einzige Ganze, womit der Mensch sich vergleichen kann, sollte nicht so gut wie der Mensch in einer Geschichte begriffen seyn oder welches eins ist, einen Geist haben? die Natur wäre nicht die Natur, wenn sie keinen Geist hätte, nicht jenes einzige Gegenbild der Menschheit, nicht die unentbehrliche Antwort dieser geheimnissvollen Frage, oder die Frage zu dieser unendlichen Antwort."

[I,105,5–11] "Wie seltsam, dass gerade die heiligsten und reitzendsten Erscheinungen der Natur in den Händen so todter Menschen sind, als die Scheidekünstler zu seyn pflegen! sie, die den schöpferischen Sinn der Natur mit Macht erwecken, nur ein Geheimniss der Liebenden, Mysterien der höhern Menschheit seyn sollten, werden mit Schaamlosigkeit und sinnlos von rohen Geistern hervorgerufen, die nie wissen werden, welche Wunder ihre Gläser umschliessen."

[I,106,26–107,3] "Vorzüglich hatte sie jene heilige Sprache gelockt, die das glänzende Band jener königlichen Menschen mit überirdischen Gegenden und Bewohnern gewesen war, und von der einig Worte, nach dem Verlaut mannichfaltiger Sagen, noch im Besitz einiger glücklichen Weisen unter unsern Vorfahren gewesen seyn mögen. Ihre Aussprache war ein wunderbarer Gesang, dessen unwiderstehliche Töne tief in das Innere jeder Natur eindrangen und sie zerlegten. Jeder ihrer Namen schien das Loosungswort für die Seele jedes Naturkörpers. Mit schöpferischer Gewalt erregten diese Schwingungen alle Bilder der Welterscheinungen, und von ihnen konnte man mit Recht sagen, dass das Leben des Universums ein ewiges tausendstimmiges Gespräch sey; denn in ihrem Sprechen schienen alle Kräfte, alle Arten der Thätigkeit auf das Unbegreiflichste vereinigt zu seyn."

[I,110,#1] "Der geognostische Streit der Volkanisten und Neptunisten ist eigentlich der Streit: Ob die Erde sthenisch oder asthenisch debütirt hat."

Hymnen an die Nacht

[I,134,170–196] "Einst, da ich bittre Thränen vergoss— / Da in Schmerz aufgelösst meine Hoffnung zerrann / und ich einsam stand an dem dürren Hügel, der in engen / dunkeln Raum die Gestalt meines Lebens begrub, Einsam, / wie noch kein Einsamer war, von unsäglicher Angst ge-trieben, Kraftlos, nur ein Gedanke des Elends noch,— / Wie ich da nach Hülfe umherschaute, Vorwärts nicht könnte / und rückwarts nicht— und am fliehenden, verlöschten Leben / mit unendlicher Sehnsucht hing—da kam aus blauen Fernen, / Von den Höhen meiner alten Seligkeit ein Dämmerungs Schauer— / Und mit einemmale riss das Band der Geburt, des / Lichtes Fessel—Hin floh die irrdische Herrlichkeit und / meine Trauer mit ihr. Zusammen floss die Wehmut / in eine neue unergründliche Welt—Du Nachtbegei-sterung, Schlummer des Himmels kamst über mich. / Die Gegend hob sich sacht empor—über der Gegend / schwebte mein entbundner neugeborner Geist. Zur Staubwolke / wurde der Hügel und durch die Wolke sah ich die / verklärten Züge der Geliebten—In Ihren Augen / ruhte die Ewigkeit—ich fasste ihre Hände und die / Thränen wurden ein funkelndes, unzerreissliches / Band. Jahrtausende zogen abwärts in die Ferne, / wie Ungewitter—An ihrem Halse weint ich dem / neuen Leben entzückende Thränen. Das war der / Erste Traum in dir. Er zog vorüber aber sein Abglanz / blieb der ewige unerschütterliche Glauben an den / Nachthimmel und seine Sonne, die Geliebte."

[I,135,25–27] "Es war der erste einzige Traum—und erst seitdem fühl ich ewigen, unwandelbaren Glauben an den Himmel der Nacht und sein Licht, die Geliebte."

Geistliche Lieder

[I,163,33–36,#3] "Was du verlohrst, hat er gefunden;
Du triffst bey ihm, was du geliebt:
Und ewig bleibt mit dir verbunden,
Was seine Hand dir wiedergiebt."

[I,164,1–24,#4] "Unter tausend frohen Stunden,
So im Leben ich gefunden,
Blieb nur eine mir getreu;
Eine, wo in tausend Schmerzen
Ich erfuhr im meinem Herzen,
Wer für uns gestorben sey.

"Meine Welt war mir zerbrochen,
Wie von einem Wurm gestochen
Welkte Herz und Blüthe mir;
Meines Lebens ganze Habe,
Jeder Wunsch lag mir im Grabe,
Und zur Qual war ich noch hier.

"Da ich so im stillen krankte,
Ewig weint' und wegverlangte,
Und nur blieb vor Angst und Wahn:
Ward mir plötzlich, wie von oben
Weg des Grabes Stein gehoben,
Und mein Innres aufgetan.

"Wen ich sah, und wen an seiner
Hand erblickte, frage Keiner,
Ewig werd' ich diess nur sehn;
Und von allen Lebensstunden
Wird nur die, wie meine Wunden
Ewig heiter, offen stehn."

Heinrich von Ofterdingen

[I,196,32–197,7] "Er tauchte seine Hand in das Becken und benetzte seine Lippen. Es war, als durchdränge ihn ein geistiger Hauch, und er fühlte sich innigst gestärkt und erfrischt. Ein unwiderstehliches Verlangen ergriff ihn sich zu baden, er entkleidete sich und stieg in das Becken. Es dünkte ihn, als umflösse ihn eine Wolke des Abendroths; eine himmlische Empfindung überströmte sein Inneres; mit inniger Wollust strebten unzählbare Gedanken in ihm sich zu vermischen; neue, niegesehene Bilder entstanden, die auch in einander flossen und zu sichtbaren Wesen um ihn wurden, und jede Welle des lieblichen Elements schmiegte sich wie ein zarter Busen an ihn. Die Flut schien eine Auflösung reizender Mädchen, die an dem Jünglinge sich augenblicklich verkörperten."

[I,198,12–27] "Träume sind Schäume, mögen auch die hochgelahrten Herren davon denken, was sie wollen, und du thust wohl, wenn du dein Gemüth von dergleichen unnützen and schädlichen Betrachtungen abwendest. Die Zeiten sind nicht mehr, wo zu den Träumen göttliche Gesichte sich gesellten, und wir können und werden es nicht begreifen, wie es jenen auserwählten Männern, von denen die Bibel erzählt, zu Muthe gewesen ist. Damals muss es eine andere Beschaffenheit mit den Träumen gehabt haben, so wie mit den menschlichen Dingen.

"In dem Alter der Welt, wo wir leben, findet der unmittelbare Verkehr mit dem Himmel nich mehr Statt. Die alten Geschichten und Schriften sind jetzt die einzigen Quellen, durch die uns eine Kenntniss von der überirdischen Welt, so weit wir sie nöthig haben, zu Theil wird; und statt jener ausdrücklichen Offenbarungen redet jetzt der heilige Geist mittelbar durch den Verstand kluger und wohl gesinnter Männer und durch die Lebensweise und die Schicksale frommer Menschen zu uns."

[I,198,30–199,19] "Aber, lieber Vater, aus welchem Grunde seyd Ihr so den Träumen entgegen, deren seltsame Verwandlungen und leichte zarte Natur doch unser Nachdenken gewisslich rege machen müssen? Ist nicht jeder, auch der verworrenste Traum, eine sonderliche Erscheinung, die auch ohne noch an göttliche Schickung dabey zu denken, ein bedeutsamer Riss in den geheimnissvollen Vorhang ist, der mit tausend Falten in unser Inneres hereinfällt? In den weisesten Büchern findet man unzählige Traumgeschichten von glaubhaften Menschen, und erinnert Euch nur noch des Traums, den uns neulich der ehrwürdige Hofkaplan erzählte, und der Euch selbst so merkwürdig vorkam.

"Aber, auch ohne diese Geschichten, wenn Ihr zuerst in Eurem Leben einen Traum hättet, wie würdet Ihr nicht erstaunen, und Euch die Wunderbarkeit dieser uns nur alltäglich gewordenen Begebenheit gewiss nicht abstreiten lassen! Mich dünkt der Traum eine Schutzwehr gegen die Regelmässigkeit und Gewöhnlichkeit des Lebens, eine freye Erholung der gebundenen Fantasie, wo sie alle Bilder des Lebens durcheinanderwirft, und die beständige Ernsthaftigkeit des erwachsenen Menschen durch ein fröhliches Kinderspiel unterbricht. Ohne die Träume würden wir gewiss früher alt, und so kann man den Traum, wenn auch nicht als unmittelbar von oben gegeben, doch als eine göttlich Mitgabe, einen freundlichen Begleiter auf der Wallfahrt zum heiligen Grabe betrachten. Gewiss ist der Traum, den ich heute Nacht träumte, kein unwirksamer Zufall in meinem Leben gewesen, denn ich fühle es, dass er in meine

Seele wie ein weites Rad hineingreift, und sie in mächtigem Schwunge forttreibt."

[I,219,24–27] "Die Sonne fing eben an, die Wipfel der alten Bäume zu vergolden, die sich mit sanftem Flüstern bewegten, als wollten sie sich gegenseitig aus nächtlichen Gesichtern erwecken, um die Sonne gemeinschaftlich zu begrüssen."

[I,229,33–230,11] "Der junge Ofterdingen ward von Rittern und Frauen wegen seiner Bescheidenheit und seines ungezwungenen milden Betragens gepriesen, und die letztern verweilten gern auf seiner einnehmenden Gestalt, die wie das einfache Wort eines Unbekannten war, das man fast überhört, bis längst nach seinem Abschiede es seine tiefe unscheinbare Knospe immer mehr aufthut, und endlich eine herrliche Blume in allem Farbenglanze dichtverschlungener Blätter zeigt, so dass man es nie vergisst, nicht müde wird es zuiederholen, und einen unversieglichen immer gegenwärtigen Schatz daran hat. Man besinnt sich nun genauer auf den Unbekannten, und ahndet und ahndet, bis es auf einmal klar wird, dass es ein Bewohner der höhern Welt gewesen sey." *w*

[I,246,9–15] "Wahrhaftig, das muss ein göttlicher Mann gewesen seyn, der den Menschen zuerst die edle Kunst des Bergbaus gelehrt, und in dem Schoosse der Felsen dieses ernste Sinnbild des menschlichen Lebens verborgen hat. Hier ist der Gang mächtig und gebräch, aber arm, dort drückt ihn der Felsen in eine armselige, unbedeutende Kluft zusammen, and gerade hier brechen die edelsten Geschicke ein."

[I,252,20–23] "Gewaltige Klänge bebten in den silbernen Gesang, und zu den weiten Thoren traten alle Creaturen herein, von denen jede ihre innere Natur in einer einfachen Bitte und in einer eigenthümlichen Mundart vernehmlich aussprach."

[I,257,13–14]   "Friedrich und Marie von Hohenzollern
          kehrten auf dieser Stelle in ihr Vaterland zurück."

[I,258,15–16] "Die Kirche ist das Wohnhaus der Geschichte, und der stille Hof ihr sinnbildlicher Blumengarten."

[I,259,13–21] ". . . . und so ist es mit den meisten Geschichtschreibern, die vielleicht fertig genug im Erzählen und bis zum Überdruss weitschweifig sind, aber doch gerade das Wissenswürdigste vergessen, dasjenige, was erst die Geschichte zur Geschichte macht, und die mancherley Zufälle zu einem angenehmen und lehrreichen Ganzen verbindet. Wenn ich das alles recht bedenke, so scheint es mir, als wenn ein Geschichtschreiber nothwendig auch ein Dichter seyn müsste, denn nur die Dichter mögen sich auf jene Kunst, Begebenheiten schicklich zu verknüpfen, verstehen."

[I,259,23–24] "Es ist mehr Wahrheit in ihren Mährchen, als in gelehrten Chroniken."

[I,264,2–5] "Heinrich blätterte in den grossen schöngemahlten Schriften;

die kurzen Zeilen der Verse, die Überschriften, einzelne Stellen, und die saubern Bilder, die hier und da, wie verkörperte Worte, zum Vorschein kamen. . . ."

[I,266,4–10] "Wie lange wird es währen, so sehn wir uns wieder, und werden über unsere heutigen Reden lächeln. Ein himmlischer Tag wird uns umgeben, und wir werden uns freuen, dass wir einander in diesen Thälern der Prüfung freundlich begrüssten, und von gleichen Gesinnungen und Ahndungen beseelt waren. Sie sind die Engel, die uns hier sicher geleiten. Wenn euer Auge fest am Himmel haftet, so werdet ihr nie den Weg zu eurer Heymath verlieren."

[I,279,5] "Sie sagte ihm ein wunderbares geheimes Wort in den Mund, was sein ganzes Wesen durchklang."

[I,284,25–30] "Manche Länder und Zeiten scheinen, wie die meisten Menschen, ganz unter der Botmässigkeit dieser Feindinn der Poësie [dumpfer Begierde] zu stehen, dagegen in andern die Poësie einheimisch und überall sichtbar ist. Für den Geschichtschreiber sind die Zeiten dieses Kampfes äusserst merkwürdig. . . . Es sind gewöhnlich die Geburtszeiten der Dichter."

Vermischte Gedichte

[I,403–04]   *Kenne dich selbst*

"*Eins* nur ist, was der Mensch zu allen Zeiten gesucht hat;
    Ueberall, bald auf den Höhn, bald in dem Tiefsten der Welt—
Unter verschiedenen Namen—umsonst—es versteckte sich immer,
    Immer empfand er es noch—dennoch erfasst er es nie.
Längst schon fand sich ein Mann, der den Kindern in freundlichen
                                  Mythen
    Weg und Schlüssel verrieth zu des Verborgenen Schloss.
Wenige deuteten sich die leichte Chiffre der Lösung,
    Aber die wenigen auch waren nun Meister des Ziels.
Lange Zeiten verflossen—der Irrtum schärfte den Sinn uns—
    Dass uns der Mythus selbst nicht mehr die Wahrheit verbarg.
Glücklich, wer weise geworden und nicht die Welt mehr durchgrübelt,
    Wer von sich selber den Stein ewiger Weisheit begehrt.
Nur der vernünftige Mensch ist der ächte Adept—er verwandelt
    Alles in Leben und Gold—braucht Elixire nicht mehr.
In ihm dampft der heilige Kolben—der König ist in ihm—
    Delphos auch und er fasst endlich das: *Kenne dich selbst*."

GERMAN TEXT OF NOVALIS QUOTATIONS FROM VOLUME II

Frühe Prosaarbeiten

[II,20,#8] *Apologie der Schwärmerey.*

Von der Begeisterung

[II,22,22–31] "Der erste Wind, das erste Lüftchen, das dem Ohre des Wilden hörbar durch den Gipfel der Eiche sauste, brachte gewiss in demselben in seinem jungen, unausgebildeten, allen äusserlichen Eindrücken noch offenen Busen eine Bewegung, einen Gedanken von dem Dasein eines mächtigen Wesens hervor, der sehr nahe an die Begeisterung grenzte und wo ihm nichts als Worte fehlten, um sein volles überfliessendes Gefühl durch sie ausströmen und es gleichsam den leblosen Gegenständen um ihn mit empfinden zu lassen, da er jetzt ohne Sprache gewiss unwillkürlich auf die Kniee sank und durch seine stumme Bewegung verriet, dass Gefühle an Gefühle in seinem Herzen sich drängten."

[II,23,3–15] "Da entstand zuerst die Dichtkunst, die Tochter des edelsten Ungestüms der erhabensten und stärksten Empfindungen und Leidenschaften, die sich zwar nachher wie ein Chamäleon nach den Organisationen der verschiedenen Erdstriche, Zeiten und Charaktere umgebildet, aber in ihrer Urbedeutung, zu ihrer grössten Stärke, Zauberei und Wirkung auf die Gemüter, ihrer Mutter, der hohen Begeisterung, noch immer nötig hat. Alles dies aber, was ich hier gesagt habe, gilt nur hauptsächlich von dem Morgenlande, dem eigentlichen Vaterlande der Menschheit, Sprache, Dichtkunst und daher auch der Begeisterung, von woher eigentlich wie vom Urstamme sich alles in die übrigen Erdgegenden und Zonen nur fortgepflanzt hat und eingepfropft worden ist."

Philosophische Studien; Erste Gruppe (Herbst bis Frühjahr 1795)

[II,142,14–17,#63] "Das analytische Ich wechselt wieder mit sich selbst—wie das Ich schlechthin—in der Anschauung—Es wechselt Bild and Seyn. Das Bild ist immer das Verkehrte vom Seyn. Was rechts an der Person ist, ist links im Bilde."

Hemsterhuis-Studien (1797)

Aristée

[II,370,#30] "Organ ist Werckzeug—Mittel zu einem bestimmten Ende. . . .

/ Jedes endliche Wesen ist Werckzeug /
ist *Organ*—Mittel zu einem Best[immten] *Ende* . . .

"Nur aus Analogie mit *unserer Kunst*, nennen wir die Theile der Natur, die vorzüglich mit ihrer Fortpflanzung und Modification sich zu beschäftigen scheinen—Organe. [p. 38]

"Wo Organisation sichtbar wird—offenbart sich zugleich Zweck—Ziel—Wo ein *Ziel* erscheint—werden wir auf ein *Ideal*, auf einen *Gedanken* getrieben, der dem Realen, der Ausführung, dem Object, *vorangehe*.

"Organisation ist jene treibende Kraft der Theile—Substanzen hervorzubringen." [p. 38/39]

Alexis

[II,373,#33] "Der Geist der Poësie ist das Morgenlicht, was die Statüe des Memnons tönen macht."

Fragmentblatt

[II,395,#54] "Der ächte philosophische Act ist Selbsttödtung; dies ist der reale Anfang aller Philosophie, dahin geht alles Bedürfniss des philosophischen Jüngers, und nur dieser Act entspricht allen Bedingungen und Merckmalen der transscendenten Handlung."

[II,395,#56] "Ich habe zu Söfchen Religion—nicht Liebe. Absolute Liebe, vom Herzen unabhängige, auf Glauben gegründete ist Religion!"

[II,395,#57] "Liebe kann durch absoluten Willen in Religion übergehn. Des höchsten Wesens wird man nur durch Tod werth. / Versöhnungstod. / "

Vermischte Bemerkungen

[II,414,#11] "Der Tod ist eine Selbstbesiegung—die, wie alle Selbstüberwindung, eine neue, leichtere Existenz verschafft. / " [Ath.292]

[II,416,#13] "Wunder stehn mit naturgesezlichen Wirckungen in Wechsel —Sie beschränken einander gegenseitig, und machen zusammen ein Ganzes aus. Sie sind vereinigt, indem sie sich gegenseitig aufheben. Kein Wunder ohne Naturbegebenheit und umgekehrt."

[II,416,#15] "Leben ist der Anfang des Todes. Das Leben ist um des Todes willen. Der Tod ist Endigung and Anfang zugleich—Scheidung and nähere Selbstverbindung zugleich. Durch den Tod wird die Reduktion vollendet."

[II,416,#16] "Wir sind dem Aufwachen nah, wenn wir träumen, dass wir träumen." [Ath.288]

[II,416,30–418,9,#17] "Die Fantasie sezt die künftige Welt ent[weder] in die

Höhe, oder in die Tiefe, oder in der Metempsychose, zu uns. Wir träumen von Reisen durch das Weltall—ist denn das Weltall nicht *in uns?* Die
Tiefen unsers Geistes kennen wir nicht—Nach Innen geht der geheimnissvolle Weg. In uns, oder nirgends ist die Ewigkeit mit ihren Welten—
die Vergangenheit und Zukunft. Die Aussenwelt ist die Schattenwelt—
Sie wirft ihren Schatten in das Lichtreich. Jezt scheints uns freylich in-
nerlich so dunkel, einsam, gestaltlos—Aber wie ganz anders wird es uns
dünken—wenn diese Verfinsterung vorbey, und der Schattenkörper
hinweggerückt ist—Wir werden mehr geniessen als je, denn unser Geist
hat entbehrt.''

[II,420,10–12,#22] ''Ohne Genialitaet existirten wir alle überhaupt nicht.
Genie ist zu allem nöthig. Was man aber gewöhnlich Genie nennt—ist
Genie des Genies.''

[II,424,#27] ''Eine merkwürdige Eigenheit Göthes bemerckt man in
seinen Verknüpfungen kleiner, unbedeutender Vorfälle mit wichtigern
Begebenheiten. Er scheint keine andre Absicht dabey zu hegen, als die
Einbildungskraft auf eine poëtische Weise, mit einem mysteriösen Spiel,
zu beschäftigen. Auch hier ist der sonderbare Mann der Natur auf die
Spur gekommen und hat ihr einen artigen Kunstgriff abgemerckt. Das
gewöhnliche Leben ist voll ähnlicher Zufälle. Sie machen ein Spiel aus,
das, wie alles Spiel, auf Überraschung und Täuschung hinausläuft.

Mehrere Sagen des gemeinen Lebens beruhn auf einer Bemerckung
dieses verkehrten Zusammenhangs—so z. B. bedeuten *böse Träume*
Glück—Todtsagen, langes Leben—ein Hase, der über den Weg läuft
Unglück. Fast der ganze Aberglaube des gemeinen Volks beruht auf
Deutungen dieses Spiels.''

[II,424,#29] ''Nur dann zeige ich, dass ich einen Schriftsteller verstanden
habe, wenn ich in seinem Geiste handeln kann, wenn ich ihn, ohne seine
Individualitaet zu schmälern, übersetzen, und mannichfach verändern
kann.'' [Ath. 287]

[II,436,31–438,3,#65] ''Alle Zufälle unsers Lebens sind Materialien, aus denen wir machen können, was wir wollen. Wer viel Geist hat macht viel
aus seinem Leben—Jede Bekanntschaft, jeder Vorfall, wäre für den
durchaus Geistigen—erstes Glied einer unendlichen Reihe—Anfang
eines unendlichen Romans.''

[II,438,#68] ''Eine Übersetzung ist entweder grammatisch, oder verändernd, oder mythisch. Mythische Übersetzungen sind Übersetzungen
im höchsten Styl. Sie stellen den reinen, vollendeten Karacter des individuellen Kunstwerks dar. Sie geben uns nicht das wirckliche Kunstwerk, sondern das Ideal desselben. Noch existirt, wie ich glaube kein
ganzes Muster derselben. Im Geist mancher Kritiken und Beschrei-
bungen von Kunstwercken trift man aber helle Spuren. Es gehört

ein Kopf dazu, indem sich poëtischer Geist und philosophischer Geist in ihrer ganzen Fülle durchdrungen haben. Die griechische Mythologie ist zum Theil eine solche Übersetzung einer Nationalreligion. Auch die moderne Madonna ist ein solcher Mythuss.

"Grammatische Übersetzungen sind die Übersetzungen im gewöhnlichen Sinn. Sie erfordern sehr viel Gelehrsamkeit—aber nur discursive Fähigkeiten."

"Zu den Verändernden Übersetzungen gehört, wenn sie ächt seyn sollen, der höchste, poëtische Geist. Sie streifen leicht in die Travestie— wie Bürgers Homer in Jamben—Popens Homer—die Französischen Übersetzungen insgesammt. Der wahre Übersetzer dieser Art muss in der That der Künstler selbst seyn, und die Idee des Ganzen beliebig so oder so geben können—Er muss der Dichter des Dichters seyn und ihn also nach seiner und des Dichters eigner Idee *zugleich* reden lassen können. In einem ähnlichen Verhältnisse steht der Genius der Menschheit mit jedem einzelnen Menschen.

"Nicht bloss Bücher, alles kann auf diese drey Arten übersezt werden."

[II,444–446,#75] "Dichter und Priester waren am Anfang Eins—und nur spätere Zeiten haben sie getrennt. Der ächte Dichter ist aber immer Priester, so wie der ächte Priester immer Dichter geblieben—und sollte die Zukunft nicht den alten Zustand der Dinge wieder herbeyführen?"

[II,440,28–443,18,#74] "Nichts ist zur wahren Religiositaet unentbehrlicher, als ein Mittelglied—das uns mit der Gottheit verbindet. Unmittelbar kann der Mensch schlechterdings nicht mit derselben in Verhältniss stehn. In der Wahl dieses Mittelglieds muss der Mensch durchaus frey seyn. Der mindeste Zwang hierinn schadet seiner Religion. Die Wahl ist caracteristisch und es werden mithin die gebildeten Menschen ziemlich gleiche Mittelglieder wählen—dahingegen der Ungebildete gewöhnlich durch Zufall hier bestimmt werden wird. Da aber so wenig Menschen einer freyen Wahl überhaupt fähig sind—so werden manche Mittelglieder allgemeiner werden—sey es durch Zufall—durch Association, oder ihre besondre Schicklichkeit dazu. Auf diese Art entstehn Landesreligionen. Je selbstständiger der Mensch wird, desto mehr vermindert sich die Quantität des Mittelglieds, die Qualität verfeinert sich—und seine Verhältnisse zu demselben werden mannichfaltiger und gebildeter—Fetische—Gestirne—Thiere—Helden—Götzen—Götter—*Ein* Gottmensch. Man sieht bald, wie relativ diese Wahlen sind und wird unvermerckt auf die Idee getrieben—dass das Wesen der Religion wohl nicht von der Beschaffenheit des Mittlers abhänge, sondern lediglich in der Ansicht desselben, in den Verhältnissen zu ihm bestehe."

[II,456,#96] "Wo Kinder sind, da ist ein goldnes Zeitalter."

Glauben und Liebe oder *Der König und die Königin*

[II,485,#1] "Wenn man mit Wenigen, in einer grossen, gemischten Gesellschaft etwas heimliches reden will, und man sitzt nicht neben einander, so muss man in einer besondern Sprache reden. Diese besondre Sprache kann entweder eine *dem Ton* nach, oder *den Bildern* nach fremde Sprache seyn. Dies letztere wird eine Tropen und Räthselsprache seyn."
[II,485,#2] "Viele haben gemeynt, man solle von zarten, missbrauchbaren Gegenständen, eine gelehrte Sprache führen, z. B. lateinisch von Dingen der Art schreiben. Es käme auf einen Versuch an, ob man nicht in der gewöhnlichen Landessprache so sprechen könnte, dass es nur *der* verstehn könnte, der es verstehn sollte. Jedes wahre Geheimniss muss die Profanen von selbst ausschliessen. Wer es versteht ist von selbst, mit recht, *Eingeweihter.*"
[II,485,#3] "Der mystische Ausdruck ist ein Gedankenreiz mehr. Alle Wahrheit ist uralt. Der Reiz der Neuheit liegt nur in den Variationen des Ausdrucks. Je contrastirender die Erscheinung, desto grösser die Freude des Wiedererkennens."

Logologische Fragmente

[II,522,#3] "❙Der Buchstabe ist nur eine Hülfe der philosophischen Mittheilung, deren eigentliches Wesen in Erregung eine bestimmten Ge- *s* danckengangs besteht. Der Redende denckt producirt—der Hörende denckt nach—reproducirt. Die Worte sind ein trügliches Medium des Vordenckens—unzuverlässige Vehikel eines bestimmten, specifischen Reitzes. . . .❙"
[II,523,#6] "❙Jedes Wort ist ein Wort der Beschwörung. Welcher Geist ruft—ein solcher erscheint.❙"

Poesie

[II,534,#34] "❙Das Gedicht der Wilden ist eine Erzählung ohne Anfang, Mittel [sic] und Ende—das Vergnügen, das sie dabey empfinden[,] ist blos pathologisch—einfache Beschäftigung, blos dynamische Belebung des Vorstellungsvermögens.

"Das epische Gedicht ist das veredelte primitive Gedicht. Im Wesentlichen ganz dasselbe.

"Der Roman steht schon weit höher—Jenes dauert fort—dieser wächst fort—in Jenem ist arythmetische, im Roman geometrische Progression.❙"

Vermischte Fragmente I (February–May 1798)

[II,541,#74] "★Zur Welt suchen wir den *Entwurf*—dieser Entwurf sind wir selbst—Was sind wir? personificirte *allmächtige Puncte*. Die Ausführung, als Bild des Entwurfs, muss ihm aber auch in der Freythätigkeit und Selbstbeziehung gleich seyn—und umgekehrt. Das Leben oder das Wesen des Geistes besteht also in Zeugung Gebährung und Erziehung seines Gleichen. Nur insofern der Mensch also mit sich selbst eine glückliche Ehe führt—und eine schöne Familie ausmacht, ist er überhaupt Ehe und Familienfähig. Act der Selbstumarmung.

"Man muss sich nie gestehen, dass man sich selbst liebt—Das Geheimniss dieses Geständnisses ist das Lebensprincip der alleinwahren und ewigen Liebe. Der erste Kuss in diesem Verständnisse ist das Princip der Philosophie—der Ursprung einer neuen Welt—Der Anfang der absoluten Zeitrechnung—die Vollziehung eines unendlichen wachsenden Selbstbundes.

"Wem gefiele nicht eine Philosophie, deren Keim ein erster Kuss ist?

"Liebe popularisirt die Personalitaet—Sie macht Individualitaeten *mittheilbar* und *verständlich.* (Liebesverständniss.)"

[II,545,#104] "Ehemals war alles Geistererscheinung. Jezt sehn wir nichts, als todte Wiederholung, die wir nicht verstehn. Die Bedeutung der Hieroglyfe fehlt. Wir leben noch von der Frucht besserer Zeiten."

Vermischte Fragmente II (February–May 1798)

[II,558,#141] "Auch die Sprache ist ein Produkt des organischen Bil-[dungs] Triebes. Sowie nun dieser überall *dasselbe,* unter den verschiedensten Umständen bildet, so bildet sich auch hier durch Kultur, durch steigende Ausbildung und Belebung, die Sprache zum tiefsinnigen Ausdruck der Idee der Organisation, zum *System der Phil[osophie].*

"Die ganze Sprache ist ein *Postulat.* Sie ist positiven, freyen Ursprungs. Man musste sich einverstehen, bey Gewissen Zeichen gewisse Dinge zu denken, mit Absicht etwas Bestimmtes in sich zu construiren."

[II,559,#148] "Rechte des Gesprächs— / absolutes Spiel. /

"Wahre Mittheilung findet nur unter Gleichgesinnten, Gleichdenkenden statt."

[II,560,#164] "Jeder Mensch hat seine eigne Sprache. Sprache ist Ausdruck des Geistes. Individuelle Sprachen. Sprachgenie. Fertigkeit in und aus andern Sprachen zu übersetzen. Reichthum and Euphonie jeder Sprache. Der ächte Ausdruck macht die *klare* Idee. Sobald man nur die rechten Namen hat, so hat man die Ideen inne. Durchsichtiger, leitender Ausdruck."

[II,561,#169] "Associationsgesetze. / Der Phil[osoph] übersezt die wirckliche Welt in die Gedankenwelt und umgekehrt, um beyden einen *Verstand* zu geben."

[II,561,#174] "Der Mensch—Metapher."

[II,562,#177] "Nur ein Künstler kann den Sinn des Lebens errathen."

[II,562,#178] "Jedes Ding hat seine *Zeit*. Übereilung."

Fragmente oder Denkaufgaben

[II,564,#197] "Was ist der Mensch? Ein vollkommner Trope des Geistes. Alle ächte Mittheilung ist also sinnbildsam—und sind also nicht Liebkosungen ächte Mittheilungen?"

Anekdoten

[II,568,#207] "★Alle Poësie unterbricht den gewöhnlichen Zustand—das gemeine Leben, fast, *wie der Schlummer,* um uns zu *erneuern*—und so unser Lebensgefühl immer *rege* zu erhalten."

Vermischte Fragmente III

[II,570,#212] "Der Roman handelt von Leben—stellt *Leben* dar. Ein Mimus wär er nur in Beziehung auf den Dichter. Oft enthält er Begebenheiten einer Maskerade—eine masquirte Begebenheit unter masquirten Personen. Man hebe die Masken—es sind bekannte Begebenheiten—bekannte Personen. Der Roman, als solcher, enthält kein bestimmtes Resultat—er ist nicht Bild und Factum eines *Satzes.* Er ist anschauliche Ausführung—Realisirung einer Idee. Aber eine Idee lässt sich nicht in einen Satz fassen. Eine Idee ist *eine unendliche Reihe* von Sätzen—eine *irrationale Grösse*—*unsetzbar* (musik[alisch])—incommensurabel. (Sollte nicht alle Irrationalitaet relativ seyn?)

"Das Gesetz ihrer Fortschreitung lässt sich aber aufstellen—und nach diesem ist ein Roman zu kritisiren."

[II,573,25–574,26] "★Wie der Mahler mit ganz andern Augen, als der gemeine Mensch die sichtbaren Gegenstände sieht—so erfährt auch der Dichter die Begebenheiten der äussren und innern Welt auf eine sehr verschiedne Weise von gewöhnlichen Menschen. . . . Dem Mahler scheint die sichtbare Natur überall vorzuarbeiten—durchaus sein unerreichbares Muster zu seyn—Eigentlich ist aber die Kunst des Mahlers so unabhängig, so ganz a priori entstanden, als die Kunst des Musikers. Der Mahler bedient sich nur einer unendlich schwereren *Zeichensprache*, als der Musiker—der Mahler mahlt eigentlich mit dem Auge—Seine Kunst ist die Kunst regelmässig, und Schön zu sehn. Sehn ist hier ganz activ—durchaus bildende Thätigkeit. Sein Bild ist nur seine Chiffer—sein Ausdruck—Sein Werckzeug der Reproduktion. . . . Fast jeder Mensch ist in geringen Grad schon Künstler—Er sieht in der That heraus und nicht herein—Er fühlt heraus und nicht herein. Der Hauptunterschied ist der; der Künstler hat den Keim des selbstbildenden Lebens in seinen Organen belebt—die Reitzbarkeit derselben *für den Geist* erhöht und ist mithin im Stande Ideen nach Belieben—ohne äussre Sollicitation—durch sie heraus zu strömen—Sie, als Werckzeuge, zu *beliebigen* Modificationen der wircklichen Welt zu gebrauchen— . . . ."

[II,579,30–580,13,#242] "Das Individuum wird das Vollkommenste, das *rein Systematische* seyn, das nur durch einen *einzigen abs[oluten] Zufall* individualisirt ist—z. B. durch seine Geburt. In diesem Zufall müssen alle seine übrige Zufälle, die unendliche Reihe seiner Zustände, eingeschachtelt liegen, oder noch besser, als seine Zufälle, seine Zustände determinirt seyn. Ableitung eines individuellen Lebens aus einem einzigen Zufalle—einem einzigen Act der Willkühr.

"Zerlegung Eines Zufalls—Eines grossen Acts der Willkühr in mehrere—in Unendliche—durch allmäliche Aufnahme—langsame, successive Eindringung—Geschehung.

"★Ein Romanschreiber macht eine Art von Bouts rimes [sic]—der aus einer gegebenen Menge von Zufällen und Situationen—eine wohlgeordnete, gesezmässige Reihe macht—der Ein Individuum zu Einem Zweck durch alle diese Zufälle, die er zweckmässig hindurchführt [sic]. Ein eigenthümliches Individuum muss er haben, das die Begebenheiten bestimmt, und von ihnen bestimmt wird. Dieser Wechsel, oder die Veränderungen Eines Individuums—in einer *continuirlichen* Reihe machen den interressanten Stoff des Romans aus."

[II,581,6–9,#242] "Je grösser der Dichter, desto weniger Freyheit erlaubt er sich, desto philosophischer ist er. Er begnügt sich mit der willkührlichen Wahl des ersten Moments und entwickelt nachher nur die Anlagen dieses Keims—bis zu seiner Auflösung."

[II,584,#250] "★Einem gelang es—er hob den Schleyer der Göttin zu Saïs—Aber was sah er? er sah—Wunder des Wunders—Sich Selbst."

[II,588,12–19,#264] "★Sprache in der 2ten Potenz. z. B. Fabel ist Ausdruck eines ganzen Gedanckens—und gehört in die Hierogly[p]histik der 2ten Potenz—in die *Ton und Schriftbilderspache²*. Sie hat poëtische Verdienste und ist nicht *rhetorisch*—subaltern—wenn sie ein vollkommener Ausdruck—wenn sie *euphonisch²*—richtig und praecis ist—wenn sie gleichsam ein *Ausdruck, mit* um des Ausdrucks willen ist—wenn sie wenigstens nicht, als Mittel erscheint—sondern an sich selbst eine vollkommene Produktion des *höhern Sprachvermögens* ist."

[II,589,#267] "★Wir wissen etwas nur—insofern wir es *ausdrücken*—i.e. *machen* können. Je fertiger und mannichfacher wir etwas *produciren*, aus-

führen können, desto besser *wissen* wir es—Wir wissen es vollkommen, wenn wir es überall, und auf alle Art *mittheilen,* erregen können—einen individuellen *Ausdruck* desselben in jedem Organe bewircken können."

[II,591,#286] "★Der Zauberer ist Poët. Der Profet ist zum Zauberer, wie der Mann von Geschmack zum Dichter."

[II,594,#316] "Alles, was wir erfahren ist eine *Mittheilung.* So ist die Welt in der That eine *Mittheilung*—Offenbarung des Geistes. Die Zeit ist nicht mehr, wo der Geist Gottes verständlich war. Der Sinn der Welt ist ver- lohren gegangen. Wir sind beym Buchstaben stehn geblieben. Wir haben das Erscheinende über der Erscheinung verlohren. Formularwesen."

[II,595,#318] "†Was in diesen Blättern durchgestrichen ist—bedürfte selbst in Rücksicht des Entwurfs, noch mancherley Verbesserungen etc. Manches ist ganz falsch—manches unbedeutend—manches schielend. Umklammerte ist ganz problematischer Wahrheit—so nicht zu ge- brauchen.

"Von dem Übrigen ist nur weniges reif zum Drucke—z. B. als Frag- ment. Das Meiste ist noch roh. Sehr—sehr vieles gehört zu Einer grossen höchstwichtigen Idee. Ich glaube nicht, dass etwas Unbedeutendes unter dem Undurchstrichnen ist. Das ★ Angestrichne wollt ich in eine Samm- lung von neuen Fragmenten aufnehmen, und dazu ausarbeiten. Das Andre soll bis zu einer weitläufigeren Ausführung warten."

Teplitzer Fragmente (Sommer 1798)

[II,599,#341] "Ein Roman ist ein *Leben,* als Buch.

"Jedes Leben hat ein Motto—einen Titel—einen Verleger—eine Vor- rede—Einleitung—Text—*Noten*—etc. oder kann es haben.

Studien zur Bildenden Kunst (August 1798)

[II,650,#481] "Die Einbildungskraft ist der wunderbare Sinn, der uns alle Sinne *ersetzen* kann—und der so sehr schon in unsrer Willkühr steht. Wenn die äussern Sinne ganz unter mechanischen Gesetzen zu stehn scheinen—so ist die Einbildungskraft offenbar nicht an die Gegenwart und Berührung äussrer Reitze gebunden."

Monolog

[II,672,] "Es ist eigentlich um das Sprechen und Schreiben eine närrische Sache; das rechte Gespräch ist ein blosses Wortspiel. Der lächerliche Irrthum ist nur zu bewundern, dass die Leute meinen—sie sprächen um der Dinge willen. Gerade das Eigenthümliche der Sprache, dass sie sich blos um sich selbst bekümmert, weiss keiner. Darum ist sie ein so wunderbares und fruchtbares Geheimniss,—dass wenn einer blos spricht, um zu sprechen, er gerade die herrlichsten, originellsten Wahrheiten ausspricht. Will er aber von etwas Bestimmten sprechen, so lässt ihn die launige Sprache das lächerlichste und verkehrteste Zeug sagen. Daraus entsteht auch der Hass, den so manche ernsthafte Leute gegen die Sprache haben. Sie merken ihren Muthwillen, merken aber nicht, dass das verächtliche Schwatzen die unendlich ernsthafte Seite der Sprache ist. Wenn man den Leuten nur begreiflich machen könnte, dass es mit der Sprache wie mit den mathematischen Formeln sei—Sie machen eine Welt für sich aus—Sie spielen nur mit sich selbst, drücken nichts als ihre wunderbare Natur aus, und eben darum sind sie so ausdrucksvoll—eben darum spiegelt sich in ihnen das seltsame Verhältnisspiel der Dinge. Nur durch ihre Freiheit sind sie Glieder der Natur und nur in ihren freien Bewegungen äussert sich die Weltseele und macht sie zu einem zarten Maasstab und Grundriss der Dinge. So ist es auch mit der Sprache—wer ein feines Gefühl ihrer Applicatur, ihres Takts, ihres musikalischen Geistes hat, wer in sich das zarte Wirken ihrer innern Natur vernimmt, und danach seine Zunge oder seine Hand bewegt, der wird ein Prophet sein, dagegen wer es wohl weiss, aber nicht Ohr und Sinn genug für sie hat, Wahrheiten wie diese schreiben, aber von der Sprache selbst zum Besten gehalten und von den Menschen, wie Cassandra von den Trojanern, verspottet werden wird. Wenn ich damit das Wesen und Amt der Poesie auf das deutlichste angegeben zu haben glaube, so weiss ich doch, dass es kein Mensch verstehen kann, und ich ganz was albernes gesagt habe, weil ich es habe sagen wollen, und so keine Poesie zu Stande kommt. Wie, wenn ich aber reden müsste? und dieser Sprachtrieb zu sprechen das Kennzeichen der Eingebung der Sprache, der Wirksamkeit der Sprache in mir wäre? und mein Wille nur auch alles wollte, was ich müsste, so könnte dies ja am Ende ohne mein Wissen und Glauben Poesie sein und ein Geheimniss der Sprache verständlich machen? und so wär' ich ein berufener Schriftsteller, denn ein Schriftsteller ist wohl nur ein Sprachbegeisterter?—''

GERMAN TEXT OF NOVALIS QUOTATIONS FROM VOLUME III

Mathematische Studien zu Bossut und Murhard

[III,123,25–124,3] ''(Worte und Figuren bestimmen sich in beständigen Wechsel—die hörbaren und sichtbaren Worte sind eigentlich Wortfiguren. Die Wortfiguren sind die Idealfiguren der anderen Figuren— Alle Figuren etc. sollen Wort oder Sprachfiguren werden—so wie die

Figurenworte—die innern Bilder etc. die IdealWorte der übrigen Ge-
dancken oder Worte sind—indem sie alle innre Bilder werden sollen.

"Der Fantasie, die die *Figurenworte* bildet, kommt daher das Praedicat
Genie vorzüglich zu.

"Das wird die goldne Zeit seyn, wenn alle Worte—*Figurenworte*—
Mythen—und alle Figuren—Sprachfiguren—Hieroglyphen seyn werden—wenn man Figuren sprech und schreiben—und Worte vollkommen plastisiren, und Musiciren lernt.

Beyde Künste gehören zusammen, sind unzertrennlich verbunden
und werden zugleich vollendet werden.)"

Das Allgemeine Brouillon (Materialien zur Enzyklopadistik 1798/1799)

Erste Gruppe (September bis Anfang/Mitte Oktober 1798)
[III,248,12–20,#52] "ARCHAEOLOGIE. Galvanism der Antiken, ihr
Stoff—Revivification des Alterthums.

"Wunderbare *Religion*, die sie umschwebt—Ihre Geschichte—die
Philosophie der Skulptur—Gemmen—menschliche Petrificationen—
Mahlerey—Portrait—Landschaften—der [Me]nsch hat immer symbo-
lische Philosophie seines Wesens in seinen Wercken und seinem Thun
und Lassen ausgedrückt—Er verkündigt sich und sein Evangelium der
Natur. Er ist der Messias der Natur—die Antiken sind zugleich *Produkte
der Zukunft und der Vorzeit.*"

[III,255,#80] "ROMANTIC. Alle Romane, wo wahre Liebe vorkommt,
sind *Mährchen—magische Begebenheiten.*"

[III,258,#96] "MINERAL[OGIE]. Steine in Potenzen—specifisch verschiedne Fossilien—dem Grad nach verschiedne Steine. Wenn man
einen philosophischen Stein hat, so hat man auch wohl einen mathematischen und artistischen Stein? etc."

[III,267,35–268,2] "GRAM[MATIK]. Der Mensch spricht nicht allein—
auch das Universum *spricht*—alles spricht—unendliche Sprachen.
/ Lehre von den Signaturen."

[III,280–81,#234] "ROMANT[IK] ETC. Märchen. Nessir und Zulima. Ro-
mantisirung der *Aline. Novellen. Tausend und Eine Nacht. Dschinnistan. La
Belle et la Bète.* Musaeus Volksmärchen. Romantischer Geist der neuern
Romane. Meister. Werther. Griechische Volksmärchen. Indische Märchen. Neue, originelle Märchen. In einem ächten Märchen muss alles
wunderbar—geheimnissvoll und unzusammenhängend seyn—alles
belebt. Jedes auf eine andre Art. Die ganze Natur muss auf eine wunderliche Art mit der ganzen Geisterwelt vermischt seyn. Die Zeit der
allg[emeinen] Anarchie—Gesezlosigkeit—Freyheit—der *Naturstand* der
Natur—die Zeit vor der *Welt* (Staat.) Diese Zeit vor der Welt liefert
gleichsam die zerstreuten Züge der *Zeit nach der Welt*—wie der Naturstand ein *sonderbares Bild* des ewigen Reichs ist. Die Welt des Märchens ist

die *durchausentgegengesezte* Welt der Welt der Wahrheit (Geschichte)—
und eben darum ihr so *durchaus ähnlich*—wie das *Chaos* der *vollendeten*
Schöpfung. (Über *die Idylle*.)

"In der *künftigen* Welt ist alles, wie in der *ehemaligen* Welt—und *doch
alles ganz Anders*. Die *künftige* Welt ist das *Vernünftige* Chaos—das Chaos,
das sich selbst durchdrang—in sich und ausser sich ist—Chaos² oder ∞.

"Das *ächte Märchen* muss zugleich *Prophetische Darstellung*—idealische
Darstell[ung]—abs[olut] nothwendige Darst[ellung] seyn. Der ächte
Märchendichter ist ein Seher der Zukunft.

"Bekenntnisse eines wahrhaften, synth[etischen] *Kindes*—eines idealischen Kindes. (Ein Kind ist weit klüger und weiser, als ein Erwach-
sener—d[as] Kind muss durchaus *ironisches* Kind seyn.)—Die Spiele
d[es] K[indes]—*Nachahmung* der Erwachsenen. (Mit der Zeit muss d[ie]
Gesch[ichte] Märchen werden—sie wird wieder, wie sie anfieng.)"

[III,281,#236] "MENSCHENL[EHRE]. Ewige Jungfrau ist nichts, als
ewiges, weibliches Kind. Was entspricht der Jungfrau bei uns Männern.
Ein Mädchen, die nicht mehr wahrhaftes *Kind* ist, ist nicht mehr
Jungfrau. (Nicht alle Kinder sind Kinder.)"

[III,281,#237] "ZUK[UNFTS] L[EHRE] D[ES] LEBENS. Unser Leben *ist*
kein Traum—aber es soll und wird vielleicht einer werden."

[III,297,#319] "GRAM[MATIK] UND LOG[IC]. Denken ist sprechen.
Sprechen und thun oder machen sind Eine nur modifizierte Operation.

"Gott sprach es werde Licht und es ward."

[III,303,#352] "THEORIE D[ES] GEMEINEN LEBENS. Gebildete Aussprache und Declamation des gewöhnlichen, *gemeinen* Lebens, als
Prosa.—Man muss sich mit Sprechen begnügen, wenn man nicht sin-
gen kann. musicalische Instrumente—poëtische Instrumente. (Platte
Einfälle = (oberflächliche) Einfälle v[on] d[er] Oberfläche.)"

[III,304,#354] "❙Roher Zufall—*Gebildeter* Zufall—Harmonie. / ❙"

[II,305,#362] "PHYS[IK] UND GRAMM[ATIK]. Ein gedämpfter, sehr
naher Ton dünkt uns *weit* zu seyn. / Lateralbewegungen der Luft beym
Schall. Figurirte Schallbewegungen wie *Buchstaben*. (Sollten die Buchstaben ursprünglich *acustische Figuren* gewesen seyn. Buchst[aben] a priori?) Lateral und figurirte Bew[egungen] des Lichts and der Wärme. Farben*bilder* sind Lichtfiguren. Der Lichtstrahl ist der Streichende Fiedel-
bogen. Was vertritt wohl hier die Stelle des Sandes? Man (*zwingt*)
eigentlich den Schall sich selbst *abzudrucken*—zu *chiffriren*—auf eine *Kup-
fertafel* zu bringen. Weitere Anwendung dieser Idee. (Bestreuung einer
Tafel mit Phosphorpulver—das die Farben des *verschiednen Lichts* an-
nähme, oder das bey einer gelinden *Erwärmung* verschiedengestalteter
und mannichfach berührter Körper in sonderbaren Figuren brennte—
und leuchtete—Bereitung eines solchen Pulvers.)

"Reflex[ion] Refraction und *Inflexion des Schalls*. / Der *schmerzhafte
Laut*—Kritzeln auf den Teller etc. Schneidender Ton. / Über das Sprechen

der *Staare.* / Natürliche, mimische, bildliche Sprache—Künstliche, zufällige, willkührliche Sprache.

"(Der Begr[iff] d[er] Caussalitaet [sic] ist z. B. ein *willkührliches Zeichen*, (transscendentales Z[eichen]) eines gewissen Verhältnisses.) Transscendentale Logik. / Jedes Wort sollte eine acustische Formel seiner Construction, seiner Aussprache seyn—die Aussprache selbst ist ein Höheres, *mimisches Zeichen* einer höhern Aussprache—*Sinnconstruction* des Worts. Alles dies hängt an den Gesetzen der *Association.* Die sog[enannten] willkührlichen Zeichen dürften am Ende nicht so willk[ührlich] seyn, als sie scheinen—sondern dennoch in einem gewissen Realnexus mit dem Bezeichneten stehn. ▌Instinktartige Sprache—Ausartung des Instinkts—conventionelle Sprache—diese soll wieder instinktartige, aber gebildete Sprache werden.▐"

[III,310,1] "*Rythmischer Sinn* ist Genie."

[III,315,#401] "PHIL[OSOPHISCHE] TELEOL[OGIE]. Die Phil[osophie] kann kein Brod backen—aber sie kann uns Gott, Freyheit und Unsterblichkeit verschaffen—welche ist nun practischer—Phil[osophie] oder Oeconomie. (Verschaffen ist *Machen*—Machen drückt nichts anderes aus)

[III,320,#418] "▌*Spielt* Gott und die Natur nicht auch? Theorie d[es] Spielens. *Heilige Spiele.* reine Spiellehre—*gemeine*—und *höhere.* Angewandte Spiellehre.▐"

Zweite Gruppe (Anfang/Mitte Oktober bis Anfang November 1798)

[III,341,#411] (Aus: Novalis, *Schriften,* Richard Samuel and Paul Kluckhohn eds. [Leipzig: Bibliographisches Institut, 1929].) "Es gibt eine Reihe idealischer Begebenheiten—die den Wirklichkeiten parallel läuft. Selten fallen sie zusammen. Menschen und Zufälle modifizieren gewöhnlich die idealische Begebenheit, so dass sie unvollkommen erscheint und ihre Folgen gleichfalls unvollkommen sind. So bei der Reformation. Statt des Protestantism kam das Luthertum hervor."

[III,364,#564] "NAT[UR] GESCH[ICHTE]. Wie alle W[issenschaften] sich einer gemeinschaftlichen—*phil[osophischen]* W[issenschaft]—mehr oder weniger nähern—und darnach eingetheilt werden können, so liessen sich auch wohl die Fossilien nach einem *phil[osophischen] Fossil* ordnen—die äussre Beschreibung dieses phil[osophischen] Fossils wäre der jetzige praeparative Theil.

"Doppelte äussre Classification der Fossilien.

"Idealisches—vollk[ommenes] äussres Fossil—*einfaches* äussres Fossil. *Formales*—*reales* Fossil. Doppeltes formales Fossil. (So auch mit d[en] W[issenschaften])"

[III,377,#620] "▌In Mährchen glaube ich am besten meine Gemüthsstimmung ausdrücken zu können.▐ (POËTIK. *Alles* ist ein *Mährchen.*)"

[III,399,12–16,#680] "Das Prädicat philosophisch—drückt *überall* die *Selbst-*

bezweckung—und zwar die *indirecte*, aus. Die directe Selbstbezweckung is ein Unding mithin—entsteht durch sie eine zerstörende, mithin *zerstörliche*—und zu zerstörende Potenz—der grobe Egoïsm."

[III,400,#691] "Die Lehre v[on] d[en] Verhältnissen gehört in die Algeber—oder die Naturgeschichte der Grössen.

"(Die Verba sind die eigentlichen Wortkräfte—die sog[enannten] *Substantiva* sind aus *Verben* entstanden—und die Verba aus Substantiven entstand[en]. Bewegung und Ruhe—Veränderliche—constante x. Alle Ruhe ist *Figur*.)"

Dritte Gruppe (Anfang November bis 10./11. Dezember 1798).

[III,409,21–410,2,#730] "Willkühr, Wunder und Zufall—hängen indirecte mit der Welt etc. zusammen. / . . . Verbindung der Wunder- und Naturwelt. Die Wunder *sollen* nach Regeln—die natürlichen Wirckungen *ohne Regeln* erfolgen—W[under] und N[atur]W[elt] sollen Eins werden. (*Regel* und *Unregel*.) Unregel ist Fantasieregel—*Willkührregel*—Zufalls—Wunderregel.

"*Regel*—*directes Gesetz*—Indirectes, (krummes) Gesetz = Unregel.

"Regel der prod[uctiven] Einb[ildungs]Kr[aft]—Synth[esis] v[on] direct[em] und indir[ectem] Gesetz—"

[III,411,19–20,#737] "Der Künstler gehört dem Wercke und nicht das Werck dem Künstler."

[III,412,33–413,4,#745] "Liesse sich nicht ein umfassenderer, kurz höhergrädiger Moment im Laocontischen Drama denken—vielleicht der, wo der höchste Schmerz in Rausch—der Widerstand in Ergebung—das höchste Leben in Stein übergeht. (Sollte der Bildhauer nicht *immer* den Moment der *Petrefaction* ergreifen—und aufsuchen—und darstellen—und auch nur diesen darstellen können?)

"Die höchsten Kunstwercke sind schlechthin *ungefällig*—Es sind Ideale, die uns nur approximando gefallen können—und *sollen*—ästhetische Imperative."

[III,414,#752] "Auch der Zufall ist nicht *unergründlich*—er hat seine Regelmässigkeit."

[III,423,27–29,#788] " / Mystizism d[er] Natur. Isis—Jungfrau—Schleyer—Geheimnissvolle Behandl[ung] der N[atur] W[issenschaft]. / "

[III,425,#793] "Die Gesetze des Zufalls—die *Veränderungsgesetze überhaupt*—die Gesetzreihen—der Gesetzcalcul."

[III,427,10–13,#804] "Vielleicht ist alle *mechanische Bewegung* nur *Sprache* der Natur. Ein Körper spricht den andern mechanisch an—dieser antwortet mechanisch—Bey beyden ist aber die mechanische Bewegung secundair and nur Mittel—Anlass zur innern Veränderung and Folge derselben."

[III,427,#809] "Zeit und Raum entstehn zugleich und sind also wohl Eins, wie Subject und Object. Raum ist beharrliche Zeit—Zeit ist fliessender, variabler Raum—Raum—Basis alles Beharrlichen—Zeit—Basis alles

Veränderlichen. Der Raum ist das Schema—die Zeit der Begriff—die Handlung (Genesis) dieses Schemas. (Allem Moment muss ich einen Vor- und Nachmoment hinzudenken)"

[III,434,#853] "Nichts ist romantischer, als was man gewöhnlich Welt und Schicksal nennt—Wir leben in einem colossalen (im *Grossen* und *Kleinen*) Roman. Betrachtung der Begebenheiten um uns her. Romantische Orientirung, Beurtheilung, und Behandlung des Menschenlebens.

[III,438,#883] "Nichts ist mehr gegen d[en] Geist des Mährchens—als ein moralisches Fatum—ein gesezlicher Zusammenhang.—Im Mährchen ist ächte Naturanarchie. / *Abstracten* Welt—Traumwelt—Folgerungen von der *Abstraction* etc. auf d[en] Zustand nach dem Tode."

[III,440,#894] "Die *Erhebung* ist das vortrefflichst Mittel, was ich kenne, um auf einmal aus fatalen Collisionen zu kommen. So z. B. d[ie] allg[e-meine] Erhebung in Adelstand—die Erhebung aller Menschen zu *Geni-es*—die Erhebung aller Phaenomène im *Wunderstand*—der Materie zu Geist—des Menschen zu Gott aller Zeit zur goldnen Zeit etc."

[III,440,#897] "Über unser ich—als *der Flamme* des Körpers in der *Seele*. Aehnlichkeit der Seele mit Oxigène. (Oxigène als Irritabilitaetspr[ocess].) Alle Synthesis ist eine *Flamme*—oder Funken—oder Analogon derselben."

[III,440,#898] "Die *allg[emeinen] Ausdrücke* der scholastischen Phil[osoph-ie] haben sehr viel Aehnlichkeit mit *den Zahlen*—daher ihr mystischer Gebrauch—ihre Personification—ihr *musicalischer Genuss*—ihre un-endlichfache Combination.

"Alles aus *Nichts* erschaffene Reale, wie z. B. die Zahlen und die abstracten Ausdrücke—hat eine wunderbare Verwandtschaft mit Din-gen einer andern Welt—mit unendlichen Reihen sonderbarer Combina-tionen und Verhältnissen—gleichsam mit einer mathem[atischen] und abstracten Welt an sich—mit einer *poëtischen mathem[atischen]* und ab-stracten Welt."

[III,441,#901] "Aller *Zufall* ist wunderbar—Berührung eines höhern We-sens—ein Problem *Datum* des thätig religiösen *Sinns*.

"(Verwandl[ung] in *Zufall*.)

"Wunderbare *Worte*—und *Formeln*. (Synth[esis] d[es] Willkührlichen und Unwillk[ührlichen].)

"(Flamme zwischen Nichts und Etwas.)"

[III,443,#913] "Sollten die *Körper* und *Figuren* die Substantiva—die Kräfte die Verba—und die Naturl[ehre]—Dechiffrirkunst seyn."

[III,446,#928] "Sonderbare Harmonie des Zufälligen im atomistischen System."

Vierte Gruppe (Dezember 1798 bis Anfang Marz 1799).

[III,449,12–13,#938] " / Üb[er] die Sprache der Körperwelt durch *Figur*. Übersetzung d[er] Qualit[ät] in Quantität und umgek[ehrt]."

[III,449,#940] "Das Mährchen ist gleichsam der *Canon* der *Poësie*—alles poëtische muss mährchenhaft seyn. Der Dichter betet den Zufall an."

[III,450,#943] "Die gew[öhnliche] N[atur]L[ehre] ist noth[wendige] *Phaenomenologie—Grammatik—*Symbolistik. / Wir sehn d[ie] Natur, so wie vielleicht d[ie] Geisterwelt, en perspect[ive].

"Der *verständigen* Einbildungskraft kommt das Geschäft des *Bezeichnens* im Allgemeinen zu—des Signalisirens—Phaenomenologisirens— Die Sprachzeichen sind nicht specifisch von den übrigen Phaenomèns unterschieden."

[III,450,#944] " / *Mystische Kriegskunst.* Der mathem[atische] Krieg—Der *poëtische* Krieg—der wissenschaftliche—der Spielkrieg etc. Der rhetorische Krieg."

[III,451,#953] "Der Poët braucht die Dinge und Worte, wie *Tasten* und die ganze Poësie beruht auf thätiger Idéenassociation—auf selbstthätiger, absichtlicher, idealischer *Zufallproduktion*—(zufällige—freye *Catenation.*) (Casuïstic—Fatum. *Casuation.*) (*Spiel.*)

[III,451,#954] "Ein Mährchen sollte ich wahrlich schreiben—Gesetze des M[ährchens]."

[III,452,#959] "Der Traum ist oft bedeutend and prophétisch, weil er eine Naturseelenwirckung ist—und *also* auf Associationsordnung beruht. Er ist, wie die Poësie bedeutend—aber auch darum unregelmässig bedeutend—*durchaus frei.*"

[III,452,#966] "*Wolkenspiel—Naturspiel* äusserst poëtisch. Die Natur ist eine Aeolsharfe—Sie ist ein musikal[isches] Instrument—dessen Töne wieder Tasten höherer Sayten in uns sind. [*Ideenassociation.*]

[III,454,#986] "Ein Mährchen ist eigentlich wie ein Traumbild—ohne Zusammenhang—ein *Ensemble* wunderbarer Dinge und Begebenheiten—z. B. eine *musicalische Fantasie*—die Harmonischen Folgen einer Aeolsharfe—die *Natur selbst.*

"Wird ein *Geschichte* ins Märchen gebracht, so ist dies schon eine fremde Einmischung—Eine Reihe artiger, unterhaltender Versuche— ein abwechselndes Gespräch—eine Redoute sind Mährchen. Ein höheres Mährchen wird es, wenn ohne den Geist des M[ärchens] zu verscheuchen irgend ein *Verstand*—(Zusammenhang, Bedeutung—etc.) hinein gebracht wird. Sogar *nüzlich* könnte vielleicht ein Märchen werden."

"Der Ton des blossen M[ärchens] ist abwechselnd—er kann aber auch *einfach* seyn. / Best[and]Th[eile] der Märchen."

[III,455,26–27,#991] "Zeit ist *innrer Raum*—Raum ist *äussre Zeit.* (Synth[ese] derselben) *Zeitfiguren* etc. R[aum] and Z[eit] entstehn zugleich."

[III,458,#1011] "Der Raum geht in die Zeit, wie der Körper in die Seele über. Simultanerzeugungsproc[ess] einer *Seite.*"

[III,461,#1034] "Eine Synthese ist ein *chronischer Triangel.* / *Die Sprache* und die *Sprachzeichen* sind a priori aus der menschlichen Natur entsprungen und die ursprüngliche *Sprache* war ächt *wissenschaftlich*—Sie wieder zu finden ist der Zweck des Grammatikers."

[III,462,#1036] "Sollte es nicht ein *Vermögen* in uns geben, was dieselbe Rolle hier spielte, wie die *Veste* ausser uns—der *Aether*—jene unsichtbar sichtbare Materie, der Stein der Weisen—der überall und und nirgends, alles und nichts ist—*Instinkt* oder Genie heissen wir sie—Sie ist überall *vorher*. Sie ist die *Fülle der Zukunft*—die *Zeitenfülle* überhaupt—in der Zeit, was der Stein der Weisen im Raum ist—Vernunft—Fantasie—Verstand und Sinn (*Bedeutung 3–5 Sinne*) sind nur ihre *einzelnen Funktionen*."

Fragmente und Studien 1799–1800:

[III,559,#28] "Die eigentliche *sichtbare* Musik sind die Arabesken, Muster, Ornamente etc."

[III,559,#30] "Der Tod ist das romantisirende Princip unsers Lebens. Der Tod ist − das Leben +. Durch den Tod wird das Leben verstärkt."

[III,562,#45] "Die Schreibart des Romans muss kein *Continuum*—es muss ein in jeden Perioden gegliederter Bau seyn. Jedes kleine Stück muss etwas abgeschnittnes—begränztes—ein eignes Ganze seyn."

[III,565,#75] "Es giebt nur Einen Tempel in der Welt und das ist der menschliche Körper. Nichts ist heiliger, als diese hohe Gestalt. Das Bücken vor Menschen ist eine Huldigung dieser Offenbarung im Fleisch.

"(Göttliche Verehrung des Lingam, des Busens—der Statuen.)"

[III,570,#102] "Sollen die Geberden wircklich grammatisch Symbolisch, oder ausdrucksvoll seyn? Ich glaube nicht, dass sie es seyn sollen—aber sie werden es seyn—wenn sie natürlich, im idealischen Sinne, Produkte der idealischen Association der innern and äussern Gliedmaassen sind— Sie gehören zum Ressort der Tanzkunst."

[III,586,12–13] "Der Historiker muss im Vortrag oft Redner werden—Er trägt ja *Evangelien* vor, denn die ganze Geschichte ist Evangelium."

[I,587,#221,17–18] "Nichts ist *poëtischer*, als alle *Übergänge* und heterogène Mischungen."

[III,588,#225] "Episches Gedicht—die franz[ösische] Exped[ition] nach *Aegypten*. Ein Vers[uch]."

[III,593,16–17] "Der innige Zusammenhang, die Sympathie des Weltalls, ist ihre Basis."

Mathematische Fragmente (Dezember 1799–Januar 1800)

[III,593,18–19] "Zahlen sind, wie Zeichen und Worte, Erscheinungen, Repraesentationen katexoxin."

[III,593,26–28] "In der Musik erscheint sie förmlich, als Offenbarung—als schaffender Idealism."

"Hier legitimirt sie sich, als himmlische Gesandtin, Kat anϑropon."

[III,594,3] "Reine Mathematik ist Religion."

Aufzeichnungen von Ende 1799 bis Herbst 1800

[III,639,#508] "Höchst sonderbar ist die Ähnlichkeit unsrer heiligen Geschichte mit *Mährchen*—Anfänglich eine Bezauberung—dann die wunderbare Versöhnung—etc. Die Erfüllung der Verwünschungsbedingung—Wahnsinn und Bezauberung haben viel Ähnlichkeit. Ein Zauberer ist ein Künstler des Wahnsinns."

[III,664,#603] "Je persönlicher, localer, temporeller, eigenthümlicher ein Gedicht ist, desto näher steht es dem Centro der Poesie. Ein Gedicht muss ganz *unerschöpflich* seyn, wie ein Mensch und ein guter Spruch.

"Was war der Parallelism der orient[alischen] Poesie?

"Was oben vom Gedicht gesagt ist gilt auch vom Roman.

"Wenn Gott Mensch werden konnte, kann er auch Stein, Pflanze[,] Thier und Element werden und vielleicht giebt es auf diese Art eine fortwährende Erlösung in der Nature."

[III,684,#659] "Wunderbarkeit der Mathematik.

"Sie ist ein *schriftliches Instrument*—was noch unendlicher Perfection fähig ist—Ein Hauptbeweis der Sympathie und Identitaet der Natur und des Gemüths."

[III,687,#680] "Wer rechten Sinn für den Zufall hat, der kann alles Zufällige zur Bestimmung eines unbekannten Zufalls benutzen—er kann das Schicksal mit gleichen Glück in den Stellungen der Gestirne, als in Sandkörnern, Vogelflug und Figuren suchen."

[III,687,#681] "Der Roman ist völlig, als Romanze zu betrachten.

GERMAN TEXT OF NOVALIS QUOTATIONS FROM VOLUME IV

Klarisse

[IV,24,13] *Sie will nichts seyn*—sie *ist* etwas."

[IV,24,20] *"Ihr Betragen gegen mich.* Ihr Schreck für der Ehe."

[IV,25,4–6] "Sie will sich nicht durch meine Liebe geniren lassen. Meine Liebe drückt sie oft. Sie ist *kalt* durchgehends."

Journal (18. April bis 6. Juli 1797)

[IV,30,26] "Der Entschluss stand recht muthig."

[IV,32,29–30] "Der Entschluss ward etwas düster angesehn."

[IV,34,33] "Früh war der Entsch[luss] sehr fern—Abends desto näher."

[IV,35,23–36,7] "Früh um 5 stand ich auf. Es was sehr schön Wetter. Der Morgen vergieng; ohne, dass ich viel that. Der Hauptmann Rockenthien und seine Schwägerin und Kinder kamen. Ich kriegte einen Brief von

Schlegel mit dem 1sten Theil der neuen Shakespeareschen Übersetzungen. Nach Tisch gieng ich spatzieren—dann Kaffee—das Wetter
trübte sich—erst Gewitter dann wolkig und stürmisch—sehr lüstern—
ich fieng an in Shakespeare zu lesen—ich las mich recht hinein. Abends
gieng ich zu Sophieen. Dort war ich unbeschreiblich freudig—aufblit-
zende Enthusiasmus Momente—Das Grab blies ich wie Staub, vor mir
hin—Jahrhunderte waren wie Momente—ihre Nähe war fühlbar—ich
glaubte sie solle immer vortreten—Wie ich nach Hause kam—hatte ich
einige Rührungen im Gespräch mit Machere. Sonst war ich den ganzen
Tag sehr vergnügt. Niebekker war Nachmittags da. Abends hatte ich
noch einige gute Ideen. Shakespeare gab mir viel zu denken.

[IV,41,10–15] "Auch hab ich bemerckt, dass es offenbar meine Bestimmung ist—ich soll hier nichts erreichen—ich soll mich in der Blüthe von
allem trennen—Erst zulezt das Beste im Wolbekannten kennen lernen—
So auch mich selbst. Ich lerne mich jezt erst kennen und geniessen—
eben darum soll ich fort."

[IV,46,5–7] "Das Engagement war nicht fuer diese Welt. Ich soll hier nicht
vollendet werden—Alle Anlagen sollen nur berührt und rege seyn."

Tagebuch

[IV,48,31] "Xstus und Sophie."
[IV,55,6] "Alles was wir Zufall nennen, ist von Gott."

Briefe von Novalis

An Caroline Just. [Tennstedt, Ende November, 1794?]
[IV,148,17–24] "Glauben Sie nicht, dass meine Unpässlichkeit blos kör-
perlich ist. Die Indisposition des Körpers traf nur mit der Indisposition
der Seele zusammen—keine von beyden *allein* würde jene hervorge-
bracht haben. Meine Fantasie war lange nicht so in lebhafter Bewegung
als nach unsrer Reise. So viel Entzückendes auf Einmal, Sophie, Ihre in
der That einzige Freundschaft, und die unendliche Aussicht, die mir sich
hier auf einmal so *bestimmt* für mein Leben und meine Bestimmung
öfnete—"

An Caroline Just. [Grüningen, Juni(?) 1795]
[IV,152,6–11] "Unsern wechselseitigen Verwandten und Freunden ma-
chen wir hierdurch unsre Verbindung am 19ten März dieses Jahrs be-
kannt und versichern uns im voraus ihrer freundschaftlichsten Theilnahme.
Schlöben: am 25sten Marz. 1798.
Fridrich von Hardenberg und
Sophie von Hardenberg geb. v. Kühn."

An Caroline Just. [Weissenfels, 24. März, 1797]
[IV,208,27–29] ". . . . Schon damals, wo der Zufall, der ihr schönes Leben endigte, so nahe war. . . ."
An Caroline Just. [Weissenfels, 28. März]
[IV,210,9–12] "Meine Mutter sagte, wie sie zum erstenmale ihre Silhouette sah—Ihr Gesicht gefällt mir unbeschreiblich—Sie sieht so from[m], so still aus—als wäre sie nicht auf dieser Welt an Ihrem Platze."

An Friedrich Schlegel. [Tennstedt, 13. April, 1797]
[IV,220,12–15] "Soviel versichre ich Dir heilig—dass es mir ganz klar schon ist, welcher himmlischer Zufall ihr Tod gewesen ist—ein Schlüssel zu allem—Ein wunderbarschicklicher Schritt."

An Karl Ludwig Woltmann. [Tennstädt, 14. April, 1797]
[IV,222,22–28] "Es ist gewiss nicht Leidenschaft—ich fühle es zu unwidersprechlich, zu kalt, zu sehr mit meiner ganzen Seele, dass sie Eine der edelsten, idealischen Gestalten war, die je auf Erden gewesen sind und seyn werden. Die schönsten Menschen müssen ihr ähnlich gewesen seyn. Ein Bild von Raphael in der Physiognomik hat die treffendste Aehnlichkeit von ihr, die ich noch fand, unerachtet es gewiss kein vollkommnes Bild von ihm ist."

An den Bruder Karl. [Tennstedt, 16. April, 1797]
[IV,223,6–8] ". . . . sey getrost, Erasmus hat überwunden; die Blüthen des lieben Kranzes lösen sich einzeln hier auf, um ihn sich dort schöner und ewiger zusammenzusetzen. . . ."

An August Wilhelm Schlegel. [Weissenfels, 30. November, 1797]
[IV,237,12–33] "Er ist unter den Übersetzungen, was W[ilhelm] Meister unter den Romanen ist. Giebts denn schon eine Ähnliche? So lange wir Deutschen übersetzen, so national dieser Hang des Übersetzen ist, indem es fast keinen deutschen Schriftsteller von Bedeutung giebt—der nicht übersezt hätte, und warlich darauf soviel sich einbildet, als auf Originalwercke, so scheint man doch über nichts unbelehrter zu seyn, als über das Übersetzen. Bey uns kann es zur Wissenschaft und zur Kunst werden. Ihr Shakespeare ist ein trefflicher Canon für den wissenschaftlichen Beobachter. . . . Es gehört poëtische Moralität, Aufopferung der Neigung, dazu, um sich einer wahren Übersetzung zu unterziehn—Man übersezt aus ächter Liebe zum Schönen, und zur vaterländischen Litteratur. Übersetzen ist so gut dichten, als eigne Wercke zu stande bringen—und schwerer, seltner.

"Am Ende ist alle Poësie Übersetzung. Ich bin überzeugt, dass der deutsche Shakespeare jezt besser, als der Englische ist."

An August Wilhelm Schlegel. [Freyberg, 12. Jänner, 1798]

[IV,246,25–29] "Aber sie bleibt Poësie—mithin den wesentlichen Gesetzen ihrer Natur getreu—Sie wird gleichsam ein organisches Wesen— dessen ganzer Bau seine Entstehung aus dem Flüssigen, seine ursprünglich elastische Natur, seine Unbeschränktheit, seine Allfähigkeit verräth."

An Caroline Just. [Freyberg, 5. Februar, 1798]

[IV,249,28–250,7] "Je öfter ich da gewesen bin—je mehr haben die beyden Mädchen bey mir gewonnen. Sie sind einigermaassen das für mich, was Sie und Carolinchen Kühn für mich sind. Die älteste ist klug, in allen Dingen geschickt, und ein durchaus eingenthümliches, höchstlebhaftes Wesen—ächtes ionisches Blut, wenn Sie mir diesen Platnerischen Ausdruck verzeihen—der so viel ausdrückt, wie Sanguinisch und hübscher, wie mich dünckt, ist—Sie ist für alles empfänglich, und weiss meiner Schwachheit laut zu denken, sehr gut zu schmeicheln. Julchen ist ein schleichendes Gift—man findet sie, eh man sich versieht, überall in sich und es ist um so gefährlicher, je angenehmer es uns däucht. Als ein junger Wagehals würde ich einmal eine solche Vergiftung probiren—So aber, abgestumpft, wie ich bin, reizt es meine alten Nerven nur so eben zu leichten, frölichen Vibrationen, und erwärmt stundenlang mein starres Blut. In zarten, kaum vernehmbaren Empfindungen begegnet man ihr und ist gewiss, dass das Schönste von Ihr zu erst bemerckt, gethan, und bewahrt wird."

An August Wilhelm Schlegel. [Freyberg, 24. Februar, 1798]

[IV,251,26–29] "Ich habe noch . . . einen Anfang, unter dem Titel, der Lehrling zu Saïs—ebenfalls Fragmente—nur alle in Beziehung auf Natur."

An Friedrich Schlegel. [Freyberg, 20. Jänner, 1799]

[IV,273,4–12] "Ich habe Dir viel zu sagen—die Erde scheint mich noch viele Zeiten hindurch festhalten zu wollen. Das Verhältniss, von dem ich Dir sagte, ist inniger und fesselnder geworden. Ich sehe mich auf eine Art geliebt, wie ich noch nicht geliebt worden bin. Das Schicksal eines *sehr liebenswerthen* Mädchens hängt an meinem Entschlusse—und meine Freunde, meine Eltern, meine Geschwister bedürfen meiner mehr, als je. Ein sehr interressantes Leben scheint auf mich zu warten—indess aufrichtig wär ich doch lieber todt."

An Caroline Schlegel. [Freyberg, 27. Februar, 1799]
[IV,279,20–281,19] "Vielleicht gibt es nur wenig individuellere Bücher. Man sieht das Treiben seines Innern, wie das Spiel der chymischen Kräfte in einer Auflösung im Zuckerglase, deutlich, und wunderbar vor sich. Tausend mannichfaltige, helldunkle Vorstellungen strömen herzu und man verliert sich in einem Schwindel, der aus dem denkenden Menschen einen blossen Trieb—eine Naturkraft macht—uns in die wollüstige Existenz des Instinkts verwickelt. . . .

"Die Idealisierung der Vegetation hat mich vorzüglich interressirt. Merckwürdig verschieden hat auf uns beyde die höchste Liebe gewirckt. Bey mir war alles im Kirchenstyl—oder im dorischen Tempelstyl componirt. Bey ihm ist alles corynthischer. Jezt ist by mir *bürgerliche Baukunst*.

"Ich bin dem Mittage so nahe, dass die Schatten die Grösse der Gegenstände haben—und also die Bildungen meiner Fantasie so ziemlich der wircklichen Welt entstprechen.

"Soviel seh ich unsre ersten Romane werden himmelweit verschieden. Der Meinige wird diesen Sommer wahrscheinlich in Toeplitz oder Carlsbad fertig. Indess, wenn ich sage, fertig—so heisst dies der erste Band—denn ich habe Lust mein ganzes Leben an Einen Roman zu wenden—der allein eine ganze Bibliothek ausmachen—vielleicht Lehrjahre einer *Nation* enthalten soll. Das Wort *Lehrjahre* ist falsch—es drückt ein bestimmtes *Wohin* aus. Bey mir soll es aber nichts, als—*Übergangs Jahre* vom Unendlichen zum Endlichen bedeuten. Ich hoffe damit zugleich meine historische und philosophische Sehnsucht zu befriedigen. Eine Reise nach Süden und Norden ist mir, als Vorbereitung hiezu, noch unentbehrlich—"

An die Schwester Sidonie. [Churprinz, 9. Juli, 1799]
[IV,291,8–23] "Ich bin ziemlich wol hier am Sonntag angekommen—traf aber zum Unglück Julien nicht an, die nach Dresden gereist war. Ich war sehr ärgerlich and sehr—betrübt und schickte gleich einen Boten nach Dresden, um ihre Rückkunft zu beschleunigen. Gestern Abend kam das herrlich, gute Mädchen und seit der Zeit weiss ich nicht, ob ich noch auf Erden, oder im Himmel bin. . . . Lebtwohl—Ihr Guten—Neues ist nichts—ausser dass ich Julien unendlich liebe—und sie mich. . . ."

An Friedrich Schlegel. [Weissenfels, 31. Jänner, 1800]
[IV,318,3–8] "Das Neueste von mir ist ein bald fertiger *Roman*—
Heinrich von Afterdingen.

"Wenn nicht alles entgegen ist, so kommt er schon Ostern. Sobald ich fertig bin, erhälst Du ihn im M[anu]sc[ri]pte. Ich habe jezt nichts im Kopfe, als Romane, und Lustspiele. Der Lehrling zu Saïs kommt nach der Vollendung des obigen R[omans] sogleich an die Arbeit."

An Ludwig Tieck. [Weissenfels, 23. Februar, 1800]
[IV,323,2–5] "Um so besser ist es, dass die Lehrlinge ruhn—die jezt auf eine ganz andre Art erscheinen sollen—Es soll ein ächtsinnbildlicher, Naturroman werden. Erst muss Heinrich fertig seyn—Eins nach den Andern, sonst wird nichts fertig."

Chronology

1772   Georg Friedrich Phillip von Hardenberg is born May 2 to Heinrich Ulrich Erasmus Freiherr von Hardenberg and his wife Auguste Bernhardine née von Bölzig, on the family estate in Oberwiederstedt, Thuringia; their first son and second child of eleven. He is preceded by an older sister, Caroline, who was born 1771 and dies 1801, the same year Novalis dies.

1774   August 9, Novalis's brother Erasmus is born. He dies 1797, the same year as Sophie von Kühn.

1776   March 13, Novalis's brother Carl is born. He dies 1813.

1779   May 16, Novalis's sister Sidonie is born, who dies in 1801, the same year as her brother Novalis and their sister Caroline.

1780   Novalis falls seriously ill with dysentery; an unexceptional and even rather slow student who needs to be enticed into learning by having his older sister Caroline instructed with him, he becomes, after recuperation, an exceptionally good student who quickly outgrows his tutors.

1781   July 28, Novalis's brother Georg Anton is born. He dies in 1825.

1783   April 1, Novalis's sister Auguste is born, who dies in 1804. Following Auguste's birth Novalis's mother becomes physically and emotionally seriously ill.

1784   Novalis's father is appointed director of the Saxonian salt mines of Dürrenberg, Kösen, and Artern.

1785   The family moves from Oberwiederstedt to Weissenfels.

1786   Novalis stays with his uncle, the province administrator (Landkomptur) of the Deutschritter order, Gottlob Friedrich Wilhelm von Hardenberg, at the manor house and estate of Lucklum in Braunschweig. His uncle's well-stocked library much advances Novalis's education in the literature of the time.

1787   February 5, Novalis's brother Bernhard is born, who dies in 1800, the year before Novalis's death.

1788   Novalis writes his first poems.

1789   In May, Novalis meets Gottfried August Bürger in Langendorf near Weissenfels. Novalis writes poems, rhymed tales, and translations.

1790   June–October Novalis studies at the Luther-Gymnasium in Eisleben, where Christian David Jani is headmaster.
       October 23, Novalis matriculates at the University of Jena, where he meets both Friedrich von Schiller and Karl Leonhard Reinhold.

1791   Novalis develops a friendly relationship to Friedrich von Schiller.
       In April, Novalis's first publication, the poem "Klagen eines Jünglings," appears in Wieland's *Der Neue Deutsche Merkur.*
       In September, Novalis leaves the University of Jena.
       In October, Novalis matriculates at the University of Leipzig.
       November 26, Novalis's brother Peter Wilhelm is born. He dies in 1811.

1792   In January, Novalis first meets Friedrich von Schlegel, in Leipzig, with whom he develops a close friendship.
       In December, Novalis falls in love with Julie Eisenstück.

1793   In March, he ends the affair under family pressures and leaves the University of Leipzig.
       In April, he moves to Wittenberg.
       In May, Novalis matriculates at the University of Wittenberg to study jurisprudence.
       August 19, Novalis's sister Amalie is born. She dies in 1814. Novalis keeps a journal of his journey to Wernigerode, in which his very wide range of interests is clearly in evidence.

1794   June 14, Novalis receives his degree in law.
       June–October, Novalis is in Weissenfels.
       October 25, Novalis moves to Tennstedt, where he takes up lodgings in the house of the country bailiff (Kreisamtmann) Just. There he meets the bailiff's niece, Caroline Just, with whom he forms a close friendship.
       November 8, Novalis begins his training as assistant (Aktuarius) to the Kreisamtmann Just.
       November 17, while on a business trip in Grünningen near Tennstedt, Novalis meets the then twelve and a half year old stepdaughter of Hauptmann Rockenthien, Sophie von Kühn, born March 17, 1782.
       December 19, Novalis's brother Hans Christoph is born. He dies in 1816.

1795   March 15, Novalis becomes secretly engaged to Sophie von Kühn.
       In May, Novalis meets Fichte and Hölderlin in the home of Professor Friedrich Immanuel Niethammer in Jena.

In the fall, Novalis begins his serious studies of Fichte's works.

November 9, Sophie's illness first becomes apparent.

December 30, Novalis is appointed assistant (Akzessist) to the directorate in Weissenfels of the Saxonian saltworks.

1796   In January, Novalis takes a two-week chemistry course with Johann Christian Wiegleb, in Langensalza.

In February, Novalis leaves Tennstedt and returns home to Weissenfels, where he takes up his new position as assistant administrator (Akzessist) of the salt mines of Saxony under his father.

In May, Novalis visits the castle Hardenberg, near Nörten.

July 5, Sophie von Kühn has her first operation in Jena.

In August, Friedrich von Schlegel visits Weissenfels; further mutual visits in Jena and Weissenfels follow.

In December, Sophie von Kühn returns to Grünningen.

Novalis studies the works of Spinoza and Zinzendorf.

1797   March 1–10, Novalis, for the last time before her death, visits Sophie von Kühn in Grünningen.

March 19, Sophie von Kühn dies.

April 14, Erasmus, Novalis's oldest and closest brother, dies.

April 18, Novalis starts the diary of his mourning and resolve to "die after" Sophie.

May 13, Novalis has the mystical vision at Sophie's grave.

In the summer, Novalis meets August Wilhelm and Caroline von Schlegel in Jena, but he spends most of his time in Tennstedt mourning and reading Goethe's *Wilhelm Meisters Lehrjahre,* Shaftesbury, Furguson, Eschenmayer, and A. L. Hülsen's essay "Popularity in Philosophy."

In September, Novalis decides to matriculate at the Mining Academy in Freiberg.

In October and November Novalis returns to the serious study of the works of Kant, Hemsterhuis, and Fichte.

In December, Novalis, while on his way to Freiberg, meets Friedrich Wilhelm Joseph Schelling, in Leipzig. In Freiberg, he begins his scientific studies, particularly of chemistry, physics, mathematics, and geology, under Abraham Gottlob Werner. He also reads a good many alchemical texts, John Brown's medical studies, Galvani's observations on electricity, Volta's experiments in galvanism, Johann Wilhelm Ritter's studies of galvanism, and Franz von Baader's works on natural philosophy.

1798   In January, Novalis meets Julie von Charpentier.

Novalis travels to Dresden and Siebeneichen.

March 22, Novalis writes the poem "The Stranger" ("Der Fremdling").

March 29, Novalis, together with August Wilhelm von Schlegel, meets Goethe in Weimar; in the evening he visits Schiller in Jena.

In April, the Schlegels publish the collection *Blüthenstaub* in the first issue of their journal *Athenäum.* It appears with the pen-name

"Novalis"—the first occasion of its use. Novalis begins to write *Die Lehrlinge zu Sais.*

June–July, the *Jahrbücher der Preussischen Monarchie* publishes *Blumen* and *Glauben und Liebe.* Novalis makes notations for an additional collection of fragments on Romantic philosophy and poetry. He also writes *Dialogen* and the *Monolog.*

July 15–mid-August, Novalis spends in Teplitz taking the cure and writing the "Teplitzer Fragmente."

August 25–26, Novalis visits the Dresden Art Gallery with the brothers Schlegel and with Schelling.

In September, Novalis begins notes for the *Allgemeine Brouillon.*

In October, Novalis meets Johann Paul Friedrich Richter, better known by his pseudonym Jean Paul.

In December, Novalis becomes engaged to Julie von Charpentier, who was born March 16, 1776, and who dies on September 2, 1811, at the age of thirty-five, surviving Novalis by 10 years.

1799   In January, Novalis announces his engagement publicly.

In May, Novalis returns to Weissenfels.

May 20–June 15, Novalis, working as the official record keeper for Julius Wilhelm von Oppels, makes an inspection tour of the saltworks of Saxony.

July 17, Novalis meets Ludwig Tieck in Jena, who accompanies him on a visit to Herder. Novalis develops a close friendship with Tieck, who introduces him to the writings of Jacob Boehme.

July 21, Novalis visits Goethe for the second time. Novalis writes the first of his *Geistliche Lieder.*

In late August, Novalis visits his future brother-in-law, Friedrich von Rechenberg, in the Oberlausitz.

September–October, Novalis studies Schleiermacher's *Reden über die Religion* and writes marginal notes to Schlegel's *Ideen.*

October–November, Novalis writes *Die Christenheit oder Europa,* and additional *Geistliche Lieder.*

November 11–14, Novalis participates in the "Meeting of the Romantics" at the house of August Wilhelm von Schlegel in Jena and reads his *Geistliche Lieder* and *Die Christenheit oder Europa* to them. Others who participate at the meeting are: Friedrich von Schlegel, Schelling, Tieck, and Ritter [Jean Paul].

Late November, Novalis begins to write his *Heinrich von Ofterdingen* in Artern.

December 7, Novalis is appointed an associate (Salinen-Assessor) to the directorate of the saltworks of Saxony.

In December, Novalis begins to work on the *Hymnen an die Nacht.*

1800   In January, Novalis finishes the manuscript of the *Hymnen an die Nacht.* Novalis undertakes to study the works of Jacob Boehme seriously.

April 5, Novalis finishes working on the first part of *Heinrich von Ofterdingen.*

April 10, Novalis applies for a position as bailiff (Amtshauptmann) in the county of Thuringia.

June 1, Novalis, on behalf of Gottlob Werner, begins, together with the student Friedrich Traugott Michael Haupt of the Mining Academy in Freiberg, a geological survey tour of the region around Zeitz, Gera, Borna, and Leipzig, in Saxony.

July 20–22, Tieck visits Weissenfels.

In July–September, Novalis plans the second part of his *Heinrich von Ofterdingen* together with some poems for it, among them the "Lied der Toten"; he makes notations on religious, philosophical, and medical problems.

In August, the *Hymnen an die Nacht,* in edited form, are published in the 6th issue of the journal *Athenäum*. Novalis ceases to make any literary notations or entries in his journals.

September 28, Novalis mails off a writing sample in application for the position of Amtshauptmann.

Novalis becomes seriously ill with tuberculosis.

October 13, Novalis undertakes a journey to Siebeneichen, Meissen, and Dresden to seek medical help.

October 28, Novalis's brother Bernhard dies.

On December 6, Novalis is appointed circuit director (Supernumerar-Amtshauptmann) for the Thuringian county of the saltworks administration.

1801   On January 20–24, Novalis is taken home to Weissenfels from Dresden.

On March 23, Friedrich Schlegel arrives in Weissenfels.

On March 25, Novalis dies in Weissenfels while Friedrich Schlegel is by his side and his brother Karl plays the piano for him.

Notes

INTRODUCTION

1. The letter in which Novalis writes to his brother Erasmus that a quarter of an hour determined him has not been preserved. But Erasmus's response of November 28, 1794, has come down to us, and in it he quotes Novalis: "You write to me that a quarter of an hour has determined you; how can you find out a girl in a quarter of an hour?" [IV,367,1–2]

In Novalis's own hand we have the lines he wrote to Caroline Just on November 17, 1794: "Don't believe that my indisposition is only physical. The indisposition of the body only coincided with the indisposition of the soul—*alone* neither would have been able to produce the other. It has been a long time since my imagination has been as lively and active as after our trip. So much that is enchanting all at once, Sophie, your indeed singular friendship, and the infinite vista which here all at once so determinately opened for my life and my determination—" [IV,148,17–24] This letter was written within the week of Novalis's return from a business trip to Clingen near Greussen, on which he accompanied the bailiff (*Kreisamtmann*) Just and his niece Caroline. It was during this "expedition" that Novalis was taken to Grüningen to be introduced to the Rockenthien family; there he met Sophie von Kühn, Rockenthien's stepdaughter. Overwhelmed by the impression Sophie made on him, Novalis appears to have confided his emotions to Caroline Just while they were still on the trip. Feeling indisposed by the very urgency of his desire to see Sophie again, and being inhibited, by considerations of propriety and prudence, from confessing himself to her directly, Novalis, in order to speak to somebody of what so deeply moved him, wrote Caroline Just even though they lived in the same house, namely her uncle's. As a result of her early role as his confidant, Caroline became a close friend to both Novalis and Sophie. After Sophie's death many of Novalis's most heartfelt letters were addressed to her.

2. "We herewith make known to our mutual relatives and friends our union

on March the 19th of this year and are assured in advance of their most loving interest.

Schlöben, the 25th of March, 1798.

Fridrich von Hardenberg and
Sophie von Hardenberg, neé von Kühn."
[IV,152,6–11]

This playful, entirely fictional, and unusually double-dated announcement contains, in fact, not only the date of Sophie's death, but also that of Novalis himself: March 25.

3. In his biographical notes on Novalis, August Coelestin Just writes of the time shortly after Sophie's death that for Novalis ". . . the continued life of his loved ones (Novalis's oldest brother Erasmus, to whom he had been very close, had died only a few weeks after Sophie) and his reunion with them, were the ruling thoughts in his soul. . . . His phantasy flattered him with the hope, which to his apparent consolation became a certainty for him, that within the year he would once more rejoin his loved ones." [IV,543,34–42]

In his diary of the days and weeks after Sophie's death, Novalis himself speaks of both the "thought that is my goal" (Mein Zielgedanke) and of his "decision" (mein Entschluss), and chronicles for himself the degree of resolve with which he pursues that goal or decision: "The resolve stood quite bravely." [IV,30,26] Or: "The decision was considered somewhat gloomily." [IV,32,30] And similarly: "In the morning the resolve was very distant—in the evening that much closer." [IV,34,33] The very problem that his resolve presented to Novalis is evidence for the seriousness with which he pursued his set goal. His aim was not to commit suicide, but to follow Sophie into death within the year by dying of natural causes, that is, he quite simply hoped to will his own death.

4. Novalis remarks in a fragment of June 1799: "Death is the romanticizing principle of our life. Death is − life +. By death life is strengthened." [III,559,#30]

5. In refreshing contrast to those who tend to mystify Novalis, Peter Küpper observes correctly that Novalis "does not know the concept of the 'poetical' or 'romantical' in the sense of an anti-bourgeois life style. Family, state, the traditional institutions, the civic virtues of simplicity and modesty are for him what constitutes the attributes of the poetical. He did not live or desire to live a 'poetical life' as did Friedrich Schlegel or Tieck and later on Brentano or Wackenroder who despaired over this issue. He rather preferred to pursue such obviously 'unpoetical' goals as marriage and a profession." (Peter Küpper, *Die Zeit als Erlebnis des Novalis* [Köln Graz: Böhlau Verlag, 1959].)

6. In the *Logologische Fragmente*, for instance, Novalis remarks: "Everything we come to know is a *communication*. Thus is the world, indeed, a *communication*—revelation of the spirit. The time is no longer when we understood the spirit of God. The meaning of the world has been lost. We stopped at the letter. We lost that which appears for the sake of the appearance. Formular-being." [II,594,#316]

But when in *Heinrich von Ofterdingen* a similar thought is voiced, it is spoken by Heinrich's father, who represents the rational and far more pragmatic approach of the older generation which Heinrich supersedes, as Novalis for himself hopes to overcome the heritage of the Enlightenment: "At the world age we live in, the immediate intercourse with heaven no longer takes place. The old stories and texts are now the only sources that impart to us knowledge of the higher world as much as we need it; and instead of those immediate revelations, the holy spirit now speaks to us through the mediation of the understanding of judicious and well-meaning men and through the conduct and destinies of pious human beings." [I,198,20–27]

7. The very Protestant Just remarks, in this respect, that Novalis had a "preference for aesthetic beauty. Even as his inner man was not yet attuned to the rational holiness of the Christian religion, even then did he, nevertheless, love and value the Bible because of its aesthetic beauty; but, of course, for the same reason he also could fall in love with such a religion as that which offered a mother of God, a Madonna for one's adoration." [IV,541,8–13]

CHAPTER ONE

1. Thomas Carlyle, "Novalis" in *Critical and Miscellaneous Essays* (London: Chapman and Hall, Ld., 1869) vol. II, p. 183 ff. Hereafter referred to as *TCE*.

2. René Wellek observes: "The sources of many phrases of the most characteristic 'Carlylese' have been revealed. Such stock formulas as the 'Worship of sorrow' or the 'Open Secret' come from Goethe, the concept of 'self-annihilation' is a translation of Novalis' 'Selbsttötung.'" Even though Wellek continues by saying that such "borrowings are not of much importance" he only means to deny the linguistic importance of these "verbal loans." For further on in his essay Wellek says of Carlyle's relation to Novalis that "Novalis exerted a much greater charm on Carlyle. He pays him deep respect and expresses his gratitude: 'Novalis is an Anti-Mechanist—a deep man—the most perfect of modern spirit seers. I thank him for somewhat.' [sic] (two Note Books, ed. Norton, p. 140) Though Carlyle could not and would not understand the fragmentary mind of a Coleridge he felt drawn to the German mystic for the power of his personal charm." René Wellek, *Confrontations* (Princeton, N.J.: Princeton University Press, 1965), p. 37 and p. 56. See also Henry A. Pochmann, *German Culture in America* (Madison, Wis.: The University of Wisconsin Press, 1957). p. 97. Hereafter referred to as *PGA*.

One of Novalis's fragments reads: "The true philosophical act is self-annihilation; this is the real beginning of all philosophy, toward this end tend all needs of the philosophical apostle, and only this act fulfills all the conditions and characteristics of the transcendental deed. [II,395,#54] And similarly, an aphorism of the *Vermischte Bemerkungen* states: "Death is a victory over oneself—which like all self-surmounting, brings about a new, easier existence. / [II,414,#11] (See chapter 7.)

3. Charles Frederic Harrold, *Carlyle and German Thought* (Hamden and London: Archon Books, 1963), vol. 82, *Yale Studies in English*. Hereafter referred to as *HCG*.

4. Carlyle read Novalis's *Die Lehrlinge zu Sais, Die Christenheit oder Europa, Heinrich von Ofterdingen, Hymnen an die Nacht,* and the *Fragmente.* [*HCG*,15.]

Harrold also says that Carlyle came to know what he knew of Kant's and Fichte's philosophy by way of Novalis's fragments and the writings of the brothers Schlegel. [*HCG*,12–14]

5. Although Carlyle was not the only early transmitter of German Romantic thought into English, he was the most important and the most proficient. Others were George Eliot, De Quincy, Henry Crab Robinson and also Coleridge.

6. Emerson, in fact, became quite fluent in German although he never knew how to pronounce it and only learned to read it. In 1861 Emerson wrote to Grimm: "I read German with some ease, and always better, yet I never shall speak it." Quoted by Stanley M. Vogel, in *German Literary Influences on the American Transcendentalists* (New Haven, Conn.: Yale University Press, 1955), vol. 127, *Yale Studies in English*, p. 80–81. Hereafter referred to as *VGI*.

Most of the Transcendentalists attempted to learn some German: Thoreau knew a little but never enough to read it with ease; Clarke and Fuller both took up German, but Margaret Fuller clearly mastered it better and, in fact, often helped those who were less proficient. She, for instance, gave pronunciation lessons to Emerson, [*VGI*,80] while herself receiving help in this respect from Channing. Theodore Parker and Sarah Ripley both learned German; Nathaniel Hawthorne, who found Tieck's works in Sarah Ripley's library, set out to study German, as he wrote to Longfellow, but never advanced very far in it. [*VGI*,82–84]

7. "From the Boston Atheneum Library, Emerson twice took out the two-volume edition of *Novalis Schriften*, Berlin 1826, edited by Ludwig Tieck and Fr. Schlegel; once on August 2, 1836, and again on September 12, 1851." Percy Matenko, *Ludwig Tieck in America*, vol. 12, *University of North Carolina Studies in Germanic Languages and Literatures* (Chapel Hill, N.C.: The University of North Carolina Press, 1954), p. 55.

8. "As early as in 1830 in one of his blotting books he [Emerson] copied numerous long quotations, not only from Goethe's works such as *Wilhelm Meister, Dichtung und Wahrheit* and *Die Wahlverwandtschaften*, but also from Fichte and Novalis." [*VGI*,86]

9. "When he [Emerson] was able to obtain a good translation, he did not refuse it. 'I should as soon think of swimming across Charles River when I wish to go to Boston,' he once said, 'as of reading all my books in originals when I have them rendered for me in my mother tongue.' (Emerson, Works, 7, 204)" [*VGI*,81]

10. "Before the publication of *Nature* Emerson read for the first time or re-read, excluding Goethe's works, the writings of Novalis, the Schlegels, Karl Müller, Jung-Stilling's *Autiobiography*, Mendelssohn's *Phaedo*, Herder's *Outlines of the History of Man*, Heeren, Fichte, Tieck, Lessing, Schleiermacher, Schelling, (Coleridge's *Aids to Reflection* was his first source of Schelling's philosophy. Alcott was also impressed with this book) Richter [Jean Paul], Wieland (whose letters to Merck he found charming), Boerne, Winckelmann, Zelter's *Correspondence with Goethe*, Schiller's *Correspondence with Goethe*, Friedrich Wolf, Camper and Tischbein. By 1838 he added to his reading list the names of Spinoza, Niebuhr, Herschel and Bettina von Arnim." [*VGI*,86]

It is remarkable with how few exceptions this list could have been drawn up also by Novalis. While in part this is due to the literary climate of the time, it is also a reflection of some basic similarity of intellectual temperament between Emerson and Novalis.

11. Pochmann even goes so far as to say that in its ideas the essay contains little that was not derived from Carlyle's article on Novalis: "The relation of

Carlyle's essay to Emerson's *Nature* is close . . . Indeed, except for the illustrations drawn from natural science and the homespun phrases and figures, Emerson's *Nature* contains few ideas that have not their counterparts in Carlyle's words on Novalis or in the quotations from Novalis that are adduced for illustrative purposes." [*PGA*,607,n.418]

12. R. W. Emerson, "Nature" in *The Collected Works of Ralph Waldo Emerson*, 2 vols., R. E. Spiller, A. R. Ferguson, J. Slater and J. F. Carr, eds. (Cambridge, Mass.: The Belknap Press of Harvard University Press, 1971) vol. 1, p. 13.

I trust that the following chapters will establish that Emerson's essay is indeed closely related to both *Die Lehrlinge zu Sais*, and to the *Fragmente*. (Compare especially Pt. II, chap. 6.) Meanwhile here are a few examples of how Novalis's ideas sound when expressed in Emerson's idiom:

"Every man's condition is a solution in hieroglyphic to those inquiries he would put. He acts it as a life before he apprehends it as a truth." [Ibid.,7]

"We are thus assisted by natural objects in the expression of particular meanings. But how great a language to convey such pepper-corn informations . . . Whilst we use this grand cipher to expedite the affairs of our pot and kettle, we feel that we have not yet put it to its use, neither are able . . . Whilst we see that it always stands ready to clothe what we would say, we cannot avoid the question whether the characters are not significant of themselves. Have mountains, and waves, and skies, no significance but what we consciously give them when we employ them as emblems of our thoughts? The world is emblematic. Parts of speech are metaphors, because the whole of nature is a metaphor of the human mind. [Ibid.,16]

"The sensual man conforms thought to things, the poet conforms things to his thoughts. The one esteems Nature as rooted and fast; the other, as fluid, and impresses his being thereon. [Ibid.,31]

"The happiest man is he who learns from Nature the lesson of worship." [Ibid.,37]

"The world proceeds from the same spirit as the body of man. It is a remoter and inferior incarnation of God, a projection of God in the unconscious." [Ibid., 38]

"To the wise, therefore, a fact is true poetry, and the most beautiful of fables." [Ibid.,44]

13. See Friedrich Nietzsche, *Sämtliche Werke: Kritische Studienausgabe*, eds. Giorgio Colli and Mazzino Montinari (München: Deutscher Taschenbuch Verlag, 1980), vol. 9, p. 666–72.

14. The same year John Owen's translation of *Heinrich von Ofterdingen* was published in Cambridge.

15. Margaret Fuller found it soothing to turn from the overwhelming writings of Goethe to the spiritually more akin nature of Novalis. His more one-sided "imperfection and glow of mind" she thought "refreshingly human." [*PGA*,444]. Similarly, Thoreau, although he did not own any of Novalis's writings, seems to have enjoyed them: "Another German romanticist who appealed to Thoreau was Friedrich von Hardenberg, better known as Novalis . . . and the *Hymns to the Night* [*Hymnen an die Nacht*] made some impression on Thoreau." [*VGI*,81]

16. The journals with a transcendental perspective were generous in their

German offerings. To name some of the most prominent: the *Dial*, *The Western Messenger*, the *Harbinger*, the *North American Review*, and the *Christian Examiner*. [VGI,158] Novalis had 24 poems appear in translation between 1830 and 1899. For an author by author breakdown see *PGA*, 327–48.

17. *Novalis, Schriften*, Richard Samuel and Paul Kluckhohn, eds. (Leipzig: Bibliographisches Institut, 1929) vol. III, p. 341, #411.

For a detailed discussion of Poe's translation of and familiarity with the German language and this fragment see *PGA*, 388–97 and appended notes.

18. Pochmann remarks that "there is evidence that Poe knew and admired the writings of Novalis. Harrison and Woodberry both think Poe was influenced by Novalis. The former speaks of Novalis as one of 'Poe's masters across the German sea' (Works I, 134), and the latter regards Poe's 'prose poem' *Eureka* as growing out of a 'single phrase of Novalis' (Poe, I, 93). Since there was no complete translation of Novalis in Poe's day, and the fragments translated by Mrs. Austin cover only seven small pages of her booklet, it seems reasonable to assume that Poe knew Novalis in the original . . . While all three of Poe's quotations from Novalis are taken from the *Fragmente*, they are taken from widely separated sections of the book. It would seem that Poe not only had access to a copy of at least this one work of Novalis but read it." [*PGA*,712] Since Poe's indebtedness to German Romanticism is also traceable to August Wilhelm von Schlegel, the brother of Friedrich von Schlegel, who was Novalis's best friend, it is likely that Poe's familiarity with Novalis's works was deepened by this connection as well.

The other two fragments Poe used are, in the *Marginalia:* "The artist belongs to his work not the work to the artist." [III,411,#737,19–20] And in *The Tale of the Ragged Mountains* he quoted from the *Vermischte Bemerkungen* (possibly taken from Carlyle's article): "We are near waking when we dream that we dream." [II,416,#16]

19. Whereas both Novalis and Poe lost brothers whom they felt close to and loved to the slow death of tuberculosis, only Poe nursed the dying sibling and saw him through his last hours. And whereas both Novalis and Poe fell deeply in love with women who still were children—Novalis's Sophie being twelve-and-one-half years at the time of their meeting and Poe's Virginia not yet fourteen at their wedding—Novalis lost and idealized only Sophie, while Poe's life was marked by many similar losses. Poe's young and beautiful mother died of tuberculosis before he was quite three years old; the secret engagement to his first love, the fifteen-year-old Sarah Elmira Royster, was thwarted when her father intercepted his letters to her and without telling Poe married her off at seventeen to the well-to-do merchant Shelton; Frances Allan, Poe's adored foster-mother, the ally, friend, and protector against the ill-will of his foster-father, died in 1829 in Poe's twentieth year; and finally, after eleven years of marriage, Poe's young wife, Virginia, died of tuberculosis after years of suffering during which Poe nursed her and attempted to ease her pain. It is then not surprising that Poe's reaction to so much pain, suffering, and loss is much blacker than Novalis's and that his view of fate and his idealization of the beloved have a dark and threatening aspect that is quite missing in Novalis. Nevertheless it would appear that Poe, despite his several mental breakdowns and bouts of depression, had more of a stomach for reality and its pains than Novalis did. For while Novalis fled from the scenes of pain—he

left Sophie's house nine days before her death and only returned some three weeks after her funeral—Poe endured and suffered through the agonies of those he loved.

20. Pochmann says to this: "In view of Poe's interest in others of Novalis' works, it seems reasonable to conclude that he drew suggestions for his theory of coincidences, his 'Calculus of Probabilities,' from Novalis' *Fragmente.*" [*PGA*,393]

21. Comparing E.T.A. Hoffmann's and Novalis's relation to nature Heine writes: "Novalis saw everywhere only miracles and lovely miracles; he listened in on the conversation of flowers, knew the secret of the young rose, identified himself finally with the whole of nature, and when autumn came and the leaves fell, he died. Hoffmann, on the contrary, only saw ghosts everywhere. They nodded at him from every Chinese teapot and from every Berlin wig; he was a magician who transformed people into beasts and these even into royal Prussian courtiers; while he was able to conjure the dead from their graves, life itself cast him out as a dark apparition. This he felt; he felt that he himself had become a specter, all of nature now was to him a badly cut mirror in which he saw only his own deathmask in thousandfold distortions. His works are nothing more than a terrible cry of fear in twenty volumes . . . Properly witty and poetical natures wanted no part of him. They much preferred Novalis. But actually Hoffman was far more important as poet than Novalis. For the latter with his ideal constructions was forever hovering in the blue yonder, while Hoffman with all his bizarre grimaces held fast to earthly reality. But, as the giant Antaeus remained unconquerably strong as long as he touched mother Earth with his feet, and lost all his strength when Hercules lifted him up high, thus also the poet remains strong and powerful only so long as he does not leave the sphere of reality, he becomes powerless as soon as he floats enthusiastically in mid-air . . . The great similarity between the two poets apparently consists in the fact that their poetry was actually a sickness. In this respect it was said that the evaluation of their writings was properly not the business of a critic, but of a physician. The rosy glow in the literary works of Novalis is not the color of health, but of tuberculosis, and the purple fire in Hoffmann's pieces of fantasy is not the flame of genius but of fever."

But Heine relents and questioningly adds: "Yet, are we entitled to such remarks, we who are not blessed altogether with health? And particularly now when literature looks like a large hospital? Or is poetry perhaps itself a sickness of man, as the pearl is actually only the ailment causing matter the oyster suffers from?" Heinrich Heine, "Romantische Schule," (1833) in *Sämmtliche Werke* (Hamburg: Hoffmann und Campe, 1861) vol. 6, pp. 172–74.

22. See "German Wit: Henry Heine," in George Eliot, *The Essays of George Eliot,* ed. Nathan Sheppard (New York: Funk and Wagnalls, 1883), pp. 99–140.

23. Pochmann puts it this way: "Heine's attacks, together with a swing of the pendulum away from the Transcendentalist intuitionism and idealism, put a halt to the growth of interest in such writers as Novalis, Tieck, and Hoffmann. Infrequently discussed in the journals they were dismissed as 'morbid,' 'hypermystic,' 'intensely egoistic,' and 'lacking in intellectual balance and symmetry.' [*PGA*,338] And in a footnote to this passage Pochmann remarks: "Even Professor Boyesen, writing for the *Atlantic* (XXXVI, vi, Dec. 1875, 689–98) regretted their [the Romantics] unconventional lives and represented their striving as 'extreme and largely

futile.' At most he had a condescending interest in Novalis, whose poems, he said, 'possess a potent charm and even a kind of unity' . . . An article in the *Methodist Review* (LIII, v, Sept. 1893, 721–34), on the other hand, was full of praise for the Christian mysticism of Novalis." [*PGA*,684]

24. Ronsard (1524–1585), known as the "prince of poets," conceived the ambition of becoming for France what Homer and Pindar had been for Greece. After a youth at court and in the service of several ambassadors with whom he visited Scotland and England, Flanders, Holland, and Germany, Ronsard, recovering from an illness that left him deaf, joined the Collège de Coqueret, studying literature under Daurat. Here he met other poets with whom he founded a brotherhood first known as the "Brigade," which was dedicated to the pursuit of classical learning. But soon, in order to stress the group's understanding of itself as perpetuating classical forms of poetry and literature, Ronsard renamed the group and called it the "Pléiades," in commemoration of the group of ancient Alexandrian tragic poets called the "Pleiad" who worked during the third century B.C. (Lycophron of Chalcis, Alexander of Aetolia, Dionysiades of Tarsus, Homer of Byzantium, Sosiphones of Syracuse, Sositheus of Alexandria Troas, and Philicus of Corcyra.) But the French "Pléiades," in contrast to the Alexandrian "Pleias," and the seven-starred constellation from which both derived their name, did not limit themselves to seven members. For the group at one time or another included: Ronsard, de Baïf, du Bellay, Belleau, Deportes, Jordelle, Jamin, Thiard, and also Muret and Daurat.

25. Claude Binet, *La Vie de Pierre de Ronsard*, édition critique, Paris 1909, p. 40. As quoted by Werner Vordtriede, *Novalis und die französischen Symbolisten* (Stuttgart: W. Kohlhammer, 1963) p. 9. Hereafter referred to as *VNS*.

I owe much of my information about Novalis's influence on French poetry, and particularly on the Symbolist movement, to Vordtriede's interesting account.

26. "Nos pleurs et notre sang sont l'huile de la lampe / Que Dieus nous fait porter devant le genre humain." Alphonse de Lamartine (1790–1869). *Premières Méditations poétiques*, (Paris, 1879) p. 155. [*VNS*, 10].

27. "La terre me disait: Poète! / Le ciel me répétait: Prophète! / marcher! parler! enseigne! bénis!" Victor Hugo (1802–1885), *Les Chants due Crépuscle*, XXVI. Quoted in *VNS*, 11.

28. See Vordtriede's discussion of this point *VNS*, 12.

29. Not only were the *Tales of Hoffmann* phenomenally successful in France, but Baudelaire held a conception "of mystic *Correspondance* between the world of sense and that of symbol, a theory which may suggest the later Symbolists, but which he derived from Swedenborg and Hoffmann." (W. Nitze and E. P. Dargan, *A History of French Literature*, third ed. [New York: Holt, Rinehart and Winston, 1960] p. 604.) Thus while both Novalis and Baudelaire read and were influenced by Swedenborg, Novalis influenced Hoffmann, whereas Baudelaire was influenced by him—for instance, in the images of artificial, inorganic, and mineral plants and gardens, which Hoffmann encountered first in Novalis's *Klingsohr* tale, and which abound in Baudelaire's poems.

In addition, Baudelaire not only admired Poe but translated his work into French: "European critics were far more astute in recognizing his [Poe's] significance . . . his work marks him not simply as a precursor of the Symbolist school in France, but as a direct and major influence on Baudelaire, Mallarmé, Verlaine and Rimbaud." (Edgar Allan Poe, *Selected Writings*, with an introduction by David Galloway, ed. [Harmondsworth, Middlesex, England: Penguin Books, 1978] p. 12.) But since Poe was influenced by Novalis, Novalis however indirectly also affected Mallarmé, Verlaine, and Rimbaud. "Baudelaire's translation of the tales, which comprise five of the twelve volumes of his collected works, are remarkable for their strict authenticity and adherence, wherever idiom permits, to Poe's phraseology. Poe's poetry—which Baudelaire despaired of rendering accurately in French—received its most influential translation in Mallarmé's edition, where the form of the prose poem made a direct and major contribution to the *vers libre* movement . . . " [*Ibid.*] Yet, as Heinz Ritter has so convincingly shown, the form of the *vers libre* is *the* mode of a good deal of Novalis's "prose." (Heinz Ritter, *Der unbekannte Novalis* (Göttingen: Sachse und Pohl Verlag, 1967).

Finally, Blaze de Bury, who translated Novalis's "Miners' Song" (see pt. II, chap. 7), was probably personally acquainted with Baudelaire. In any case, as Vordtriede points out, Baudelaire's "Rêve parisien" is not only written in the same, and for the *Fleurs du Mal* unusual, meter, but it exhibits the same turn inward that the "Miners' Song" metaphorically chronicles. See *VNS*, 44–48.

30. Madame de Staël was advised extensively by August Wilhelm von Schlegel, the older brother of Novalis's best friend, Friedrich von Schlegel. Together the brothers von Schlegel edited the *Athenäum*, in which Novalis's works were first published. Madame de Staël speaks of Novalis as a "mystic" and gives a paraphrased account of *Die Lehrlinge zu Sais.*

31. Even though Carlyle's essay on Novalis was published four years before Heine's often politically motivated critique, its effect on the French understanding of Novalis was felt only several years later. It continued to shape French thought about Novalis and German philosophy after 1837, when Novalis's works (in the one volume publication edited by Tieck and Schlegel) became available in Paris, and even after 1840, when this edition was distributed fairly widely. See *VNS* 39–40.

32. During the second half of the nineteenth century French writers often went to British and American sources to enrich the horizon of their own literary world. Thus for instance both Verlaine and Rimbaud traveled in England, and Mallarmé, who translated Poe into French, spent some time there during his youth. In addition, these writers read British and American authors, as well as reviews and journals.

33. Henri Albert, "Conte de Jacinthe et de Feuille-de-Rose" in *L'Idee libre*, Sep. 10, 1893, [*VNS*, 185].

34. Maurice Maeterlinck, *Les Disciples à Sais* in *Le Réveil*, 1894. [Ibid.]

35. *Les Disciples à Sais et les fragments de Novalis*, (Bruxelles: 1895) [Ibid.]

36. Maurice Maeterlinck, *On Emerson and other Essays* (New York: Dodd, Mead, and Co., 1912). Hereafter referred to as *MEE.*

37. Novalis wrote most of his mathematical notations during September and October of 1798 and the *Arythmetica Universalis* during October and November of the same year.

38. Most extreme among these is the claim that comes out of the Rudolf Steiner school of Novalis interpretation. It asserts that Novalis is the reincarnation

of Raffael, who in turn is said to be the reincarnation of St. John. But both the link to St. John and to Raffael are older. Tieck in his biographical notes compares Novalis to St. John. Carlyle chooses to translate this passage and to quote it in his Novalis essay: "In outline and expression his face strikingly resembled that of the Evangelist John, as we see him in the large noble painting by Albrecht Dürer, preserved at Nürnberg and München." [*TCE*,200] Novalis himself on the other hand says that Sophie resembles Raffael as he appears in one of his self-portraits.

39. Thus for instance Nietzsche, even when he means to praise Novalis, does so only in an ironical voice and backhandedly by claiming his true insight to be expressed with naive delight: "Novalis, by experience and instinct an authority in questions of holiness, once expressed the whole secret with naive delight: 'It is sufficiently surprising, that the association of lust, religion, and cruelty has not long since made people aware of their intimate relationship and common tendency.'" (Friedrich Nietzsche, *Sämtliche Werke, Kritische Studienausgabe*, eds. Giorgio Colli and Mazzino Montinari [München: Deutscher Taschenbuch Verlag, 1980] vol. 2, p. 138.) but there is, in fact, nothing naive about this statement. Rather it is one of Novalis's truly admirable qualities that he never shrinks from calling a spade a spade—as the saying goes. And precisely because he is indeed in religious matters somewhat of an expert, he is not shocked by the conjunction of lust, faith, and cruelty. He, therefore, is not nearly as perverse or insignificant as Nietzsche would make him out to be when he writes: "the typical hatred of the sick against the perfect—e.g. Novalis against Wilhelm Meister, who finds the book odious. 'With straw and with rags the garden of poetry is imitated.' 'The understanding in it is like a naive devil.' 'Artistic atheism is the spirit of this book.'—And that at a time when he was enthusiastically taken with Tieck, who then just seemed to present himself as a disciple of Jacob Boehme." (Ibid., vol. 13, p. 496.) This is not to say that Nietzsche is not right about the relative literary value of Novalis and Goethe. There can be no doubt that Novalis's talent is not anywhere near the scope of Goethe's. But how many among Germans—indeed among writers anywhere, of that or any other age—have the measure of that giant? And Novalis is the first to acknowledge this!

40. Hugo Friedrich, *Die Struktur der modernen Lyrik*, Rowohlts Deutsche Enzyklopädie, ed. Ernesto Grassi, 6th ed. (Hamburg: Rowohlt Taschenbuch Verlag, 1956). Hereafter referred to as *FML*.

Prior to Friedrich and as early as 1891 Jean Thorel had already noted the connection between Novalis and the Symbolists. The thought was then taken up by Tancrède de Visan in 1910 in his classic article on the subject, "L'attitude du lyricisme contemporain" (Mercure de France, 1911), p. 399. In Germany it was Stefan George who as early as 1892 suggested that the roots of French Symbolism were to be found in German Romanticism in general and particularly in Novalis. But Jean Thorel, Tancrède de Visan, and Stefan George all wrote about French Symbolism. Hugo Friedrich is the first to widen the subject sufficiently to address the question of modern poetry in Europe. As a result he comes to consider Novalis in his own right, not merely as a precursor of the Symbolists, and nevertheless remains very much aware of Novalis's importance for that movement.

41. Recently, for instance, Vietta wrote an interpretation of Novalis's theory of language that is indebted to Friedrich and also makes this point. (see: Silvio

Vietta, *Sprache und Sprachreflexion in der modernen Lyrik,* vol. III, Literatur und Reflexion, ed. Beda Alleman (Bad Homburg: Verlag Dr. Max Gehlen, 1970). Hereafter referred to as *VSS.* Since Vietta numbers both his chapters and paragraphs I will use the following convention: the first numeral gives the page number, the second the chapter number, and the following two numerals the paragraph numbers.

42. The positive and negative importance of the concept of nature, and its relationship to art, for Novalis, is discussed in pt. II.

43. The star indicates that Novalis in the course of later revisions singled out this passage for a "collection of new fragments" that he meant to work on. See II, 595, #318, 15–17.

44. The importance of the concept chance or *Zufall* is discussed in pt. I, chap. 2.

45. For an account of the French Illuminati Friedrich refers us to his article "Die Sprachtheorie der französischen Illuminaten, insbesondere Saint Martins," *Deutsche Vierteljahresschrift für Literaturwissenschaft und Geistesgeschichte* 13 (1935): 293–310. Here Claude de Saint-Martin and Martinez de Pasqually are named as the main figures of that movement in France. But only the former can properly be said to have possibly influenced Novalis's thought on language, since the latter did not develop a language theory of his own.

46. As readers of Hegel doubtless know, it is difficult to translate the German word *Geist.* Its range of meaning includes "spirit," "mind," "intellect," "wit,"— and not unlike the English word "spirit," even "ghost." In fact, Geist and "ghost"—as well as "aghast" and "ghastly"—are etymologically related. The Indo-Germanic root *gheis* (angry) develops into the Gothic *usgeisnan* and *usgaisjan* (to be terrified and to terrify). From the original meaning of terror, dismay, excitement, of being stirred in general, eventually develop the significations "spirit," "soul," and "heart," all of which tend to be used as something that is standing in opposition to body. As a result the later signification of supernatural being develops. In 1366 Heinrich Seuse used the adjectival form *geistreich* to translate the Latin *spiritualis.* "Geistreich" thus came to function prominently in the German mystical tradition. In 1526 Martin Luther used the word in the phrase "geystreiche Prediger" and in 1534 in "geistreicher Poet," meaning respectively preacher and poet filled with the spirit of the Holy Ghost. In the Renaissance and in the Enlightenment the meaning of "geistreich" became secularized. In 1624 Opitz spoke of the *homo spiritualis poeticus* as "geistreich," and in 1682 Leibniz broadened its signification to include the intellect. During the Classic and Romantic periods "geistreich" even became a fashionable word, yet during the latter its significance changed, and it often took on the negative meanings of "fragmented" or "nonproductive." Although Novalis is a Romanticist, he deliberately turns to the older Medieval usage of "geistreich" as he found it in Luther and the Mystical tradition. Novalis, contrary to the spirit of his own times then, does not mean "mind" or "intellect" when he says "Geist" but has "spirit" or indeed "supernatural being" in mind. I believe, therefore, it is more nearly correct to translate "Geist" as "spirit," although the significations of "mind," "intellect," and even "wit" are certainly also vibrating as associated meanings within the horizon of the idea of "Geist." (See Alexander Kluge, *Etymologisches Wörterbuch* [Berlin: Walter de Gruyter and Co., 1967.])

47. The bars indicate that in the course of later revisions Novalis had second thoughts about this fragment: "What in these pages is crossed out—requires even in respect of the draft still quite some improvements etc. Some is totally wrong— some insignificant—some wall-eyed. What is in bars is of entirely problematic truth—thus it is useless." [II,595,#318]

As a result we must ask what status a fragment should be awarded that Novalis, in the course of later revisions, decided to cross out, as he did this aphorism on the incantatory power and nature of words. The inclusion of such fragments in the collected works is obviously indicated in a critical edition. Yet their status is problematic. On the one hand, they become in this fashion unques- tionably part of Novalis's oeuvre; on the other hand, their being a part of it is the very thing that is denied by the fact that the author's dismissal of them is being noted. And so we are to think them absent while they are present, much like evidence in a trial that has been ruled inadmissible and that the jury is instructed to disregard. Clearly neither the jury nor we are able to forget what we have heard or seen. Yet it seems singularly unfair to treat such a fragment as if its status were equal with that of fragments the author had approved of or selected for publica- tion. Who, for instance, would want to take one of the many sketches for the Fifth Symphony Beethoven wrote but discarded and play it as an equally valid version? Why should we be any less strict in our judgments concerning literary aphor- isms? If such a fragment is to be used at all as support for one's interpretation of Novalis's views, then it is clearly of no little interest that Novalis had second thoughts about it and in fact decided against it. Therefore, while the fragment may still bear interesting evidence about the way Novalis worked, its power to support a specific view of Novalis is surely diminished, and the reader ought to be made aware of this.

48. If, indeed, we are meant to read the fragment on incantation as pertaining to the autonomy of language by understanding the calling spirit to be that of language herself—a reading that may, in fact, be more interesting, although I do not believe that it accurately reflects Novalis's intention, unless a great deal more is said about just how we are to understand the nature of that spirit of language!— then the fragment says nothing about the poet's extraordinary powers of will and imagination by which he is able to create for his audience an entire world indepen- dent of the outer senses and their stimulation. For then it is not the poet's will and imagination, but that of language herself that conjures for the reader this sense- independent world, and the poet is nothing more—nor less—than the conduit through whom poetic language herself speaks to us. But this makes of the poet a possessed or inspired servant of language rather than the radically free and self- willed writer that Friedrich for instance insists he is.

49. In the creation of all art, chance occurrences play a legitimate role. From ancient times artists have used happenstance configurations to spur their imag- ination or have gratefully incorporated lucky accidents into the overall intentional design of their work. Thus, for instance, as classic an artist as Leonardo da Vinci in his *Treatise on Painting* writes a chapter entitled "A Way of Developing and Arous- ing the Mind to Various Inventions," in which he says: "I cannot forbear to mention among these precepts a new device for study which, although it may seem but trivial and almost ludicrous, is nevertheless extremely useful in arousing

the mind to various inventions. And this is, when you look at a wall spotted with stains, or with a mixture of stone, if you have to devise some scene, you may discover a resemblance to various landscapes, beautiful with mountains, rivers, rocks, trees, plains, wide valleys and hills in varied arrangement; or, again, you may see battles and figures in action; or strange faces and costumes and an endless variety of objects which you could reduce to complete and well-drawn forms. And these appear on such walls confusedly, like the sound of bells in whose jangle you may find any name or word you choose to imagine." (Leonardo da Vinci, *Codex Urbinas* [Vatican Library, 1270]. Selections from this text appear in *A Documentary History of Art*, 2 vols., ed. Elisabeth Gilmore Holt [Princeton, N. J.: Princeton University Press, 981], I: 283.)

Similarly the late Romantic poet Justinus Kerner used Rorschach-like inkblots to fire his imagination and then wrote poems on the strange figures and phantoms he projected onto these "entirely accidental" images. (Justinus Kerner, *Kleksographien*, in *Justinus Kerners sämtliche poetische Werke*, 4 vols., ed. Josef Gaismaier [Leipzig: Hesse und Becker Verlag, 1905], II: 199 ff.)

But in neither case is the resulting work entirely a product of sheer, haphazard chance. The artists who follow Leonardo's and Justinus Kerner's instructions merely use accidental configurations in order to get started, but then proceed with deliberate control in the execution of their work. Kerner himself seems ambivalent about his own active part in the creation of the *Kleksographien*. In the foreword he advises the reader how he can, by deliberately folding paper over a bit of carefully splattered ink, make images that leave room for the imagination to play with, and also suggests that one can always give fantasy a helping hand by adding to the accidental images with pen and ink what they lack: "thus, for instance, an image of a man may come about in his entire shape and clothing, but perhaps without head, hand etc., then, as has also happened in what follows, what is missing may, here and there, be easily added." [202] But Kerner then warns "that we can never bring about what we desire and that frequently the opposite of what we expect appears." [202] Similarly, some lines accompanying one of his inkblot images read: "Out of the night of ink, / even before the images of Hades / (not thoughts of my own heart) / arose the messengers of death." [206] He repeats this sentiment in the introduction, saying: "The pictures here given, the so-called images of Hades, did also not come about as a result of my will and power, I am completely incapable of drawing. On the contrary, they came about entirely as the result of making ink-blots in the manner described above, and often required no assistance, often only a little, by having a few lines added or faces traced artificially." [203] But even if Kerner is unclear about his own involvement, about how much these images are accidental products, or works of the deliberate imagination after it has been stimulated into activity by the amorphous shapes of the blots, there can be little doubt for an unbiased observer: the images have been extensively reshaped by the pen! And sometimes—or so it appears—even by a pair of scissors. No doubt at all can exist about the poems that accompany the blots. Having been written as captions or illustrative texts to the images, there is nothing accidental about them.

50. Reinhardt, who in his essay on the language philosophy of Novalis also cites this fragment, seems to be aware of its limitations, for he says: "The paradox

of a deliberately brought about chance, first of all, means to say no more than that the adequate word, as lucky windfall, is found by chance, but that it can be induced only by a very highly raised consciousness." (Heinrich Reinhardt, *Integrale Sprachtheorie* [München: UNI-Druck, 1976], p. 8.) Reinhardt, here, as in his reading of Novalis in general, is clearly aware of the philosophic and religious background against which Novalis must be understood.

51. It was to this thought that Edgar Allan Poe responded when he set the Novalis quotation as motto at the beginning of "The Mystery of Marie Rogêt." See pt. I, chap. 1, above.

52. For a discussion of the meaning fairy tales and dreams held for Novalis see pt. II, chap. 8.

CHAPTER TWO

1. Søren Kierkegaard, *Either/Or*, (Princeton, N. J.: Princeton University Press, 1971), pp. 231–245. Hereafter referred to as *E/O*.

2. Thus, Hugo Friedrich as well as Silvio Vietta, for instance, speak of Zufall in connection with the freedom of both fantasy and language.

3. See pt. I, chap. 1, above.

4. For a more detailed discussion of this fragment, see pt. I, chap. 4 and also, particularly, endnote 6 below.

5. Thus, for instance, Huizinga says: "The agon in Greek life, or the contest anywhere else in the world, bears all the formal characteristics of play and as to its function belongs almost wholly to the sphere of the festival, which is the play sphere. It is quite impossible to separate the contest as a cultural function from the complex 'play-festival-rite.'" Johan Huizinga, *Homo Ludens*, (Boston: Beacon Press, 1950), p. 31. Hereafter referred to as *HHL*. The essential connection between the realms of the agon and of games is here fully discussed.

6. Although this is one of those fragments Novalis crossed out in later revisions, it still shows that he was aware of the more than *merely* playful nature of games.

7. Friedrich von Schiller, *Schillers Sämtliche Werke* (Leipzig: Der Tempel Verlag) vol. 4, letters 14 and 15, pp. 249–55.

8. Consider in this respect also the *Monolog*, where "proper conversation" is said to be a "mere word game." See pt. I, chap. 4.

9. In the *Hemsterhuis Studien*, partly copying and partly commenting on Hemsterhuis, Novalis, for instance, notes: "Organ is instrument—means to a determined end. . . . / Every finite being is instrument / is *organ*—means to a determined end. . . . Only in analogy with *our art* do we call those parts of nature which appear especially to serve its procreation and modification—organs. Where organization becomes apparent—at once a purpose is revealed—*an end*— Where an *end* appears—we are driven to an *ideal*, to a *thought*—which *precedes* the real, the execution, the object. Organization is that driving force of the parts—to bring forth substances." [II,370,#30]

Hemsterhuis here reverses the relation of art and nature that Plato suggests when he says: "Any discourse ought to be constructed like a living creature, with its own body, as it were; it must not lack either head or feet; it must have a middle and extremeties so composed as to suit each other and the whole." [264c] (Plato, *Phaedrus*, in *The Collected Dialogues of Plato*, Edith Hamilton and Huntington Cairnes, eds. [Princeton, N. J.: Princeton University Press, 1973] p. 510.)

No doubt it was this passage that led Aristotle, in chapter seven of *The Poetics*, to say: ". . . a tragedy is an imitation of an action that is complete in itself, as a whole of some magnitude . . . Now a whole is that which has beginning, middle, and end . . . A well constructed plot, therefore, cannot either begin or end at any point one likes . . . to be beautiful, a living creature, and every whole made up of parts, must not only present a certain order in its arrangement of parts, but also be of a certain definite magnitude. Beauty is a matter of size and order, and therefore impossible either (1) in a very minute creature . . . or (2) in a creature of vast size . . . " [1450b23–39] (Aristotle, *The Basic Works of Aristotle*, Richard McKeon, ed. [New York: Random House, 1971])

It is commonly thought that Novalis's concentrated study of Kant does not include a reading of the *Critique of Judgement*. Yet Novalis's thinking of the causal efficacy of chance in analogy to the causal interrelation of the parts or elements in an organized being not only echoes Plato and Aristotle but also strongly resembles Kant's notion of "purposiveness without a purpose," as put forth in the *Critique of Judgement*, where the notion suggests an organic interconnectedness in the beautiful object and, therefore, leads to a view of beauty as an "organized being": "This principle, which is at the same time a definition, is as follows: *An organized product of nature is one in which every part is reciprocally purpose [end] and means*. In it nothing is vain, without purpose, or to be ascribed to a blind mechanism of nature. . . . We may therefore describe the aforesaid principle as a *maxim*, for judging of the internal purposiveness of organized beings." (Immanuel Kant, *Critique of Judgement* [New York: Hafner Press, 1974], pp. 222–23). Insofar a' chance, for Novalis, is involved in the creation of beautiful art then, it raises the possibility of his having been familiar with the third critique. (For an account of Novalis's reading of Kant see II, 334, 35; there Hans-Joachim Mähl in the introductory essay to Novalis's *Kant Studien* remarks that the *Fichte Studien* of 1795–96 already presuppose that Novalis had a thorough knowledge of Kant's main works and that he returns again to a serious study of Kant in 1797.)

10. Although this is one of the fragments Novalis crossed out, it still shows that he distinguished between *mere* and meaningful chance.

11. See fragment III, 409, #730 cited pt. I, chap. 1 above.

12. See III, 425, #793 cited above in this chapter.

13. David Hume, *An Enquiry Concerning Human Understanding*, sect. X, pt. 1.

14. In my English rendition of this fragment I translate "aufheben" as "cancelling." While this translation is correct as far as it goes, it is incomplete, since the German aufheben, for Novalis, has the same dual nature that it came to have for Hegel. Particularly when aufheben occurs in conjunction with the idea of synthesis, it always implies in the cancelling also a raising to a higher level. The etymological nearness of "aufheben" to "erheben" or "Erhebung" makes this dual meaning not only evident, but also especially significant for Novalis. Theo-

dor Haering bases his claim that Novalis not only foreshadowed Hegel but actually evolved a proper Hegelian dialectic before Hegel in part on this fact. (Theodor Haering, *Novalis als Philosoph* [Stuttgart: W. Kohlhammer, 1954]).

Novalis also points in fragment 730 itself to the conjunction of miracles and natural events: "Arbitrary will, miracles and chance—are indirectly connected to the world, etc. / . . . Interrelatedness of the world of miracles and of nature. Miracles *shall* take place according to laws—natural effects *without laws*—the world of miracles and the world of nature shall become one. (*Rule* and *non-rule*.)" [III, 409,21–29,#730]

That miracles and natural effects not only supplement each other, but become one—that is, become interchangeable with each other—is the project for the Golden Age in which—as the method of Erhebung even now attempts—the conjunction of all opposites is the paradisical promise.

15. Historically the notion developed out of the beliefs and practices of stellar religions in the Near East. The stars, although considered to be divine beings, were nevertheless in their unchanging behavior seen to be subject to a higher will and purpose and were thought to make that purpose known by the various orbits that they draw against the night sky. In the regularity of their movements, in the eternal periodicity of their cycles, and in the rationality of the heavenly motions as a whole, that is, in the qualitatively understood manner of their behavior, the stars were thought to reveal a system of cosmic meaning, and whereas the stars served as quantitative cosmic clocks measuring time (*chronos*), they were also thought to be the qualitative cosmic interpreters of the meaning of times (*kairos*). In the Egyptian tradition, for instance, which left its influence on other stellar religious systems, it was thought that the star-god imparts his *ka* or essence to the spaces and periods of time he traverses. Out of this notion arose the idea of a star-ruler who determines the character of particular time intervals.

Thinking of a star that after a time of invisibility rises again in the East as being newly born and linking its reappearance with the birth of a human being at the same moment generated not only the idea of a star companion in fate and of a stellar guardian with which the idea of a guardian was later associated, but also allowed the individualization of the hitherto largely general and cosmic oracles. Thus a man's destiny was thought to be established by the lot he drew at the beginning of his life, that is, by the star that rose over the eastern horizon at the moment of his birth. Known as the *katarchian horoscopos*, the star was personified as the Moira Lachesis who rules a man's fate by choosing and determining his lot. As a newborn star the katarchian horoscopos was thought to possess all the strengths and powers of life that come with the freshness of youth. And it was therefore believed to be the strongest factor shaping our destiny. The star in the meridian at the moment of our birth was, like Clotho, the ruler over the evolving thread of our life. And the star just setting in the western sky, analogically thought to be dying, was believed to determine, like Atropos, the time and manner of our death. The goddesses of fate, accordingly, were understood as emanations of the planets and the stars. They came down to Earth to guide us during the course of our life and in this way determine our destiny. But whereas the Moirai watch over the general development and fundamental order of life, Fortuna-Tyche presides over the sudden moments of change when good fortune unexpectedly turns into disaster or disaster turns seemingly inexplicably into a blessing. Moirai and Tyche are two elements of a rather intricately structured notion of fate, to which yet other aspects belong—such as, for example, the personal Daimon as the reflection of one's own nature and Potmos, the limiting otherness of the yoke of circumstances into which we are born. The Moirai, as the lot we draw, rule over the inevitability of physical changes as part of the organic laws of nature in general. Tyche, on the other hand, enters whenever we meet a challenge with daring and the outcome of our actions is uncertain. The concept of destiny personified in the Moirai, thus, is one of a linear, continuous development; in contrast, Tyche names fate's instantaneous shifts and changes. In the momentary nature of Tyche our actions meet the ordained order and are therefore decided not by the skill with which they are executed but by a divine will manifesting itself at that particular moment.

For a full treatment of the subject see Wilhelm Gundel, *Sternglaube, Stern-religion, Sternorakel* (Leipzig: Quelle und Meyer, 1933); Wilhelm Knappich, *Geschichte der Astrologie* (Frankfurt, a. M.: Vittorio Klostermann, 1967); and Hans Strohm, *Tyche. Zur Schicksalsauffassung bei Pindar and den frühgriechischen Dichtern* (Stuttgart: Cottasche Buchhandlung Nachfolger, 1944).

16. Plato, *Laws*, trans. A. E. Taylor, in *The Dialogues of Plato*, ed. Edith Hamilton and Huntington Cairns, Bollingen Series LXXI (Princeton, N. J.: Princeton University Press, 1973), 709b–c.

17. See John Smith's short but incisive article on the subject, "Time, Times, and the 'Right Time': Chronos and Kairos," *Monist* 53 (January 1969): 1–13.

18. The metaphor of navigation dominates the Moira-Tyche-Kairos nexus of ideas. Not only is our life seen as a voyage across the sea in which we might be shipwrecked—that is, meet an ill fate or have ill fortune—but the Latin translation of kairos, which is *opportunitas*, is compounded of *ob*, "toward," and *portus*, "harbor," and therefore literally means "a favorable wind blowing toward port," from which the meaning "favorable moment" or "opportunity" derives. *The Odes of Pindar*, trans. Sir John Sandys, Loeb Classical Library, (Cambridge, Mass.: Harvard University Press, 1978), *Olympian* XII: 1–7.

19. Novalis seems to have been very much aware of the wide horizon of the agonistic sphere and of its connection to game or play, as well: " / *Mystical art of war*. The mathematical war—The *poetical* war—the scientific—the game of war etc. The rhetorical *war*." [III,450,#944] For an imaginative and interesting discussion of this subject see Johan Huizinga's *Homo Ludens*.

20. Pindar has some striking examples of the idea of the word as missile in his poetry: "But now, from the bow of the far-darting Muses, do thou shoot a shower of such shafts of song as these, at Zeus, the Lord of the ruddy lightening. . . . And speed thou to Pytho also a winged arrow sweet, for not unto the ground shall fall the words thou shalt essay, while trilling the lyre in honor of the wrestling of the hero from famous Opûs." [*Olympian* IX: 5–21] Or: "From the gods come all the means of mortal exploits; thanks to the gods are men wise and brave and eloquent. And, while I am eager to praise my hero, I trust I may not fling, as it were, outside the lists the bronze-tipped javelin which I brandish in my hand, but may fling it afar, and thus surpass my foes." [*Pythian* I: 41–45] Or: "Oh father Zeus, I pray that I may sound the praises of this deed of prowess by the favour of the

Graces, and that I may excel many a bard in honouring victory by my verses, shooting my dart of song nearest of all to the mark of the Muses." [*Nemean* IX: 53–55].

21. A haunting example of the adoration of chance and its connection to a challenging and combative attitude is provided by Kierkegaard. I hope that this rather lengthy quotation may be excused on the grounds that it bears witness to how much the ancient idea of chance was still alive during the early nineteenth century.

"Accursed chance never have I cursed you because you appeared. I curse you because you do not appear at all. Or is this perhaps a new invention of yours, unfathomable being, barren mother of all, sole remnant of the past, when necessity gave birth to freedom, when freedom was again lured back into its mother's womb? Accursed chance, you, my only confidante, the only being whom I consider worthy of being my ally and my enemy, always the same by forever being different, always incomprehensible always a riddle! You whom I love with all my soul in whose image I mold myself, why do you not show yourself? I do not humbly entreat you to show yourself in this manner or that; such worship would be idolatry not acceptable unto you. I challenge you to battle, why do you not appear? Or has the pendulum of the world system stopped, is your riddle solved, so that you too have hurled yourself into the sea of eternity? Terrible thought, for thus the world comes to a standstill from boredom! Accursed chance I await you. I shall not overcome you with principles nor with what foolish people call character; no, I will be your poet! I will not be a poet for others; show yourself! I will be your poet! I consume my own verse, and that will sustain me. Or do you think I am not worthy? Like a Bayadère dancing to the honor of the Gods, so have I devoted myself to your service. Nimble, thinly clad, agile, unarmed I renounce everything for you. I own nothing, I desire to own nothing, I love nothing, I have nothing to lose, but I am not therefore more worthy of you, you who long ago must have wearied of tearing human beings away from what they love, tired of their cowardly sighs, and cowardly petitions. Take me by surprise, I am ready. No stakes, let us fight for honor. Show her to me, show me a possibility which seems an impossibility; show her to me among the shades of the underworld, I shall fetch her up, let her hate me, despise me, be indifferent to me, love another, I am not afraid; only let the waters be troubled, the silence be broken. To starve me in this way is paltry of you, you who imagine that you are stronger than I am." [*E/O*,322ff.]

This passage from *Either/Or* ostensibly expresses the seducer's desire accidentally—or rather by chance—to see and meet Cordelia, the girl whose love he is attempting to win. Yet this passionate plea clearly goes beyond the specific literary situation. In the speaker's vow to be the poet of chance, we are given a clue: the seduction is the poet's attempt to seduce the muse. He does battle with chance in order to win the muse, he entreats chance to let him meet her, see her, or retrieve her from the underworld as Orpheus, the first poet, attempted to fetch his muse, Eurydice, from Hades. Viewed from this perspective, the *Diary of a Seducer* becomes a chronicle of the poet's service to and conflict with chance for the gift of the muse on the occasion of a particular creative act. When it is completed he moves on, leaving this particular effort and involvement behind him absolutely.

As W. H. Auden remarks: "Just as a good man forgets his deed the moment he has done it, a genuine writer forgets a work as soon as he has completed it and starts to think about the next one; if he thinks about his past work at all, he is more likely to remember its faults than its virtues. (W. H. Auden, "Writing," in *20th Century Criticism*, ed. David Lodge, [London: Longman Group Ltd., 1972.] p. 637.)

In the poet's ambivalent feelings toward chance and in the inversion of the classical attitude, in which it was chance that challenged the protagonist to battle and bestowed on him the gifts of the muse, Kierkegaard reveals his essentially Romantic stance and character: for to challenge chance, to want to bend her to *his* will and consider himself stronger than her kairotic nature, is not only hybris but an attempt to overcome the limitations of time and to reach for infinity. Yet ultimately the poet cannot challenge chance; he cannot coerce her or the muse. Indeed, he cannot even seduce them! If he tries to do so anyway, and whether it appears as if he has succeeded in his attempt or not, the "silence will not be broken"; the muse, and therefore the poet's *true* voice, will remain mute. But this is not to suggest that the poet ought to be entirely passive or subservient. For as Auden says: "It is true that, when he is writing a poem, it seems to a poet as if there were two people involved, his conscious self and a Muse whom he has to woo or an Angel with whom he has to wrestle, but, as in an ordinary wooing or wrestling match, his role is as important as Hers. The Muse, like Beatrice in *Much Ado*, is a spirited girl who has as little use for an abject suitor as she has for a vulgar brute. She appreciates chivalry and good manners, but she despises those who will not stand up to her and takes a cruel delight in telling them nonsense and lies which the poor little things obediently write down as 'inspired' truth." (Ibid, p. 638.)

22. Compare Novalis's *Heinrich von Ofterdingen*, chap. 6 [I,279,5], where in a dream Mathilde, who is Heinrich's muse as well as his fiancée, "spoke a miraculous, secret word into his mouth, and it sounded through his entire being."

23. Novalis owned two different editions and translations of Pindar's works and tried his hand at translating the "Eleventh Olympian Ode." But the reflection of the notion of Tyche in Zufall is not the only parallel to Pindar. For Novalis found the essentially agonistic character of the poet's task to be mirrored in the life of Heinrich von Afterdingen, one of the contestants in the battle at the Wartburg.

Novalis first came across Afterdingen's story in 1799 in old chronicles in the library of the historian Major Funk in Artern: namely, the *Düringische Chronic* of Johannes Rothe, who died in 1434, the *Legend of the Holy Elisabeth*, written in rhymed verse by the town clerk of Eisenach, and the *Mansfeldische Chronica*, written by Cyriacus Spangenberg and published in 1572. In all these chronicles Heinrich's name is given as von A̲fterdingen, and this is how it appears in all of Novalis's manuscripts. Only the posthumous first edition of this tale in 1802 gives the title and name of its hero as O̲fterdingen. In doing so it follows Bodmer, whose edition of the *Minnesinger* of 1757 gives Heinrich's name as O̲fterdingen, no doubt in order to avoid any embarrassing associations to *anus* (*After*). But Novalis had not been familiar with this book when he started to work on his tale; he was introduced to it only later by A. W. Schlegel. [I,183–84] Nor do I think it likely that Novalis would have been guided by prudish considerations in selecting his protagonist's name, particularly since according to the *Sachsenspiegel* "Afterding" designates the continuation, convening fourteen days later, of the true *Ding* (judicial assembly), which was held according to Franconian law regularly every six weeks and comprised all the free citizens of the region who gathered, presided over by the landgrave, to decide questions of life, liberty, and landed property. The agonistic association of the name surely would have appealed to Novalis more than any prudish considerations might have dissuaded him from using it— even more so since in Afterdingen's story such a postponement, continuation, and reconvening of the agon on the *Wartburg* is of central concern and importance!

Der Wartburgkrieg (The War of Wart Castle) is the story of the legendary contest of poets that is supposed to have taken place in 1207 on the Wartburg, near Eisenach in Saxony. This contest was first described in a polemic poem of the thirteenth century. Here it is said that the five troubadours Walther von der Vogelweide, Wolfram von Eschenbach, Biterolf, Reinmar von Zweter, and Heinrich von Afterdingen fought with well-measured verses in honor of their princes. Heinrich von Afterdingen, who sang the praises of Leopold of Austria, lost the contest to Walther von der Vogelweide, who praised the Landgrave of Thuringia. As the loser in this combat of words, Heinrich von Afterdingen was condemned to die by the hangman's hand. He was saved from the noose only by the intervention of the landgrave's lady Elisabeth, and the contest was rescheduled for a later date to give Heinrich von Afterdingen time to consult with his liege, Leopold of Austria. But since Heinrich after this first defeat is supposed to have sought the help of the Hungarian magician Klingsor, instead, the poetic riddle describing the latter's verbal bout with Wolfram von Eschenbach was added and incorporated into the polemic poem. Thuringian chroniclers of the thirteenth century believed both the poem and the riddle to describe a historical situation and used them as historical sources. Besides Novalis, E. T. A. Hoffmann in his *Kampf der Sänger* and Richard Wagner in his opera *Tannhäuser* reworked the material and theme of the poem. In 1858 Simrock edited and prepared the poem for publication. *Der Wartburgkrieg*, ed. and trans. Karl Joseph Simrock (Stuttgart: J. G. Cotta, 1858.)

24. In *Heinrich von Ofterdingen*, for example, Novalis says: "And this is how it is with most writers of history, who may be sufficiently accomplished in narrating, and tiresomely profuse, but nevertheless forget what is most worthy of being known, namely that which alone makes history into history, and unites the many chance events into a pleasant, instructive whole. As I carefully consider all this, it seems to me that a historian should necessarily also be a poet, for only poets may understand the art by which events are properly intertwined." [I,259,13–21]

25. Also in *Heinrich von Ofterdingen* we find the following: "Some countries and times seem like most people to be ruled entirely by the enemy of poetry [dull desire], others, to the contrary, give poetry a home and it can be seen everywhere. For the historian the times of this conflict are the most remarkable . . . they are usually the times at which poets are born." [I,284,25–30]

26. The "Self-active, intended, ideal chance production," mentioned in fragment 953 then, can be understood in part also as the production of chance by the method of *Erhebung*. See fragment 953, pt. I, chap. 1, and also pt. I, chap. 2 above.

27. Paul Tillich, *Systematic Theology* (Chicago: University of Chicago Press, 1963), III: 370.

28. In evaluating the works of the imagination as more likely sources for truth than are merely factual historical accounts, Novalis expresses an opinion that a few years later was echoed by Schopenhauer: "The poet, however, apprehends the Idea, the inner being of mankind outside all relation and all time, the adequate objectivity of the thing-in-itself at its highest grade. Even in that method of treatment necessary to the historian, the inner nature, the significance of phenomena, the kernel of all those shells, can never be entirely lost, and can still be found and recognized by the person who looks for it. Yet that which is significant in itself, not in the relation, namely the real unfolding of the Idea, is found to be far more accurate and clear in poetry than in history; therefore, paradoxical as it may sound, far more real, genuine, inner truth is to be attributed to poetry than to history." (Arthur Schopenhauer, *The World as Will and Representation,* trans. E. F. J. Paine [New York: Dover Publications, 1969], I: 245).

Obviously both Schopenhauer's and Novalis's views about the relation of history and poetry to truth are in the tradition of Aristotle's exemplary passage on this subject. Novalis would have been aware of Aristotle's dictum that "poetry is both a more philosophic and a more real thing than history; for poetry tells rather the universal, history the particular" [Aristotle, *Poetics,* XCVI], even if he had not read the *Poetics,* since Shaftsbury cites this passage and says about it that "some considerable wits have recommended the best poems as preferable to the best histories; and better teaching the truth of characters and nature of mankind." [*Characteristics,* pt. IV, sect. III] Novalis, it would appear, ordered Shaftsbury's *Characteristiken,* translated by C. A. Weichmann, with notes by Leibniz, from Hensius. [IV,960]

Schopenhauer's speaking of a "far more real, genuine, *inner* truth," though, seems to align him, in this instance, far more closely with Novalis and the Romantic tradition than with Aristotle, and that despite his often biting critique of the Romantics.

29. Because of his dependence on the imagination, the writer, according to Novalis, is subject to the rule of indirect or "crooked" laws. This series of laws allows the reversal of time—at least in poetry and art—by permitting backward directed inferences. It is mostly because of this relationship to time that Novalis considers the poet to be a magician. In this connection compare Goethe's *Faust,* where in the witch's kitchen, when Faust first enters the world of fantasy and imagination, the natural order of cause and effect is reversed, future and past become interchangeable, and all natural temporal sequences are suspended, so that the witch's animals can desire Mephistopheles to repair what has as yet not been broken. (Johann Wolfgang von Goethe, *Faust,* Part One, 11. 2450–53)

30. For a discussion of the word "geistreich," (spiritual) see p. 253, note 46.

31. *Blüthenstaub* was published in May 1798, and most of it was written during the year 1797.

32. Addison, *The Spectator,* ed. Alexander Chalmers (New York: D. Appelton, 1879), V: 21.

33. Novalis owned Johann Georg Sulzer's *Allgemeine Theorie der schönen Künste*

in einzeln, nach alphabetischer Ordnung der Kunstwörter aufeinander folgenden Artikeln abgehandelt. (Erster–Zweyter Theil. Leipzig: Weidmann und Reich, 1771–1774.) In 1790 Novalis lists the work as one of those to be sent to Schlöben during his stay in Jena. [Booklist 1a, IV, 692, #32] We can therefore assume that Novalis was well acquainted with the complex general discussion of the term "genius" that took place during the eighteenth century. But despite Novalis's belief in the artist's superior spirit or genius, his recognition of the importance of skill for the creative artist—be he a poet, musician, or painter—was unwavering. In fact, Gadamer's observation describes Novalis's attitude well: "The concept of genius is conceived, fundamentally, from the point of view of the observer. This classical idea seems convincing not to the creative, but to the critical spirit. What is experienced by the observer as an inexplicable miracle of accomplishment is reflected for him in the marvelous nature of creation through the inspiration of genius. Creative individuals may then, insofar as they observe themselves, use the same form of understanding. The cult of genius of the 18th century, therefore, was doubtlessly also nourished by creative artists. Yet they have never gone as far in their self-apotheosis as bourgeois society would have allowed them to. The self-understanding of the artist remains far more down-to-earth. He sees possibilities of making and capabilities and questions of 'technique' even where the observer seeks inspiration, mystery, and deeper meaning. (Hans-Georg Gadamer, *Wahrheit und Methode* [Tübingen, I. C. B. Mohr ⟨Paul Siebeck⟩, 1975] pp. 88–89)

34. As pointed out earlier, it is among other things this relation to time that makes of the poet a magician.

CHAPTER THREE

1. Cited by Roy Harris, "Theoretical Ideas," in *Times Literary Supplement* 202, no. 4 (14 October 1983): 1119.

2. Johann Gottfried Herder, *Über die neuere Deutsche Literatur. Eine Beilage zu den Briefen, die neueste Literatur betreffend. 1766/1767. Erste Sammlung.* In *Sämmtliche Werke*, ed. Bernhard Suphan, 33 vols. (Berlin: Weidmannsche Buchhandlung, 1877–99], I: 240) Hereafter referred to as *HSW*.

George Eliot, who like Herder was a good translator, puts it this way when making excuses for giving some verses in their original German version: "It is not fair to the English reader to indulge in German quotations, but in our opinion poetical translations are usually worse than valueless." (George Eliot, "German Wit: Henry Heine," in *The Essays of "George Eliot,"* ed. Nathan Sheppard, [New York: Funk and Wagnalls, 1883], p. 135.)

3. George Steiner, "The Feast of Dissemination," *Times Literary Supplement* 202. no. 4 (14 October 1983): 1117.

4. *Ibid.*

5. In an essay on translation, Roy Harris, in speaking of the notion of equivalence at work in the idea of translation, remarks that "When the Red Queen asks 'What's the French for fiddle-de-dee?,' Alice replies 'Fiddle-de-dee's not English.' 'Who ever said it was?' is the Red Queen's retort. Whereupon Alice plays the translation theorist's trump card: 'If you'll tell me what language fiddle-de-dee is, I'll tell you the French for it.' Why one needs to know what language *fiddle-de-dee* is

in order to say what the French for it is Alice does not explain; but the implication is that unless one knew *that*, one could not be sure what *fiddle-de-dee* meant." Harris then goes on to say that "having ascertained the role played by *fiddle-de-dee* in its proper linguistic system, the translator may proceed to inquire whether there is a corresponding role played by any linguistic expression in French." Harris now suggests that this search for equivalence is due in part to the way we come to learn foreign languages: "How could any relevant correspondences be recognizable independently of a prior process of translation, namely the process typically involved in the translator's learning the foreign language in the first instance? For do we not learn foreign languages by being told e.g. that *chien* is the French for *dog?*" (Roy Harris, "Theoretical Ideas," *Times Literary Supplement* 202, no. 4 [14 October 1983]: 1119.) But while it is true that we learn foreign languages by setting up such equivalences—or at least do so when we first approach a new language—this is not the way we learn the meaning of words, expressions, and phrases in our mother tongue. Here we become aware of contextual wholes, of entire spheres of meaning, from which particular words and expressions must be abstracted if they are to be understood in isolation. The approach Novalis suggests for translating into a foreign language—to move to the idea that constitutes the wholeness of the work of art and to give it a new expression in a new idiom—closely resembles, then, the process by which translation into linguistic expression in one's own language occurs in the first place.

6. Like the English word *translation*, which derives from *translatus*, the past participle of *transferre*, meaning "to carry across" or "to transfer," the German *übersetzen* basically refers to being ferried across a divide. But since *über* also carries the meaning of "above," *übersetzen* can easily be made to connote both a lateral transfer and one that raises what is being carried across to a higher level.

7. James Grieve, "Taking Liberties," in *Times Literary Supplement* 202, no. 4 (14 October 1983): 1117.

8. I am indebted to Rita Terras for the observation that Tieck, in fact, did none of his own translating and that what usually is thought to be his contribution to the Schlegel/Tieck translation of 1822–23 is actually the work of his daughter Dorothea. Between 1797 and 1810, August Wilhelm Schlegel translated sixteen of Shakespeare's plays, with some of the proofreading being done by Dorothea Schlegel (née Mendelssohn). After 1810 he was no longer involved with the translation at all, and Tieck took over the supervision of it and occasionally assisted in the translation of eighteen more plays. Six of these were translated by his daughter Dorothea, the remaining twelve by her husband, Count Wolf von Baudissin. For further information see L. M. Price, *Die Aufnahme der englischen Literatur in Deutschland, 1500–1960* (Bern, 1961), and *Der deutsche Shakespeare*, with contributions by Walter Muschg, Hans Schmid, and others, vol. 7 of *Theater unserer Zeit*, ed. Reinhold Grimm (Basel, Hamburg, Wien: Basilius Presse, 1965).

9. The idea of a transformational translation finds a parallel and point of departure in Novalis's later studies of alchemy and its transformational process-philosophy, thus leading Novalis to see the alchemical project as a hermeneutical enterprise.

10. In this respect compare for instance Goethe's poem *Prometheus*, in which

the following lines occur: "Gods? I am no God, / And think myself as much as one. / Infinite?—Allmighty?— / What can they do? . . . / They want to share with me and I think, / I have nothing to share with them. / That which I have they cannot rob me of, / And what they have, they better guard. / Here mine and theirs, / And so we part. . . . / Look down Zeus, / Upon my world: it lives! / I formed them in my image, / A people, to resemble me, / To suffer, cry, to indulge and to enjoy themselves, / And not to pay Thee heed, / Like me! . . . [lines, 33–36, 70–75, 243–50]

11. Auden suggests that this recognition factor is due to the unique personality expressed by each writer in his works: "Frost's definition of poetry as the untranslatable element in language looks plausible at first sight but, on closer examination, will not quite do. In the first place, even in the most rarefied poetry, there are some elements which are translatable. The sound of the words, their rhythmical relations, and all meanings and association of meanings which depend upon sound, like rhymes and puns, are, of course, untranslatable, but poetry is not, like music, pure sound. Any elements in a poem which are not based on verbal experience are, to some degree, translatable into another tongue, for example, images, similes, and metaphors which are drawn from sensory experience. Moreover, because one characteristic that all men, whatever their culture, have in common is uniqueness—every man is a member of a class of one—the unique perspective on the world which every genuine poet has survives translation. If one takes a poem by Goethe and a poem by Hölderlin and makes literal prose cribs of them, every reader will recognize that the two poems were written by two different people. In the second place, if speech can never become music, neither can it ever become algebra. Even in the most 'prosy' language, in informative and technical prose, there is a personal element because language is a personal creation. Ne pas se pencher au dehors has a different feeling tone from Nichthinauslehnen. [sic] ('Do not lean out,' in French and German respectively.) A purely poetic language would be unlearnable, a purely prosaic not worth learning." W. H. Auden, "Writing," in 20th Century Literary Criticism, ed. David Lodge, (London: Longman Group Limited, 1972) p. 643.

12. Interestingly, Herder, despite his belief in the essential untranslatability of poetry, sees the task of the translator, if it is dispatched conscientiously, as a form of interpretation. In Über die neuere Deutsche Literatur . . . 1766/1767. Zwote Sammlung, he says: "Therefore, we shall not at all imitate miserably . . . if we rouse ourselves to study the oriental poems [by which Herder means the Books of the Bible] as history, and learn to explain them and to make them known. For it is impossible for us to translate and imitate them without understanding them. And the oriental philology that has now for some little time been blossoming in Germany, will, if it is joined to taste, scatter bad and foolish imitators. The best translator must be the best commentator. If this pronouncement were reversible, we could hope soon to have a book with the title 'Poetical Translation of the Oriental Poems which Explicates Them in Terms of the Country, History, Opinions, Religion, Conditions, Customs, and Language of Their Nation, and Transplants Them into the Genius of Our Own Time, Mentality, and Language'. . . . But we also consider this translation to be an original piece of work which can

influence our literature more than ten original works. . . . It is a paradigm of imitation that remains original. . . . Where is the translator who is, at once, a philosopher, poet, and philologist: he shall be the morning-star of a new era in our literature! But alas!" [*HSW*,I,274]

Herder, I think, is closer to Novalis's approach to translation than one might believe at first glance: his apparent indifference to the distinction between translation and imitation, his willingness to treat them often as interchangeable concepts, shows how much for him, too, translation is a *Nachdichtung*.

13. Walter Benjamin, *Illuminations* (New York: Schocken Books, 1976], p. 81.

In this respect it might be interesting to consider how translating into a language that is not one's mother tongue may allow one greater freedom in manipulating expressions and in pushing the limits of conventions beyond what a native speaker may feel possible. Being originally at home in a third language or in the language from which one translates may, therefore, enhance one's ability to find fresh approaches to the language into which one is translating.

14. On this point George Steiner correctly observes: "Imagine modernity if Kierkegaard was available solely in Danish, if only the speaker-reader of Norwegian could know Ibsen, if Marx or Freud remained encased in German." (George Steiner, "The Feast of Dissemination," *Times Literary Supplement* 202, no. 4 [14 October 1983]: 1117.)

15. It is for this reason that *Fabel*—being both a character in the *Klingsohr* Märchen and the German translation of Mythos—is said to be the spirit of the Golden Age and is indeed the agent by whose efforts that age is brought about.

16. How closely the structure of alchemy resembles, for Novalis, the structure of poetry and language cannot be discussed here in detail. Let it suffice to say that Francis Bacon, for example, whose works Novalis knew, thinks the shape-changer of Greek mythology, Proteus, is a symbol for the mutability of matter, while Novalis himself uses this mythic figure to indicate the changeability of philosophical ideas because of historical interpretation. [III,#468; III,#886; III,#977] Novalis also describes the nature of poetry and language with allusions to the transformational character associated with Proteus. See pt. II, beginning of chapter 7.

17. That this screen is, indeed, removable for Novalis will become apparent when, in the second part of this essay, the symbolism of the veil of Isis comes under consideration.

CHAPTER FOUR

1. The idea of the East as *the* place of origin does not refer only to the biblical Middle East, rather, it includes India, Egypt, and even Spain as Moorish domain. The East, therefore, names not a geographical location but a spiritual idea. To the Baroque tradition, on which Novalis draws heavily particularly in his *Lehrlinge zu Sais* and *Heinrich von Ofterdingen*, the East is the place of the Hebrew Bible, of the fairy tales of the Arabian Nights, of the Persian poetry of Firdowsi, of the Indo-Persian myth of Zarathustra, of the heroic epic of the history of Moorish Spain, and of the Egyptian sacred writings of Isis and Osiris recorded in the secret

symbols of the hieroglyphs. Thus the East is the true land of mythos, or fable, and therefore not only *ex oriente lux* but also *ex oriente lingua!* And for Novalis this means both poetry as prayer and prayer as poetry.

It was Hamann who in 1762 in his *Aesthetica in nuce* first suggested that literature ought to turn to the Orient to renew the dead languages of nature. In 1767, Herder picked up on this suggestion in his *Fragmente über die neuere deutsche Literatur* by speculating that either Hebrew or Arabic must have been the first language of mankind. Both men are concerned with rediscovering man's original language. For Hamann this means finding our way back to the universal language spoken before the confusion of tongues that was visited upon man in punishment for his building the tower of Babel.

2. Alexander Kluge, *Etymologisches Wörterbuch* (Berlin, Walter de Gruyter, 1967).

3. *VSS*,36,3.4.1. Similar claims are made by Hugo Friedrich.

4. One of the few interpreters of the *Monolog* who is acutely aware of the importance of its linguistic form is Strohschneider-Kohrs. (Ingrid Strohschneider-Kohrs, *Die Romantische Ironie in Theorie und Gestaltung* [Tübingen: Max Niemeyer Verlag, 1960]). She gives a fine analysis, particularly of the presence of irony in the *Monolog*. It is her insight that first alerted me to its importance for a proper understanding of the *Monolog*. While I find myself in agreement with Strohschneider-Kohrs, my own interpretation will take a somewhat different tack.

5. Compare fragment II, 559, #148, quoted in pt. 1 above. See also p. 270, endnote 15 below.

6. How much Novalis, in general, doubts the reliability and adequacy of language when it is used as a mere instrument for the expression of thoughts is not entirely clear. He seems to have been ambivalent in his feelings on this question, for while he considers this subject in the *Logologische Fragmente*, he discarded the paragraph during later revisions: "❙The letter is only an aid to philosophical expression, the essential nature of which consists in the excitation of a particular process of thought. The speaker considers, produces—the listener reconsiders, reproduces. Words are a deceptive medium for the instigation of thought—they are unreliable vehicles for a determined, specific stimulus.❙" [II,522,#3] But it would appear that this inadequacy is an aspect of language only when it is not poetical, that is, inspired speech. Novalis, in the *Allgemeine Brouillon*, discussing the distinction between the common or prosaic and the poetical life, says: "THEORY OF THE COMMON LIFE. The educated pronunciation and declamation of the ordinary. *common* life as prose—one has to settle for speaking, if one cannot sing. Musical instruments—poetical instruments. (Trivial ideas = [superficial] ideas from the surface.) [III,303,#352]

The German for "trivial ideas" here is *platte Einfälle*. Novalis's own spinning out of this term into notions of "superficial ideas" or ideas "from the surface" points to his awareness of the relation *Einfall* has to *Zufall*. Both words entered the German language by way of the theological writings of German mystics who translated the scholastic *incidere* with *einfallen* and *accidere* with *zufallen*, or rather, with middle high German *invallen* and *zuovallen*, respectively. (See Alexander Kluge, *Etymologisches Wörterbuch*). For Novalis the two terms have a parallel function: where the poet gathers the true insights that fall to him from the depth beyond the everyday of human life, common man must make do with what falls to him from its surface and, therefore, is merely a flat or superficial idea. Thus, common talk no less than poetical speech depends on something that comes to the speaker from outside his own person. But whereas to the poet the gift comes from the very depth of all being, it comes to the man of common talk, or idle chatter, merely from its surface, from the appearance of being, rather than from its essence.

7. Käte Hamburger, "Novalis und die Mathematik," in *Romantikforschung*, vol. 16, *Deutsche Vierteljahresschrift für Literaturwissenschaft und Geistesgeschichte*, ed. P. Kluckhohn and E. Rothacker (Halle/Saale: Max Niemeyer, 1929), pp. 113–184.

8. "The wonderfulness of mathematics. It is a *written instrument*—which is still capable of infinite perfectability—A main proof of the sympathy and identity of nature and the soul." [III,684,#659]

9. Thus Novalis says, for example, also of the young Heinrich von Ofterdingen, that his appearance, his handsome "figure was like the simple word of a stranger which one nearly misses hearing, until long after his departure it slowly opens its deep, simple bud and finally shows a beautiful flower in all the brilliancy of the color of its densely set petals, so that one never again can forget it, and never becomes tired of repeating it, and has in it an inexhaustible and ever-present treasure. One now remembers the stranger more clearly and divines and wonders, until suddenly it becomes clear that he was an inhabitant of the higher world." [I,230,3–11]

This is not simply poetic imagery. In the very reversal of the representational relationship—for usually it is the word that is thought to be like the object it represents, rather than that the object is thought to resemble its name—Novalis points to the essential likeness of sign and object and, therefore, to the mutuality holding, for him, in all representational relationships, but particularly in those that have "a kinship with things of another world."

10. *VSS*,36,3.4.1. I do not mean to single out Vietta for disagreement; rather, he stands in a tradition of Novalis interpretation with which I disagree and for which I take him to be an eloquent spokesman.

11. Thus, in the *Blüthenstaub* collection, for instance, Novalis says: "In the beginning poet and priest were one, only later times separated them. But the true poet always remained a priest, just as the true priest always remained a poet. And why should the future not return again the ancient condition?" [II,441,#71] But it is important to realize that for Novalis this relationship is one of a hierarchical difference, in which the prophet stands on a lower rung than the poet. Compare, for instance, the following fragment: "★The magician is a poet. The prophet stands to the magician as the man of taste to the poet." [II,591,#286] The magician and the poet exceed respectively the powers of the prophet and the man of taste, since they not only appreciate and understand (that is, have a passive relationship to the world), but can also actively interfere in the world and shape it in accordance with their own desire. How strongly Novalis felt the truth of this proposition is shown by the fact that he selected this fragment for publication. Yet, this is

not all: in his *Heinrich von Ofterdingen*, which presents the apotheosis of the poet, Novalis planned, ultimately, to show the truly godlike nature of the poet-magician.

12. Compare the following fragment: "The *general terms* of scholastic philoso-phy have much in common with *numbers*—for that reason their mystical usage—their personification—their *musical pleasure*—their infinite combinations. Every-thing *real* created from *nothing,* as e.g. the numbers and the abstract terms—has a wonderful kinship with things of another world—with the infinite series of pecu-liar combinations and relationships—as it were with a mathematical and abstract world in itself—with a *poetical mathematical* and abstract world." [III,440,#898]

13. Søren Kierkegaard, *The Concept of Anxiety* (Princeton, N. J.: Princeton University Press, 1980), pp. 129–30.

14. See pt. I, chap. 2; and p. 257, endnote 14 above.

15. Paul Radin, *The Trickster* (New York: Schocken Books, 1978), p. xxiv. Here-after referred to as *PRT*. The decisive trickster figure for the early European con-sciousness is Hermes, of whom Karl Kerényi in his postscript to Radin's book says that to him belong "Chance and mischance the Hermetic substance; its transfor-mation, through 'finding and thieving,' into Hermetic art (not unmixed with artifice), into riches, love, poetry, and all the ways of escape from the narrow confines of law, custom, circumstance, fate: all these are not *just* psychic realities. They are the world around us, and, at the same time, a world revealed to us by Hermes. The reality of this Hermes world at least proves the existence of a stand-point from which it may be glimpsed; indeed, it testifies to some active force which, seen from that point, is no empty vision, but something that forcibly brings the variegated forms of Hermetic art and artifice into reality. The source from which we gain this experience of the world, once we have reached that standpoint, is—whether we name him or not—Hermes. It must possess the full Hermetic span, ranging from the phallic to the psychopompic." [*PRT*,190]

Wandering freely between the upper realm of the gods and the underworld, and being equally at home in either, as well as in the world of man, Hermes is one of those liminal figures or threshold beings who—like language for Novalis—can break through the apparent boundaries. In claiming that Hermes does not merely represent a psychic reality, but an aspect of the world around us, Kerényi's re-sponse to the trickster parallels Novalis's assertion that the tricksterish element in language, no less than language itself, represents the world. That Kerényi also points to Hermes' "finding and thieving" that from which he fashions his art, riches, love, and poetry makes this mythic figure truly paradigmatic for the poetic enterprise. For poets, too, are finding and thieving that from which they fashion their poetry. Thus, an undue concern with influence (or even plagiarism) is more the critic's concern than the poet's. As Goethe remarked to Eckermann: "One might as well ask a well-nourished man about the oxen, sheep, and pigs he ate and that gave him strength!" (J. P. Eckermann, *Gespräche mit Goethe*, ed. L. Geiger [Leipzig: Max Hesse Verlag] p. 239) But insofar as language represents the world, it, too, makes use of what it finds there and takes from it what suits its needs of expression. And so not only poetry but language itself finds and thieves like the trickster.

There are trickster figures other than Hermes who are similarly meant to be a mirror of the world for us: for instance the folk hero Till Eulenspiegel; and the Hans-Wurst figure of the *Kasperle Theater*; and Punch and Judy all are images of the trickster that are meant to represent aspects not only of our experience of the world, but of the world itself; and so does Reineke Fuchs, of the folk fable that served as inspiration for Goethe's dramatic poem, and elements of which go back to Aesop's fables. Here the trickster's animal shape, like that of many other animals in myths and wonder tales, "is only the phenomenal form, with the real form—glimpsed by the eye of the myth-maker—shining through." [*PRT*,187–88]

C. G. Jung, in his essay for the Radin book, turns away from the mythical image and toward man himself to give an example of tricksterism, finding "something of the trickster in the character of the shaman and medicine man." [*PRT*,196] Here in the early magician-priests the tricksterish element is most obviously tied to language: in the riddlelike conjuring formulas and spells; in the contrariness of healing songs; and, most importantly, in the tales of the trickster told and exemplified by the shaman himself.

16. See quotation II, 23, 3–15 above in this chapter.

17. As I noted before, it is this quality of language that leads Novalis to see in the transformational processes of alchemy a parallel to the transformational character of language.

18. Compare fragment II, 589, #267 quoted in pt. I, chap. 1 above.

19. Compare the *Monolog* quoted above in this chapter.

20. Hugo Friedrich, for instance, belongs to this tradition; as we have seen, he was, in fact, one of those who first established it.

21. Martin Heidegger, "The Way to Language," in *On the Way to Language* (New York: Harper and Row, 1971), p. 134.

In denying Novalis's claim about the monological nature of language by a gesture of dismissal toward absolute idealism, Heidegger is making things a bit too easy for himself. For Novalis has not made Fichte's thoughts the limits of his own. As will become apparent in the second part of this essay, Novalis's concept of nature, for instance, is presupposed and is not first to be realized by the imagination. Yet his understanding of the ideas of nature and earth is pivotal for his philosophy of language and makes any interpretation of him as "within the horizon of absolute idealism," on the one hand, far too beholden to the tradition of Novalis interpretation as it existed earlier in the century and, on the other hand, a hurdle to thinking through Novalis's project.

22. *Ibid.*, pp. 134–35.

23. Why Heidegger misread Novalis and found in Hölderlin a stronger echo for his own thinking about language is, I think, a question of some interest. It cannot be answered simply by asserting that Heidegger plainly liked Hölderlin better, preferred him as a poet, and more highly esteemed his poetry, although all of this is, in fact, quite true. But in addition, I think, there is considerable kinship of thought between Heidegger and Novalis (and not only on the subject of language and poetry), while at the same time their style and approach differ greatly. As a result it seems likely that Heidegger felt Novalis to be something of an interference for the development of his own thought and, therefore, rather decidedly, even if not necessarily consciously, turned away from him, and misread him decisively in the essay in which he does consider his thinking.

CHAPTER FIVE

1. [II,22,#9] See also chap. 4, pp. 61–62.

2. Johann Gottfried Herder, *Abhandlung vom Ursprung der Sprache.* [*HSW*,V,1–154]. We know Novalis had a copy of this treatise since it appears on a list that Richard Samuel believed represented the inventory of the very young Friedrich von Hardenberg's library. [IV,687ff.] Most likely Novalis owned the first edition of this text (Berlin: Voss, 1772). [IV,1049,#61] When in October 1790, he moved to Jena for his first semester at the university, he seems not to have taken the essay with him, since on the inventory listing the book was not marked for shipment to Jena. [IV,1033–34] The fact that it was left behind and that its influence can be felt in *Von der Begeisterung* allows us to assume that Novalis read the treatise before the summer of 1790.

It is possible that Novalis met Herder in Jena as early as during the academic year 1790–91 [I,7], but he certainly visited him with Tieck in November 1799. Rudolf Köpke, writing in 1855 about Tieck's friendship with Novalis, says that "Tieck unhappily followed Novalis's invitation to accompany him on a visit to Herder." [IV,633,20–23]

3. For a discussion of the influence of Condillac on Herder see Hans Aarsleff, *From Locke to Saussure* (Minneapolis, Minn.: University of Minnesota Press, 1982), pp. 194–99.

4. "Von der Sprachfähigkeit und vom Ursprunge der Sprache," in Johann Gottlieb Fichte, *Sämtliche Werke*, 11 vols., ed. J. H. Fichte (Berlin: Verlag von Veit, 1846), VIII: 301–41. Hereafter referred to as *FSW*.

Hans-Joachim Mähl, in his introduction to Novalis's "Fichte Studien," says we can deduce that "Novalis had a more particular knowledge" of the following works by Fichte: *Über den Begriff der Wissenschaftslehre oder der sogenannten Philosophie* (1794); *Grundlage der gesammten Wissenschaftslehre* (parts 1 and 2, 1794; part 3, 1795); *Einige Vorlesungen über die Bestimmung des Gelehrten* (1794); *Grundriss des Eigenthühmlichen der Wissenschaftslehre, in Rücksicht auf das theoretische Vermögen* (1795); and *Von der Sprachfähigkeit und vom Ursprunge der Sprache* (*Phil. Journal*, 1, 1795). Finally, Mähl finds evidence in Novalis's later manuscripts that he also knew Fichte's *Grundlage des Naturrechts nach Prinzipien der Wissenschaftslehre* (part 1, 1796). [II,31]

5. For a short review of Fichte's and Herder's main essays on language with respect to Novalis, see Appendices A and B, respectively.

6. See Appendix A.

7. Herder does not distinguish between speech and language. See Appendix B.

8. *Von der Begeisterung.* [II,22–23] See also pt. I, chap. 4, pp. 61–62 above.

9. Martin Buber, *I and Thou* (New York: Charles Scribner's Sons, 1970), p. 57.

CHAPTER SIX

1. See Appendix B.

2. This fragment seems to reflect not only Novalis's interest in the language of nature, but also his reading of Leibniz.

3. Novalis undertook several walking tours with the purpose of surveying and categorizing the stone formations and mineral deposits of the region. His reports, in the form of two long letters to his former teacher at the mining academy at Freiberg, Professor Abraham Gottlob Werner, can be found in volume III, pp. 775–90 and 794–98.

These tours were undertaken on behalf of the Saxon government as part of a project to investigate the coal deposits of the region. Werner had expanded this project to a full cartographic recording of the geological characteristics of Saxony. Novalis was accompanied on these journeys by Friedrich Traugott Michael Haupt, a student of Werner's at the academy, who completed the report of their findings only after Novalis's death. This report is still on file today in the archives of the bureau of mines of Saxony and was confirmed in its results by later research. [III,700–02] For further details on Novalis's activities as a mining official see Gerhard Schulz's introduction to Section XIII. [III,697–712] Other reports, notes, plans, and correspondence of Novalis's career as a mining administrator can also be found in Section XIII. [III,713–808]

4. Goethe to J. H. Merck, October 11, 1780 (*Werke*, XVIII, 538).

5. Novalis knew Lessing's essay *Laocoön* and obviously takes a position in opposition to it. Lessing advises the sculptor, in contrast to the poet, to seek the quieter moments of all emotions since, when represented in pictorial form, intense emotional expressions are ugly and require a distortion of the human face into a grimace and into a caricature. According to Lessing, beauty, art's most important quality, is thus lost and art becomes ineffective as artistic expression.

6. Quoted by Charles W. Lemmi, in *The Classic Deities in Bacon* (Baltimore: The Johns Hopkins Press, 1933), p. 98. Novalis refers to Bacon several times in his fragments, and his name appears on one of Novalis's book lists. [IV,690]

7. F. W. J. v. Schelling, *Sämmtliche Werke* (Stuttgart: Cotta'scher Verlag, 1857), II: 56.

8. J. W. v. Goethe, *Faust*, Part One, Philip Wayne, trans. (Harmondsworth: Penguin Books, 1951), p. 48 ll. 510–517.

9. J. W. v. Goethe, "Essay on Granite," in *Werke*, vol. II (Weimar, 1784), pt. 9, p. 174.

10. "The predicate 'philosophical'—expresses *everywhere self-purposiveness*—and, in fact, an *indirect* one. Direct self-purposiveness is an abomination with which arises a destructive and, thus, *destructible* force to be destroyed—unmitigated selfishness." [III,399,#688,12–16]

11. Kurt Sprengel, *Versuch einer pragmatischen Geschichte der Arzneikunde*, pt. 1–5 (Halle: Gebauer, 1792–1803).

12. Jacob Boehme, *De Signatura Rerum oder von der Geburt und Bezeichnung aller Wesen* (1622) in *Sämtliche Schriften*, 11 vols., ed. Will-Erich Peuckert (Stuttgart: Fromanns Verlag, 1957), VI: 1–244.

13. Despite the fact that Novalis came to know Boehme's works quite a bit later than when he first undertook to write *Die Lehrlinge zu Sais*, a similar attitude toward the role and meaning of nature is evident in them. Boehme's influence on Novalis, therefore, was more in the manner of confirming him in his own views than in setting him on a new road.

14. I will say more about this when I consider Novalis's theory of time and its

relation to his understanding of the importance of wonder-tales and dreams. But let me point out now that insofar as Novalis's philosophical considerations have a strong psychological component, it is interesting to note that the contemporaneous presence of all the parts of time is also a significant part of Freud's understanding of the unconscious.

15. The physicist E. F. F. Chladni (born 1756) discovered the so-called sound-figures (*Klangfiguren*), which appear when plates of glass or pitch are covered with sand and are then made to sound by being stroked with the bow of a fiddle. Novalis owned Chladni's book, *Entdeckungen über die Theorie des Klanges* (Leipzig, 1787). [IV,697,#81]

16. An interesting account of Novalis's philosophy of time and its relation to Kant and Fichte is given by Manfred Frank, *Das Problem der Zeit in der Deutschen Romantik* (München: Winkler Verlag, 1972), pp. 130-233.

17. Immanuel Kant, *Critique of Pure Reason* (New York: St. Martin's Press, 1965), p. 77.

18. In the *Allgemeine Brouillon* Novalis says: "*Time* is *inner space*—space is *outer time* (synthesis of these) *time figures* etc. Space and time come into being at once." [III,455,#991,26-27]

19. In one of the fragments from June 1799, Novalis attempts to set up a similar equivalence of acoustic and visual signs or expressions for art. "The arabesques, patterns, ornaments, etc., are actual *visual* music." [III,559,#28]

20. Memnon was thought to be the son of Eos, the dawn, and Tithonus, King of Ethiopia. In Egyptian Thebes he was identified with one of the two colossal statues of Amenophis III. After the statue was partially broken by an earthquake about 26 B.C., it started to "sing" at sunrise—an appropriate time for the son of the dawn to raise his voice. In Roman times the statue became a great attraction for travelers. But when Septimus Severus, the Roman emperor, had it repaired toward the end of the second century A.D.. the statue fell silent. Presumably the passages through which the warm air escaped and produced the famous sounds were then blocked off.

21. In *Alexis ou de l'âge d'or*, Hemsterhuis says that "The spirit of poetry is the morning light that makes the statue of Memnon sound." [158] Novalis excerpted this line in his *Hemsterhuis Studien*. [II,373,#33]

22. For a thorough discussion of Novalis's theory of representation see Theodor Haering, *Novalis als Philosoph*, chap. 6, pp. 162-94. Haering stresses the mutuality that according to Novalis holds in all representational relations.

23. See the entire fragment pp. 94-95, above in this chapter.

24. Although künstlich would now be translated best as artificial, in Novalis's texts it still is used to mean "artful" or "artistic."

25. Novalis was also intrigued by this campaign and jotted down the following note: "An epic poem—The French expedition to *Egypt*. An attempt." [III, 588,#225]

26. In 1748, an accidental but lucky find led to more systematic searches of both Pompeii and Herculaneum. Particularly successful were the excavations of 1763 and 1775. About the former Johann Joachim Winkelmann wrote the *Sendschreiben von den herculanischen Entdeckungen* (Dresden, 1762); *Nachricht von den neuesten herculanischen Entdeckungen* (Dresden, 1764); and his *Briefe an Bianconi*,

which were meant for the prince elector of Saxony and his wife, and which were published after Winklemann's death in 1768 in the *Antologia Romana* (1779).

27. It is interesting that Freud also speaks in archeological metaphors of the psyche and the psychoanalytic enterprise. He claims, for instance, that in "mental life nothing which has once been formed can perish . . . that in suitable circumstances . . . it can once more be brought to light." He then goes on to compare this "bringing once more to light" with the excavation of ancient Rome. Freud's explanation for using this analogy is that "If we want to represent historical sequences in spatial terms we can only do it by juxtaposition in space: the same space cannot have two different contents." But Freud then disclaims his own attempt to represent "the characteristics of mental life" in "pictorial terms," saying that they "seem to be an idle game." (Sigmund Freud, *Civilization and Its Discontents* [New York: W. W. Norton, 1962], pp. 16–18.) Novalis might have agreed with Freud that such attempts indeed were games. But never would he have called them *idle*. For, as we have seen, to Novalis, no game is ever merely idle. But not only that, Freud's focus on the word as the proper tool for representing the mental life leads him even when he addresses what is decidedly an imagistic aspect of our mind—namely dreams—to an approach that primarily uses words. Translating the images into discursive verbal accounts, he frequently proceeds to analyze the account as if it were a story rather than a verbal description of an image. Novalis's tendency, on the contrary, is to seek verbal configurations that *are* images. And the significance of dreams is, for him, that they are man's most purely pictorial mental product and, therefore, non-discursive representation in which the restrictions of succession are all but eliminated.

28. See: Kluge, *Etymologisches Wörterbuch der Deutschen Sprache* (Berlin: Walter de Gruyter, 1967). Also Eric Partridge, *Origins, A Short Etymological Dictionary of Modern English*, (New York: Macmillan Publ. Co., 1979).

29. Gravestones in their origin were primarily meant to weigh down the dead sufficiently to prevent them from rising again. To be able to lift the gravestone was considered a sign of extraordinary spiritual power—either good or evil—on the part of the dead soul. The traditional icon of the raised stone associated with the depiction of the resurrection of Christ is therefore a symbol for his divine powers. The gravestone, thus, served only secondarily as a commemorative monument.

30. See chap. 7 below for a comparison with Heidegger's use of the idea of earth.

31. I am very well aware of the shortcomings of this translation. But I have decided to use it as a compromise solution that, on the one hand, gives a feeling for its ditty-like simple rhythms, and, on the other hand, preserves its meaning faithfully.

As the editors of Novalis's collected works point out, this poem was published in thirty-two different collections of songs for miners. Novalis is thought to have modeled it after a "song of descent" that appeared in the miner's calendar of 1790. [I,630,n.248]

32. The idea of sexual union was of primarily philosophical, religious, and psychological significance also in the alchemical tradition.

33. Since in the alchemical tradition gold, the symbol of purity, is often called "the king," Novalis seems to play here with a double possibility of meaning.

34. Goethe, *Faust*, Part One, ll. 382–85. Not unlike Novalis, Goethe here, too, seems to set seeing in opposition to spoken language, with words being able to give merely mediated knowledge while the "vision clear," the image, allows an immediate understanding.

35. For an account of these beliefs and traditions, see Mircea Eliade, *The Forge and the Crucible* (New York: Harper and Row, 1971).

36. Examples of how this nexus of ideas pertaining to the miner and his relation to the earth works itself out in the literary tradition after Novalis are: Hugo von Hofmannsthal, *Das Bergwerk zu Falun*; E. T. A. Hoffmann, *Die Bergwerke zu Falun*; Richard Wagner, *Tannhäuser*.

37. After speaking of the intoxication of the Dionysian mood, Nietzsche, for instance, says: "Under the charm of the Dionysian, not only is the union between man and man affirmed, but nature which has become alienated, hostile, or subjugated celebrates once more her reconciliation with her lost son, man. Freely earth proffers her gifts and peacefully the beasts of prey of the rocks and desert approach. . . . For the rapture of the Dionysian state with its annihilation of the ordinary bounds and limits of existence contains, while it lasts, a *lethargic* element." Friedrich Nietzsche, *The Birth of Tragedy*, trans. W. Kaufmann (New York: Random House, 1967), pp. 37 and 59, respectively.

38. Only in the *Hymnen an die Nacht*, which are hymns of death, does light have a predominantly negative value for Novalis. The hymns' earliest passages were written shortly after Sophie died and Novalis had the mystical experience of her grave's translucency. (See chap. 7 and endnote 2 below.) Before this experience and again not long after Novalis met Julie von Charpentier, light usually has the traditional positive meaning. (For a detailed interpretation of this development see Heinz Ritter, *Novalis' Hymnen an die Nacht* [Heidelberg: Carl Winter, 1974].) In his last work, *Heinrich von Ofterdingen*, Novalis has a decidedly positive orientation toward light without giving to darkness, its polar opposite, a purely negative value.

39. Nothing of the traditional association of evil with the earth exists for Novalis. The earth is not the home of the devil; rather it is a symbolic image of man and of man's way to God.

40. For further information on the genesis of *Die Lehrlinge zu Sais* see the editors' introduction to it in the *Schriften*. [I,71–78]

41. See p. 274, and endnote 15 above.

42. According to Paracelsus, alcahest, or rather alkahest, is the name used by the later alchemists for the liquifier of all matter, for the universal solvent. According to Helmont, it is sometimes an acid liquid, sometimes a salt or the essential nature of all salts. It is said to transform all mineral, vegetative, and animalic substances into a liquid as clear as water, "as hot water dissolves snow." (*Brockhaus' Konversationslexikon* [Berlin: F. A. Brockhaus, 1898].) Or as Ashmole puts it in his *Theatrum Chemicum Britannicum* (pp. 135–36), "The aim of this [solution] is to reduce the hard and dry compactyon to become 'intenuate'— thin liquid. 'Every metall was ons [once] water mynerall, / Therefore wyth Water they turne to Water all." (Cited by Wayne Shumaker, *The Occult Sciences in the Renaissance* [Berkeley: University of California Press, 1979] p. 171.)

At first glance we may be surprised at Novalis's negative use of the liquid condition the alkahest produces. For liquidity is a decidedly positive quality for him when he is speaking about poetry and poets. But what is a positive symbol with respect to poets and their privileged relation to the flux of time becomes a negative ascription when applied to the philosopher of nature, whose concern is space and the solid bodies it contains.

43. Friedrich Murhard, *System der Elemente der Allgemeinen Grössenlehre* (Lemgo, 1798). See III, 115–124.

44. Novalis's view here obviously foreshadows Hegel's. For a detailed discussion of the many similarities that hold between Novalis and Hegel see Haering's *Novalis als Philosoph*.

45. The ice-skating image is not Novalis's, but mine. For in English the term "figure-skating" easily leads to a clearer understanding of what Novalis has in mind. In German that is not so, because figure-skating in German is called artistic skating (*Kunsteislauf*)—nevertheless, I think, this explanation serves Novalis's meaning well.

46. Already earlier, on May 26, Novalis had written: "I have also noticed that it is apparently my fate—that I shall not achieve anything here—I shall be separated from everything in my prime—only at the end shall I come to know the best in the familiar—so also myself. I only now have come to know and appreciate myself—just because of this I am to leave." [IV,41,10–15]

And again on Easter Sunday, April 16, 1797, consoling his brother Karl about the death of their brother Erasmus, Novalis remarks: "Be confident Erasmus has overcome; the blossoms of the dear wreath drop off singly here, there to join more beautifully and more eternally." [IV,223,6–8]

Similarly in *Heinrich von Ofterdingen*, the completion of love for Mathilde and Heinrich takes place only after her death—as Novalis felt his love for Sophie would find its fulfillment only after he, too, had died.

47. In 1791, Georg Forster published his translation of the Indian drama *Sakontala*, which he brought back from England in Jones's translation. He attached to it a sort of dictionary of important Indian concepts. In the entry for Sanskrit he writes: "Even if the origin of the original Sanskrit remained as dark as it is now, we still could not help admiring the organization of this language which, according to a learned linguist, is more perfect than Greek and richer in words than Latin. (Sir William Jones in *As. Research*, p. 422) In addition, it reached a much higher philosophical polish and refinement than either. Nevertheless it has with both a not merely accidental agreement in the roots of its verbs and its grammatical forms. No philologist can examine these without coming to the conclusion that all three derive from one common (probably no longer existing) source. . . . Now, Sanskrit can be found only in books in which it has achieved this high grammatic formation that deserves the name *Sanskrit*, the *perfect* (*Sam*, or as prefix *San*, complete; and *skrita*, finished made, done). The script in which this language and all Indian dialects are written is called *Nágari* (of *Nagar* or *Nagara*, a town) and sometimes it is prefixed by the word *Deva*, because the Godhead itself taught it and is said to have prescribed its artful order." (Georg Forster, *Werke*, ed. Gerhard Steiner [Berlin: Akademie Verlag, 1963], VII: 419–20.) Novalis on several occasions refers to *Sakontala* and, therefore, was obviously familiar with Forster's translation.

48. In the *Allgemeine Brouillon*, for instance, Novalis says: "The ordinary doctrine of nature is necessary *phenomenology—grammar*—science of symbols. / We see nature, as well as perhaps the world of spirits, perspectivally. In general the

understanding imagination has the task of *signifying*—of signaling—of phe-
nomenologizing—the signs of language do not specifically differ from other phenomena." [III,450,#943] Here also Novalis's kinship to Hegel, particularly to the
Phenomenology of Mind, is once more evident.

49. William Faulkner, *As I Lay Dying* (New York: Random House, 1964),
pp. 163–64.

50. Ibid., p. 166. One cannot help marveling at the magnificent display of the
power of language with which that power is here denied.

51. Hugo von Hofmannsthal, "The Letter of Lord Chandos," in *Gesammelte
Werke, Prosa*, ed. Herbert Steiner (Frankfurt a. M.: S. Fischer, 1929), II: p. 8.

52. Ibid., p. 10–11.

53. Goethe, *Faust*, Part One, trans. Philip Wayne (Harmondsworth: Penguin
Books, 1951), p. 95, ll. 1936–41. The lines are part of the so-called *Urfaust* (original
Faust) and therefore were written between 1773 and 1775.

54. The editors of the *Schriften* point out that Novalis here is referring primarily to Johann Wilhelm Ritter's experiments with galvanism on frog legs.
[I,595]

55. Benedict de Spinoza, *Ethics* (New York: Hafner, 1949), p. 269, pt. V, prop.
XXV. For comments by Novalis on Spinoza see II, 159–60, #159; III, 382, #633; III,
443, #914; III, 451, #958; and III, 465, #1067.

CHAPTER SEVEN

1. Lionel Trilling remarks in his essay "Freud and Literature" how much the
theme of the opposition between the hidden and the visible became a common
characteristic of both Freud and Romanticism, and that the "idea of the hidden
thing went forward to become one of the dominant notions of the age. The hidden
element takes many forms and it is not necessarily 'dark' and 'bad'; for Blake the
'bad' was the good, while for Wordsworth and Burke what was hidden and
unconscious was wisdom and power, which work in despite [sic] of the conscious
intellect." Lionel Trilling, "Freud and Literature," in *20th Century Criticism*, ed.
David Lodge, (London: Longman Group Lit., 1972.) We might add that for
Novalis the hidden was sometimes light and sometimes dark but always good;
and the good was both wisdom and power, but only when power was the power
of wisdom and of love in their transcendent nature—as we shall see.

2. Even when nature is not thought to hide her truth behind a veil, the
imagery in which her secretiveness is described still depends on articles of
clothing. Explaining why the philosophers—and in the Middle Ages that always
also included the alchemists—speak of nature's secrets in such fantastic language, Macrobius writes: "But in treating of the other gods and Soul, as I have
said, philosophers make use of fabulous narratives; not without a purpose however, nor merely to entertain, but because they realize that a frank, open exposi-
tion of herself is distasteful to Nature, who, just as she has withheld an understanding of herself from the uncouth senses of men by enveloping herself in
variegated garments, has also desired to have her secrets handled by more pru-
dent individuals through fabulous narratives." (Quoted by George D. Economou,

The Goddess Natura in Medieval Literature [Cambridge: Harvard University Press, 1972], p. 20.)

3. Athanasius Kircher, *Oedipus aegyptus* (Rome: Vitalis Mascardi, 1652), I: 189, as cited by Wayne Shumaker, *The Occult Sciences in the Renaissance* (Berkeley: University of California Press, 1979), p. 247.

4. Apuleius, *The Golden Ass*, trans. Robert Graves (New York: Farrar, Straus and Giroux, 1969), pp. 262–65. Novalis owned Apuleius's *Golden Ass*. See book list 1a of September 1797, item 3. [IV,692]

5. Cited by Charles W. Lemmi, *The Classic Deities in Bacon* (Baltimore: The Johns Hopkins Press, 1933), pp. 91–92.

6. In this, again, Novalis seems to prefigure Heidegger. For a comparison of Novalis's and Heidegger's use of the idea of earth see pp. 139–148.

7. Novalis not only revered Schiller deeply, but also studied with him in Jena and on his advice agreed to follow his parents' wishes to study jurisprudence rather than philosophy and poetry. (See Novalis's letters to Schiller, as well as his letter to Karl Leonhard Reinhold, in which Novalis speaks at length about Schiller. [IV,8.9–102]) Because Novalis also read the *Horen* and *Thalia* journals, I consider it very unlikely that he did not know Schiller's thoughts on this subject.

8. "Das verschleierte Bild zu Sais," in *Die Horen*, 1795, 9. Stück.

9. "Die Sendung Moses," in *Thalia*, 1791, 10. Stück.

10. I am not claiming scholarly accuracy for Schiller's account, but am quoting it at length solely because it is a very likely source for Novalis's understanding of the subject and because I consider it to be a representative sample of the view generally held at the time.

11. Friedrich von Schiller, *Sämtliche Werke*, 13 vols., ed. Julius Zeitler (Leipzig: Der Tempel Verlag), IX:288–94.

12. *Glauben und Liebe oder Der König und die Königin.* [II,485–503]

13. Compare Macrobius' comments given in endnote 2 of this chapter.

14. Considering that this aphorism is given as the second motto prefacing *Glauben und Liebe (Faith and Love)*, which was received by the Prussian court as if it were written in a foreign language, one must conclude that Novalis's thought-experiment was conducted and resoundingly proved his point. The essay *Glauben und Liebe* was first published in the *Jahrbücher der Preussischen Monarchie* under the reign of Friedrich III (ed. F. E. Rambach [Berlin: Unger, 1798], II, June issue, pp. 184 ff.) As the editors of the *Schriften* remark, the "Prussian king read and did not understand *Glauben und Liebe*. He passed the essay on to his Adjutant General Köckeritz, who also did not understand it and who gave it to *Konsistorialrat* Niemeyer who did not understand it any better, but was 'most indignant' about it and conjectured that one of the brothers Schlegel had to be the author. . . . Finally, *Kabinetsminister* Count Schulenburg is dispatched to Unger in order to ascertain the true name of the author (to what purpose is not entirely clear), but Unger does not divulge it and maintains that the author lives in Russia! Nevertheless the hunt for the true identity of the author is partially successful: it is rumored to be one of the nephews of the Minister von Hardenberg." In any case, censorship intervenes and the publication of the *Political Fragments*, which were meant to be the second part of *Glauben und Liebe*, does not take place.

15. That Novalis chooses the central place of the unity of things to be sym-

bolized by a pebble or small stone surely is meant to evoke associations to the most mysterious stone of all, the philosopher's stone.

16. Ovid, *Metamorphoses*, 2 vols., trans. F. J. Miller (Cambridge: Harvard University Press, 1977), I: 325–29.

17. Schiller, *Das verschleierte Bild zu Sais* ("The Veiled Image at Sais"), in *Sämtliche Werke* (Leipzig, Temple Verlag), I: 335–36.

18. See pt. II, chap. 6 p. 101 above.

An illustration of the kinship of this notion of an inner world of either man or earth with the thinking of the alchemists can be found in Michael Maier's second emblem of *Atalanta Fugiens*, which depicts an Isis-like figure for whom, on the one hand, the world is her body and, on the other hand, is also inside that body.

19. *Fragmente und Studien*, 1799–1800.

20. Novalis's desire to lift the veil and see the "naked" truth must be distinguished, however, from the project of the Enlightenment, in which "signs" are understood as value free and neutral expressions that unlike signatures—or similes, metaphors, and allegories, all of which are products of the imagination—are a product of reason and, therefore, better equipped to express the *plain* truth, the *unadorned* truth, the *naked* truth. Such truth is to be logically provable and is supposedly arrived at by reasoning that is entirely devoid of analogical thinking. But it is this attitude toward language that ultimately finds signs—that is, words in general even when not used in an imagistic manner—inadequate as means for both thought and expression. Here all language is understood as an unreliable tool for the truth. Knowledge of objective reality is seen to be beyond the reach of language, which deceptively hides the naked truth of things behind a veil of words. Both Locke and Berkeley, for instance, speak therefore of the mist or of the veil of words, while Bacon not only wants to put nature on the rack to torture the truth from her, but also wants that truth to be naked.

21. Heinz Ritter, *Novalis's Hymnen an die Nacht* (Heidelberg: Carl Winter, 1974), p. 211.

22. Eventhough the fourth of the *Spiritual Songs* speaks of only *one* joyful hour: "Among thousands of good hours / That I found throughout my life, / Only one kept faith with me; / One in which through myriad pains / In my heart I comprehended / Who it was that died for us. / / Broken was my world for me, / As if eaten by a worm / Did my heart and blossom wilt; / Everything I had in life, / Ev'ry wish lay in that grave, / I, to my torment remained, / / As in silence I was ailing, / ever cried and longed away / And remained for fear and madness: / Suddenly, as from above / was the tombstone raised for me / And my inmost heart was opened, / / Who I saw and who beheld Him / leading by the hand, ask not, / Ever shall I see just this; / Of the hours of my life / only this one, like my wounds / shall remain joyfully open." [I,164] But here the emphasized "one" does not appear to have a numerical meaning, rather it seems to speak of the quality of eternal openness in time by the metaphor of the oneness of the hour.

23. "Xstus and Sophie" is the heading for his entry of June 30, 1797. [IV,48,31]

24. A similar thought is expressed by Hölderlin: "What is God? unknown, yet full of his qualities is the face of the sky. For the lightnings are the wrath of God. The more something is invisible, the more it yields to what's alien." To this Heidegger remarks: "Into this, which is intimate to man but alien to the God, the

unknown imparts himself, in order to remain guarded within it as the unknown . . . the genuine image which as a sight or spectacle lets the invisible be seen and so imagines the invisible in something alien to it . . . " [*PLT*,p.225–26]

25. Novalis is rather a careful observer and whatever the power of his imagination might have been and however the strain of the days after Sophie's death might have affected him, it seems unlikely that he misremembered what his mother's first reaction was to the woman he loved.

26. As the editors of the *Schriften* point out, Lavater had published a copper engraving of Raphael's self-portrait in his *Physiognomic Fragments*. As explanation to this portrait, Lavater writes that Raphael is an apostolic artist and in comparison with other painters was what the apostles were in comparison with people in general.

27. In a fragment of the *Allgemeine Brouillon* Novalis writes: "ANTHROPOLOGY. An eternal virgin is nothing else but an *eternal, female child*. What corresponds to the virgin in us men. A girl who no longer is truly a *child*, is no longer virgin. (Not all children are children)." [III,281,#236]

The child for Novalis plays a major symbolic role in his idea of the Golden Age. It is, therefore, also only with the arrival of the child in the midst of the novices of Sais, for instance, that the clumsy student changes and finally finds the central pebble. (For an analysis of the role of the child in the bringing about of the Golden Age see Hans-Joachim Mähl, *Die Idee des goldenen Zeitalters im Werke des Novalis* [Heidelberg: Karl Winter, 1965].) To Novalis Sophie is clearly such a virginal child. Her religious role of mediation for the poet Novalis is, then, that she is the muse of the Golden Age—just as the child Fabel is in *Heinrich von Ofterdingen*.

28. Novalis was well aware of this distinction. Yet his first mention of Julie in a letter to Caroline Just on February 5, 1798 is rather ambivalent: "The more frequently I have been there [at the Charpentiers]—the more the two girls gained my esteem. They roughly mean to me what you and Carolinchen Kühn do. The oldest is intelligent, handy in all things, and an entirely individual, very lively character—genuine ionic blood, if you will pardon this Platnerian expression—which says as much as sanguine and is, I believe, prettier—she is open to everything and knows very well to flatter my weakness of thinking out loud. Julchen is a lingering poison—before one is aware of it one finds her everywhere in oneself and it is the more dangerous the more pleasant it appears to us. As a young adventurer I would try such a poisoning once—But dulled as I am it excites my old nerves only to slight, happy vibrations and warms my frozen blood for hours. One encounters her with fine hardly noticeable feelings and is certain that whatever is most beautiful is first observed by her, done by her, and preserved by her." [IV,249,28–250,7] Not quite a year later though, on January 20, 1799, Novalis writes in an already very different tone to Friedrich Schlegel: "I have much to tell you—the earth seems to want to hold me for quite some time yet. The relationship of which I spoke to you has become deeper and more binding. I find myself loved in a manner I have not been loved before. The fate of a *very lovable* girl depends on my decision—and my friends, my parents, my brothers and sisters need me now more than ever. A very interesting life seems to await me—nevertheless, in truth, I would rather be dead." [IV,273,4–12] The avowal rather to be dead, strikes me as disingenuous and as far more

telling an expression of Novalis's relation to Schlegel than of his feelings for either Julie or his life. Thus, a letter written only a few months later, on July 9, 1799, to his sister Sidonie has none of the darker tones: "I arrived here quite well on Sunday—but unfortunately did not find Julie home, she had gone to Dresden, I was very angry and very sad and immediately sent a messenger to Dresden to speed up her return. Yesterday evening the magnificent, good girl arrived and since then I do not know whether I am still on earth or in heaven. . . . So long—my dears—there is nothing new—except that I infinitely love Julie— and she me—" [IV,291,8–23]

29. Søren Kierkegaard, *Fear and Trembling*, trans. Howard V. and Edna Hong (Princeton, N. J.: Princeton University Press, 1983), pp. 41–44.

30. In "Poetically Man Dwells," Heidegger writes: "Man exists as a mortal. He is called mortal, because he can die. To be able to die means: to be capable of death as death. Only man dies—and indeed continually, so long as he stays on this earth, so long as he dwells." [PLT,p.22]

31. William Faulkner, *As I Lay Dying* (New York: Random House, 1964) p. 161.

32. Martin Heidegger, *The Origin of the Work of Art*, in *Poetry, Language, Thought* (New York: Harper and Row, 1975), pp. 15–87. Hereafter referred to as *PLT*.

33. Martin Heidegger, *Being and Time* (New York: Harper and Row, 1962), pp. 242–43.

34. Here, once again, Novalis's position calls Hegel's philosophy to mind. The kinship between their views is often startling, and although, as I said before, I do not entirely agree with Haering's interpretation of Novalis, I certainly see why the impetus to such an interpretation arises.

35. Friedrich Nietzsche, *The Birth of Tragedy*, trans. Walter Kaufmann, (New York: Random House, 1967), p. 95. Kaufmann's choice of "science" and "scientific community" for *Wissenschaft* and *die Wissenschaftlichen* is an unhappy one. "Scientific" in English has come to mean "pertaining to the natural sciences," and this is *not* what Nietzsche meant. "Scholarly community" comes closer to Nietzsche's intended meaning.

36. Martin Heidegger, "Hölderlins Himmel und Erde," in *Hölderlin Jahrbuch 1958–1960*, p. 22, fn. 3.

37. Martin Heidegger, *Die Selbstbehauptung der deutschen Universität* (Breslau: W. G. Korn, 1933)

38. Martin Heidegger, *Remembrance of the Poet*, in *Existence and Being* (Chicago: Henry Regnery Company, 1949), pp. 248–49.

39. Novalis, *Heinrich von Ofterdingen*, trans. Palmer Hilty (New York: Frederick Ungar, 1978), pp. 79–80. I am using Hilty's translation of this poem only because it does give a feeling for the meter and rhythm. Unfortunately, though, Hilty takes rather too great a liberty with its meaning. A translation of the poem that is faithful to its meaning—though it foregoes rhythm and rhyme—reads as follows: I still remain gladly in the valley / Smiling in the dark of night, / For love's full chalice / Is offered to me daily. // Love's holy droplets lift / My soul upward high, / And in this life I stand / Drunken at heaven's gate. // Cradled in blessed gazing / No pain frightens my soul. / Oh, the queen among women / Gives me her faithful heart. // Anxiously cried-away years / Have transfigured this worthless

clay, / And engraved in it an image / That grants it eternity. // Those great many days / appear a mere moment; / When one day I am carried from here / I will yet look back gratefully. [I,254–255]

40. *Glauben and Liebe* has this issue as its subject matter.

CHAPTER EIGHT

1. Vladimir Propp, "Fairy Tale Transformations" in *Readings in Russian Poetics*, Ladislav Matejka and Krystyna Pomorska, eds. (Ann Arbor, Mich: The University of Michigan, 1978) p.96.

2. Henry and Mary Garland, *The Oxford Companion to German Literature* (Oxford and New York: Oxford University Press, 1986) p. 593.

The preceding account is indebted to several authors and books, foremost among these is Max Lüthi, *Märchen* (Stuttgart: Metzlersche Verlagsbuchhandlung, 1962).

3. Ibid., pp. 13–14.

4. Thus Vladimir Propp, for instance, observes that: "The basic forms are those connected with the genesis of the fairy tale. Obviously the tale is born out of life; however, the fairy tale reflects reality only weakly. Everything that derives from reality is of secondary formation." Vladimir Propp, "Fairy Tale Transformations," in *Readings in Russian Poetics*, p. 96.

5. Even though Italy does not have many real Märchen of its own, the history of the recording of Märchen begins in Italy. The exaltation of the light of reason, which during the Renaissance became the dominant intellectual mood of Europe, exerted a twofold pressure on the storytelling tradition: on the one hand, it undercut the esteem in which the oral tradition of the telling of magical and marvelous tales was held; on the other hand, the newly awakened interest in ancient sources set the stage so that a recording of one's own oral tradition could appear as a worthy and scholarly enterprise. Thus, at the very moment that storytelling became regarded as belonging to the lower classes and, therefore, came to be thought of as a lesser enterprise, story recording became a respectable undertaking. Coupled with the need to find new avenues of expression for the imagination and for the darker non-rational interests of man, the recorded collections of these stories, ironically, served the upper classes as entertainment.

As early as 1550, Francesco Straparola gathered tales told among his people and elsewhere and presented them under the title *Tredeci Piacevoli Notti*. A little later in the century, Giovanni Baptista Basile published the *Pentamerone*, a high point in the art of recorded folktales.

As the spirit of the Renaissance moved north, it not only changed and took on the character of the new regions that fell under its spell, but also ever greater emphasis was put upon the role of reason. And although Pascal opposed Descartes's rational doubt with his "reasons of the heart that reason cannot know," it was Descartes, and not Pascal, who shaped the main tradition of Western philosophy and, thus, of the intellectual climate of the sixteenth and seventeenth century. Needless to say, an intellectual attitude that questioned everything as possible illusion, except the existence of thought itself, and that found its self-evident truths only in those thoughts that were both clear and distinct, cannot be well disposed toward exploring the depth of the non-rational and imaginative. Thus, in France, too, the satisfaction and knowledge derived from sources other than discursive and rational thought moved to humbler quarters. The recording of folk and fairy tales for consumption by the upper classes began here as well. In 1697, a good hundred years after the *Pentamerone* appeared in Italy, Charles Perrault published the *Contes de ma mère l'Oye*, which contained many of the tales we enjoy to this day: *Blue Beard, Little Red Riding Hood, Cinderella,* and *Sleeping Beauty*.

In 1698, the Countess d'Aulnoy published a collection of tales under the title *Contes de Fées*, and impressed her own courtly style and personality on the traditional lore. Refining the rough and robust nature of the true folktale, she presented the old stories newly tailored to the elegant tastes of the court of Louis XIV. With Galland's translation of the Arabian folktales of *1001 Nights* into French in 1704, the folktale added many Oriental images, poetic conventions, and romantic moods to its repertory.

When the "pastoral" or "shepherd's tale," which originated in the games and plays of courtiers, filtered down to the level of the common folk and brought with it the courtly version of rustic simplicity and romance, the gallant love-story was born. Thus, literary influence circled back on itself: the true folktale had contributed through Perrault's collection to the literary tastes and traditions of the upper classes, only to be shaped in turn by these tastes and traditions as they made their way back down from the court and salons to the cafés and the marketplace.

By the middle of the eighteenth century a polemic tendency began to dominate a good deal of literature. A pragmatically oriented rationalism, influenced by empiricist developments coming from England, fought prejudice and superstition with reason. And even in poetry, aesthetic effects yielded to critical and instructive aims, as for instance with Voltaire who, although he often used the form of the fairy tale to make his points, allowed little of the tradition-rich fantasy and symbolic imagery of the true folktale to find its way into his creations. Consequently his stories were mundane, witty, and entirely transparent works of reason, rather than darkly meaningful creations of the unconscious and non-rational forces of the soul, or of man's relation to such forces in his life and in the world.

The polemic against superstition had been so successful that the fairy and folktale, with its fantastic creatures, its ghosts, elves, giants, dwarves, and witches, in other words, in its genuinely folkloristic form, became thought of as being fit fare for children only. And yet in Austria even its use in the nursery was outlawed. For it was thought to do damage to the rational development of the child by filling its head with all sorts of nonsense and fantasies, instead of with facts.

It is to this exaggerated overestimation of reason that the Romantic school of poets and writers opposed the artistic Märchen. Following Voltaire's example, they deliberately created folkloristic tales, but in contrast to Voltaire, they let their imagination, rather than their reason, be the guide and impulse of their stories. Particularly in Germany, the wonder tale, or Märchen, became the proper occupation of the poets: Tieck; Wackenroder; Brentano; von Arnim; and of course Novalis, to name but a few, all wrote Kunstmärchen. In fact, even as classic a writer as Goethe was not above trying his hand at this art form. The Germans finally decided to heed Herder's emphatic pleading for the necessity to throw light on the history and heritage of the German myths and Märchen when the brothers Grimm began their painstaking collecting of Germanic folklore. And just in time, too, for the deluge of literary or artistic tales threatened to drown the genuine folk traditions. But even the brothers Grimm could not deny the influence of their literary education or of the social norms of their day. As a result their folk tales often reflect folk traditions as they appear when filtered through an aesthetic and moral sensibility far more "refined"—and "confined"—than the original peasant tale had been. As Ruth Bottigheimer observes: "One aspect of Grimm's *Fairy Tales* is arguably related to this larger social phenomenon as well as to the history of German literature. Despite the ancient and international lineage of many of the tales, the process of editing, codifying, and translating them produced a distinctly nineteenth-century text, incorporating the gender-related assumptions of Grimms' informants and of Wilhelm Grimm himself." (Ruth B. Bottigheimer, "Silenced Women in the Grimms' Tales: The 'Fit' Between Fairy Tales and Society in Their Historical Context" in *Fairy Tales and Society: Illusion, Allusion and Paradigm*, Ruth B. Bottigheimer, ed., [Philadelphia: University of Pennsylvania Press, 1986]). Compare also Jack Zipe's account of the evolution and change of the social and sociological elements in the story of "Little Red Riding Hood." (Jack Zipes, *The Trials and Tribulations of Little Red Riding Hood: Versions of the Tale in Socio-Cultural Context* [London: Heinemann, 1982]).

6. Consider, for example, the many criticisms Walt Disney's film *Snow White* received from folklorists when it was first shown. Whatever the problems of its slick and commercial presentation may be, it certainly proved to have a profound effect on its audience and to be a popular and rather enduring version—two criteria it shares with proper folktales! Similarly, the recent black movie version of Cinderella caused some eyebrow raising.

7. Distinguishing the genesis of folkloric works from works of literature, Roman Jacobson writes: "The point at which an author puts down his completed piece of writing is the moment of birth of a literary work; this is the type of creativity most often encountered by the student of literature. By analogy, he is inclined to consider the birth of a work in folklore to be the first expression of that work by some person. In fact, however, the work belongs to folklore only from the moment it is adopted by the community . . . Preliminary censorship by the community is a prerequisite for the existence of a folklore work. All those products of individual creativity which are denied socialization by the community do not become facts of folklore: they are condemned to obliteration . . . A literary work is objectivized, it exists concretely apart from the reciter. Each subsequent reader or reciter returns directly to the work . . . for a folklore work the only path leads from implementer to implementer. If bearers of a given folklore tradition die, the resurrection of that tradition is no longer possible; whereas, on the contrary the reactualization of the literary works of a distant past is not uncommon, even when such works may have temporarily lost their vitality." (Roman Jacobson and Petr Bogatyrev, "On the Boundary Between Studies of Folklore and Literature" in *Readings in Russian Poetics*, pp. 91–92.)

8. For an account of the Cinderella tale see: Alan Dundes, ed., *Cinderella: A Casebook* (New York: Wildman Press, 1983). For its possible origin in China see the following contributions: R. O. Jameson, "Cinderella in China" (pp. 71–97) and Ann Brigitta Rooth, "Tradition Areas in Eurasia" (pp. 129–47).

9. Particularly in the French version of Cinderella, the good fairy is a rather late courtly embellishment of the story, for she really resembles the fine ladies at the court a good deal more than she does the liminal creatures who originally were the agencies of fate.

10. My interpretation of the Märchen as an image of the working of chance, as the fated moment of the qualitative aspect of time, does not deny the possibility of psychological interpretations such as, for instance, von Franz's, Jung's, or Bettelheim's. (Marie-Louise von Franz, *Problems of the Feminine in Fairytales* [New York: Spring Publications, 1972], and *An Introduction to the Psychology of Fairytales* [New York: Spring Publications, 1978]; Carl Gustav Jung, *Symbols of Transformation*, vol. 5 of *Collected Works of C. G. Jung*, Bollingen Series XX [Princeton, N. J.: Princeton University Press, 1976]; Bruno Bettelheim, *The Uses of Enchantment: The Meaning and Importance of Fairy Tales* [New York: Vintage Books, 1977].) But it does claim that such interpretations do not deal with the Märchen's most basic or ultimate icon, except insofar as our developmental changes are experienced by us as coming upon us with the same kind of obscure unpredictability that events of chance do, and are, therefore, at first felt to be alien intrusions. In other words, it is my contention that psychological interpretations of the effectiveness of the Märchen depend on and are grounded in the Märchen's metaphysical foundation, in its being an icon of chance—in Novalis's sense of this concept. The Freudian tradition's reduction of the symbolic meaning of Märchen to the psychosexual sphere works insofar as our sexual growth and sexual being are experienced as being part of inexorable and fated occurrences in the world. Thus, for instance, Snow White's reawakening from her poison-death sleep, for Bettelheim, is a symbol of a young girl's awakening to sexuality from the sleep of the latency period, since the agency of her return to life is the kiss of a handsome young prince. Yet ultimately the mystery is that we all awaken to life by means of a kiss—since it is part of the act that stands at the beginning or inception of life. And so it is, indeed, a symbol for the gift of chance! Here a turn, a shift, a sudden change from nothing to being occurs—a leap across the abyss of naught.

Thus, while I do not doubt the psychological acuity of Bettelheim's interpretation, I do think that it stops short of the final meaning of the Märchen. In addition, I think that Jung's more future-bound interpretations, which understand man as a project rather than as a Prometheus bound by the past, are more in line with the Märchen's own orientation and evolution of meaning as well as with its expectation that the tale's truth always shines forth on the occasion of its last telling. Man as a project of chance finds himself adequately mirrored by the project of the Märchen, which is an icon of chance.

Similarly, I do not dispute the value of the many interesting literary, anthropological, and sociological investigations, interpretations, and analyses of Märchen and folktales. In fact, I have enjoyed many of these accounts and greatly profited by them. Particularly the following works come to mind: K. M. Briggs, *The Fairies in Tradition and Literature* (London: Routledge and Kegan Paul, 1977); Ruth B. Bottigheimer, ed., *Fairy Tales and Society: Illusion, Allusion, and Paradigm* (Philadelphia: University of Pennsylvania Press, 1986); Alan Dundes, *Cinderella: A Casebook* (New York: Wildman Press, 1983); Max Lüthi, *Märchen* (Stuttgart:

Metzler, 1974). and *The Fairytale as Artform* (Bloomington: Indiana University Press, 1984), and *Volksmärchen und Volkssage* (Bern, München: A. Francke, 1966); Hedwig von Rocques-von Beit, *Symbolik des Märchens: Versuch einer Deutung* (Bern: A. Francke, 1965–67); Vladimir Propp, *Morphology of the Folktale* (Austin: University of Texas Press, 1983); Jack Zipes, *Fairy Tales and the Art of Subversion* (New York: Wildman Press, 1983), and *Breaking the Magic Spell* (New York: Methuen, 1979), and *The Trials and Tribulations of Little Red Riding Hood: Versions of the Tale in Socio-Cultural Context* (London: Heinemann, 1982).

11. In the *Allgemeine Brouillon*, Novalis says: "I really ought to write a *Märchen*—Laws of *Märchen*." [III,451,#954].

12. Mary McCarthy, "Novel, Tale, Romance," in *The New York Review of Books*, May 12, 1983. pp. 53–54.

13. Anthony Burgess, *The Novel Now* (New York: Pegasus, 1970) pp. 13–14.

14. Gero von Wilpert, *Sachwörterbuch der Literatur* (Stuttgart: Alfred Körner Verlag, 1969) pp. 650–57.

15. Novalis here plays with the sound similarity of the plural of "Satz" (Sätze) and the verb "setzen" (to posit or put). Thus in the acoustic configuration of the statement "unsetzbar" he lets us *hear* the impossibility of putting an idea into one sentence.

16. The proper etymological derivation of *Versöhnung* is from the medieval *suene*, the modern *Sühne* (atonement); the prefix *ver-* belongs to that series of meanings indicating an annihilation of something (namely of the sin, guilt, or quarrel), which the stem *Sühne* (restitution, judgment) alludes to as well. See A. Kluge, *Etymologisches Wörterbuch*.

17. *Heinrich von Ofterdingen*, trans. Palmer Hilty (New York: Fredrick Ungar, 1978) p. 18.

18. *Ibid.*, p. 19.

19. "The Märchen is, so to speak, the *canon of poetry*—everything that is poetical must be like a Märchen. The poet adores chance." [III,449,#940]

20. The entire fragment reads: "❚I believe I can best express the attunement of my soul in Märchen.❚ (POETICS. *Everything* is a *Märchen*." [III,377, 620].

21. See Alexander Kluge, *Etymologisches Wörterbuch*.

Mary McCarthy, discussing Don Quixote's interruption of Sancho Panza's tale, in which keeping track of how many goats have already been ferried across the river is crucial to the tale's continuing narration, remarks: "There in fact the tale ends. Like somebody in a fairy story, Don Quixote, heedless of Sancho's warning, has broken the spell. It is like the legend of Cupid and Psyche. As Sancho remarks philosophically, 'as far as my tale is concerned there's nothing more to add, for it ends where the mistake in the counting of the goats begins.' In short, being a true tale, it is endless and can only be stopped." (Mary McCarthy, "Novel, Tale, Romance," in *The New York Review of Books*, May 12, 1983. p. 50. Mary McCarthy thus sees a thematic—and not just an etymological—kinship between the telling of tales and the telling of money: both are at bottom an adding of always another element. While this view, at first glance, seems to contradict Novalis's emphasis of the qualitative nature of time in fairy tales, I wonder whether it paradoxically is not also a denial of the importance of chronos time and an assertion both of the significance of time's kairotic nature and of the tale's iconic character, since the ultimate outcome of such a process of addition always is *one* sum. It is, for instance, the very monotony of the counting toward a sum of sheep ferried across the river in Sancho's 'account' that prompts Don Quixote, who is used to the chronicling of varied adventures in the more modern and more novel-like style of the romance, to interrupt the tale. Don Quixote is a man caught up in chronos time. Accustomed to the ever-changing flux of events as it occurs in the romance, he is impatient and, therefore, incapable of understanding and appreciating the repetitious and, thus, less changing, more static nature—and, therefore, imagery—of the tally or tale.

22. Gotthold Ephraim Lessing, *Laocoön*, trans. Edward Allen McCormick (Baltimore: Johns Hopkins University Press, 1984), pp. 74–79. *Laocoön* originally was published in 1766. Novalis knew the essay well. His own fragment on the petrification-like nature of the sculptor's work is obviously in response to the passage quoted here. For Novalis's short discussion of Lessing's essay see II, 379, 1–20.

APPENDIX A

1. "The German phrase which I translate as "arbitrary signs" is *willkürliche Zeichen*. But Fichte uses "willkürlich" sometimes to mean "arbitrary" and sometimes to mean "voluntary," and sometimes he seems to have both meanings at once in mind. In the following pages I translate willkürlich mostly as "arbitrary" but add remarks about the voluntary nature of language where this seems appropriate.

2. In contrast, our most loving and obedient household pets never learn to perform this simple feat: a dog or cat, for example, will fix all its eager attention on the pointing finger, but never on the thing pointed at.

3. Monroe C. Beardsley, *Aesthetics* (Indianapolis and Cambridge: Hackett, 1981) p. 116.

4. Awe before the power of the letter was at the time not an unusual attitude, although it is more commonly found in connection with religious views of language. Johann Peter Süssmilch, for instance, wrote in 1766 that it is a mark of the divine order that all known languages can be expressed in twenty letters. *Versuch eines Beweises, dass die erste Sprache ihren Ursprung nicht vom Menschen, sondern vom Schöpfer erhalten habe* [Berlin: Buchladen der Realschule, 1766].) Herder took issue with Süssmilch on this point: "No quick-sounding language may be completely expressed in letters, and certainly not in twenty: to this one and all languages bear witness. The articulations of the tools of language are so manifold, each sound is intoned in so many ways that, for example, Mr. Lambert in the second part of his *Organon* has been able to show with good reason that there are many fewer letters than sounds and that as a result the former express the latter most inadequately. . . . Where do all the peculiarities and oddities of orthography arise from, if not from the awkwardness of writing as one speaks? Which living language may in its tones be learned from the letters in a book, and which dead language may thus be reawakened?" [*HSW*,V,11]

APPENDIX B

1. "If an angel or heavenly spirit had invented language, how could it be otherwise than that its entire structure would have to be impressed with the mode of thought of this spirit. For how could I recognize the image of an angel except by its angel-like, supernatural features? But where in our language can this be found? The structure and plan, indeed, even the cornerstone of this palace betrays (*verräth*) its humanity." [*HSW*,V,51]

2. Genesis, 2:19. [*HSW*,V,51]

3. The German *dichten*—of which the past tense is *gedichtet*—not only has the meaning of "condensing," but also of "making a poem." Here Herder clearly makes use of this double nature of the word to good advantage.

Bibliography

Works preceded by an "*" were included in various of Novalis's booklists and therefore most likely were read by him. Works preceded by an "†" I found especially helpful or interesting.

†Aarsleff, Hans. *From Locke to Saussure*. Minneapolis: University of Minnesota Press, 1982.

Abrams, M. H. *The Mirror and the Lamp: Romantic Theory and the Critical Tradition*. London, Oxford, New York: Oxford University Press, 1979.

Addison, Joseph. *The Spectator*. Ed. Alexander Chalmers. New York: D. Appleton, 1879.

Agricola, Georgius. *Bermannus sive de re metalica*. Basel, 1530.

––––––. *De animantibus subterraneis*. Basel, 1549.

Albrecht, Luitgard. *Der magische Idealismus in Novalis' Märchentheorie und Märchendichtung*. Hamburg: Hansischer Gildenverlag, 1948.

Apuleius. *The Golden Ass*. Trans. Robert Graves. New York: Farrar, Straus and Giroux, 1969.

Aristotle. *Poetics*. In *The Basic Works of Aristotle*. Ed. R. McKeon. New York: Random House, 1941.

Auden, W. H. "Writing." In *20th Century Criticism*. Ed. David Lodge. London: Longman, 1972.

Beardsley, Monroe C. *Aesthetics*. Indianapolis and Cambridge: Hackett, 1981.

Beck, Hans-Joachim. *Friedrich von Hardenberg "Oeconomie des Styls": Die Wilhelm Meister Rezeption im "Heinrich von Ofterdingen"*. Bonn: Bouvier Verlag Herbert Grundmann, 1976.

Benjamin, Walter. *Illuminations*. New York: Schocken, 1976.

Bettelheim, Bruno. *The Uses of Enchantment: The Meaning and Importance of Fairy Tales*. New York: Vintage, 1977.

Birrell, Gordon. *The Boundless Present: Space and Time in the Literary Fairy Tales of Novalis and Tieck*. Chapel Hill: University of North Carolina Press, 1979.

†Blumenberg, Hans. *Arbeit am Mythos*. Frankfurt a.M.: Suhrkamp, 1979.

†————. *Schiffbruch mit Zuschauer: Paradigma einer Daseinsmetapher*. Frankfurt a.M.: Suhrkamp, 1979.

†————. *Die Lesbarkeit der Welt*. Frankfurt a.M.: Suhrkamp, 1981.

Bodomer. *Minnesinger*. 1757.

*Boehme, Jacob. *Theosophische Send-Briefe*. Amsterdam, 1682.

*————. *Clavis oder Schlüssel etlicher vornemen Puncten und Wörter*. Amsterdam, 1682.

*————. *Morgenröte im Aufgang*. Amsterdam, 1682.

————. *De Signatura Rerum oder von der Geburt und Bezeichnung aller Wesen* (1622). In *Sämtliche Schriften*. 11 vols. Ed. Will-Erich Peuckert. Stuttgart: Fromanns Verlag, 1957.

Boethius. *The Consolation of Philosophy*. Trans. Richard Green. Indianapolis: Bobbs-Merrill, 1962.

Bottigheimer, Ruth B., ed. *Fairy Tales and Society: Illusion, Allusion and Paradigm*. Philadelphia: University of Pennsylvania Press, 1986.

————. "Silenced Women in the Grimms' Tales: The 'Fit' Between Fairy Tales and Society in Their Historical Context." In *Fairy Tales and Society: Illusion, Allusion and Paradigm*. Philadelphia: University of Pennsylvania Press, 1986.

Briggs, K. M. *Fairies in Tradition and Literature*. London, Boston, and Henley: Rutledge and Kegan Paul, 1967.

Brockhaus Konversationslexikon. Berlin: F. A. Brockhaus, 1898.

Buber, Martin. *I and Thou*. Trans. Walter Kaufmann. New York: Charles Scribner's Sons, 1970.

Buchan, John. *The Novel and the Fairy Tale*. Oxford: Oxford University Press, 1931.

Burgess, Anthony. *The Novel Now: A Guide to Contemporary Fiction*. New York: Pegasus, 1970.

Carlyle, Thomas. "Novalis." In *Critical and Miscellaneous Essays*, vol. II. London: Chapman and Hally, 1869.

*Chladni, E. F. F. *Entdeckungen über die Theorie des Klanges*. Leipzig, 1787.

Dick, Manfred. *Die Entwicklung des Gedankens der Poësie in den Fragmenten des Novalis*. Bonn: Bouvier, 1967.

Dilthey, Wilhelm. *Das Erlebnis und die Dichtung: Lessing, Goethe, Novalis, Hölderlin*. Leipzig: B. G. Teubner, 1921.

Dundes, Alan, ed. *Cinderella: A Casebook*. New York: Wildmann, 1983.

Eckermann, Johann Peter. *Gespräche mit Goethe*. Ed. L. Geiger. Leipzig: Max Hesse, n.d.

Economou, George D. *The Goddess Natura in Medieval Literature*. Cambridge: Harvard University Press, 1972.

Eliade, Mircea. *The Forge and the Crucible*. New York: Harper and Row, 1971.

Eliot, George. *The Essays of George Eliot*. Ed. Nathan Sheppard. New York: Funk & Wagnalls. 1883.

Emerson, Ralph Waldo. "Nature." In *The Collected Works of Ralph Waldo Emerson*. 2 vols. Ed. R. E. Spiller, A. R. Ferguson, J. Slater, J. F. Carr. Cambridge: The Belknap Press of Harvard University Press, 1971.

Faber, Richard. *Novalis: Die Phantasie an die Macht*. Stuttgart: Metzler, 1970.

Faulkner, William. *As I Lay Dying*. New York: Random House, 1964.

Feilchenfeld, Walter. *Der Einfluss Jacob Böhmes auf Novalis*. Berlin: E. Ebering, 1922.

Fichte, Johann Gottlieb. *Von der Sprachfähigkeit und vom Ursprunge der Sprache*. In *Sämtliche Werke*, vol. VIII. Ed. J. H. Fichte. Berlin: Verlag von Veit. 1846.

Forster, Georg. *Werke*. Ed. Gerhard Steiner. Berlin: Akademie Verlag, 1963.

Frank, Manfred. *Das Problem der Zeit in der deutschen Romantik*. Munich: Winkler, 1972.

Franz, Marie-Louise von. "The Dream of Descartes." In *Timeless Documents of the Soul*. Evanston: Northwestern University Press, 1968.

―――. "Bei der schwarzen Frau." In *Studien zur analytischen Psychologie C. G. Jungs*, vol. II. C. G. Jung Institute ed. Zürich: 1955.

―――. *An Introduction to the Psychology of Fairytales*. Irving, Tex.: Spring Publications, 1978.

―――. *Problems of the Feminine in Fairytales*. New York: Spring Publications, 1972.

Freud, Sigmund. *Civilization and Its Discontents*. New York: W. W. Norton, 1962.

Friedrich, Hugo. *Die Struktur der modernen Lyrik*. Rowohlts Deutsche Enzyklopädie. 6th ed. Ed. Ernesto Grassi. Hamburg: Rowohlt, 1956.

―――. "Die Sprachtheorie der französischen Illuminaten, insbesondere Saint Martins." In *Deutsche Vierteljahresschrift für Literaturwissenschaft und Geistesgeschichte* 13(1935):293–310.

†Gadamer, Hans-Georg. *Wahrheit und Methode*. Tübingen: J. C. B. Mohr (Paul Siebeck), 1975.

Gade, Ernst-Georg. *Eros und Identität: Zur Grundstruktur der Dichtung Friedrich von Hardenbergs (Novalis)*. Marburg: N. G. Elwert, 1974.

Gaier, Ulrich. *Krumme Regel: Novalis' Konstruktionslehre des schaffenden Geistes und ihre Tradition*. Tübingen: M. Niemeyer, 1970.

Garland, Henry and Mary, eds. *The Oxford Companion to German Literature*. Oxford and New York: Oxford University Press. 1968.

Goethe, Johann Wolfgang von. *Faust*. Trans. Philip Wayne. Harmondsworth: Penguin, 1951.

———. *Prometheus*. In *Werke*, Vol. II. Frankfurt a.M.: Insel, 1966.

†Grassi, Ernesto. *Kunst und Mythos*. Hamburg: Rowohlt, n.d.

†———. *Die Macht des Bildes: Ohnmacht der rationalen Sprache; zur Rettung des Rhetorischen*. Cologne: M. DuMont Schauberg, 1970.

†———. *Die Macht der Phantasie: Zur Geschichte abendländischen Denkens*. Königstein/Ts.: Athenäum, 1979.

†———. *Rhetoric as Philosophy: The Humanist Tradition*. University Park and London: The Pennsylvania State University Press, 1980.

Grassi, Ernesto, and Hugo Schmale. *Das Gespräch als Ereignis: Ein semiotisches Problem*. Munich: Wilhelm Fink, 1982.

Grieve, James. "Taking Liberties." In *Times Literary Supplement* 202, no. 4(14 October 1983):1117.

Grimm, Reinhold, ed. *Der deutsche Shakespeare*. With contributions by Walter Muschg, Hans Schmid, and others. Vol. 7. *Theater unserer Zeit*. Basel, Hamburg, Vienna: Basilius, 1965.

Grob, Karl. *Ursprung und Utopie: Aporien des Textes; Versuch zu Herder und Novalis*. Bonn: Bouvier Verlag Herbert Grundmann, 1976.

Grützmacher, Curt. *Novalis und Phillip Otto Runge; Drei Zentralmotive und ihre Bedeutungssphäre: Die Blume, das Kind, das Licht*. Munich: Eidos, 1964.

Gundel, Wilhelm. *Sternglaube, Sternreligion, Sternorakel*. Leipzig: Quelle und Meyer, 1933.

†Haering, Theodor. *Novalis als Philosoph*. Stuttgart: W. Kohlhammer, 1954.

Hamburger, Käte. "Novalis und die Mathematik." In *Romantikforschung*, (D. V. Buchreihe, vol. 16). Halle/Saale: Max Niemeyer, 1929, repeated in Käte Hamburger *Philosophie der Dichter* (Stuggart, Berlin, Cologne: Kohlhammer Verlag, 1966.

———. *Philosophie der Dichter: Novalis, Schiller, Rilke*. Stuttgart, Berlin, Cologne, Mainz: W. Kohlhammer, 1966.

Harris, Roy. "Theoretical Ideas." *Times Literary Supplement* 202. no. 4(14 October 1983):1119.

Harrold, Charles Frederic. *Carlyle and German Thought. Yale Studies in English*, vol. 82. Hamden and London: Archon, 1963.

Haywood, Bruce. *Novalis, the Veil of Imagery: A Study of the Poetic Works of Friedrich von Hardenberg, 1772–1801*. Cambridge: Harvard University Press, 1959.

†Heftrich, Eckhard. *Novalis: Vom Logos der Poesie*. Studien zur Philosophie und Litteratur des neunzehnten Jahrhunderts, vol. 4. "Neunzehntes Jahrhundert" Forschungsunternehmen der Fritz Thyssen Stiftung. Frankfurt a.M.: Vittorio Klostermann, 1969.

Hegener, Johannes. *Die Poetisierung der Wissenschaften bei Novalis dargestellt am Prozess der Entwicklung von Welt und Menschheit: Studien zum Problem enzyklopädischen Welterfahrens*. Bonn: Bouvier, 1975.

Heidegger, Martin. *Being and Time*. New York: Harper and Row, 1962.

———. "The Way to Language." in *On the Way to Language*. New York: Harper and Row, 1971.

———. "Remembrance of the Poet." In *Existence and Being*. Chicago: Henry Regnery, 1949.

———. *Die Selbstbehauptung der deutschen Universität*. Breslau: W. G. Korn, 1933.

———. "Hölderlins Himmel und Erde." In *Hölderlin Jahrbuch*, 1958–1960.

———"The Origin of the Work of Art." In *Poetry, Language, Thought*. New York: Harper and Row, 1975. Pp. 15–87.

†Heilfurth, Gerhard, unter Mitarbeit von Ina-Maria Greverus. *Bergbau und Bergmann in der deutschsprachigen Sagenüberlieferung Mitteleuropas*. Marburg: N. G. Elwert, 1967.

Heine, Heinrich. "Romantische Schule." In *Sämmtliche Werke*, vol. 6. Hamburg: Hoffmann und Campe, 1861.

Heine, Roland. *Transzendentalpoesie: Studien zu Friedrich Schlegel, Novalis und E. T. A. Hoffmann*. Bonn: Bouvier, 1974.

Herder, Johann Gottfried. "Über die neuere deutsche Literatur: Eine Beilage zu den Briefen, die neueste Literatur betreffend. 1766/1767." Erste Sammlung. In *Sämtliche Werke*. 33 vols. Ed. Bernhard Suphan. Berlin: Weidmannsche Buchhandlung, 1877–99.

———. "Über die neuere deutsche Literatur . . . 1766/1767." Zwote Sammlung. In *Sämtliche Werke*. 33 vols. Ed. Bernhard Suphan. Berlin: Weidmannsche Buchhandlung, 1877–99.

———. *Abhandlung vom Ursprung der Sprache*. In *Sprachphilosophische Schriften*. Ed. Erich Heintel. Hamburg: Felix Meiner, 1960.

*———. *Abhandlung über den Ursprung der Sprache*. Berlin: Voss, 1772.

*———. *Zerstreute Blätter: Erste–Sechste Sammlung*. Gotha: Ettinger, 1785–97).

*———. *Auch eine Philosophie der Geschichte zur Bildung der Menschheit: Beytrag zu vielen Beyträgen des Jahrhunderts*. Riga: Hartknoch, 1774.

———. Ideen zur Philosophie der Geschichte der Menschheit. Erster–Vierter Theil. Riga and Leipzig: Hartknoch, 1784–91.

Hermann, Martin Gottfried. *Handbuch der Mythologie aus Homer mit erläuternden Anmerkungen begleitet.* Nebst einer Vorrede des Herrn Hofrath Christian Gottlob Heyne. Erster–Dritter Bd. Berlin and Stettin: Nicolai, 1787–95.

Herttwig, Christoph. *Neues und Vollkommenes Berg-Buch.* Dresden and Leipzig: 1734.

Hiebel, Friedrich. *Novalis; der Dichter der blauen Blume.* Bern: A. F. Francke, 1951.

———. *Novalis: German Poet, European Thinker, Christian Mystic.* (A condensed version of the author's *Novalis: Dichter der blauen Blume*, in English.) Chapel Hill: University of North Carolina Press, 1954.

Hofmannsthal, Hugo. *Gesammelte Werke in Einzelausgabe: Prosa,* vol. II. Ed. Herbert Steiner. Frankfurt a.M.: S. Fischer, 1929.

Holt, Elisabeth Gilmore, ed. *A Documentary History of Art.* 2 vols. Princeton: Princeton University Press, 1981.

Huizinga, Johan. *Homo Ludens.* Boston: Beacon, 1950.

Hume, David. *An Enquiry Concerning Human Understanding.* In *On Human Nature and the Understanding.* Ed. Anthony Flew. New York: Collier, 1962.

Ingarden, Roman. *The Literary Work of Art: An Investigation on the Borderlines of Ontology, Logic, and Theory of Literature.* Evanston: Northwestern University Press, 1973.

*Iselin, Isaak. *Philosophische Mutmassungen über die Geschichte der Menschheit.* Bd. 1–2. Frankfurt and Leipzig: Harscher, 1764.

Jacobson, Roman. *Poetik: Ausgewählte Aufsätze 1921–1971.* Ed. Elmar Holenstein and Tarcisius Schelbert. Frankfurt a.M.: Suhrkamp, 1979.

Jacobson, Roman, and Petr Bogatyrev. "On the Boundary Between Studies of Folklore and Literature." In *Readings in Russian Poetics.* Ladislav Matejka and Krystyna Pomorska, eds. Ann Arbor: The University of Michigan Press, 1978.

Janz, Rolf-Peter. *Autonomie und soziale Funktion der Kunst: Studien zur Ästhetik von Schiller und Novalis.* Stuttgart: J. B. Metzler, 1973.

Jong, H. M. E. de. *Michael Maier's Atalanta Fugiens.* Leiden: E. J. Brill, 1969.

Jordans, Wilhelm. *Der germanische Volksglaube von den toten Dämonen im Berg und Ihre Beschwichtigung: Die Spuren in England.* Bonn: Hanstein, 1933.

Jung, Carl Gustav. *Symbols of Transformation. Collected Works of C. G. Jung,* vol. 5. Bollingen Series XX. Princeton: Princeton University Press, 1976.

Kant, Immanuel. *Critique of Pure Reason.* New York: St. Martin's, 1965.

———. *Critique of Judgement.* New York: Hafner, 1974.

*———. *Zum ewigen Frieden: Ein philosophischer Entwurf.* Königsberg: Nicolovius, 1795.

Kayser, Wolfgang. *Das sprachliche Kunstwerk: Eine Einführung in die Literaturwissenschaft.* Bern and Munich: Francke, 1978.

Kerner, Justinus. "Kleksographien." In *Sämtliche poetische Werke.* 4 vols. Ed. Josef Gaismaier. Leipzig: Hesse und Becker, 1905.

Kierkegaard, Søren. *Either/Or.* 2 vols. Trans. D. F. and L. M. Swenson. Princeton: Princeton University Press, 1971.

———. *The Concept of Anxiety.* Trans. and ed. Reidar Thomte and Albert B. Anderson. Princeton: Princeton University Press, 1980.

———. *Fear and Trembling.* Trans. Howard V. and Edna Hong. Princeton: Princeton University Press, 1983.

Kluge, Alexander. *Etymologisches Wörterbuch der deutschen Sprache.* Berlin: Walter de Gruyter, 1967.

Knappich, Wilhelm. *Geschichte der Astrologie.* Frankfurt a.M.: Vittorio Klostermann, 1967.

Kuhn, Hans Wolfgang. *Der Apokalyptiker and die Politik: Studien zur Staatsphilosophie des Novalis.* Freiburg i.Br.: Rombach, 1961.

†Küpper, Peter. *Die Zeit als Erlebnis des Novalis.* Cologne and Graz: Böhlau, 1959.

Lemmi, Charles W. *The Classic Deities in Bacon.* Baltimore: The Johns Hopkins University Press, 1933.

Leonardo da Vinci. *Codex Urbinas* (Vatican Library, 1270). In *A Documentary History of Art,* vol. I. Ed. Elisabeth Gilmore Holt. Princeton: Princeton University Press, 1981.

Lessing, Gotthold Ephraim. *Laocoön.* Trans. Edward Allen McCormick. Baltimore: The Johns Hopkins University Press, 1984.

Link, Hannelore. *Abstraction und Poesie im Werk des Novalis: Studien zur Poetik und Geschichte der Literatur.* Ed. Hans Fromm, Hugo Kuhn, Walter Müller-Seidel, Friedrich Sengle. Stuttgart, Berlin, Cologne, Mainz: W. Kohlhammer, 1971.

Lukacs, Georg. *The Theory of the Novel: A Historico-Philosophical Essay on the Forms of Great Epic Literature.* Cambridge: The MIT Press, 1978.

Lüthi, Max. *Märchen.* Stuttgart: Metzlersche Verlagsbuchhandlung, 1962.

———. *Volksmärchen und Volkssage: Grundformen erzählender Dichtung.* 2. durchges. Aufl. Bern, Munich: Francke, 1966.

———. *Once Upon a Time: On the Nature of Fairy Tales.* Lee Chadeayne and Paul Gottwald, trans. Introd. and reference notes by Francis Lee Utley. Bloomington: Indiana University Press, 1967.

———. *The Fairytale as Art Form and Portrait of Man.* Jon Erickson, trans. Bloomington: Indiana University Press, 1984.

Lützeler, Paul Michael, ed. *Romane und Erzählungen der deutschen Romantik: Neue Interpretationen.* Stuttgart: Philipp Reclam jun., 1981.

Maeterlinck, Maurice. *On Emerson, and Other Essays.* New York: Dodd, Mead, 1912.

Mähl, Hans-Joachim. *Die Idee des goldenen Zeitalters im Werke des Novalis.* Heidelberg: Karl Winter, 1965.

Mahoney, Dennis F. *Die Poetisierung der Natur bei Novalis: Beweggründe, Gestaltung, Folgen.* Bonn: Bouvier, Verlag Herbert Grundmann, 1980.

†Mahr, Johannes, *Übergang zum Endlichen: Der Weg des Dichters in Novalis's "Heinrich von Ofterdingen."* Munich: Fink, 1970.

Malsch, Wilfried. *"Europa," poetische Rede des Novalis: Deutung der französischen Revolution and Reflexion auf die Poesie in der Geschichte.* Stuttgart: Metzler, 1965.

Matenko, Percy. *Ludwig Tieck in America. University of North Carolina Studies in Germanic Languages and Literatures,* vol. 12. Chapel Hill: University of North Carolina Press, 1954.

Mathesius, Johann. *Sarepta.* Nuremberg: 1562.

———. *Diluvium.* Nuremberg: 1587.

McCarthy, Mary. "Novel, Tale, Romance." In *The New York Review of Books,* May 12, 1983, pp. 49–56.

*Meiners, Christoph. *Kurzer Abriss der Psychologie zum Gebrauch seiner Vorlesungen.* Göttingen and Gotha: Dieterich, 1773.

*———. *Vermischte Philosophische Schriften; Erster–Dritter Theil.* Leipzig: Weygand, 1775–76.

*Mendelssohn, Moses. *Phaedon oder Über die Unsterblichkeit der Seele, in drey Gesprächen.* Berlin and Stettin: Nicolai, 1767.

*———. *Philosophische Schriften; Erster–Zweyter Theil.* Berlin: Voss, 1761.

*———. *Kleine Philosophische Schriften.* Ed. Johann Georg Müchler. With a sketch of his life and character by Daniel Jenisch. Berlin: Vierweg, 1789.

*Murhard, Friedrich. *System der Elemente der allgemeinen Grössenlehre.* Lemgo, 1798.

*Musäus, Johann Karl August. *Volksmärchen der Deutschen, Erster bis Fünfter Theil.* Gotha: Ettinger, 1782–88.

Neubauer, John. *Bifocal Vision: Novalis's Philosophy of Nature and Disease.* Chapel Hill: University of North Carolina Press, 1971.

———. *Novalis.* Boston: Twayne, 1980.

Nietzsche, Friedrich. *Sämtliche Werke: Kritische Studien Ausgabe.* Ed. Giorgio Colli and Mazzino Montinari. Munich: Deutscher Taschenbuch Verlag, 1980.

———. *The Birth of Tragedy.* Trans. W. Kaufmann. New York: Random House, 1967.

Nitze, William, and Dargan, E. Preston. *A History of French Literature.* 3rd ed. New York: Holt, Rinehart and Winston, 1960.

Novalis. *Novalis: Schriften.* 4 vols. Ed. Richard Samuel und Paul Kluckhohn. Leipzig: Bibliographisches Institut, 1929.

————. *Schriften: Die Werke Friedrich von Hardenbergs.* 3rd ed. 4 vols. Ed. Paul Kluckhohn and Richard Samuel. Stuttgart: W. Kohlhammer, 1977.

—. *Henry von Ofterdingen.* Trans. Palmer Hilty. New York: Frederick Ungar, 1978.

Ovid. *Metamorphoses.* 2 vols. Trans. F. J. Miller. Cambridge: Harvard University Press, 1977.

Partridge, Eric. *Origins: A Short Etymological Dictionary of Modern English.* New York: Macmillan, 1979.

Pindar. *The Odes of Pindar.* Trans. Sir John Sandys. Loeb Classical Library. Cambridge: Harvard University Press, 1978.

*————. *Carmina selecta, cum scholiis selectis suisque notis, in usum academiarum et scholarum.* Friedrich Gedike, ed. Berlin: Unger, 1786.

*————. *Pythische Siegshymnen: Mit erklärenden und kritischen Anmerkungen.* Trans. Friedrich Gedike. Berlin and Leipzig: Dekker, 1779.

*————. *Olympische Siegshymnen.* Trans. Friedrich Gedike. Berlin: Dekker, 1777.

*————. *Pythische, Nemeische und Isthmische Sieges-Lieder, aus dem Griechischen des Pindars übersetzt, und mit Anmerkungen versehen von Christian Tobias Damm.* Berlin und Leipzig: Ringmacher, 1774.

Plato. *Laws.* Trans. A. E. Taylor. In *The Dialogues of Plato.* Ed. Edith Hamilton and Huntington Cairns. Bollingen Series LXXI. Princeton: Princeton University Press, 1973.

————. *Phaedrus.* Trans. R. Hackforth. In *The Dialogues of Plato.* ed. Edith Hamilton and Huntington Cairns. Bollingen Series LXXI. Princeton: Princeton University Press, 1973.

Pochmann, Henry A. *German Culture in America.* Madison: The University of Wisconsin Press, 1957.

Poe, Edgar Allan. *Selected Writings.* Ed. and with an introduction by David Galloway. Harmondsworth: Penguin, 1978.

Praz, Mario. *The Romantic Agony.* Oxford: Oxford University Press, 1978.

Price, L. M. *Die Aufnahme der englischen Literatur in Deutschland, 1500–1960.* Bern, 1961.

Propp, Vladimir. *Morphology of the Folktale.* Laurence Scott, trans. With an introd. by Svatava Pircova-Jacobson. 2d ed., rev. and edited with a pref. ty Louis A. Wagner, and a new introd. by Alan Dundes. Austin: University of Texas Press, 1970.

————. "Fairy Tale Transformations." In *Reading in Russian Poetics.* Ladislav Matejka and Krystyna Pomorska, eds. Ann Arbor: The University of Michigan Press, 1978.

Radin, Paul. *The Trickster.* New York: Schocken, 1978.

Rehm, Walther. *Orpheus, der Dichter und die Toten: Selbstdeutung und Totenkult bei Novalis, Hölderlin, Rilke.* Düsseldorf: L. Schwann, 1950.

Reinhardt, Heinrich. *Integrale Sprachtheorie.* Munich: UNIDRUCK, 1976.
†Ritter, Heinz. *Novalis' Hymnen an die Nacht: Ihre Deutung nach Inhalt und Aufbau auf textkritischer Grundlage.* Heidelberg: Carl Winter, 1974.
†————. *Der unbekannte Novalis: Friedrich von Hardenberg im Spiegel seiner Dichtung.* Göttingen: Sachse und Pohl, 1967.
Rocques-von Beit, Hedwig von. *Symbolik des Märchens: Versuch einer Deutung.* vol. 3. Bern: A. Francke, 1965–67.
Röhrich, Lutz. *Märchen und Wirklichkeit.* 2. erw. Aufl. Wiesbaden: F. Steiner, 1964.
————. *Sage und Märchen: Erzählforschung heute.* Freiburg: Herder, 1976.
*Rothe, Johannes. *Düringische Chronic des Johannes Rothe.* n.d. (15th cent.).
Ruder, Klaus. *Zur Symboltheorie des Novalis.* Marburg: N. G. Elwert, 1974.
Schanze, Helmut. *Romantik und Aufklärung: Untersuchungen zu Friedrich Schlegel und Novalis.* Nuremberg: Hans Carl, 1966.
Schelling, F. W. J. von. *Ideen zu einer Philosophie der Natur* (1797). In *Sämtliche Werke,* vol. II. Stuttgart: Cotta'scher Verlag, 1857.
————. *Schellings Werke: Nach der Originalausgabe in neuer Anordnung.* Ed. Manfred Schröter. Munich: C. H. Beck'sche Verlagsbuchhandlung, 1968.
Schiller, Friedrich von. *Sämtliche Werke.* 13 vols. Ed. Julius Zeitler. Leipzig: Der Tempel Verlag, n.d., IX:288–94.
Schlegel, August Wilhelm. *Kritische Schriften und Briefe, 7.* Hrsg. Edgar Lohner. Stuttgart: W. Kohlhammer, 1962.
Schlegel, Friedrich. *Literary Notebooks, 1797–1801.* Hans Eichner, ed. Toronto: University of Toronto Press, 1957.
————. *Kritische Friedrich Schlegel-Ausgabe.* Ed. Ernst Behler, with the collaboration of Jean-Jacques Anstett und Hans Eichner. Munich: F. Schöningh, 1958.
Schlegel, Johann Elias. *On Imitation and Other Essays.* Indianapolis: Bobbs-Merrill, 1965.
Schleiermacher, Friedrich. *Werke.* With a preface by August Dorner. hrsg. and with an introduction by Otto Braun und Joh. Bauer. Leipzig: F. Meiner, 1910–13?.
Schulz, Gerhard. *Novalis Beitrag zu Werk und Persönlichkeit Friedrich von Hardenbergs.* Darmstadt: Wissenschaftliche Buchgesellschaft, 1970.
Schopenhauer, Arthur. *The World as Will and Representation.* Trans. E. F. J. Paine. New York: Dover, 1969.
*Shaftesbury, Earl of (Anton Ashley Cooper). *Characteristicks, oder Schilderung von Menschen, Sitten, Meynungen und Zeiten.* Trans. C. A. Wichmann, nebst einem Schreiben des Übersetzers, welches die Anmerkungen des Freyherrn von Leibnitz enthält. Leipzig: Heinsius, 1768.

Shumaker, Wayne. *The Occult Sciences in the Renaissance*. Berkeley and Los Angeles: University of California Press, 1979.

Simrock, Karl Joseph, *Der Wartburgkrieg*. Stuttgart: J. G. Cotta, 1858.

†Smith, John. "Time, Times, and the 'Right Time': Chronos and Kairos." *Monist* 53(January 1969):1–13.

Sommer, Wolfgang. *Christologie des jungen Schleiermacher und ihre Beziehung zum Christusbild des Novalis*. Bern: Herbert Lang, 1973.

*Spangenberg, Cyriacus. *Mansfeldische Chronica*. 1572.

Spinoza, Benedict de. *Ethics*. New York: Hafner, 1949.

Sprengel, Kurt. *Versuch einer pragmatischen Geschichte der Arzneikunde*. Teil 1–5. Halle: Gebauer, 1792–1803.

Stadler, Ulrich. *Die Theuren Dinge: Studien zu Bunyan, Jung-Stilling und Novalis*. Bern und Munich: Francke, 1980.

Steiner, George. "The Feast of Dissemination." *Times Literary Supplement* 202, no. 4(14 October 1983).

Strohm, Hans. Tyche. *Zur Schicksalsauffassung bei Pindar und den frühgriechischen Dichtern*. Stuttgart: Cottasche Buchhandlung Nachfolger, 1944.

†Strohschneider-Kohrs, Ingrid. *Die Romantische Ironie in Theorie und Gestaltung*. Tübingen: Max Niemeyer, 1960.

Süssmilch, Johann Peter. *Versuch eines Beweises, dass die erste Sprache ihren Ursprung nicht vom Menschen, sondern vom Schöpfer erhalten habe*. Berlin: Buchladen der Realschule, 1766.

Thalmann, Marianne. *Zeichensprache der Romantik, mit 12 Strukturzeichnungen*. Heidelberg: Stiehm, 1967.

Tillich, Paul. *Systematic Theology*. 3 vols. Chicago: University of Chicago Press, 1951–63.

Timm, Hermann. *Die heilige Revolution; Das religiöse Totalitätskonzept der Frühromantik: Schleiermacher - Novalis - Friedrich Schlegel*. Frankfurt a.M.: Syndikat Autoren- und Verlagsgesellschaft, 1978.

Tismar, Jens. *Kunstmärchen*. Stuttgart: Metzler, 1977.

Todorov, Tzvetzan. *Theories of the Symbol*. Catherine Porter, trans. Ithaca: Cornell University Press, 1982.

Unger, Rudolf. *Herder, Novalis und Kleist: Studien über die Entwicklung des Todesproblems im Denken und Dichten vom Sturm und Drang zur Romantik*. Frankfurt a.M.: M. Diesterweg, 1922.

Vico, Giambattista. *The New Science of Giambattista Vico: Unabridged Translation of the Third Edition (1744) with the Addition of "Practic of the New Science*. Trans. Thomas Goddard Bergin and Max Harold Fisch. Ithaca: Cornell University Press, 1984.

Vietta, Silvio. *Sprache und Sprachreflexion in der modernen Lyrik. Literatur und Reflexion*, vol. III. Ed. Beda Alleman. Bad Homburg: Verlag Dr. Max Gehlen, 1970.

Vogel, Stanley M. *German Literary Influences on the American Transcendentalists. Yale Studies in English*, vol. 127. Ed. Benjamin Christie Nangle. New Haven: Yale University Press, 1955.

Vordtriede, Werner. *Novalis und die französischen Symbolisten*. Stuttgart: W. Kohlhammer, 1963.

Walch, Johann Georg. *Philosophisches Lexikon*. Leipzig: 1733.

Wedew, Rolf. *Zur Sprachlichkeit von Bildern: Ein Beitrag zur Analogie von Sprache und Kunst*. Cologne: DuMont Buchverlag, 1985.

Wellek, René. *Confrontations*. Princeton: Princeton University Press, 1965.

Wilpert, Gero von. *Sachwörterbuch der Literatur*. Stuttgart: Alfred Körner, 1969.

Winkelmann, Johann Joachim. *Sendschreiben von den herculanischen Entdeckungen*. Dresden, 1762.

———. *Nachricht von den neuesten herculanischen Entdeckungen*. Dresden, 1764.

———. "Briefe an Bianconi." In *Antologia Romana*. 1779.

Zipes, Jack. *Breaking the Magic Spell*. New York: Methuen, 1979.

———. *The Trials and Tribulations of Little Red Riding Hood: Versions of the Tale in Socio-Cultural Context*. London: Heinemann, 1982.

———. *Fairy Tales and the Art of Subversion*. New York: Wildman, 1983.

*Zoroaster. *Zend-Avesta, Zoroasters Lebendiges Wort*. Trans. from the French translation of Anquetil by J. F. Kleuker. Erster–Dritter Theil. Riga: Hartknoch, 1770–77.

Zurlinden, Luise. *Gedanken Platons in der deutschen Romantik*. Hildesheim: Verlag Dr. H. A. Gerstenberg, 1976.

Index